Property and Casualty Insurance

License Exam Manual

PROPERTY AND CASUALTY INSURANCE
LICENSE EXAM MANUAL, 1ST EDITION, REVISED

If you find imperfections or incorrect information in this product, please visit www.kfeducation.com and submit an errata report.

Published in April 2010 by Kaplan Financial Education.

Printed in the United States of America.

ISBN: 1-4277-2506-3

PPN: 1000-0557

Contents

UNIT 4 The Insurance Transaction 55

UNIT 5 Introduction to Property Insurance 69

UNIT 6 Introduction to Liability Insurance 93

UNIT 7 Dwelling Insurance 111

UNIT 8 Homeowners Insurance 141

UNIT 9 Personal Auto Insurance 177

UNIT 10 Miscellaneous Personal Insurance 207

UNIT 11 The Commercial Package Policy 227

UNIT 12 The Businessowners Policy 237

UNIT 13 Commercial Property Insurance 271

UNIT 14 Ocean and Inland Marine Insurance 307

UNIT 15 Commercial General Liability Insurance 339

UNIT 16 Commercial Auto Insurance 367

UNIT 17 Commercial Crime Insurance 391

UNIT 18 Workers' Compensation 413

UNIT 19 Miscellaneous Commercial Insurance 427

Introduction

Important: Check for Updates

States sometimes revise their exam content outlines unexpectedly or on short notice. To see whether there is an update for this product because of an exam change, please go to **www.kfeducation.com** and check the Insurance Licensing Blog. If there is an update, it will be clearly noted in the blog entries.

We suggest that you check for updates when you first receive the course, again during your study period, upon completion of your studies, and one last time just before you take your insurance license exam.

Hints for Successful Exam Preparation

An examination must be taken and passed before an insurance producer's license is issued. This examination is designed to measure your basic knowledge of insurance coverages and practices to ensure that the public is served in a professionally responsible manner. The examination will also test your understanding of state laws and regulations pertaining to the insurance industry.

The Licensing Examination

All examination questions are four-part multiple-choice. The number of questions on the exam and the amount of time allowed to complete the exam varies depending on the state and the exam provider. Your exam may contain anywhere from 50–150 questions and have a time limit of 1–3 hours. Check with your state's license exam administrator for details.

Be sure to read each question carefully. While several of the possible answers may be partially correct, you must select the best answer to each question. Watch for words such as *all*, *never*, and *always*. They may help you eliminate some of the choices.

There is no penalty for guessing. If you can narrow the choice of four answers down to three or even two logical possibilities, you have a good chance of making an educated guess and picking the right answer.

Do not spend too much time on any one question. It is best to skip very difficult questions and return to them after you have completed all of the easier ones. Other questions on the exam may contain information that helps you answer more difficult questions.

Study Techniques

You may have a lot of experience taking training courses and their examinations or it may have been years since you've taken a course. Here are a couple tips we recommend to make your study most effective.

Read the Entire Course

Study the material in each unit until you understand it. A firm grasp of the material in the course is the best preparation for passing the exam.

Look for Question Areas as You Read Each Assignment

You can prepare for the exam by paying attention to the questions that appear throughout the course. They point to important areas that you should master. More importantly, study with the exam in mind. What questions would you put in the exam if you were creating it to test a student's knowledge of the material? This exercise will help you master the important material in the course and pass the exam.

UNIT

1

Principles of Insurance

1.1. LEARNING OBJECTIVES

After completing Unit 1—Principles of Insurance, you will be able to do the following:

- Define risk and describe various methods used to manage risk
- Explain the basic purpose of insurance
- Describe how the law of large numbers is used by the insurance industry
- Identify factors that determine whether a risk is insurable, including whether a risk is speculative or pure and whether insurable interest exists
- Explain the difference between a peril and a hazard
- Identify the different types of hazards

1.2. OBJECTIVES OF THIS COURSE

Congratulations on your decision to become a part of the challenging property-casualty insurance industry. As an insurance professional, you will have broad responsibilities to your company, the industry, and the public that you will serve.

This course will prepare you to begin these new responsibilities with confidence. You will learn about the principles underlying insurance and how the insurance industry operates. You will become familiar with all of the major categories of property-casualty products, the kinds of situations they are designed to cover, and the characteristics that make them unique.

Of course, no one training program will tell you everything you'll ever want to know about insurance. *Property-Casualty Concepts* will give you the knowledge you need to take your first career steps and prepare you for the challenges and training opportunities that lie ahead.

1.3. RISK, EXPOSURE

To understand what insurance is and how it works, you must first understand something about risk. Risk means the same thing in insurance that it does in everyday language. **Risk** is the chance or uncertainty of loss. For instance, the possibility that your house might be burglarized or that you might be hit by a car while crossing the street represents uncertainty of loss. Both are risks.

Now notice that risk is not the loss itself but the *uncertainty of loss.* There are some losses that are certain to occur eventually, such as when a rug finally wears out after years of use or a car runs out of gas. Such losses are not risks because they represent a certainty, instead of an uncertainty, of loss.

Another term that means almost the same thing as risk is exposure. An exposure is a condition or situation that presents a possibility of loss. For example, a home that is built on a flood plain is *exposed* to the possibility of flood damage.

1.4. MANAGING RISK

We spend our entire lives coping with risk: crossing the street, going swimming, buying a new house, traveling by plane. These risks sometimes result in small losses, such as a stubbed toe or a lost pocket comb, that we accept as a normal part of life. But risks may also result in serious financial losses, such as when a house burns down or a person is injured in a car accident. The consequences of such serious financial losses can be quite severe and far reaching.

People have developed several different methods for managing the risk of serious financial loss. One method is simply to **avoid risk**. For example, you can avoid the risk of being in an auto collision by never getting into a car.

But it isn't practical to avoid all risks. Fortunately, that isn't the only method of managing risk. You can also **control risk** to some extent. For example, training workers in the safe use of welding tools can curtail the frequency of fires on the job. Risk control techniques that curtail loss frequency come under the heading of loss prevention. Or, installing a sprinkler system in a factory won't prevent a fire from occurring, but it will limit the severity of any fire that does occur. Risk control techniques that limit loss severity come under the heading of risk reduction.

In some cases, people simply **retain a risk**. That is, if any loss occurs, they will pay for it themselves. Sometimes people retain only a portion of a risk—the portion that remains after other means of managing the risk have been employed. If people are aware of a risk and decide to retain it (or a portion of it), then they do so intentionally. If people are not aware of a risk, they may retain it unintentionally, and they may be surprised if a loss occurs.

The final method of managing risk is to **transfer it**. This option includes, but is not limited to, insurance. For example, a **hold harmless agreement** may shift liability from an owner or contractor to a tenant or subcontractor. (A hold harmless agreement is a contractual arrangement where one party assumes the liability of a situation and relieves the other party of responsibility.) However, for many risks, the best way to transfer them is through insurance. We'll focus on this way of handling the possibility of loss in the rest of this unit.

Exercise 1.A

Match the method of managing risk on the left with its correct description on the right.

____ 1. Avoid risk	A. George always wears his seat belt in the car.
____ 2. Control risk	B. Terry's car is not insured.
____ 3. Retain risk	C. Gretchen doesn't own a car because she doesn't know how to drive.

Exercise answers can be found at the end of the Unit 1 answers and rationales.

1.5. INSURANCE

You learned that one way of managing risk is to transfer it. This is what insurance does. The purpose of insurance is not to avoid or eliminate risk but to transfer risk. To see how it works, let's look at the hypothetical town of Middlefield.

Middlefield has 200 homes, each worth $100,000. Usually, one home in Middlefield burns to the ground each year. If the homeowner has to pay for the house, the owner will suffer a $100,000 loss. However, if that loss were divided among each of Middlefield's homeowners, it would be only $500. Wouldn't you agree to pay $500 knowing that if your house burned down, you would receive $100,000?

This is basically how insurance works. Instead of paying each other, people pay insurance companies, thus transferring the risk and responsibility for paying for any losses that occur to the company in exchange for a premium. The insurance company accumulates these premiums to provide the funds to pay for losses. This means that even though people don't pay each other directly, they still share in the cost of each other's losses.

So, a formal definition of **insurance** would be a contract or device for transferring risk from a person, business, or organization to an insurance company that agrees, in exchange for a premium, to pay for losses through an accumulation of premiums.

1.6. LAW OF LARGE NUMBERS

Overall, we're a pretty safe group of people. Everyone doesn't have a loss all the time. For this reason, by predicting the number of losses that will occur, an insurance company can provide large amounts of insurance for relatively little money. To help them predict their losses accurately so they can charge the proper premiums needed to accumulate adequate funds, insurance companies rely on the law of large numbers. The law of large numbers says that the more examples used to develop any statistic, the more reliable the statistic will be.

Consider these statistics.

- Four out of five homes have defective wiring. To determine this, 15 homes were checked.
- Three out of four automobiles will suffer some form of tire damage each year. Five million auto owners were surveyed.

The law of large numbers tells us that the tire statistic will be more accurate than the wiring statistic in predicting what will happen in the future because the tire statistic is based on many more examples.

1.7. ELEMENTS OF INSURABILITY

1.7.1. Pure Risk, Speculative Risk

Although theoretically almost anyone could purchase insurance to cover almost any risk, there are certain rules that establish a practical basis regarding who can be insured and for what.

For instance, insurance cannot be used to handle speculative risks. **Speculative risks** are risks in which there exists both the possibility of gain and the possibility of loss. A poker game is an example of a speculative risk. Insurance can be used to manage only **pure risks**, which involve only the possibility of loss. A person can buy insurance to protect against loss if a fur coat is stolen (pure risk) but not to protect against loss if the price of stock goes down (speculative risk).

Exercise 1.B

For each of the examples listed below, indicate whether it is a pure risk (P) or a speculative risk (S).

____ 1. Harry feels lucky, so he buys a lottery ticket at the neighborhood convenience store.

____ 2. Joan hopes her fur coat is safe at the storage warehouse.

____ 3. The lightning rods aren't up on Frank's new house yet, and a severe thunderstorm has been predicted.

____ 4. Donna purchases several shares of stock in a computer company.

Exercise answers can be found at the end of the Unit 1 answers and rationales.

1.7.2. Insurable Interest

A basic rule concerning who can be insured states that before you can benefit from insurance, you must have a chance of financial loss or a financial interest in the property. This is called an **insurable interest.** You have an insurable interest in your own home but not your neighbor's home.

1.7.3. Other Elements of Insurable Risks

There are additional rules that govern what risks are considered suitable subjects for insurance. Risks that do not meet these criteria are probably better handled using an alternate method of risk management.

- The risk of loss must be definite as to time and place and difficult to counterfeit or falsify. Death is probably the best example of a definite loss.
- The risk must be unexpected. In fact, as we mentioned earlier, if the results are expected, it does not qualify as a risk. The risk of a train wreck could be insured, whereas the risk that your suitcase will eventually wear out is not really a risk at all and, therefore, is not insurable.
- The risk must be large enough to create a financial hardship for the individual involved. A financially insignificant risk, such as the chance that you might lose a pair of inexpensive sunglasses, is not insurable.
- The loss must be calculable. In addition to requiring adequately large risks, only risks for which the cost of loss is calculable may be insured. Risks that involve loss that can't be assigned a financial value are uninsurable.
- The cost of the insurance must be affordable to the insured. If the risk is so severe that it requires the insurance company to charge prohibitively high premiums to accumulate enough money to pay losses, it is not an insurable risk. Even if the person purchasing the insurance could afford to pay it, the cost should be only a fraction of the value of the item itself.
- There must be a large number of persons with a similar potential loss available for the insurance so that overall, losses become predictable. The law of large numbers applies here. To accumulate adequate funds to pay losses, the insurance company must be able to predict losses. Accurate predictions are possible only when there are sufficient numbers of potential insureds with a similar chance of loss.
- The loss must not happen to a large number of insureds at the same time. Although insurance companies do want to insure a large number of persons, if a great number of these insureds were to suffer a loss at the same time, it would be catastrophic for the insurance company.

For instance, suppose an insurance company were to insure every home in a single town. A rapidly spreading fire could destroy the entire town. So instead of insuring every person in a single town, a company will want to insure several people in many towns. This is known as **spread of risk.** The greater the spread of risk, the less likely that there will be a catastrophic loss for the insurance company.

1.8. OTHER INSURANCE TERMS

1.8.1. Peril

You've learned that risk is the uncertainty of loss. A **peril** is the cause of loss. Fire and collision are both examples of perils.

1.8.2. Hazard

Now that you understand the difference between risk and peril, let's discuss another important term: hazard. A **hazard** is anything that increases the chance of loss.

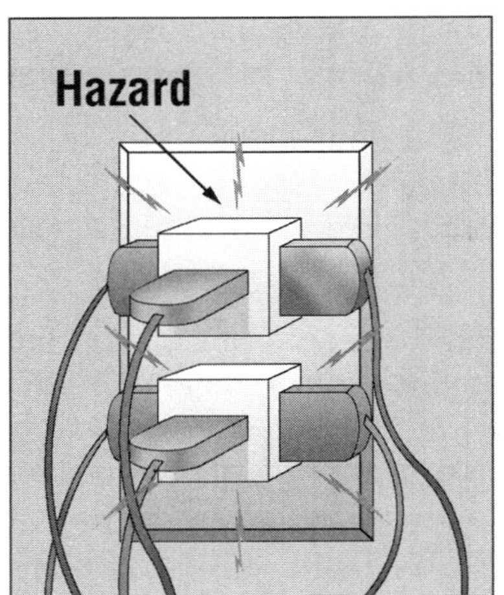

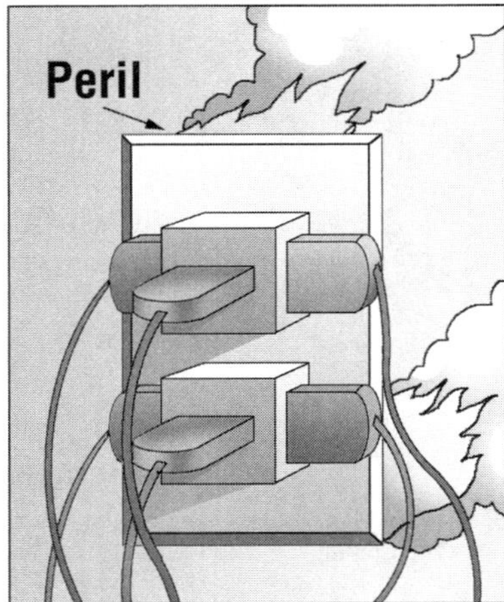

Suppose Georgia was injured when a furnace exploded as the result of a poorly tightened gas connection. The peril was explosion; the hazard was a poorly tightened gas connection.

1.8.2.1. Physical, Morale, and Moral Hazards

There are three different types of hazards.

A **physical hazard** is a hazard that arises from the condition, occupancy, or use of the property itself. An example of a physical hazard is a skateboard left on the porch steps.

The second type of hazard is called a **morale hazard.** This means that an individual, through carelessness or by irresponsible actions, can increase the possibility for a loss. An example of a morale hazard is a person who drives a car carelessly because he knows a loss will be insured if an accident occurs.

The third type of hazard, closely related to the morale hazard, is the **moral hazard.** A moral hazard means that a person might create a loss situation on purpose just to collect from the insurance company. An example of a moral hazard is a prearranged, faked theft of an older vehicle so the owner could collect the insurance money and buy something new.

Exercise 1.C

Read through the examples that follow and mark each as a physical, morale, or moral hazard.

1. Jerry is having serious business difficulties. He plans to burn down the building in which his business operates so he can collect on the insurance.

   ____

2. Bill leaves his car unlocked whenever he goes shopping. He figures that the car is insured and there is no reason to worry.

   ____

3. The Starfire Equipment Company, which is occupied in a very old building, has had several serious fires in the last two years. An inspector says that a worn-out furnace may have caused the fires.

   ____

Exercise answers can be found at the end of the Unit 1 answers and rationales.

UNIT TEST

Throughout this course, as you complete each unit, you will have a chance to review what you have learned by working through some review exercises. After you have completed them, be sure to review any that you missed and, if necessary, reread the appropriate section of the text.

Note that unit review questions are drawn from all topics discussed in a particular unit. Students who are taking this course to prepare for producer licensing exams may see questions on topics that were not included on their state exam syllabuses. If you wish to tailor your review to your particular state's licensing exam, we recommend that you purchase Kaplan's Property and Casualty InsurancePro QBank™. Go to www.kfeducation.com for details.

1. Match each word below with its appropriate definition.

1. Risk	____	A. Increases the chance of loss
2. Insurance	____	B. A means of transferring the risk of loss
3. Peril	____	C. The chance of loss
4. Hazard	____	D. The cause of loss

2. Which of the following represent pure risks?
   A. Terry places a bet on the outcome of a basketball game.
   B. Margaret's dog is temperamental. She's afraid it will bite a neighbor someday, and she will be held responsible.
   C. Both A and B.

3. The law of large numbers
   A. prohibits insurance with extremely high premiums
   B. states that there must be an adequate spread of risk for insurance to be effective
   C. states that the more examples used to develop a statistic, the more reliable the statistic will be

4. LaTonya purchases a house from John. She borrows $75,000 from First City Bank which, along with her $25,000 down payment, equals the $100,000 purchase price of the home. Who has an insurable interest in this home?
   A. LaTonya
   B. John
   C. LaTonya's son, who would like to inherit the home some day
   D. First City Bank

5. Describe four of the criteria a risk must meet to be insurable.
   A. ______________________________
   ____
   ____
   B. ______________________________
   ____
   ____
   C. ______________________________
   ____
   ____
   D. ______________________________
   ____
   ____

6. Highpoint Industries has an automatic sprinkler system installed in its office building. This is an example of which risk management method?
   A. Avoidance
   B. Reduction
   C. Control

7. Benson Pharmaceutical Company decides not to manufacture a new drug after determining that it has serious potential side effects. This is an example of which risk management method?
   A. Transfer
   B. Retention
   C. Avoidance

8. Since she has always been in good health, Donna decides to cancel her health insurance policy. This is an example of which risk management method?
   A. Retention
   B. Control
   C. Avoidance

9. Determine the peril involved in each of the following losses.
   A. Mr. Reed's home was destroyed in a fire.

      ____

      ____

   B. Suzanne's house was damaged in a flood.

      ____

      ____

   C. Jim's automobile collided with Sue's.

      ____

      ____

10. Veronica forgets to lock her front door when she leaves for work. Later that day, a thief enters her apartment and steals her television.
    A. What was the peril?

       ____

       ____

    B. What was the hazard?

       ____

       ____

ANSWERS AND RATIONALES TO UNIT TEST

1. 4 A.; 2 B.; 1 C.; 3 D. Risk is the chance or uncertainty of loss. Insurance is a contract or device for transferring the risk of loss from a person, business, or organization to an insurance company that agrees, in exchange for a premium, to pay for losses through an accumulation of premiums. A peril is the cause of loss. A hazard is something that increases the chance of loss.

2. **B** A pure risk is one that involves only the possibility of loss. Choice A is an example of a speculative risk in which there exists both the possibility of gain and the possibility of loss.

3. **C** The law of large numbers says that the more examples used to develop a statistic, the more reliable the statistic will be. Insurers use the law of large numbers to predict the number of losses that will occur so they can charge the correct premium.

4. A and D are correct. Insurable interest exists when there is an actual economic interest in the safety or preservation of the subject of the insurance from loss or destruction or financial damage or impairment. LaTonya has an insurable interest in the home because she owns it. First City Bank has an insurable interest as long as it carries a mortgage on the home.

5. Any four of the following: Insurable interest; pure risk, not speculative; loss must not happen to a large number of insureds at the same time; risk of loss must be definite; loss would cause financial hardship; cost of loss is calculable; cost of insurance covering the risk is affordable; large number of persons with similar potential for loss.

6. **B** A sprinkler system can reduce the severity of fires, but it does not prevent them altogether or reduce the number that occur.

7. **C** By not producing the drug, Benson avoids the risk of being sued by consumers who are injured by the drug.

8. **A** By not carrying health insurance, Donna is retaining the risk of financial loss from unexpected medical expenses.

9. A peril is the cause of loss. In these exercises, the perils are: A. Fire; B. Flood; C. Collision.

10. A peril is the cause of loss. In question A, the peril is theft. A hazard is something that increases the chance of loss. In question B, the hazard is leaving the door unlocked.

UNIT 1 EXERCISE ANSWERS

Exercise 1.A

1. **C**
2. **A**
3. **B**

Exercise 1.B

1. **S**
2. **P**
3. **P**
4. **S**

Exercise 1.C

1. Moral
2. Morale
3. Physical

UNIT 2

The Insurance Contract

2.1 LEARNING OBJECTIVES

After completing Unit 2—The Insurance Contract, you will be able to do the following:

- Describe the elements of a legally valid contract and how those elements apply in an insurance transaction
- Identify special characteristics associated with insurance contracts, including the principle of indemnity
- Explain the role of the five sections found in most insurance policies: declarations, insuring agreements, conditions, exclusions, and definitions
- Describe how insurance policies may be organized
- Explain the purpose of endorsements

2.2 ELEMENTS OF A VALID CONTRACT

Now that you're familiar with some of the principles of insurance, let's look more closely at the insurance contract itself.

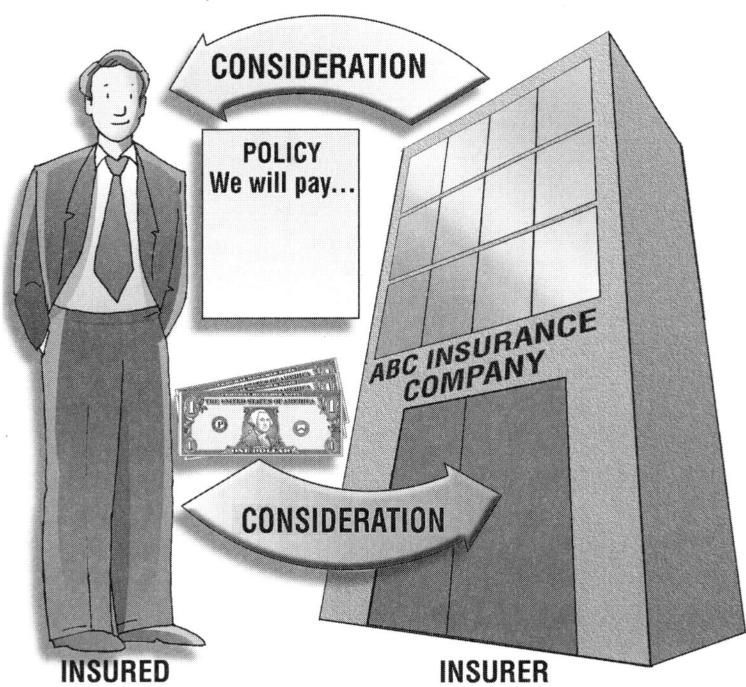

You're probably familiar with the term *contract*. A **contract** is a legal agreement between two competent parties that promises a certain performance in exchange for a certain consideration. When an insurance company agrees to pay for an insured's losses in exchange for a certain premium, the two parties have entered into a contract. Although a contract of insurance may be oral, it is usually written in the form of an insurance policy.

Insurance contracts, like all other contracts, must exhibit certain characteristics to be legally enforceable. These characteristics are:

- competent parties;
- legal purpose;
- offer and acceptance (agreement); and
- consideration.

2.2.1. Competent Parties

A contract is not valid unless it is made between two parties who are considered competent under the law. In most cases, a person who is a minor, insane, or under the influence of alcohol or drugs is considered incompetent.

2.2.2. Legal Purpose

The second requirement for a valid contract is that it be formed for a legal purpose. A contract that is against public policy (offensive to the best interests of the public) or in violation of the law is not enforceable.

2.2.3. Offer and Acceptance

The third element of a valid contract, **offer and acceptance**, means that the contract involves two parties: one who makes an offer and one who accepts it. This is also called **agreement**. An offer is a promise that requires an act or another promise in exchange. Acceptance occurs when the other party agrees to the offer or does what was proposed in the offer.

Exercise 2.A

Ted fills out an application for auto insurance and sends it to the XYZ Insurance Company, which agrees to provide the insurance to Ted.

1. Which party made an offer?

   A. Ted
   B. XYZ Insurance Company

2. Which party accepted the offer?

   A. Ted
   B. XYZ Insurance Company

Exercise answers can be found at the end of the Unit 2 answers and rationales.

2.2.4. Consideration

The last requirement for a valid contract is that it involve consideration. Consideration is a thing of value exchanged for the performance promised in the contract. With insurance, the consideration that the insured gives is the premium payment. The consideration that the insurer gives is the promise to pay for certain losses suffered by the insured.

2.3 CHARACTERISTICS OF AN INSURANCE CONTRACT

2.3.1. Principle of Indemnity

In addition to the characteristics an insurance contract shares with other valid contracts, it also has some special features of its own.

Principle of Indemnity

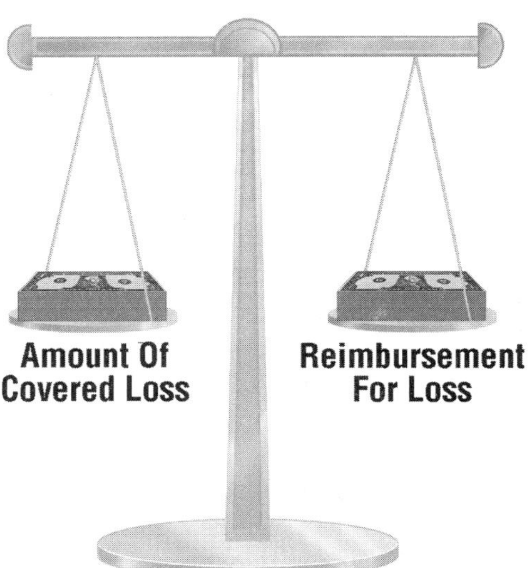

One of the most important characteristics of an insurance contract is that it is a contract of indemnity. The principle of indemnity states that when a loss occurs, an individual should be restored to the approximate financial condition he was in before the loss, no more and no less. Let's consider two examples.

- The insured bought an automobile four years ago for $15,000. Today it is worth $6,000. According to the principle of indemnity, the insured should receive no more than $6,000 if the car is demolished.
- You lend your laptop computer to a friend, and it is destroyed in a fire at your friend's house. Your friend offers to pay for the computer. You also have insurance that would cover the loss. According to the principle of indemnity, you should not be able to collect the full amount of this loss from both your friend and the insurance company.

The principle of indemnity is closely related to both the requirement of an insurable interest and the exclusion of speculative risks that we discussed earlier. An insured may only be indemnified to the extent of his insurable interest. Insurance is not gambling—the insured doesn't win or lose. The insured may only be returned to the approximate financial condition he occupied before the loss occurred.

Suppose Harry Arne and his cousin each own 50% of a $160,000 duplex. Suppose Harry purchases $160,000 of insurance on the home. If it burns to the ground, Harry could not collect more than $80,000.

2.3.2. Personal

An insurance contract does not insure property; it insures the person who owns the property. This means it is a **personal** contract.

2.3.3. Aleatory

An insurance contract is **aleatory**, which means it is contingent on an uncertain event (a loss) that provides for unequal transfer of value between the parties. An insured can pay premiums for many years without having a covered loss. On the other hand, insureds who suffer a loss often get a great deal more from the insurance company than they've paid in premiums.

2.3.4. Adhesion

When we say that insurance contracts are **adhesion** contracts, we mean that one party has greater power over the other party in drafting the contract. The provisions of the contract are prepared by one party—the insurer. The other party, the insured, does not take part in the preparation of the contract. Although the insured may request special provisions or coverages, it is the insurance company that ultimately draws up and issues the policy.

A problem that sometimes arises in insurance contracts is ambiguity, which occurs when the insurer doesn't make the terms and agreements of the policy perfectly clear. Since an insurance policy is an adhesion contract, the courts usually resolve any ambiguity in policy wording in favor of the insured. When doing so, the courts may rely on the **doctrine of reasonable expectations**, which states that a policy includes coverages that an average person would reasonably expect it to include, regardless of what the policy actually provides.

2.3.5. Unilateral

An insurance policy is a unilateral contract. **Unilateral** means one sided. An insurance policy is one sided because only the insurance company is legally bound to perform its part of the agreement. If an insured pays a premium and a loss occurs, the insurer is legally bound to pay for the loss under the terms of the policy. However, insureds are not legally obligated to pay premiums. If insureds stop paying premiums, the insurance company can cancel coverage, but it can't take them to court for breaking the contract. On the other hand, if an insured fails to comply with conditions and duties specified in the contract, the insurance company may deny an insured's claim.

2.3.6. Contract of Utmost Good Faith

Another characteristic of an insurance contract is that it is a **contract of utmost good faith**. The insurance company relies on the truthfulness and integrity of the applicant when issuing a policy. In return, the insured relies on the company's promise and ability to provide coverage and pay claims.

2.3.7. Conditional

An insurance policy includes a number of conditions that both the insured and the insurer must comply with. For example, if a covered loss occurs, the insured must notify the insurer about the loss, and the insurer must use the valuation methods specified in the policy to settle the loss. For this reason, an insurance policy is a **conditional** contract.

2.4 PARTS OF THE INSURANCE CONTRACT: DECLARATIONS, INSURING AGREEMENTS, CONDITIONS, EXCLUSIONS, AND DEFINITIONS

Since an insurance policy is a legal contract, it must be very specific about the agreements between the insured and the insurer. To do this, most policies contain five parts: declarations, insuring agreements, conditions, exclusions, and definitions.

The declarations, which are almost always on the first page of the policy, contain such information as the name of the insured, the address, the amount of coverage provided, a description of the property, and the cost of the policy.

The insuring agreements, the heart of the policy, state in general what is to be covered or, in other words, the losses for which the insured will be indemnified. This section also describes the type of property covered and the perils against which it is insured.

The conditions state the ground rules for the policy. They describe the responsibilities and the obligations of both the insurance company and the insured.

The exclusions describe the losses for which the insured is not covered. If an excluded loss occurs, the insured will not be indemnified.

Finally, the definitions section clarifies the meanings of certain terms used in the policy.

Exercise 2.B

Read the following policy excerpts and label them as **declarations, insuring agreements, conditions, exclusions,** or **definitions.**

1. Named insured and mailing address: Leah Bachman, 11491 Bretson Road, Elysium, Anystate 01001

 ____

2. In this policy, **property damage** means physical injury to or destruction of property.

 ____

3. This policy does not cover any loss caused by earthquake.

 ____

4. This policy may be canceled if the insured does not pay premiums when due. ______________________________

5. This policy covers personal property owned or used by the insured.

 ____

Exercise answers can be found at the end of Unit 2 answers and rationales.

2.4.1. Policy Organization

Although all insurance contracts contain these elements, policies can be organized in a number of different ways.

Some policies contain the declarations, insuring agreement, conditions, definitions, and exclusions all in one single, continuous page.

Another format uses a policy jacket, also called a skeleton policy, that contains general conditions and the declarations. To complete the policy, a policy form or coverage form containing the insuring agreements, exclusions, definitions, and additional coverages must be attached.

Still another format features a declarations page, a coverage form containing the coverages and certain exclusions, definitions and conditions, a separate general conditions form, and a causes of loss form listing the perils insured against and additional exclusions. Later in this course, you will have an opportunity to learn more about specific policies and see how they are constructed.

Because our lives are subject to so many changes and because each policyholder is different, it is often necessary to modify or change the original policy in some way, such as broadening coverage, restricting coverage, or changing the name of an insured. This is accomplished by adding an endorsement, which is attached to the policy itself.

UNIT TEST

1. For each of the following examples, write in which of the four elements of a valid contract is missing: competent parties, legal purpose, offer and acceptance, or consideration.
   - A. Jack agrees to burn down Albert's house for $10,000.________________
   - B. Susan's insurance policy is canceled for nonpayment of premium.

     ____
   - C. JAG Insurance Company denies George's application for auto insurance.

     ____
   - D. Andrea, age 15, signs a lease for an apartment in Highview Estates.

     ____

2. Match the following terms describing insurance contracts with the statements that explain them.

1. Conditional	____	A.	Prepared by one party, with little or no opportunity for bargaining by the other party
2. Indemnity	____	B.	Insurer relies on insured's statements and insured relies on insurer's ability to fulfill its promises
3. Personal	____	C.	Dependent on an uncertain event
4. Aleatory	____	D.	Insures a person
5. Adhesion	____	E.	After a loss occurs, an individual is restored to the approximate financial condition she was in before the loss
6. Unilateral	____	F.	One-sided contract; only the insurance company is legally bound to perform under the contract
7. Utmost good faith	____	G.	Includes conditions that both the insured and the insurer must comply with

3. List the purpose of each part of an insurance policy.
   - A. Declarations: ____________________
   - B. Insuring agreements: ____________________
   - C. Conditions: ____________________
   - D. Exclusions: ____________________
   - E. Definitions: ____________________
   - F. Endorsements: ____________________

ANSWERS AND RATIONALES TO UNIT TEST

1. **A.** Legal purpose. One of the requirements for a valid contract is that it be formed for a legal purpose. A contract that is in violation of the law—such as this example, which involves arson—is not enforceable.

   B. Consideration. A valid contract must involve consideration—a thing of value exchanged for the performance promised in the contract. With insurance, the consideration that the insured gives is the premium payment. Since Susan did not pay the premium, there is no consideration involved.

   C. Offer and acceptance. A contract involves two parties: one who makes an offer and one who accepts it. Since JAG Insurance did not accept George's offer (an application for insurance), no contract exists.

   D. Competent parties. A contract is not valid unless it is made between two parties who are considered competent under the law. In most cases, a person who is a minor is considered incompetent.

2. 5. A.; 7. B.; 4. C.; 3. D.; 2. E.; 6. F.; 1. G. Insurance contracts have a number of special characteristics. An insurance contract is a conditional contract because it contains a number of conditions that both parties must comply with. An insurance contract is a contract of indemnity because when a loss occurs, the insured is restored to the approximate financial condition he occupied before the loss occurred, no better or no worse. An insurance contract is a personal contract because it insures a person, not property. An insurance contract is aleatory because it is contingent on an uncertain event (a loss). An insurance policy is an adhesion contract because one party (the insurer) has more power than the other party in drafting the contract. An insurance contract is unilateral because it is one sided—only the insurance company is legally bound to perform its part of the agreement. Another characteristic of an insurance contract is that it is a contract of utmost good faith. The insurance company must be able to rely on the honesty and cooperation of the insured, and the insured must rely on the company to fulfill its obligations.

3. **A.** The Declarations list who is insured, what property or risk is covered, when and where coverage is effective, and how much coverage applies.

   B. Insuring agreements describe what is covered and the perils the policy insures against.

   C. The conditions explain the rights and duties of the insured and the insurer under the policy.

   D. The exclusions list property, perils, persons, or situations that are not covered by the policy.

   E. Definitions clarify the meaning of certain terms used in the policy.

   F. Endorsements are documents attached to the policy that change the policy in some way.

UNIT 2 EXERCISE ANSWERS

Exercise 2.A

1. **A**
2. **B**

Exercise 2.B

1. Declarations
2. Definitions
3. Exclusions
4. Conditions
5. Insuring agreements

U N I T

3

Insurance Company Organization and Regulation

3.1. LEARNING OBJECTIVES

After completing Unit 3—Insurance Company Organization and Regulation, you will be able to do the following:

- Describe the most common types of insurance companies
- Define the four broad categories of insurance
- Explain the difference between personal and commercial insurance
- Describe the duties an agent has to insureds and insurance companies
- Identify the four basic distribution systems used to market insurance
- Explain the roles of other insurance professionals, such as solicitors, brokers, and consultants
- Describe major functions of insurance companies, such as underwriting, claims, and loss control
- Describe how state insurance departments regulate the insurance industry and its agents

3.2. TYPES OF INSURANCE ORGANIZATIONS

3.2.1. Stock and Mutual Companies

Now that we've talked about the insurance contract in general, we want to look more closely at the organizations that issue these contracts. There are several types of insurance companies that represent different ways in which companies raise the money necessary to begin business and enroll their prospects for insurance.

The first type is called a **stock** company. When a stock company first forms, it sells stock to stockholders to raise the money necessary to operate the business. Stockholders are not necessarily insured by the company, and insureds do not necessarily own stock in the company. The company is in the business to sell insurance to the insured. Profits attributed to the operation of the company are returned as dividends to the stockholders, not the insureds.

The second type, a **mutual** insurance company, functions differently than a stock company. In a mutual company, the insureds are also owners of the company. As owners, they can vote to elect the management of the company. Profits are returned to the insureds in the form of dividends or reductions in future premiums.

Most mutual companies are advance premium companies that charge nonassessable premiums. As a result, they are required to set money aside in a reserve in case their claims experience is higher than expected. A small number are **assessment** companies, providing primarily fire and windstorm insurance for small towns and farmers. Assessment mutuals charge members a pro rata share of losses at the end of each policy period.

3.2.2. Reciprocals and Lloyd's Associations

The third form of company organization, although not as common as a stock or mutual, is known as a **reciprocal** company. The word *reciprocate* means "to give and take." A member of a reciprocal agrees to share the insurance responsibilities with all other members of the unincorporated group. In a sense, all members insure each other and share the losses with each other. A reciprocal is managed by an **attorney-in-fact** who is empowered to handle all of the business of the reciprocal.

Another type of insuring organization is called a **Lloyd's Association**. Perhaps you have heard of Lloyd's of London. It may surprise you to know that Lloyd's of London is not an insurance company. It is a voluntary association of individuals, or groups of individuals, who agree to share in insurance contracts. Each individual, or "syndicate," is individually responsible for the amounts of insurance they write. There are also a limited number of Lloyd's Associations in the United States.

3.2.3. Fraternal Benefit Societies

Another type of insuring organization is a **fraternal benefit society**. A fraternal benefit society is an incorporated society or order, without capital stock, that is operated on the lodge system and conducted solely for the benefit of its members and their beneficiaries and not for profit. Fraternals offer insurance that is available only to their members. Most write only life and health insurance.

3.2.4. Risk Retention Groups and Purchasing Groups

In 1981, Congress passed the Liability Risk Retention Act to give product manufacturers more options when insuring against product liability. To facilitate this process, the act allowed product manufacturers to establish group self-insurance programs or group captive insurance companies, called **risk retention groups (RRGs)**, to protect them against product liability exposures and to purchase liability insurance on a group basis through **purchasing groups (PGs)**. The act accomplished this by limiting the states' authority to regulate product liability insurance. Risk retention groups and purchasing groups are regulated in the states where they are domiciled, but they can transact business in all other states. This exempts them from state insurance regulation and guaranty funds. The Liability Risk Retention Act of 1986 amended the 1981 act by giving the right to form RRGs and PGs to nearly all businesses. They are prohibited from writing workers' compensation and personal lines insurance.

3.2.5. Self-Insurance

Some companies and individuals choose to **self-insure**. With this option, part or all of the risk of loss is borne without the benefit of insurance coverage to fall back on if a loss occurs. Some large companies are self-insured because they have the resources to withstand losses and their claims experience demonstrates that it is cheaper to be self-insured than to pay for insurance coverage.

3.2.6. Private, Government Insurers

Insurance companies may be privately owned or operated by the state or federal government.

The government sometimes steps in to provide insurance that is not ordinarily available from private insurers. This type of insurance is sometimes called **residual market insurance**. The federal government provides:

- war risk insurance;
- nuclear energy liability insurance;
- flood insurance; and
- federal crop insurance.

At the state level, the government is involved in providing unemployment insurance and may provide workers' compensation benefits through state funds.

3.3. LINES OF INSURANCE

3.3.1. Four Lines of Insurance

Another way of classifying insurance companies is by the type of insurance policies they write. There are four broad categories, or **lines**, of insurance:

- Property
- Casualty
- Life
- Health and disability

An insurance company that writes only one line of insurance is referred to as a **monoline** company. An insurance company that writes more than one line of insurance is called a **multiline** company.

3.3.1.1. Life and Health

Now, let's look a little closer at these four lines of insurance.

Life insurance is designed to handle the risk of premature death or the risk that an individual may outlive his or her financial resources. **Health and disability insurance** is designed to handle the risk of medical bills and loss of income resulting from injury or sickness. In this course, we will not deal with these lines of insurance, although your company or agency may offer them.

3.3.1.2. Property and Casualty

The remaining two lines of insurance make up the property and casualty industry. We'll be concentrating on the kinds of insurance that are a part of the property and casualty field for the remainder of this course.

Property insurance is relatively simple to define. It includes many types of insurance designed to handle property risks—risks that we will suffer financial loss because something we own is damaged or destroyed. The following types of insurance are generally considered to be property insurance:

- Dwelling
- Homeowners
- Commercial property
- Inland marine
- Ocean marine
- Crime

We'll look more closely at each of these types of insurance later.

Casualty insurance is more difficult to define because it includes a wide variety of basically unrelated insurance products.

One of the most important risks covered by the casualty line is the **liability** risk—the risk that we will suffer financial loss as a result of our actions toward others. A good example is the all-too-familiar auto accident in which Allen backs out of his driveway, hits Blanca's car, and causes $500 in damage. If the accident was Allen's fault, he is liable for the damage he caused to Blanca or her auto.

Although insurance against the liability risk is an important casualty coverage, there are many other types of insurance that have historically been classified as casualty:

- Aviation
- Auto
- Workers' compensation
- Surety bonds

You'll learn more about these coverages later in the course.

Exercise 3.A

1. Bonnie drives a school bus. She drives very carefully because she knows she's responsible for the lives of the children on board. This is an example of a (property/casualty) ______________________ risk.
2. Bart lives in the Midwest and wants to insure his home against damage by a tornado or windstorm. This is an example of a (property/casualty) ____________________________ risk.

Exercise answers can be found at the end of the Unit 3 answers and rationales.

3.3.2. Personal and Commercial Lines

Insurance can be written to meet the needs of an individual or family as well as the needs of a business. **Personal lines** are property and casualty coverages that protect an individual or family. **Commercial lines** are coverages designed for businesses.

Exercise 3.B

Label each of the following as a personal line **(P)** or commercial line **(C)**.

1. ____ Mabel wants insurance protection for her home.
2. ____ Willoby Industries would like to purchase property insurance for its new warehouse.
3. ____ The Jensens have insurance coverage for their two family cars.
4. ____ Toyland, Inc., has insurance that protects it against liability arising out of the toys it manufactures.

Exercise answers can be found at the end of the Unit 3 answers and rationales.

3.4. INSURANCE COMPANY ORGANIZATION

3.4.1. Introduction

Whether an insurance company is monoline or multiline, whether it specializes in personal lines or commercial lines, an insurance company is made up of people.

In this section, we'll consider how an insurance company is organized and the various functions people perform within the company. Although you may not find your specific position listed, this review should give you an idea of where you fit in the total picture.

3.4.2. The Agent

3.4.2.1. Duties

The first person most people think of when they think of insurance is the **insurance agent**. The insurance agent, who represents the insurance company, is the direct link between the company and its insureds. As such, the agent has many responsibilities, including:

- selling insurance;
- issuing and countersigning policies;

- collecting premiums; and
- providing a link between the insured and the insurance company.

Most of these duties are self-explanatory, but you may be curious about countersigning. **Countersigning** means the agent signs each new policy prepared by the company before delivering it to the insured. In most states, the agent's countersignature is required to validate the contract.

The agent's duty to provide a link between the insured and the insurance company involves a number of responsibilities.

The agent is responsible for **field underwriting** each risk. This means using preestablished criteria to seek out the type of business that is likely to be acceptable to the company. Although the company underwriter makes the final decision to accept a risk, the agent also has a responsibility to seek out quality business.

Before selling a policy, the agent must obtain information on the prospect's particular exposures and review existing policies. The agent must analyze the prospect's coverage needs and make recommendations as to the amount and type of coverage appropriate for each exposure.

The agent may prepare a **quotation** that will show the prospect what the premium for the proposed coverage will be. When the prospect buys, the agent must complete a detailed **application**. The application must be carefully, completely, and accurately filled out and submitted on a timely basis.

The agent must make sure the client understands the type of coverage being purchased and what the insured's responsibilities are under the policy, as well as the services that will be provided by the agent and the insurance company. The agent may also be expected to deliver the policy.

Once a policy is in force, the agent has a continuing responsibility toward the insured. At least once a year, the agent should review the client's coverage and evaluate the adequacy of the coverage provided. The agent must also stay current with new coverages that might be appropriate for the client. An agent should maintain a **suspense** or **diary system** that alerts the agent before the policy renewal time. This is an appropriate time for the agent to ensure that the insured's coverage is still adequate and that there have been no significant changes in the risk.

At any time during the policy year, the agent must be available to assist the insured with **service needs**, such as a name change or a change in the method of premium payment, and maintain accurate records of all such changes requested by the insured. The agent may also help the insured file and follow up on claims. Some companies give the agent authority to settle certain types of claims.

Not only does the insurance agent have a moral obligation to fulfill these duties, but there are legal obligations as well. Agents who are negligent in meeting their responsibilities may be liable for their inadvertent errors. Later in the course, we'll discuss **errors and omissions (E&O) insurance**. E&O insurance should be purchased by agents to protect themselves against legal liability arising from inadvertent errors or omissions.

The insurance business is constantly changing, so it's critical that insurance professionals maintain lifelong educational programs to keep their professional knowledge and skills up to date.

Many states have continuing education laws that require producers to take a certain number of hours of insurance-related course work before their licenses can be renewed. In states that do not have continuing education laws, insurance professionals must assess their own needs for continuing education and engage in ongoing improvement of their knowledge and skills.

Insurance professionals may also earn **professional designations** from educational organizations such as the American Institute for Chartered Property Casualty Underwriters and the Insurance Institute of America. These organizations have developed a variety of programs to meet the educational needs of insurance professionals. Some of the designations offered by the institutes include Chartered Property and Casualty Underwriter (CPCU), Accredited Adviser in Insurance (AAI), and Associate in Personal Insurance (API).

Agents also have responsibilities toward the insurance company or companies they represent. Agents must:

- be loyal to the insurer's interests and avoid engaging in any business activity that competes or interferes with the insurer's business;
- obey all legal instructions provided by the insurer;
- deposit funds belonging to the insurer in a separate account in the insurer's name;
- perform all duties with the degree of care and skill that a reasonably prudent person would exercise in the same circumstances; and
- keep the insurer informed of all facts related to the agency relationship.

3.4.2.2. Authority: Express, Implied, Apparent

An **agency** relationship exists when one party (an **agent**) is authorized to act on behalf of another (a **principal**). In the insurance business, the principal is the insurance company and the agent is a person authorized to act on the company's behalf. Principals grant certain powers, or authority, to their agents, and when agents act under these powers, their acts are considered to be the acts of the principal. These acts include making contracts and accepting money.

Even the knowledge of the agent is held to be the knowledge of the principal. For example, suppose the applicant tells the agent something very important about the applicant's insurability. The agent does not list this information on the application. According to the law of agency, the applicant is revealing the information to the insurance company through the knowledge of the agent.

There are actually three separate levels of agent authority. **Express authority** is the authority specifically given to an agent, either orally or in writing, by the principal. Written authority is usually provided through an agency agreement that allows the agent to countersign, issue, and deliver policies and provide other customary services on all contracts accepted by the insurer from the agent.

Implied authority is authority given by the insurance company to the agent that is not formally expressed or communicated. This implied authority allows the agent to perform all of the usual and necessary tasks to sell and service insurance contracts and to fully exercise the agent's express authority.

Apparent authority is a doctrine that holds that an agent may have whatever authority a reasonable person would assume the agent has. In the public's eye, an agent acting under apparent authority binds the company as fully as under expressed or implied authority.

3.4.3. Insurance Marketing Systems

There are four basic distribution systems used to market insurance:

- Exclusive agency system
- Direct writer system
- Direct response system
- Independent agency system

Insurance Marketing and the Internet

Advertising and selling insurance through the Internet is a relatively recent development in insurance marketing. Insurance company Websites offer information about insurers; the various lines of insurance provided; and links to regulatory information, financial rating, and quotation services as well as locator services to put consumers in touch with local agents. Some companies use the Internet to solicit leads, accept applications, and even issue insurance policies. Some insurance agencies have also developed home pages that advertise products and services over the Internet.

These practices raise some interesting questions about the regulation of Internet sales. Because the Internet essentially dissolves state geographic boundaries, at issue is whether the insurance company is licensed to do business in the state, and whether the agent is properly licensed and appointed for the companies represented. Other challenges include how to track premium taxes, how to ensure the security of disclosed personal information, how to audit Internet transactions, whether Internet advertisements comply with state laws, and what the implications are for state guaranty associations. The NAIC has established an Internet Marketing Issues Working Group to further explore these issues.

In an **exclusive** or **captive agency system,** the insurance company contracts with agencies, which are independent businesses, to represent and sell insurance only for that insurance company.

In the **direct writer system,** the insurance company's agents are actually employees. They may receive a salary, be paid by commission or a combination of both.

In the **direct response system,** there are no agents. These companies sell through direct mail or over the phone.

In the **independent agency system,** agencies that are independent contractors contract with several different companies to represent and sell insurance for those companies. An agent who represents more than one company is called an **independent** or **nonexclusive agent.** Several companies may authorize the agent to sell insurance for them, but the agent remains an independent businessperson. Agents collect commissions on the policies sold but collect no salary from the companies they represent.

In the exclusive agency, direct writing, and direct response systems, the insurance company owns and controls its accounts, policy records, and renewals. If the agency or employment relationship terminates, that person loses all rights and interest in company business and related commissions.

In contrast, in the independent agency system, the agent owns and controls accounts, policy records, and renewals. If an independent agent's contract with a particular insurer terminates, that agent retains rights to active accounts and may place them with another insurer and continue to receive commissions.

3.4.4. Other Insurance Professionals

Perhaps you have also heard the terms *solicitor*, *broker*, *excess* or *surplus lines agent*, and *producer* used in conjunction with a person who sells insurance. Although not every state recognizes these classifications, we'll explain briefly how these positions differ from that of an agent.

A **solicitor**, like an agent, sells insurance and may even be authorized to collect premiums. However, a solicitor cannot issue or countersign policies—this responsibility can only be handled by an agent. So a solicitor, who often works with or for an agent, has more limited authority than the agent.

Both agents and solicitors represent the insurance company. A **broker**, on the other hand, represents the insured. A company that is seeking insurance could contact a broker, who in turn might contact several insurance companies to find the insurance that is best for the client. Although a broker may sometimes act as an agent of the insurer in certain activities, such as policy delivery, a broker does not have the authority to bind an insurer to an insurance contract.

Excess or **surplus lines** are highly specialized insurance coverages, such as auto racing liability and tuition refund insurance, that are often not available from any company admitted to do business in a state. An **excess** or **surplus lines agent** is an agent licensed by the state to handle the placement of such coverages with nonadmitted companies (ones that are not authorized to conduct business in the state under ordinary circumstances).

Producer is a general term used to describe someone who sells insurance, such as an agent, broker, or solicitor.

Another type of insurance professional you might encounter is an insurance **consultant**. A consultant is someone who, for a fee, offers advice on the benefits, advantages, and disadvantages of various insurance policies. Consultants don't actually sell insurance; they sell advice.

Exercise 3.C

Mark the following as examples of an excess lines agent, consultant, solicitor, or broker.

1. Garraway Construction wants insurance to cover its multimillion dollar foreign construction project. The company contacts a professional to represent Garraway in finding the best coverage for the money.

   ____

2. Janice provides advice about various insurance policies for a fee. She does not sell insurance.

 ____

3. Bill is licensed to handle highly specialized insurance coverages. He is authorized to obtain these coverages from insurance companies not admitted to do business in the state where he works.

 ____

4. Jim, an employee of the Goodwill Agency, spends his days collecting premiums and finding prospective clients. He has no authority to issue or countersign policies.

 ____

Exercise answers can be found at the of the Unit 3 answers and rationales.

3.4.5. Other Insurance Functions

Of course, an agent would have nothing to sell if it weren't for the other functions taking place in the insurance company—at both its central, or home, office and its regional, or branch, offices.

Loss, Expense, and Combined Ratios

An insurance company evaluates its overall book of business for given periods to measure its financial performance during those periods and to look for trends that may have occurred over an extended time. An insurer uses three ratios to evaluate its book of business: loss ratio, expense ratio, and combined ratio.

The **loss ratio** is used to compare the company's operations from year to year. It shows the percentage of losses the company incurred for every dollar of earned premium. It is calculated by dividing the amount of incurred losses by the amount of earned premium. Here is the loss ratio as a formula:

$$\text{Loss ratio} = \frac{\text{incurred losses}}{\text{earned premiums}}$$

Earned premium is the premium the company actually earned by providing insurance protection for the designated period. **Incurred losses** include amounts paid on claims for covered losses and various expenses related to handling claims.

The **expense ratio** indicates the cost of doing business. The formula is:

$$\text{Expense ratio} = \frac{\text{underwriting expenses}}{\text{written premium}}$$

Underwriting expenses are the costs required to acquire and maintain a book of business. They include expenses for advertising, commissions, salaries, and other administrative costs and regulatory costs such as taxes and licensing fees.

Written premium is the gross amount of premium income on the company's books. It includes both earned and unearned premium. Premiums for new business, renewals, and policy endorsements make up written premium.

The **combined ratio** is simply the sum of the loss ratio and the expense ratio:

Combined ratio = loss ratio + expense ratio

Traditionally, 100% is considered to be the breakeven point. A combined ratio of less than 100% indicates that the company had an underwriting profit; a ratio of greater than 100% indicates a loss.

Underwriting Department: **Underwriting** is the process of selecting certain types of risks and rejecting others so the insurance company will have a book of business that will produce the company's desired results. The underwriting department is usually made up of many individual underwriters, who decide whether to accept or reject the applications sent in by agents on the basis of the company's standards and their own judgment. They may also be called on to review loss experience, provide judgment rates, and specify the particular policy forms required to provide the coverages applicants have requested.

Policy Issue and Administration: Once the underwriter has approved a new application or a change to a current policy, the application is checked by a **policy analyst** or **screener** to make sure all information is correct and complete. It then goes to a **rater**, who computes the premium to be charged. The policy forms may be printed by computer or assembled in an **assembly and filing area**. Copies of the policy will be mailed to the agent, the insured, or both.

In many companies, policy rating, policy issue, and assembly are combined with the underwriting function in a single unit. Each unit has responsibility for all of these functions within a specific geographic region or territory.

Claims Department: The claims department sees that the company's insureds are adequately indemnified for their losses. **Claim adjusters** or **representatives** are used to inspect a loss, determine whether there is coverage for the loss, estimate indemnification, and, in some cases, pay for the loss immediately. Large companies have their own claim adjusters, whereas smaller companies may use the services of **independent adjusters**.

Actuarial and Statistical Department: The actuarial and statistical department is the numbers department. Using the tremendous amount of data generated by computer, together with statistics available from other companies, **actuaries** determine the rates to be charged for various types of insurance.

Accounting Department: As with any profit-oriented business, the determination of financial condition is a very important function in an insurance company. However, insurance companies must place special emphasis on this area because their finances are closely regulated by the state—for example, premiums must be credited to specific accounts, agents must be paid commissions, and proper reserves must be maintained. All of these functions are handled by the accounting department.

Investment Department: The investment department oversees the funds the company needs to invest to make sure adequate funds will be on hand to pay claims. The investment department attempts to maintain a healthy rate of return while maintaining the safety of the investment. Because money must be on hand to pay future obligations, highly speculative stocks are not appropriate, and at least some of the investments must be readily convertible to cash, as needed.

Legal Department: Because insurance policies are legal contracts, it is not surprising that insurance companies maintain a legal staff. This department interprets the various state insurance laws and helps the company keep its policies and practices in compliance. A key role is the department's involvement with court cases arising from claims. The legal department is instrumental in helping determine fair indemnification for insureds and is involved in the company's other legal actions.

Audit Department: For certain insurance coverages, a premium is determined after or during the policy term, instead of at the beginning of the policy term. These after-the-fact premiums may be based on a number of factors such as payroll, number of employees, or amount of receipts. The audit department checks the accounting records of these insureds at the required intervals to obtain the necessary information used to determine these types of premiums.

Loss Control Department: Although insureds are glad when insurance pays for a loss, they would rather have no loss at all. This is why prevention and control of losses are very important aspects of the insurance business. The loss control department, or engineering department as it may be called in some companies, inspects factories, certifies boilers, and makes recommendations to insureds as to how risks may be avoided or reduced.

Agency Department: This department works very closely with, and directs the operations of, the agents who represent the company. Its responsibilities include recruiting, appointing, and training, especially if an agent will be an exclusive agent. The department must monitor the sales and marketing efforts of these agents and make sure that the number and quality of agents are closely tuned to the market the company serves.

Marketing Department: Closely related to the agency department, the marketing department helps determine the company's overall marketing strategy. It develops advertising and sales aids or works closely with a separate advertising department to accomplish these goals.

Reinsurance Department: Insurance companies themselves often purchase insurance to cover their own exposure to loss. This is called **reinsurance**. Reinsurance helps protect insurance companies from catastrophic losses and from wild fluctuations in underwriting results. This coverage may be obtained on a policy-by-policy basis or on the basis of a whole block of policies. The reinsurance may cover the initial insurer for losses above a certain amount or may call for losses to be shared on a pro rata basis.

Support Departments: Like other businesses, insurance companies have departments whose contributions help all other departments operate smoothly. They include **personnel**, **training**, **information systems**, **administration**, **forms and filings**, and **building and maintenance**.

Exercise 3.D

Match the name of the department listed in the left-hand column with the function it performs listed in the right-hand column.

____ 1. Decides whether to accept or reject applications on the basis of company standards	A.	Underwriting
____ 2. Determines the rates to be charged for various types of insurance	B.	Policy issue and administration
____ 3. Oversees the company's investments to ensure that there are adequate funds to pay claims	C.	Claims
____ 4. Performs a variety of functions such as checking applications for accuracy and completeness, rating policies, and printing and assembling policies	D.	Actuarial and statistical
____ 5. Makes sure insureds are properly indemnified for losses	E.	Accounting
____ 6. Handles transactions related to the company's financial condition	F.	Investment

Exercise answers can be found at the end of the Unit 3 answers and rationales.

3.5. REGULATION

3.5.1. State Insurance Regulation

Because of the long-term nature of the insurance contract and the principle of utmost good faith on which such contracts are based, insurance is closely regulated for the good of the insurance industry and the general public. And because insurance needs and practices differ from one area to another, it is the states that regulate the insurance business conducted within their boundaries.

Each state has an **insurance department** headed by an official charged with the responsibility for controlling insurance matters within that state.

These officials are called **Directors**, **Superintendents**, or **Commissioners of Insurance**, depending on the state in which they hold office, but they all perform similar duties.

The Commissioners of each of the states together make up the **National Association of Insurance Commissioners (NAIC)**, which meets at regular intervals to exchange information and provide coordination of the regulatory measures of each state. Through its recommendations, much of the nation's insurance laws take shape. Although nonbinding on individual states, the NAIC's recommendations are generally followed.

3.5.2. Regulation and the Company

3.5.2.1. Admitted (Authorized) and Nonadmitted (Unauthorized) Companies

A state insurance department has four areas of responsibility:

- Companies
- Agents
- Ratification
- Enforcement

We'll first consider the department's duties with regard to companies.

One of the duties of an insurance department is to determine which insurance companies will be allowed to do business in the state. A company that meets the insurance department's standards and is authorized to do business in a state is called an **admitted** or **authorized insurer**. An insurance company that is not authorized to do business in a state is a **nonadmitted** or **unauthorized insurer**. A nonadmitted insurer may only do business in the state under special circumstances.

3.5.2.2. Domestic, Foreign, Alien

Although a company may conduct business in several states, it is formed and incorporated in only one state. Within its home state, an insurance company is known as a **domestic** company. Within states other than the state in which it is incorporated, an insurance company is a **foreign** company. A company that is incorporated in a country other than the United States but doing business in the states is known as an **alien** company.

For example, Amalgamated Indemnity is incorporated in the state of Ohio. Within Ohio, Amalgamated is known as a domestic company. In all other states in which Amalgamated is admitted to do business, Amalgamated is considered a foreign company.

Another insurer, Rio Grande Insurance Company, is incorporated in Mexico but writes some business in Ohio. In Ohio, Rio Grande is referred to as an alien company.

3.5.2.3. Financial Regulation

In addition to examining and authorizing companies to conduct business within the state, the state insurance department keeps close watch over the financial health of all companies doing business within its boundaries.

Various regulations are designed to preserve insurance company solvency, detect financial problems, and protect insureds in the event of insolvency. State laws impose capital and surplus requirements on insurers, require the preparation of annual financial statements, and require periodic examinations of insurers. These laws establish initial financial requirements and help in the early detection of financial problems. If an insurer falls into a hazardous financial condition, the insurance department attempts to rehabilitate the company. If an insurer becomes insolvent, the insurance department will handle the liquidation. In many states, the public is also protected by one or more **insurance guaranty associations**, which provide funds for payment of unpaid claims when an insurer becomes insolvent.

3.5.2.4. Independent Rating Services

There are several organizations that rate the financial strength of insurance carriers on the basis of an analysis of a company's claims experience, investment performance, management, and other factors. These organizations include A.M. Best, Inc., and Standard & Poor's. These ratings are one of the most widely used indicators of financial health (or the lack of it) in the insurance industry.

The approach taken by A.M. Best, Inc., illustrates one approach to evaluating companies. Best uses nine alphabetical ratings for insurers to which it gives an assigned rating and uses other designations to evaluate financial health, which are explained in the following.

A++, A+	Superior—strongest position
A, A–	Excellent
B++, B+	Very good
B, B–	Good
C++, C+	Fair
C, C–	Marginal
D	Below minimum standards
E	Under state supervision
F	In liquidation

Various **modifiers** (one of eight lowercase letters) may be added to assigned ratings, which are shown in upper case, to qualify the status of a rating. For example, *g* is used to indicate a group rating involving a pool of affiliated companies. The letter *e* indicates a parent company rating, when the financial strength of the parent is used to evaluate a newly affiliated company. Caution is signaled by a *w*, which means "watch list": some decline has occurred but not enough to cause a drop in the assigned rating. An overall rating might look like this:

B+w: Very good, but watch

3.5.3. Regulation and the Agent

3.5.3.1. Licensing

The state insurance department devotes much of its time to working with insurance agents. One of its most important duties with regard to agents is licensing. It is illegal for someone to sell insurance without first obtaining a license from the state to do so.

To make sure agents will be prepared to undertake their substantial responsibilities, each state requires its agents to pass a licensing exam to receive a license.

3.5.3.2. Codes Regulating Agents

In addition to licensing, the state is responsible for the way agents conduct business within the state. State insurance codes are very specific about the standards agents must meet. Although we won't try to cover each of the many types of laws governing agent conduct, we'll introduce you to some important terms.

Fiduciary: A fiduciary is a person who stands in a special relationship of trust to another person. Agents have fiduciary duties toward their clients, especially regarding handling premiums. Agents also owe a fiduciary responsibility to the insurer and must always make decisions in the insurer's best interest.

Misrepresentation: Agents may not misrepresent or falsely advertise the terms or benefits of a policy or the financial condition of the company. The agent must make complete, accurate statements about the product being sold.

Twisting: Twisting is a form of misrepresentation in which the agent convinces the client to cancel already-existing insurance and buy another policy from the agent, to the detriment of the insured. Twisting is illegal.

Rebating: Rebating is giving or offering some benefit other than those specified in the policy, such as cash, gifts, or securities, to induce a customer to buy insurance. For example, an agent might kick back part of a commission to the customer, thus lowering the price of the insurance, in return for the business. Rebating is illegal in all but two states.

Unfair Discrimination: Agents can be in violation of the law if they unfairly discriminate against insureds. This means that an insured cannot be given a lower or higher rate than another insured in identical circumstances. It also means that the agent cannot accept a bribe from a client to provide insurance or lower the premium.

Exercise 3.E

Identify each of the following examples as twisting **(T)**, rebating **(R)**, failure of fiduciary responsibility **(F)**, misrepresentation **(M)**, or unfair discrimination **(U)**.

1. ____ Joe agrees to split the commissions he earns with his clients. He's able to sell more insurance this way.
2. ____ Ann receives a check from the insurance company that is a refund to one of her insureds. She cashes the check herself and pockets the money.
3. ____ Allen tells an applicant that her new policy covers earthquake damage, although it does not.
4. ____ May agrees to offer an insured a lower premium if he will agree to direct other family members to May.
5. ____ George persuades a prospect to let her current policy lapse and buy insurance through him. He tells the prospect that his company's policy provides more coverage at a lower premium, even though this is not true.

Exercise answers can be found at the end of the Unit 3 answers and rationales.

3.5.4. Ratification

3.5.4.1. Forms and Rates

Another important function performed by state insurance departments is approval, or **ratification**, of the policy forms, endorsements, and rates used by companies doing business in their states.

In some states, called **prior approval** states, the insurance company must obtain official approval before using new forms and rates.

In **file and use** states, a company may begin using forms and rates as soon as they have been filed. The state eventually reviews the filing and officially accepts or rejects it.

In **use and file** states, insurers must file rates and forms within a certain period after they are first used.

Open competition states allow the companies to compete openly with the forms and rates they select, subject only to requirements of adequacy and nondiscrimination (we'll discuss these two requirements in a moment).

In some states, for some lines of insurance, the use of unique state forms or rates may be mandatory for any company doing business in the state.

You've learned that the state insurance department must also approve the rates each company uses. **Rates** are the basic charges an insurance company sets for various types of insurance.

When a company establishes a rate it will use, it calculates a rate that will be adequate to pay:

- the cost of losses that will have to be paid;
- the cost of conducting the business; and
- a small profit.

Insurance companies collect extensive data in each of these areas to help them calculate rate levels. Data are collected on a large number and variety of risks. Within a specific line of insurance, risks with similar characteristics are grouped together in classes, and rates are determined for each class.

When the state examines rates for approval or rejection, it requires that the rates be adequate for the company to meet its obligations to insureds. It also requires that the rates be **nondiscriminatory**, meaning the insurer cannot charge different rates for the same class of insureds, and **not excessive**, meaning the rates cannot be so high as to allow the company to make a windfall profit or make insurance an unrealistic purchase.

3.5.4.2. Rating Organizations

Some states establish their own rates for certain types of insurance and require all companies to use these mandatory rates. For most types of insurance, however, the company must establish the rates and submit them to the state.

We've already indicated that this involves collecting extensive and accurate financial, operational, and loss records. To help the insurance company collect these statistics, central **service bureaus** have been established. These organizations, made up of numerous individual insurance companies, gather, pool, and analyze statistics from all of the member companies. The bureau then establishes **loss costs** based on these combined figures and files them with individual states. Loss costs represent the key component of an insurance rate—how much an insurance company needs to collect to cover expected losses.

Member companies may use these loss costs, combined with factors covering their own expenses and profit margins, to establish finished rates. Companies must file rates with the state but may do this by referencing the service bureau's loss costs and filing their own individual factors that reflect expenses and profit. Some companies do not belong to a service organization; they collect their own statistics and file independently.

Companies that use bureau filings sometimes deviate from the published rates by charging something either higher or lower than the recommended rate. Deviations are usually permitted within a specified range, provided that the insurer is consistent in applying the same deviation to all similar risks.

One of the largest services bureaus is the **Insurance Services Office (ISO)**. ISO files both loss costs and standardized forms on behalf of its member companies. The **National Council on Compensation Insurance (NCCI)** is a rating bureau with jurisdiction over workers' compensation. The **Surety Association of America** functions as a rating bureau for surety bonds. There are numerous other rating bureaus.

3.5.5. Enforcement

The final area of regulatory responsibility for state insurance departments is enforcement. We've already talked about many of the rules that apply to the conduct of the companies, agents, and types of insurance transacted within the state. The department is responsible for seeing that the insurance business within the state is in compliance with these codes and standards. Reported violations must be investigated and appropriate penalties assessed. Violations can result in fines, license suspension or revocation, suspension or revocation of a company's authority to do business in the state, and, in some cases, imprisonment.

3.5.6. Federal Regulation

Although most insurance operations are primarily regulated by the states, there are some areas where the federal government has some regulatory impact on insurers.

For example, federal law imposes penalties for fraud and false statements made in connection with insurance transactions. Anyone engaged in the insurance business who makes a false material statement or report or willfully and materially overvalues any land, property, or security in connection with financial reports or documents presented to an insurance regulatory official or agency for the purpose of influencing their actions will be punished accordingly. The punishment for this offense is a fine, imprisonment for up to 10 years, or both. The term of imprisonment may be up to 15 years if the statement, report, or overvaluing of land, property, or security jeopardized the safety and soundness of an insurer and was a significant cause of the insurer being placed in conservation, rehabilitation, or liquidation by an appropriate court.

Any insurance officer, director, or agent who willfully embezzles, abstracts, purloins, or misappropriates any of the moneys, funds, premiums, credits, or other property of an insurer may be punished accordingly. The punishment may consist of a fine, imprisonment for up to 10 years, or both. If the crime jeopardizes the safety and soundness of an insurer and was a significant cause of the insurer being placed in conservation, rehabilitation, or liquidation by an appropriate court, imprisonment may be up to 15 years. If the amount or value does not exceed $5,000, whoever violates this section will be fined, imprisoned for up to one year, or both.

Any insurance professional who knowingly makes any false entry of material fact in any book, report, or statement of a person engaged in the insurance business with intent to deceive another person about the financial condition or solvency of the business may be punished accordingly. The punishment for this offense is a fine, imprisonment for up to 10 years, or both. If the false entry jeopardized the safety and soundness of an insurer and was a significant cause of an insurer being placed in conservation, rehabilitation, or liquidation by an appropriate court, imprisonment may be up to 15 years.

Anyone who threatens, forces, or corruptly influences, obstructs, or impedes the due and proper administration of the law under any proceeding involving the insurance business may be fined and/or imprisoned for up to 10 years.

An insurance professional who has been convicted of any criminal felony involving dishonesty or a breach of trust or who has been convicted of an offense under this section may be fined, imprisoned for up to five years, or both. After committing a felony of this nature, offenders may only engage in the business of insurance if they have the written consent of an insurance regulatory official. (18 USC 1033–1034)

3.5.6.1. Prohibited Persons in Insurance—Federal Violent Crime Control and Law Enforcement Act (18 USC Sect 1033, 1034)

The Federal Violent Crime Control and Law Enforcement Act expanded federal law in several ways:

- It prohibits anyone who has been convicted of a state or federal felony involving dishonesty or breach of trust from engaging in the insurance business without a consent waiver from the Commissioner.
- There is no statute of limitations.
- It prohibits fraud, embezzlement, falsification of company records, or coercion in insurance transactions in interstate commerce.
- Penalties range from $5,000 to $10,000, imprisonment from 10 to 15 years, or both fine and imprisonment. Violations may result in both civil (monetary, regulatory) and criminal (fines and/or jail) penalties.

3.5.6.2. USA PATRIOT Act (Uniting and Strengthening America by Providing Appropriate Tools Required to Intercept and Obstruct Terrorism of 2001)

This law gives the federal government broad power to curtail attempts to launder money and finance terrorist activities, and includes the following:

- Stronger anti-money laundering provisions
- Broad enforcement discretion to government officials
- Guidance to US financial institutions

- Forfeiture of laundered assets
- Appropriate regulation across the financial services industry
- Stronger ability of financial institutions to maintain integrity of employees
- Requirement of reports of potential money-laundering transactions to authorities
- Prevention of use of US financial system for personal gain by corrupt non-US political figures and officials

Almost all financial institutions are subject to review. The law requires institutions to:

- develop a compliance program and train personnel to follow it;
- designate an anti-money laundering officer;
- share information with other institutions; and
- adopt procedures to verify identity of any person opening an account.

3.5.6.3. National Do Not Call Registry

The National Do Not Call Registry is a list of phone numbers from consumers who have indicated their preference to limit the telemarketing calls they receive. The registry is managed and enforced by the Federal Trade Commission (FTC), as well as the Federal Communications Commission (FCC), and state officials.

The National Do Not Call Registry applies to any plan, program, or campaign to sell goods or services through interstate phone calls, including insurance. This includes telemarketers who solicit consumers on behalf of third parties. It also includes sellers who provide, offer to provide, or arrange to provide goods or services to consumers in exchange for payment.

Calls from or on behalf of political organizations, charities, and telephone surveyors are still permitted, as well as calls from companies that have the express written permission of the consumer. Calls are also permitted to consumers with whom the company has established a business relationship, as follows.

- A consumer can establish a business relationship with an insurer by requesting information from it or submitting an application to it. In this case the business can call for three months from the date of inquiry or application. For example, a person contacts an insurance company to request information about types of policies offered by the company. That insurance company has the right to call the person for three months, even if the person did not purchase a policy or product.
- A company with which a consumer has an established business relationship may call for up to 18 months after the consumer's last purchase or last delivery, or last payment, unless the consumer asks the company not to call again.
- Telemarketers and sellers are required to search the registry at least once every 31 days and drop from their call lists the phone numbers of consumers who have registered.

A consumer who receives a telemarketing call despite being on the registry will be able to file a complaint with the FTC, either online or by calling a toll-free number. Violators could be fined up to $11,000 per incident.

UNIT TEST

1. A mutual insurance company
   A. is managed by an attorney-in-fact
   B. pays dividends to its stockholders
   C. is owned by its insureds
   D. is a voluntary association of individuals that shares in writing insurance contracts for a variety of risks

2. Beneficient Insurers writes homeowners, auto, and liability insurance for individuals and families. Beneficient is a (mono-/multi-) ______________________ line company that specializes in (personal/commercial) ____________ lines.

3. One of the most important risks covered by insurance policies in the casualty line is the risk that
   A. you will outlive your financial resources
   B. you will become liable for damage to others
   C. property you own will be damaged
   D. you will become disabled

4. A nonexclusive agent
   A. represents a single insurance company
   B. works for a direct writer
   C. is an independent businessperson
   D. does not collect commissions

5. Solicitors may not
   A. issue or countersign policies
   B. sell insurance
   C. collect premiums
   D. sign an application

6. At DEF Insurance Company, agents are employees of the company who are paid a salary plus commissions. This is an example of what type of insurance marketing system?
   A. Captive
   B. Independent
   C. Direct writer
   D. Direct response

7. An agent has all of the following responsibilities to applicants and insureds EXCEPT
   A. preparing quotations for prospects
   B. countersigning policies
   C. reviewing insureds' coverage on a regular basis
   D. representing the insured in the insurance transaction

8. The actuarial department
   A. performs inspections and certifications
   B. examines the financial and bookkeeping records of insureds to determine after-the-fact premiums
   C. determines the company's overall marketing strategy
   D. collects and analyzes data to determine the rates to be charged for insurance

9. Which insurance company department is responsible for accepting and rejecting applications on the basis of company standards?
   A. Underwriting
   B. Loss control
   C. Claims
   D. Agency

10. Which insurance company department is responsible for paying insureds' covered losses?
   A. Audit
   B. Claims
   C. Underwriting
   D. Reinsurance

11. Perfect Policies, Inc., is an insurance company incorporated in Idaho.
   A. In Idaho, Perfect Policies is a/an (domestic/foreign/alien)__________________ company.
   B. Perfect Policies is also authorized to do business in Montana. In Montana, Perfect Policies is (admitted/nonadmitted) ______________________ and is a(n) (domestic/foreign/alien) __________________ company.

12. Who is responsible for licensing insurance agents?
    A. Lloyd's Associations
    B. State insurance department
    C. Interstate Commerce Commission
    D. Insurance Services Office

13. Blondell is offering a free television to every applicant who agrees to buy insurance through his agency. In most states, this is an illegal practice known as
    A. rebating
    B. twisting
    C. misrepresentation
    D. failure of fiduciary responsibility

14. State insurance departments are responsible for approving or rejecting
    A. rates
    B. policy forms
    C. both A and B

15. Match the method of rate and form regulation listed in the left-hand column with its correct description in the right-hand column.

____ A. Prior approval	1. Insurers compete with one another with the forms and rates they select, subject only to requirements of adequacy and nondiscrimination.
____ B. File and use	2. Insurers must obtain official approval from the state before using forms or rates.
____ C. Use and file	3. Insurers must use state's unique forms or rates.
____ D. Open competition	4. Insurers begin using rates and forms as soon as they are filed with the state.
____ E. Mandatory	5. Insurers must file rates and forms for approval within a certain period after they are first used.

16. J&M Industries does not have a group health insurance plan for its employees. Instead, it pays employees' medical expenses out of a fund specifically created for this purpose. This is an example of
    A. fraternal insurance
    B. self-insurance
    C. reinsurance

17. What is the primary reason the state or federal government becomes involved in providing insurance?

____

____

18. If an insurance company's agent makes an error, can the company be held liable? ( ) Yes ( ) No Explain your answer.______________________

____

19. Which of the following statements concerning regulation of the insurance industry is CORRECT?
   A. The insurance industry is regulated by the federal government.
   B. The insurance industry is very loosely regulated.
   C. The state insurance department is responsible for controlling insurance matters within the state.
   D. The state insurance department serves only the interests of the insurance industry.

20. Give three reasons that state insurance departments regulate insurance companies' financial situations.
   A. ______________________________________
   ____
   ____
   B. ______________________________________
   ____
   ____
   C. ______________________________________
   ____
   ____

ANSWERS AND RATIONALES TO UNIT TEST

1. **C.** In a mutual company, insureds are also owners of the company. They can vote to elect the management of the company. Profits are returned to insureds in the form of dividends or reductions in future premiums.

2. multi-, personal. A multiline company is one that writes more than one line of insurance. Personal lines are property and casualty coverages that protect an individual or family.

3. **B.** Casualty insurance includes a wide variety of basically unrelated insurance products. One of the most important risks it covers is the risk of suffering financial loss as a result of our actions toward others.

4. **C.** A nonexclusive, or independent, agent represents more than one company. This type of agent collects commissions on the policies sold but collects no salary from the companies the agent represents.

5. **A.** A solicitor, who often works with or for an agent, has more limited authority than the agent. A solicitor sells insurance and may even be authorized to collect premiums. However, a solicitor cannot issue or countersign policies.

6. **C.** In the direct writer system, the insurer's agents are actually employees. They may receive a salary, be paid on commission, or both.

7. **D.** Under the law of agency, an insurance agent represents the insurance company. A broker represents the insured.

8. **D.** Choice A describes the loss control department. Choice B describes the audit department. Choice C refers to the marketing department.

9. **A.** Underwriting is the process of selecting certain types of risks and rejecting others so the insurer will have a profitable book of business.

10. **B.** The claims department sees that the company's insureds are adequately indemnified for their losses. Claim adjusters determine the cause of loss, whether the loss is covered by the policy, the value of the loss, and the amount of loss payable by the policy.

11. A. domestic; B. admitted, foreign. An insurance company is known as a domestic company in the state in which it was formed and incorporated. A company that is authorized by a state's insurance department to do business in that state is an admitted insurer. An insurance company is known as a foreign company while it is doing business in states other than the state in which it was formed and incorporated.

12. **B.** State insurance departments devote much of their time to working with insurance agents. One of their most important duties is agent licensing.

13. **A.** Rebating is giving or offering some benefit other than those specified in the policy, such as cash, gifts, or securities, to induce a customer to buy insurance. Rebating is illegal in all but two states.

14. **C.** One of the functions performed by state insurance departments is approval, or ratification, of the policy forms, endorsements, and rates used by companies doing business in their states.

15. 2 A.; 4 B.; 5 C.; 1 D.; 3 E. State insurance departments use several methods to ratify forms and rates used in their states. In prior approval states, the insurance company

must obtain official approval before using new forms and rates. In file and use states, a company may begin using forms and rates as soon as they have been filed. The state eventually reviews the filing and officially accepts or rejects it. With use and file states, insurers must file rates and forms within a certain period after they are first used. In open competition states, the state allows the companies to compete openly with the forms and rates they select, subject only to requirements of adequacy and non discrimination. In some states, for some lines of insurance, the use of unique state forms or rates may be mandatory for any company doing business in the state.

16. **B.** With self-insurance, part or all of the risk of loss is borne without the benefit of insurance coverage to fall back on if a loss occurs.

17. To provide insurance that is not available from private insurers. The government sometimes steps in to provide insurance that is not available from private insurers. Flood insurance and federal crop insurance are examples of insurance provided by the federal government. At the state level, the government is involved in providing unemployment insurance and may provide workers' compensation benefits through state funds.

18. **Yes.** Under the principles of agency, actions or knowledge of the agent are considered actions or knowledge of the principal.

19. **C.** Insurance is regulated by the states. It is closely regulated for the good of the insurance industry and the general public.

20. In any order: To preserve solvency; To detect financial problems; To protect insureds if insolvency occurs. A state insurance department monitors the financial health of all companies doing business within its boundaries. Various regulations are designed to preserve insurance company solvency, detect financial problems, and protect insureds if insolvency occurs.

UNIT 3 EXERCISE ANSWERS

Exercise 3.A

1. Casualty
2. Property

Exercise 3.B

1. **P**
2. **C**
3. **P**
4. **C**

Exercise 3.C

1. Broker
2. Consultant
3. Excess lines agent
4. Solicitor

Exercise 3.D

1. **A**
2. **D**
3. **F**
4. **B**
5. **C**
6. **E**

Exercise 3.E

1. **R**
2. **F**
3. **M**
4. **U**
5. **T**

UNIT

4

The Insurance Transaction

4.1. LEARNING OBJECTIVES

After completing Unit 4—The Insurance Transaction, you will be able to do the following:

- Explain the role of applications and binders in insurance transactions
- Explain how the federal Fair Credit Reporting Act and the principle of adverse selection affect the underwriting process
- Describe the different methods used to rate insurance policies
- Explain how misrepresentation, fraud, concealment, warranties, and waiver and estoppel may affect an in-force contract
- Define material fact, certificate of insurance, and representation
- Describe the rights and responsibilities of insureds and insurance companies when an insurance policy is canceled or nonrenewed

4.2. APPLICATION

Before an insurance policy can be issued, the prospective insured must apply to the insurance company. The agent and the applicant fill out an **application** form that is then forwarded to the insurance company. The application is the insured's offer. (Remember that an offer is one of the necessary elements of a contract.)

The application contains underwriting information to help the company decide whether it should accept or reject the prospect's offer to become an insured. The application also contains rating information that will help the insurance company decide how much the insured will be charged if the policy is issued.

Because the application represents the company's primary source of information about the risk to be insured, it is vitally important that the agent fill out the application completely and accurately. The agent must make sure to ask the prospect every question on the application form, faithfully recording answers and questioning information that seems vague or inaccurate to provide as clear a picture of the risk as possible. Failure to do so can be expensive for the company, the prospect, and the agent.

4.3. BINDERS

After the agent has completed the application, he may have the authority to issue a **binder** for insurance. This is an oral or written statement made by the agent that the insured has immediate protection that is valid for a specified time. If it is an oral statement, it must be backed up in writing as soon as possible.

A binder can also be issued by the insurance company. This is often done to let the insured know that there is coverage but that the actual policy will be issued in a few days.

A binder does not guarantee that a policy will be issued; it only guarantees temporary coverage. The insurance company has access to additional information that is not readily available to an agent. This information might convince the company to refuse to issue the policy, even though the agent has already issued a binder. In this case, coverage under the binder may be canceled by a formal cancellation or rejection notice. However, if no formal cancellation is made, coverage remains in effect until the binder expires. If the policy is issued, coverage under the binder ceases as of the effective date of the policy.

Suppose John gets an oral statement from his agent on July 6 that he is "bound" effective that date for 90 days. The insurance company reviews the application and decides not to issue the policy. However, it does not send John a formal notice of cancellation. On July 21, John has a loss that would have been covered under the policy. Because the agent issued a binder, John will have coverage for this loss.

4.4. UNDERWRITING THE POLICY

When the application comes to the insurance company, underwriters review it for its acceptability to the company. In addition to the application, underwriters may turn to other sources of information to help them evaluate the risk. These include:

- inspection services;
- government bureaus, such as the Bureau of Motor Vehicles;
- insurance industry bureaus, such as the Automated Property Loss Underwriting System;
- financial information services, such as Standard & Poor's;
- previous insurers; and
- the company's own claim files.

4.4.1. Fair Credit Reporting Act

When an application is submitted to an insurance company, a consumer reporting agency is often hired to obtain information about the applicant. Reports that have traditionally been called credit reports are actually consumer reports. In addition to a consumer's credit standing, the reports explore personal character, reputation, habits, and lifestyle. Public reaction to the misuse of personal information led to the enactment of the federal **Fair Credit Reporting Act**. This act protects consumers by requiring that the consumer be notified in certain situations and by establishing provisions for the removal of outdated and incorrect information. One of the purposes of the act is to ensure that credit reporting agencies exercise their responsibilities with fairness, impartiality, and a respect for the consumer's right to privacy.

The act applies to the preparation and use of two types of reports: **regular** consumer reports and **investigative** consumer reports. The two contain similar types of information, but the investigative report gathers data through personal interviews with friends, neighbors, and associates of the consumer.

Under the act, reporting agencies may furnish reports only for specific purposes, which are spelled out in the law. A report may be provided to someone who intends to use the information for insurance underwriting purposes or in connection with employment, credit transactions, or other types of personal business transactions.

Consumer reporting agencies are specifically prevented from putting information in their reports about:

- bankruptcies over 10 years old;
- suits and judgments over seven years old or in which the statute of limitations has expired, whichever period is longer;
- paid tax liens or accounts placed for collection or charged to profit that are over seven years old;
- arrests, indictments, or conviction of crime reports; and
- any other adverse information that took place seven years before the report.

These restrictions are not applicable when the consumer credit report is used in connection with a credit transaction of $150,000 or more, a life insurance policy of $150,000 or more, or when it concerns employment of an individual earning $75,000 or more.

Before or shortly after an investigative report (but not a regular report) is ordered, the consumer must be informed in writing that the report may be made and that additional information about the nature and scope of the report is available upon written request. The initial written notice must be sent to the consumer no later than three days after the report is ordered. Many insurers provide prenotification by stating on the insurance application that an investigative report may be ordered. If a consumer requests the additional information about the nature of the report, the disclosure must be made within five days.

Postnotification of an adverse outcome is required for both regular and investigative reports. If insurance is rejected, reduced, or written at a higher premium because of the information in the report, the consumer must be notified and provided with the name and address of the reporting agency. The consumer has the right to obtain the substance of the information in the report (but not the actual report) and to be informed of the identity of anyone who received reports within the previous six months.

If the consumer challenges any information, the reporting agency is required to reinvestigate and to change the report if necessary. If inaccurate information was given to any individuals or organizations within the previous six months, the consumer's side of the story must be provided to those parties.

Both reporting agencies and users of reports are subject to civil and criminal penalties for failure to comply with the provisions of the act. For negligent noncompliance, the consumer may recover any actual damages from the guilty party, although such damages may be difficult to prove. For willful noncompliance, criminal penalties of up to two years in prison, a fine, or both may be imposed. Anyone who knowingly and willfully obtains consumer information from a reporting agency under false pretenses as well as officers or employees of reporting agencies who knowingly and willfully provide consumer information to anyone not authorized to receive it can be subject to criminal charges.

4.4.2. Adverse Selection

Underwriters are responsible for protecting the insurer against adverse selection.

Adverse selection is the tendency for people with a greater-than-average exposure to loss to purchase insurance. For example, certain parts of the country are very prone to earthquakes, so people in those areas are likely to want earthquake insurance to protect their property against loss. On the other hand, people who live in areas that are not prone to earthquakes would have no need for such coverage. An insurance company that wrote a large amount of insurance in earthquake-prone areas would be subject to adverse selection. This means the company may experience large financial losses and decreased profitability.

4.4.3. Basic Types of Construction

For property risks, a building's construction type is considered when underwriting and rating a policy. The construction of the building is determined by the types of materials used in the building and roof of the insured structure. Construction materials are also found in the building's interior finish and insulation. Other construction factors that an underwriter considers include the number of fire divisions in the building, the adequacy of electrical circuits for the occupancy, the number of stories, the building's age, and the type of heating system. Most underwriters recognize six construction classifications or types:

- **Class 1—Frame:** Frame structures have outside support walls, roof, and floors constructed of wood or other combustible materials. The exterior walls may be covered with stucco or brick veneer, and the interior walls are typically lath and plaster.
- **Class 2—Joisted Masonry:** Joisted masonry structures have outside support walls made of noncombustible masonry materials (such as concrete, brick, hollow concrete block, stone, or tile) and a roof and floor made of combustible materials (such as wood).
- **Class 3—Noncombustible:** A noncombustible structure is one whose exterior walls, floors, and roof are constructed of and supported by noncombustible materials such as metal, asbestos, or gypsum.

- **Class 4—Masonry Noncombustible:** Structures in this construction class have exterior walls constructed of masonry materials and a roof and floor made of metal or other non-combustible materials.
- **Class 5—Modified Fire Resistive:** Buildings that are modified fire resistive have exterior walls, floors and roof constructed of masonry or fire resistive material with a fire resistance rating of 2 hours or less.
- **Class 6—Fire Resistive:** These structures are constructed of masonry or fire resistive material with a fire resistance rating of 2 hours or more.

4.5. RATING THE POLICY

4.5.1. Judgment and Manual Rating

If the insurance company agrees to issue a policy, a premium must be determined. There are three basic ways in which a premium can be computed:

- Judgment rating
- Manual rating
- Merit rating

The oldest form of determining rates is called **judgment rating**. The premium is determined by considering the individual risk. No books or tables are used; premiums are established through careful judgment.

The second and most common method of premium determination is called **manual** or **class rating**. The company's rates for a particular state or area are obtained by consulting a manual, which is usually stored on a computer. Rates are arranged by various categories or classes. The agent or underwriter classifies the risk according to defined criteria and then looks up the appropriate rate. The printed rate, which is a rate per unit of insurance, is then multiplied by the number of units of insurance being purchased to calculate the premium. The formula looks like this:

Rate per unit × number of units = premium.

So, an insured who purchases $60,000 of insurance at a rate of $2 per $1,000 would pay a premium of $120 (2 × 60 = 120).

4.5.2. Merit Rating

Another means for determining premiums is **merit rating**. Typically, merit rating starts with class or manual rates, which are then modified to reflect the unique characteristics of the risk that are not reflected in the manual rate.

Experience rating is a form of merit rating that modifies the manual premium on the basis of the insured's **loss experience** (i.e., the dollars paid out in claims vs. the premium received) over some period, generally the three years preceding the current policy year. When past loss experience is poorer than the average loss experience expected for this class of insured, the insured will pay more than the manual premium. When the insured's past loss experience is better than average, the insured will pay less than the manual premium.

Other types of merit rating include **retrospective rating**, which bases the insured's premium on losses incurred during the policy period, and **schedule rating**, which applies a system of debits or credits to reflect characteristics of a particular insured.

4.6. CERTIFICATE OF INSURANCE

After a policy has been issued, an insured may need a **certificate of insurance** as proof that the policy has been written. A certificate of insurance, which contains a general summary of the policy's coverage, is frequently required in loan transactions and other legal matters.

4.7. MISREPRESENTATION, CONCEALMENT, AND FRAUD

Once an applicant's offer has been accepted and the policy has been rated, issued, and countersigned, the contract may only be canceled by the insurance company under very specific circumstances. State laws, as well as the policy itself, spell out these circumstances.

Since the insurance contract is a contract of utmost good faith, it is expected that the insured and the insurance company will be fair and honest in their dealings with each other. However, the insurance company can void the contract on the basis of misrepresentation, concealment, or fraud by the insured.

Misrepresentation is a written or verbal misstatement of a material fact involved in the contract on which the insurer relies. Misrepresentation will void the policy only if it concerns a material fact. A **material fact** is a fact that would cause an insurer to decline a risk, charge a different premium, or change the provisions of the policy that was issued.

Concealment is similar to misrepresentation except that it involves withholding, rather than misstating, a material fact.

Fraud is a deliberate misrepresentation that causes harm. An act of fraud contains four elements.

- Someone deliberately lies.
- The intent of the lie is for someone else to rely on that lie.
- Another person relies on that lie.
- The other person suffers harm as a result of relying on that lie.

Fraud differs from misrepresentation in that misrepresentation may be intentional or unintentional. Fraud is always intentional and involves an all-out effort by one party to deceive and cheat the other.

4.8. REPRESENTATIONS AND WARRANTIES

Most of the statements contained in the insured's application for insurance are **representations**—statements that the applicant believes are true. Under the law, a representation is not considered a matter to which the parties contract, so a policy cannot be voided on the basis of a representation.

Sometimes, however, specific agreements are made between the insured and insurer that certain conditions will be met. For example, they might require that while a business is closed, a security guard will be on duty at all times. These agreements, called **warranties**, become a part of the policy and can void the policy if they are breached, whether the breach was intentional or unintentional.

4.9. WAIVER AND ESTOPPEL

The legal definition of **waiver** is the intentional relinquishment of a known right. Sometimes an insurer or its representative knowingly overlooks a condition or exclusion that would normally have been grounds for denying coverage, increasing the premium, reducing the benefits provided in the policy, or some other material change in the policy. When the insurer or its representative relinquishes the insurer's right of denial or refusal, the act becomes a waiver. Though any policy provision may be waived, the requirement of an insurable interest may not be waived, nor may facts be waived.

If an insurance company representative intentionally or unintentionally creates the impression that a certain fact exists when it does not, and an innocent party relies on that impression and is damaged as a result, the insurance company will be **estopped** (prevented) from denying this fact. For example, if an agent states or indicates by his actions that a particular loss is covered, the insurance company will be estopped from denying that coverage.

4.10. CANCELLATION AND NONRENEWAL

Most insurance policies are issued with a definite effective date and expiration date. The **policy period** or **term**—the time between the effective date and the expiration date—may be six months, one year, or even three years. But at times, the insured or the insurance company may want to cancel the insurance before the policy expires.

The **insured** may cancel the policy by writing a letter to the insurance company or by surrendering the policy to the company. The insurance company returns any **unearned premium**; that is, any premium not yet "used up" during the policy period.

These premiums may be returned on a **short rate basis**. This means that when the insured cancels before the expiration date, the company not only keeps the premium for insurance already provided but also keeps an allowance for expenses, such as issuing the policy.

The **insurance company** does not have the same freedom to cancel that the insured does. Each state has rules governing the circumstances under which a policy may be canceled by the company. Most states do not permit arbitrary cancellation but restrict this right to such situations as nonpayment of premium. When the company does cancel, various state laws and policy provisions require that the insured be notified of the cancellation in writing within a specified number of days before the effective date of cancellation.

When the insurance company cancels the policy, unearned premium is returned to the insured on a **pro rata basis**. This means the company retains only the earned premium and is not permitted to keep an extra amount for expenses.

Occasionally, a policy is canceled by either the insured or the insurance company on its effective date. This is called **flat cancellation**.

Exercise 4.A

True or false?

1. The insurance company may cancel a policy for any reason.
   ( ) True ( ) False
2. When the insured cancels a policy, he must notify the company in writing or surrender the policy.
   ( ) True ( ) False
3. When the insurance company cancels the policy, unearned premium is returned on a short rate basis.
   ( ) True ( ) False
4. Flat cancellation occurs when the policy is canceled on its effective date.
   ( ) True ( ) False
5. An insured must give the insurance company written notice of cancellation within a specified number of days before the effective date of cancellation.
   ( ) True ( ) False
6. When the insured cancels the policy, unearned premium is returned on a short rate basis.
   ( ) True ( ) False

Exercise answers can be found at the end of the Unit 4 answers and rationales.

When a policy reaches its expiration date, it is customary to renew the policy for another term, provided both the insured and the insurer want the coverage to continue.

Of course, the insured has the option not to renew the insurance at this point. The insurance company may also decide not to renew the policy. Although **nonrenewal** provisions are usually more liberal than cancellation requirements, the insurance company may still be limited in the reasons it may nonrenew and in how and when the insured is notified of the decision not to renew.

UNIT TEST

1. Which of the following statements concerning binders is CORRECT?
   A. They guarantee that a policy will be issued.
   B. They may be issued by insurance companies but not agents.
   C. They expire on the effective date of the policy to which they apply, or on the expiration date of the binder if the policy is not issued.

2. Judgment rating is based on
   A. an evaluation of the characteristics of the individual risk
   B. manual rates developed from statistical data
   C. calculation and evaluation of the insured's past loss experience

3. What rating method makes modifications to manual rates to reflect the unique characteristics of each risk?
   A. Judgment
   B. Merit
   C. Certification

4. To void a policy, misrepresentation or concealment must
   A. concern material facts
   B. be intentional
   C. both A and B
   D. neither A nor B

5. An agreement between the insured and the insurer that certain conditions will be met is
   A. a misrepresentation
   B. a warranty
   C. an estoppel
   D. a certificate of insurance

6. An insurance policy (can/cannot) ____________ be voided on the basis of a representation made by the insured.

7. When an insured decides to cancel an insurance policy before the expiration date, the unearned premium is returned on a
   A. flat basis
   B. pro rata basis
   C. short rate basis

8. List four information sources besides the application that an underwriter might use to evaluate whether a risk is insurable.
   A. ______________________________
   ____
   B. ______________________________
   ____
   C. ______________________________
   ____
   D. ______________________________
   ____

9. Which of the following statements about the Fair Credit Reporting Act is NOT correct?
   A. Prenotification is required for both regular and investigative reports.
   B. Postnotification is required when insurance coverage is denied because of adverse information in a credit report.
   C. An agent who obtains information from a reporting agency under false pretenses may be sent to jail and fined.
   D. Consumers have the right to challenge information in investigative reports and to have incorrect information removed.

10. What is adverse selection?

____

____

11. Retrospective rating bases premiums on the insured's loss experience (before/during) ______________ the current policy period.

12. A certificate of insurance provides
    A. temporary insurance coverage until a policy is issued
    B. proof that a policy has been written

13. What is the difference between fraud and misrepresentation?

____

____

14. An agent tells an insured that a loss caused by flood damage is covered under her homeowners policy. Actually, the policy specifically excludes such losses. The insurance company
    A. may deny coverage for the loss on the basis that the homeowners policy excludes flood losses
    B. is estopped from denying coverage because the agent stated that the loss is covered

15. The insured's policy is nearing the expiration date. The insurance company doesn't want to continue the insured's coverage, so it sends the insured a notice that the policy will not continue beyond the expiration date of the policy. This is
    A. flat cancellation
    B. nonrenewal
    C. pro rata cancellation
    D. unearned renewal

ANSWERS AND RATIONALES TO UNIT TEST

1. **C.** An agent or an insurance company may issue a binder. A binder does not guarantee that a policy will be issued; it only guarantees temporary coverage. If the company decides to not issue the policy, coverage under the binder may be canceled by a formal cancellation notice; however, if no formal cancellation is made, coverage remains in effect until the binder expires. If a policy is issued, coverage under the binder ceases as of the effective date of the policy.

2. **A.** This is the oldest form of rating. The premium is determined by considering the individual risk. No books or tables are used; premiums are established through careful judgment.

3. **B.** Experience rating, retrospective rating, and schedule rating are all types of merit rating.

4. **A.** Misrepresentation is a written or verbal misstatement of a material fact. It may be either intentional or unintentional.

5. **B.** A warranty becomes part of the policy. If it is breached, the insurer can void the policy.

6. Cannot. Most of the statements contained in the insured's application for insurance are representations—statements that the applicant believes are true. Under the law, a representation is not considered a matter to which the parties contract, so a policy cannot be voided on the basis of a representation.

7. **C** This means the insurer can keep an allowance for expenses. When the insurance company cancels, unearned premium is returned on a pro rata basis, which means the company retains only the earned premium.

8. All of the following are examples of information sources an underwriter may use to evaluate a risk: inspection services, government bureaus, insurance industry bureaus, financial information services, previous insurers, and the company's own claim files.

9. **A.** Prenotification is required for investigative reports but not regular reports.

10. The tendency for people with a greater-than-average exposure to loss to purchase insurance. Adverse selection may result in large financial losses and decreased profitability for the insurer.

11. During. Retrospective rating is a type of merit rating that bases the insured's premium on losses incurred during the policy period.

12. **B.** A certificate of insurance contains a general summary of the policy's coverage. It may be used in loan transactions and other legal matters to provide proof that a policy has been issued.

13. Fraud is always intentional and involves an all-out effect by one party to deceive and cheat the other. Misrepresentation may or may not be intentional.

14. **B.** Estoppel is a legal principle that states that if one intentionally or unintentionally creates the impression that a certain fact exists, and an innocent party relies on that impression and is injured as a result, the guilty party may be legally prohibited from asserting that the fact does not exist.

15. **B.** Nonrenewal occurs when the insured or the insurer decides to not continue coverage for another policy period after the current policy period expires.

UNIT 4 EXERCISE ANSWERS

Exercise 4.A

1. False—state law restricts the circumstances under which the insurer can cancel the policy
2. True
3. False—pro rata basis
4. True
5. False—only the insurer is required to give prior written notice of cancellation
6. True

UNIT

5

Introduction to Property Insurance

5.1. LEARNING OBJECTIVES

After completing Unit 5—Introduction to Property Insurance, you will be able to do the following:

- Identify the types of information found in a policy's Declarations and Insuring Agreement
- Explain the differences between an insured, a named insured, a first named insured, and an additional insured
- Compare and contrast blanket and specific insurance, named peril and open peril policies, and direct losses and indirect losses;
- Describe the five broad categories of exclusions commonly found in property insurance policies
- Explain the purpose of policy conditions
- Describe an insured's duties when a loss occurs
- Compare and contrast various methods used to value losses under insurance policies
- Explain the purpose of coinsurance and how the coinsurance penalty may reduce loss payment
- Describe the purpose of the pair or set provision
- Compare and contrast various methods used to determine reimbursement when other insurance applies to a loss
- Explain how appraisal or arbitration may be used to determine the amount paid for a loss
- Describe the purpose of the following policy conditions:
  - salvage and abandonment,
  - subrogation,
  - liberalization,
  - assignment,
  - no benefit to bailee,
  - mortgage/loss payable,
  - policy period and policy territory, and
  - vacancy and unoccupancy
- Compare and contrast reporting and nonreporting insurance policies

5.2. STANDARDIZED POLICIES

Now that the stage is set, you'll want to learn something about the wide range of insurance products you'll be working with in your profession.

In discussing each of the major types of insurance, we'll concentrate on basic, frequently used policies. You will learn their purposes and their unique characteristics.

Now a word about standardization. Not all insurance policies are alike. Our job would be easier if every company that provided automobile insurance used the same policy. But it doesn't work that way. That's not to say that there isn't some uniformity, however. Certain policies, for instance, have been standardized by law. Any company that writes the policies must use a standard form.

A degree of standardization has also been introduced by insurance service organizations such as the **Insurance Services Office (ISO)**. Although companies may deviate from ISO's forms or use their own with state approval, it is customary for member companies to use the standardized forms.

Even when companies design their own forms for a particular coverage, there tend to be more similarities than differences between the policies used by various insurers. So don't worry if your company's policies do not match word for word with the contracts we discuss here. We're concerned with the basic concepts, which will apply no matter where you are in the insurance industry.

5.3. HOW THE REMAINDER OF THE COURSE IS ORGANIZED

Because there are so many different types of insurance contracts, there are a number of ways to organize a review of key policies. We've chosen an organization that builds logically so that each unit helps you prepare for the next.

The first part of the policy review deals with personal lines policies. We start with a personal lines property contract, the dwelling policy, and then talk about personal lines policies that combine both property and casualty coverages.

The second part of the policy review covers commercial lines policies, beginning with package policies that include both property and casualty coverages, and then commercial policies that cover individual lines of insurance.

Before you begin looking at specific policies, however, this unit will familiarize you with some of the key characteristics of property insurance that are common to both personal and commercial property policies. Then, in the next unit, you'll review some of the key principles of liability insurance. When you've finished, you'll be ready to begin your review of personal lines to see how these general principles apply in specific policies.

5.4. DECLARATIONS

5.4.1. Who Is Insured

Like all insurance contracts, property insurance contracts are made up of declarations, insuring agreements, conditions, exclusions, and definitions.

The first job of the declarations section is to state who is insured, whether it is an individual or a business. Remember, insurance contracts are personal. Even though we sometimes talk about insuring homes or other types of property, such as cars, it is the party named in the declarations who is insured, not the property.

The word *insured* can have a number of different meanings in an insurance policy. The **named insured** is the person, business, or other entity named in the declarations to whom the policy is issued. When there is more than one named insured listed on a policy, the policy may assign a higher level of duties or rights to the **first named insured**, the person listed first on the Declarations page.

In addition to the named insured, the policy may cover other specifically designated persons, businesses, or entities as insureds under the policy, such as family members. Such designations are usually found in the definition of *insured* listed in the definitions section of the policy.

In some circumstances, another individual or business may be listed on the declarations as an **additional insured**—for example, a mortgage company that has an outstanding loan (and therefore an insurable interest) on the property.

Exercise 5.A

1. John purchases an auto policy for his new car. There are no other insureds listed on the declarations. John is considered
   A. the additional insured
   B. the named insured
   C. the first named insured
2. Pedro's homeowners policy lists the mortgage company that has an outstanding loan on the home. The mortgage company is
   A. an additional insured
   B. a named insured
   C. a first named insured
3. Jamal and Pierre are co-owners of a carpet cleaning company. Both are named insureds on the company's insurance policy. Since Jamal's name appears first on the declarations, he is
   A. the additional insured
   B. the named insured
   C. the first named insured

Exercise answers can be found at the end of the Unit 5 answers and rationales.

5.4.2. What Property Is Covered and Where

The declarations also describe the property to be insured. The description can be very specific, designating a particular item to be insured (**specific insurance**), or it can be a blanket description, such as "personal property located at 1550 Willow" (**blanket insurance**). Blanket coverage may also mean that the insured's covered property is insured at any location, rather than at only a particular location.

An almost endless variety of property can be insured: buildings (real property), tangible and intangible business and personal property, property owned by the insured, and nonowned property. In addition to the brief description contained in the declarations, the insuring agreements will describe in detail the property that is covered by the policy. You'll learn more about the types of property that can be insured as you progress through the course.

5.4.3. When Property Is Insured

Insurance policies specify the date and time, including where and in what time zone coverage begins and ends. This is known as the **policy period**.

Policy Period

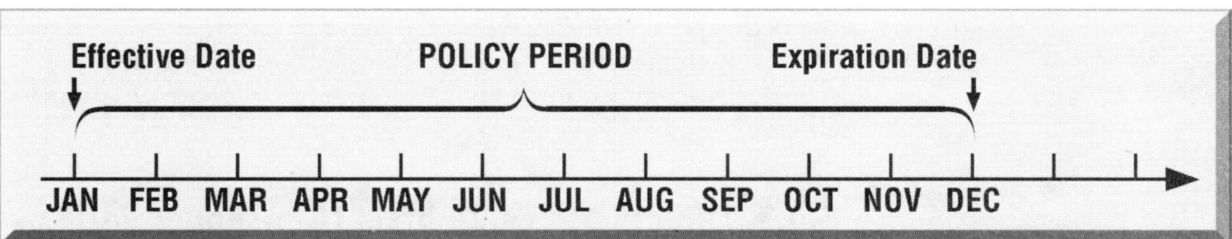

In some states, the exact time of day policies start and stop is set by law to maintain uniformity between companies and to prevent gaps in coverage when an insured changes insurance companies.

5.4.4. How Much Property Is Insured for

Finally, the declarations show the **policy limit**, also known as the **limit of coverage**, **limit of liability**, or **limit of insurance**. These limits represent the maximum amount the insurance company will pay for a loss. Within this framework, the principle of indemnity and applicable policy conditions are used to determine the exact reimbursement in the event of a loss.

For certain hard-to-value items, the insurance company will issue a **valued** or **agreed amount contract**. Valued contracts are written for a specified amount, and they list the value of the insured property as agreed to by both the insured and the insurer at policy inception. If the item is damaged, this is the amount that will be used to value the loss. This avoids the difficulty of trying to determine the value of such property after it has already been damaged or destroyed. An example of property frequently covered on a valued basis is art work.

5.5. INSURING AGREEMENT

5.5.1. Property Covered

The insuring agreement explains what property is covered and the perils the property is insured against.

Several different coverages may be provided in a single policy. The insuring agreement describes the key **policy coverages** in detail. The insuring agreement may also specify that certain **additional coverages** apply. These coverages, which may also be called **extended coverages**, **coverage extensions**, or **other coverages**, may have reduced or separate limits of liability or require the insured to meet certain policy requirements before they apply.

5.5.2. Perils Insured Against: Named Peril and Open Peril Policies

Policies that list the specific perils or causes of loss insured against under the contract, such as lightning, fire, and windstorm, are called **named peril** or **specified peril** policies. Named peril contracts insure property only against the perils specifically listed in the policy.

An **open peril** policy insures against all risks of physical loss except those specifically excluded in the policy. This type of contract is sometimes called **all-risk** or **special coverage**.

5.5.3. Direct Loss vs. Indirect (Consequential) Loss

In addition to specifying the property covered and the perils insured against, the insuring agreement will state whether it covers direct loss, indirect loss, or both.

Direct Loss

You are probably most familiar with direct loss. This is financial loss resulting directly from a loss to property, such as a house being damaged in a windstorm or a valuable piece of jewelry being stolen.

Indirect Loss

Indirect loss comes as a result, or consequence, of the original loss. For this reason, it is also known as consequential loss. For instance, suppose a hotel burns down. In the one year required to rebuild, the owner loses over $2 million in room rentals. This loss of rent would be an indirect, or consequential, loss resulting from the direct loss to the hotel by fire.

Exercise 5.B

Classify the following as direct losses **(D)** or indirect losses **(I)**.

____ 1. After a warehouse fire, an automobile agency has to rent office space from a motel until the damage can be repaired.

____ 2. A homeowner discovers that a valuable painting was stolen from her home.

____ 3. A large fire destroys a city newspaper. To continue publishing, it rents another printing press at an additional cost.

Exercise answers can be found at the end of the Unit 5 answers and rationales.

5.6. EXCLUSIONS AND LIMITATIONS

Every property insurance contract contains exclusions. In a named peril policy, any peril that is not specifically listed as covered is automatically excluded. However, named peril policies also list certain exclusions separately to explain or emphasize perils or property that is excluded from coverage.

In an open peril policy, the exclusions are especially important, because any peril not specifically listed as excluded is insured against.

Exclusions in a policy vary with the type of property or situation the contract is designed to cover. However, there are five broad categories of exclusions that are commonly found in property policies.

- **Nonaccidental losses:** Nonaccidental losses are excluded because they are certainties, not risks. Wear and tear, deterioration, rust, corrosion, and mechanical or electrical breakdown are all examples of nonaccidental losses.

Concurrent Causation

Property insurance policy provisions and policy language underwent changes in recent years to avoid confusion related to **concurrent causation.** Concurrent causation refers to a situation where two or more perils act *concurrently*—at the same time or in sequence—to cause a loss. This created significant problems for insurers when one peril was covered by a policy and the other was not.

The issue initially arose when some insurers were challenged to pay earthquake claims under collapse coverage. At the time, dwelling, homeowners, and commercial property policies included collapse of a building or structure as a peril insured against, whereas earthquake coverage was generally excluded. When an earthquake struck, claims were filed under the collapse coverage by insureds who did not have earthquake coverage. The insurers maintained that they never intended to provide earthquake coverage under the peril of collapse. Some courts concluded otherwise and held for the insured on the grounds that the loss was due to collapse of the building *whether earthquake was a concurrent or contributing cause.*

To clarify the intent of the policy, insurers removed collapse as a peril insured against and made it an additional coverage. The wording was changed to specify that collapse coverage only applies when it is caused by certain perils named in the policy, such as fire, weight of contents or people, and the use of defective construction materials.

- **Losses controllable by the insured:** Losses that can be controlled or prevented with extra care or effort on the insured's part are excluded. This encourages the insured to be responsible in the use of the property. Marring, scratching, and breaking or chipping of fragile objects are all examples of losses that are controllable by the insured.

- **Extra-hazardous perils:** Certain perils are extra hazardous. The insurance company could provide coverage, but the unique nature of the peril requires a substantial increase in the premium the insured would pay. Extra-hazardous perils are usually excluded from the policy because most insureds would not want or need the coverage. Insureds who do require the coverage can often obtain it through an endorsement to the policy, for which an extra premium is charged. An example of an extra-hazardous peril is earthquake.

- **Catastrophic losses:** Some losses are so broad in their scope that they could bankrupt any company that insured against them. Losses arising from war or nuclear disasters are generally uninsurable because of their catastrophic nature.

- **Property covered in other policies:** Property customarily covered in other insurance policies is excluded. For example, a policy covering your personal property would normally exclude your car because there is a separate automobile policy to provide coverage for your vehicle.

Some policies also include **limitations** that are less sweeping than exclusions. A limitation may eliminate or reduce coverage but only under certain circumstances or when specified conditions apply. For example, after a building has been vacant for 60 days, some types of commercial property losses will not be covered at all, while the amount paid for other types of losses will be reduced by 15%.

5.7. CONDITIONS

5.7.1. Duties Following Loss

The conditions section of a property insurance policy lists the duties and rights of both the insured and the insurer. We've already discussed the cancellation and misrepresentation provisions. Let's consider some additional conditions often included in property insurance contracts.

Most contracts include conditions that specify what the insured and insurer must do when a loss occurs. Together, these provisions may be referred to as **loss provisions**.

The **duties following loss** condition lists the insured's responsibilities after a loss, including:

- giving prompt **notice of claim** to the insurance company or agent;
- protecting the property from further damage;
- completing a detailed **proof of loss** (an official inventory of the damages);
- making the property available for inspection by the company;
- submitting to examination under oath if required; and
- assisting the insurer as required during the claim investigation procedure.

5.7.2. Valuation

The insurance company also has duties when a loss occurs. Determining adequate indemnification is an important concern. Such provisions are sometimes contained in the **valuation** or **how losses will be paid** condition.

In general, the insured can collect the lesser of:

- insurable interest;
- policy limits;
- actual cash value;

- cost to repair; and
- replacement cost.

We've already discussed the first two items on this list. The insured can never collect more than the policy limits or the insurable interest he has in the property.

Exercise 5.C

1. Burt's home is destroyed in a fire. His homeowners policy has a $150,000 limit. What is the maximum amount Burt's insurer will pay for this loss? $__________ Explain your answer.

____

____

2. George and his cousin Nadine each own 50% of a $200,000 condominium. George buys a $200,000 insurance policy to cover the condo. If it were totally destroyed, what is the maximum amount he could collect? $__________ Explain your answer.

____

____

Exercise answers can be found at the end of the Unit 5 answers and rationales.

5.7.2.1. Actual Cash Value

Many losses are reimbursed on an **actual cash value (ACV)** basis. Actual cash value is usually calculated by determining the item's replacement cost (what it would cost to buy a replacement) and subtracting an amount for depreciation, as illustrated here:

Actual Cash Value

But why isn't the insured reimbursed for the full replacement cost? Depreciation is subtracted because the insured has already had use of the property. If the full amount were reimbursed so the insured could replace it with a new item, the insured would be better off after the loss than before. This violates the principle of indemnity.

Bill has a washing machine he bought eight years ago. The machine depreciated $100 the first year, $50 the second year, and $10 each of the remaining six years. When the machine was destroyed in a fire, Bill discovered that a new one would cost $800. The actual cash value of Bill's old machine is $590: $800 – ($100 + $50 + $60), or $800 – $210.

5.7.2.2. Repair Cost

Although actual cash value is a common method for reimbursing a loss, the insured may be reimbursed on the basis of the item's **repair cost** when this amount is less than actual cash value.

5.7.2.3. Replacement Cost and Functional Replacement Cost

In some policies, the insurance company agrees to automatically pay the replacement cost for covered losses with no allowance for depreciation, provided the insured meets certain conditions. This is known as **replacement cost**. We'll discuss this more fully in a later unit.

Some policies pay losses on a **functional replacement cost basis**, in which damaged property is repaired or replaced with less expensive, but functionally equivalent, materials. This method is used most frequently for losses to antique, ornate, or custom construction.

5.7.2.4. Market Value

Occasionally, property is insured for **market value**, or what it could be sold for at the time of the loss. Market value is different from ACV or replacement cost. Suppose Ed spends $400,000 to build a fancy house in an open area, but then the land around it is zoned for heavy industry and a bad-smelling oil refinery is built nearby. Because Ed might have trouble finding a buyer, his house may only have a market value of $250,000 in that location, even though it would still cost about $400,000 to rebuild it if it were destroyed.

5.7.3. Coinsurance

Insurance companies want to encourage their policyholders to insure their property for its full value. Since partial losses are much more common than total losses, some insureds might purchase minimal insurance to take care of any possible small losses and take a chance that they would never have a total loss. If a lot of insureds were to follow this practice, the insurance company would not be able to collect enough premium to pay for the actual losses of its policyholders.

The **coinsurance** condition encourages policyholders to insure property to value. It lists the minimum amount of insurance the insured should carry on the property, which is expressed as a percentage of the property's value. For instance, a policy with an 80% coinsurance condition means the insured must insure the property for at least 80% of its value.

As long as the insured carries the amount of insurance required by the coinsurance condition at the time of a loss, the insurer will indemnify losses up to the limits of the policy. If the insured does not carry enough insurance when a loss occurs, the company will pay only a percentage of what full contract reimbursement would otherwise have been. The amount not paid by the company is sometimes called the **coinsurance penalty**. Later in this course, you'll learn a simple formula for determining the amount of reimbursement when the insured does not carry enough insurance to meet the coinsurance requirements.

Since it is sometimes difficult to predict property values accurately enough to avoid the possibility of a coinsurance penalty, some policies contain an **agreed value** or **stated amount** provision. This provision specifies a certain value that will meet the coinsurance requirement. As long as the policy limit equals or exceeds this amount, the insured will not be assessed a coinsurance penalty.

5.7.4. When Losses Are Paid

Although it may not be specifically stated in the policy, the insurer is obligated to pay covered claims promptly. Some policies provide that a claim must be paid within a certain number of days after the insurer has received proof of loss and the parties have reached agreement on the amount of the loss. Others state only that the loss must be settled within a "reasonable" time.

5.7.5. Pair or Set

The **pair or set** condition is a loss settlement condition that appears in many property contracts. It states that if part of a pair or set is lost or damaged, the loss will be valued as a fair proportion of the total value of the set, giving consideration to the importance of the damaged article to the set. The insurer is not obligated to pay for the loss of the whole set when only one part has been damaged.

Suppose burglars stole a pair of diamond earrings from the insured's home. Later, one of the earrings is found, apparently because the burglar dropped it before fleeing the home. According to the pair or set condition, the insured would be entitled to reimbursement for the stolen earring as a fair proportion of the pair's full value, recognizing the importance of the missing earring to the value of the set.

5.7.6. Deductible

Many property insurance policies have a **deductible**. This means the insured pays the first part of every loss up to the amount of the deductible. This reduces the cost of insurance by reducing the number of small claims. The amount of the deductible is specified in the declarations.

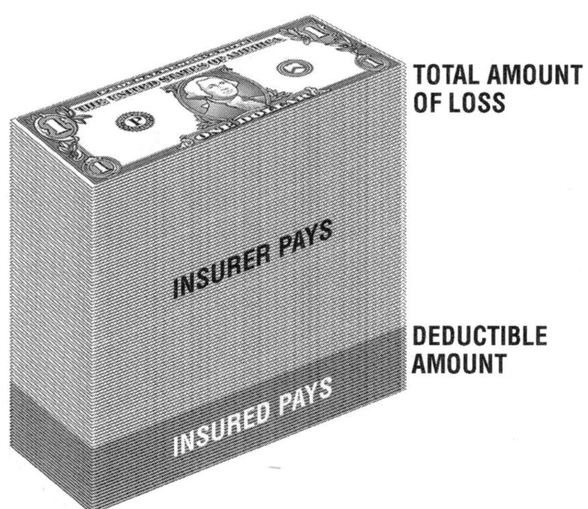

Suppose Li has insurance protection for her home. Her policy has a $500 deductible. One night, a windstorm tears off part of the roof, causing $750 in damages. The insurance company will pay Li $250 ($750 – $500).

5.7.7. Salvage and Abandonment

Many property insurance policies contain a **salvage** condition that provides that the insurance company can take possession of damaged property after payment of loss. Salvaged goods can reduce the cost of the claim to the insurance company.

While the insurance company may retain the right of salvage, it does not allow the insured to relinquish property to the company at the option of the insured. The **abandonment** condition states that the insured may not abandon property to the company and ask to be reimbursed for its full value.

Suppose the insured hits a deer, causing major damage to his 10-year-old vehicle. The abandonment condition prohibits the insured from abandoning the car to the insurance company and collecting a settlement for the total loss of the automobile. However, the salvage condition allows the company to settle with the insured by taking possession of the car and reimbursing the insured for the loss of the auto.

5.7.8. Subrogation

Most policies give the insurance company subrogation rights.

Suppose an insured suffers a loss for which he is not at fault, and the party that caused the damage has no insurance or refuses to pay for the damages. The insured's insurance company may step in and pay for the damages and then bring suit or file a claim against the other party or the other party's insurance company on the insured's behalf. This transfer to the insurance company of the insured's right of recovery against others is called **subrogation**. The subrogation condition may also be called **transfer of right of recovery against others to us**.

Suppose Mat throws a brick through the glass window at Deermont's. Mat refuses to pay the damages. Deermont's insurance company pays for the repairs and then goes to court to collect from Mat. This is an example of subrogation.

5.7.9. Appraisal and Arbitration

There are times when the insured and the insurer cannot agree on the amount of indemnification. The **appraisal** condition provides that either party may demand an appraisal of a loss. In this event, each party chooses an appraiser. The two appraisers then select an umpire. If the appraisers fail to agree on an amount, they submit their differences to the umpire. The decision agreed to by any two of the three is the final amount of indemnification. Each party pays its own appraiser and shares the costs of the umpire.

The **arbitration** condition is worded similarly, but it is not limited to disputes over the value of the loss. It may also be used to resolve other areas of disagreement between the insured and the insurance company, between the company and a third party in the case of liability insurance, or between two insurers.

Suppose an insured owned an antique organ that was destroyed in a fire. The insurance company says it will pay the insured $500. The insured believes it is worth at least $800. Two appraisers and an umpire are called in. One appraiser calculates the loss at $400, the other at $700. The umpire agrees that reimbursement should be for $700. This is the amount the insured will be paid.

5.7.10. Other Insurance

5.7.10.1. Primary and Excess

The **other insurance** condition sets out how other insurance the insured may have on the same property affects reimbursement under the policy in question when a loss occurs. This condition may also be called **other sources of recovery** or **insurance under two or more coverages**.

Some policies provide that when other insurance exists they will pay only the excess beyond what the other insurance pays for a loss. So if Company Y's policy would pay $10,000 of a $15,000 loss, Company X would pay no more that $5,000 of the loss. In this example, Company Y's policy is considered **primary insurance** and Company X's policy is **excess insurance**.

Exercise 5.D

Two policies cover the insured's $100,000 loss. ABC's policy, which is primary, has a $75,000 limit. DEF's policy is excess and has a $50,000 limit.

1. How much would the ABC policy pay for the loss?
   $________________
2. How much of the loss would be covered by the DEF policy?
   $________________

Exercise answers can be found at the end of the Unit 5 answers and rationales.

5.7.10.2. Pro Rata

Probably the most common method for handling other insurance is to agree to pay only a proportion of any loss that is also covered by other insurance. This is known as the **pro rata method**. For instance, if the insured carried 30% of the total insurance coverage on her house with Company X, Company X would not pay more than 30% of a loss.

The amount paid by each company is determined by adding the limits of all policies that cover the loss and then dividing the limit of the first policy by the total amount of insurance available. The figure that results is multiplied by the amount of the loss to determine that policy's payment amount. The previous steps are then repeated for each applicable policy. Here is how it looks as a formula:

$$\frac{\text{Policy A's limit of liability}}{\text{Policy A's limit of liability + Policy B's limit of liability}} \times \text{amount of loss} = \text{amount paid by Policy A}$$

$$\frac{\text{Policy B's limit of liability}}{\text{Policy A's limit of liability + Policy B's limit of liability}} \times \text{amount of loss} = \text{amount paid by Policy B}$$

Here's an example: Two policies cover a $50,000 loss. Policy A's limit of liability is $100,000; Policy B's is $300,000. With the pro rata method, Policy A would pay $12,500 and Policy B would pay $37,500. Here is how we calculated these amounts:

Policy A:

$$\frac{\$100{,}000}{\$400{,}000} = .25$$

$$.25 \times 50{,}000 = \$12{,}500$$

Policy B:

$$\frac{\$300{,}000}{\$400{,}000} = .75$$

$$.75 \times 50{,}000 = \$37{,}500$$

Sometimes an insured may have two or more policies on the same property that do not provide coverage to the same extent. Such an arrangement, called **nonconcurrency**, can result in coverage gaps or disputed payments and should be avoided.

Exercise 5.E

Two policies apply to an insured's $12,000 loss. Policy A has a $100,000 limit, and Policy B has a $50,000 limit. How much would each insurer pay under a pro rata other insurance condition?

1. Policy A: $_________
2. Policy B: $_________

Exercise answers can be found at the end of the Unit 5 answers and rationales.

5.7.11. Liberalization

The **liberalization** condition provides that if the insurer broadens coverage under a policy form or endorsement without requiring an additional premium, then all existing similar policies or endorsements will be construed to contain the broadened coverage.

5.7.12. Assignment

The **assignment** condition specifies that a policy may not be transferred to anyone else without the written consent of the insurer unless the named insured dies. In this case, the rights and duties under the policy are transferred to the insured's legal representative. This condition is sometimes called the **transfer of rights or duties under this policy** condition.

5.7.13. No Benefit to Bailee

A **bailee** is a person or organization that has temporary possession of someone else's personal property. Examples of bailees include dry cleaners and storage facilities. The **no benefit to bailee** condition states that the bailee is not covered under the insured's policy while the bailee has possession of the insured's property.

5.7.14. Mortgage Condition

We mentioned that lenders or mortgagees may have an insurable interest in property. The mortgagee is generally named in the declarations. The **mortgage** condition, or **loss payable** condition, specifies the rights and duties of the mortgagee, or loss payee, under the policy. For instance, if an insured fails to file a proof of loss, the mortgagee must do so after being notified by the insurer to protect its rights under the policy. In addition, the mortgagee may be expected to pay the premium if the insured fails to do so.

The policy may provide that if some condition caused by the insured would result in the insurer denying coverage for a loss it would otherwise have covered, the mortgagee may still have protection under the policy. Or the insurer may have the option of paying off the mortgage and requiring the mortgagee to assign all rights to the company, eliminating the mortgagee's interest.

5.7.15. Policy Period and Policy Territory

The **policy period** and **policy territory** provisions state that a loss will not be covered unless it occurs within the policy territory while the policy is in effect. The territory may vary, but a typical policy includes the United States, Puerto Rico, and Canada. The effective date and time of coverage are listed in the declarations.

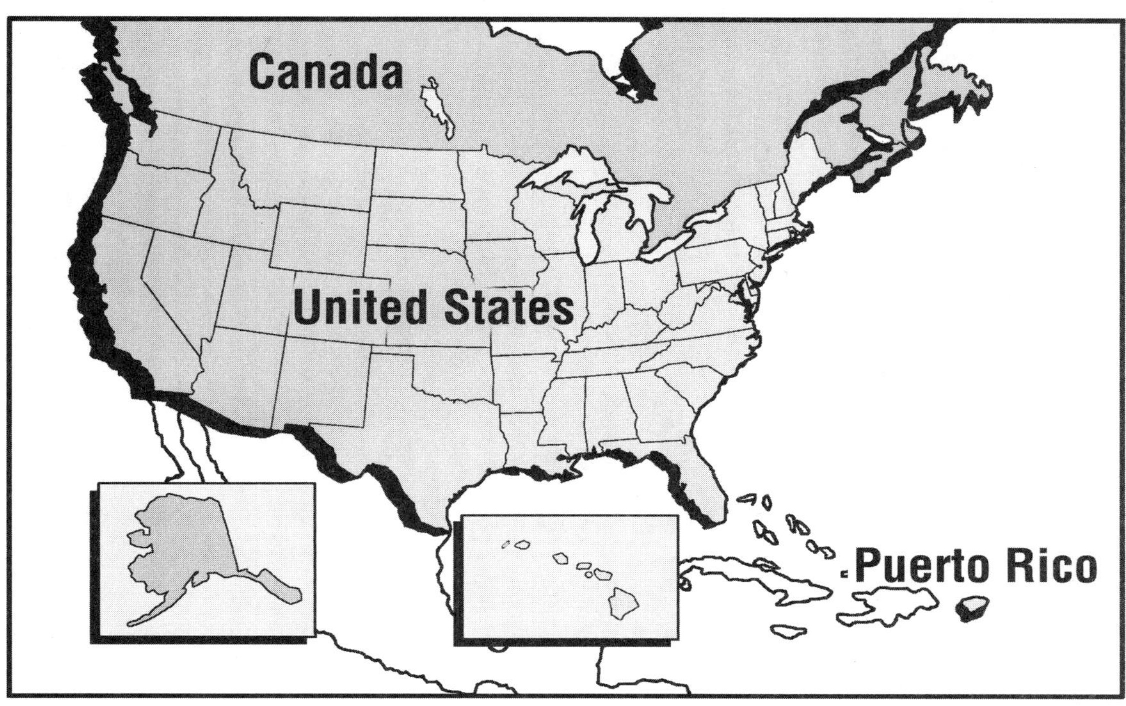

5.7.16. Vacancy and Unoccupancy

Because of the increased chance of loss, property insurance policies may exclude or limit coverage for losses when property is vacant or unoccupied. **Vacant** means the absence of both people and property from the premises; **unoccupied** is the absence of people.

5.7.17. Reporting Forms

Property contracts may be issued on a **nonreporting** or **reporting** basis. You are familiar with nonreporting policies: these are contracts for which a flat premium is charged every time the policy is renewed. Auto and homeowners policies are examples of nonreporting forms.

Policies are issued on a reporting basis when it is difficult to determine in advance what amount of coverage should be purchased. Instead of paying a flat premium, the insured pays a **deposit premium**, or **estimated premium**, and then periodically submits reports to the insurer showing the status of those factors on which the premium is based. After the insurance company has calculated the premium, it is charged against the deposit. When the deposit is used up, the insured begins to pay the premium calculated by the insurance company at the end of each reporting period.

The insurance company may conduct a **premium audit** of the insured's records before calculating a final premium and making a final adjustment.

UNIT TEST

1. A(n) (open/named) _______________ peril policy covers any loss that is not specifically excluded by the policy.

2. A(n) (open/named) ____________________ peril policy insures property against the perils specifically listed in the policy.

3. Walt and Joanna are co-owners of a bagel shop. Both are listed in the declarations of the policy that insures the business, with Joanna's name appearing first. The declarations also list First State Bank, which has an outstanding loan on the business.

   A. Who is(are) considered a named insured(s) on the policy?

      I. Walt only
      II. Joanna only
      III. Both Walt and Joanna

   B. Who is(are) the first named insured(s)?

      I. Walt only
      II. Joanna only
      III. Both Walt and Joanna

   C. Who is(are) considered an additional insured(s)?

      I. Walt
      II. Joanna
      III. First State Bank
      IV. Walt, Joanna, and First State Bank

4. When a plane hit Daryl's house, he and his family had to stay in a hotel for a week while repairs were made. The hotel bill came to $500.

   A. What was the direct loss?

      I. Plane crash
      II. Hotel bill

   B. What was the indirect loss?

      I. Plane crash
      II. Hotel bill

5. It will cost Gary $10,000 to put a new roof on his home after the old one was destroyed in a tornado. Assume the roof depreciated $300 per year and the roof was 10 years old when the loss occurred. If this loss is valued on an actual cash value basis, how much will Gary's insurance policy pay for the loss? (Assume the loss is within the policy limit.) $___________

6. Linda's sofa, television set, and entertainment center were destroyed in a fire. The total amount of the loss is $5,000; the actual cash value of the items is $3,000. If this loss is valued on a replacement cost basis, how much will Linda's insurance policy pay for the loss? (Assume the loss is within the policy limit.) $__________

7. Renata's home is demolished in a fire that started when a neighbor misdirected the fireworks he set off to celebrate the 4th of July. Renata's insurance company pays her for the damage and then files suit against the neighbor to recover the amount it paid for the loss. This is an example of the application of what policy condition?

   A. Liberalization
   B. Subrogation
   C. Abandonment

8. Byron sells his car to his friend Annette but does not notify his insurance company. Assuming that Byron's policy will transfer to her automatically, Annette doesn't buy insurance for the car. When the car is stolen, Annette files a claim with Byron's former insurer. The insurer denies the claim. This is an example of the application of what policy condition?

   A. Assignment
   B. No benefit to bailee
   C. Coinsurance

9. A heavy snowfall causes the roof over Amaya's living room to collapse. The insurance company asks her to move her belongings out of the living room to protect them from further damage and put a tarp over the roof until it can be repaired. It also asks her to complete a proof of loss form listing the items that were damaged. This is an example of the application of what policy condition?
   A. Appraisal
   B. Arbitration
   C. Duties after loss

10. Ryan has two insurance policies on his $100,000 home. Each policy has a $100,000 limit. Ryan has a $50,000 loss that is covered by both policies. How much would each policy pay for this loss if Company A's policy is primary and Company B's is excess?
    A. Company A: $______________
    B. Company B: $______________

11. Three policies apply to a $30,000 loss. Policy A's limit of insurance is $100,000, Policy B's limit is $50,000, and Policy C's limit is $150,000. Use the pro rata method to determine how much each policy would pay for the loss.
    A. Policy A: $______________
    B. Policy B: $______________
    C. Policy C: $______________

12. Following are two excerpts from sample declarations. On the basis of the language in the excerpt, decide whether the policy provides specific or blanket coverage.
    A. 1999 Toyota Camry

    ____

    B. Business property located at 3489 Beluga Street ______________

13. Which of the following would normally be *excluded* under a property contract?
    A. Catastrophic losses
    B. Nonaccidental losses
    C. Losses to personal property
    D. Losses controllable by the insured
    E. Extra-hazardous perils

14. The policy period in an insurance policy
    A. specifies the date and time coverage begins and ends
    B. may be set by state law
    C. both A and B
    D. neither A nor B

15. An indirect loss is
    A. the cause of a direct loss
    B. a type of loss that results from a direct loss
    C. an insignificant property loss
    D. not a type of property loss

16. Consuela's Homeowners policy has an 80% coinsurance condition. Her home's value is $125,000. What is the minimum amount of coverage she must carry to be indemnified for losses up to the policy limit?
    A. $125,000
    B. $100,000

17. According to the terms of the mortgage condition, the mortgagee
    A. may have to pay the premium if the insured doesn't
    B. can file a proof of loss when the insured fails to do so to protect its rights under the policy
    C. may have coverage under the policy even if something the insured does causes a claim to be denied
    D. has no insurable interest in the covered property

18. Why do property insurance policies limit or exclude coverage for losses when property is vacant or unoccupied?

    ____

ANSWERS AND RATIONALES TO UNIT TEST

1. Open. An open peril policy covers any loss that is not specifically excluded by the policy.

2. Named. A named peril policy insures property against the perils specifically listed in the policy.

3. **A.** III. The named insured is the person, business, or other entity named in the declarations to whom the policy is issued.

   B. II. When there is more than one named insured listed on a policy, the policy may assign a higher level of duties or rights to the first named insured, the person listed first on the declarations page.

   C. III. In some circumstances, another individual or business may be listed on the declarations as an additional insured. An example is a mortgage company that has an outstanding loan on the property.

4. **A.** I. A direct loss is financial loss resulting directly from a loss to property. In this example, damage to the house that occurred when it was struck by an airplane is a direct loss.

   B. II. An indirect loss comes as a result, or consequence, of the original loss. In this example, additional living expenses that resulted from the damage to the house are an indirect loss.

5. **$7,000.** Depreciation on the roof is $3,000 ($300 per year for 10 years); replacement cost is $10,000. $10,000 – $3,000 = $7,000.

6. **$5,000.** When a loss is paid on a replacement cost basis, no deduction is made for depreciation.

7. **B.** The subrogation condition transfers the insured's right to collect from a responsible third party to the insurance company.

8. **A.** The assignment condition specifies that a policy may not be transferred to anyone else without the written consent of the insurer, except in the event of the death of the named insured.

9. **C.** Most insurance policies include conditions that specify what the insured and insurer must do when a loss occurs. The insured's responsibilities after a loss include giving notice of claim to the agent or company, protecting property from further damage, and completing a proof of loss form.

10. **A.** $50,000. When two or more coverages or policies apply to the same loss, the primary policy is the one that pays first, up to its limit of liability or the amount of the loss, whichever is less.

    B. $0. The full amount of the loss was already paid by the primary policy.

11. **A.** $10,000. $100,000 ÷ $300,000 = .33; $30,000 × .33 = $10,000.

    B. **$5,000.** $50,000 ÷ $300,000 = .16; $30,000 × .16 = $5,000.

    C. $15,000. $150,000 ÷ $300,000 = .50; $30,000 × .50 = $15,000.

12. **A.** **Specific.** Specific coverage means that property is specifically listed in the declarations and covered for a specific amount.

B. **Blanket.** Blanket coverage insures more than one item of property at a single location or one or more items of property at multiple locations.

13. **A, B, D, and E.** Property insurance policies typically exclude nonaccidental losses, losses controllable by the insured, extra-hazardous perils, catastrophic losses, and property covered in other policies.

14. **C.** Insurance policies specify the date and time, including where and in what time zone, coverage begins and ends. This is known as the policy period. In some states, the exact time of day policies start and stop is set by law to maintain uniformity between companies and to prevent gaps in coverage when an insured changes insurance companies.

15. **B.** An indirect loss is one that comes as a result, or consequence, of the original loss.

16. **B.** A coinsurance condition requires an insured to carry a certain amount of insurance, which is expressed as a percentage of the property's value. In this case, Consuela must carry insurance equal to 80% of the home's value, or $100,000.

17. **A, B and C.** Lenders or mortgagees may have an insurable interest in property. The mortgage condition specifies the rights and duties of the mortgagee under the policy. For instance, if an insured fails to file a proof of loss, the mortgagee must do so after being notified by the insurer to protect its rights under the policy. In addition, the mortgagee may be expected to pay the premium if the insured fails to do so. The policy may provide that if some condition caused by the insured would result in the insurer denying coverage for a loss it would otherwise have covered, the mortgagee may still have protection under the policy.

18. These conditions increase the chance of loss.

UNIT 5 EXERCISE ANSWERS

Exercise 5.A

1. **B**
2. **A**
3. **C**

Exercise 5.B

1. **I**
2. **D**
3. **I**

Exercise 5.C

1. $150,000. The insured cannot collect more than the policy limit.
2. $100,000. George has a 50% insurable interest in the condo, so the most he can collect is 50% of the value.

Exercise 5.D

1. $75,000
2. $25,000

Exercise 5.E

1. $8,000 ($100,000/$150,000 × $12,000)
2. $4,000 ($50,000/$150,000 × $12,000)

UNIT

6

Introduction to Liability Insurance

6.1. LEARNING OBJECTIVES

After completing Unit 6—Introduction to Liability Insurance, you will be able to do the following:

- Define liability loss, tort, and negligence
- Describe the four factors used to establish negligence
- Compare and contrast common defenses against negligence
- Explain how legal liability may be imposed under absolute liability and vicarious liability
- Explain the difference between a first-party loss and a third-party loss
- Describe a typical insuring agreement in a liability insurance policy
- Describe the types of damages that may be awarded for a liability loss
- Describe how bodily injury, property damage, and personal injury are usually defined in a liability insurance policy
- Explain how defense costs, postjudgment interest, and prejudgment interest are covered under a liability insurance policy
- Identify coverages that may be provided as supplementary payments and explain how they are paid under the policy
- Compare and contrast how policy limits may apply under a liability insurance policy
- Describe common liability policy exclusions
- Explain how the duties after loss and other insurance conditions in a liability policy may differ from comparable conditions in a property policy

6.2. LIABILITY LOSSES

Picture an irate citizen creeping out from under a pile of wreckage, standing shakily erect, waving a fist and shouting, "I'm gonna sue you for everything you've got!" The irate citizen could win the suit and leave you or your business in financial ruin. It happens. To help protect people against this happening, insurance companies provide liability insurance.

As we've already mentioned, an individual may incur losses as a result of his actions toward other people or their property. Such losses are called **liability losses**. A liability loss occurs when a person is determined to have been responsible, or liable, for loss to another person or another person's property and is required to make financial restitution.

Exercise 6.A

1. Which of the following are examples of liability losses?
   A. A truck hits a school bus, seriously injuring 15 children. The truck driver caused the accident.
   B. A very expensive home is damaged in a tornado.
   C. A toy with steel-tipped arrows causes three children to lose their eyesight. The toy manufacturer was found to be at fault for producing the game.
   D. An automobile catches on fire when the car's owner drops a cigarette on the seat.

Exercise answers can be found at the end of the Unit 6 answers and rationales.

6.3. NEGLIGENCE

6.3.1. Definition

A person becomes liable to another by committing a **tort**. A tort is a civil wrong that violates the rights of another. Unlike the commission of a crime, in which the government prosecutes the wrongdoer, torts are a part of civil law and are concerned with the private relationships between people.

A tort can be either **intentional** or **unintentional**. Liability insurance generally provides no protection for the insured against liability arising out of intentional torts. It does, however, provide coverage for unintentional torts.

Another term for an unintentional tort is *negligence*. If the insured is to be held liable for a certain event or action, the individual must have been negligent. **Negligence** is the lack of reasonable care required to protect others from the unreasonable chance of harm.

6.3.2. Establishing Negligence

Generally, a court of law must determine negligence. To establish negligence, the following four factors must be involved:

- Legal duty owed
- Breach of legal duty owed
- Proximate cause
- Damages

6.3.2.1. Legal Duty Owed and Breach of That Duty

First, there must be a **legal duty owed** and a **breach of that duty.** The legal duty owed to different people varies, but as a general rule, each person owes a duty to another to protect the other's rights and property. Each person is expected to behave like a reasonable or prudent person, following those ordinary considerations that guide human affairs. This is sometimes known as the **reasonable person rule.**

The duty owed by one person to another is sometimes expressed as a **degree of care** or **standard of care**. For instance, a property owner owes the greatest degree of care to an **invitee**, a person invited onto the premises involving potential benefit to the property owner. A little less responsibility is owed to a **licensee**, a person on the premises with the owner's consent but for the sole benefit of the visitor. The least degree of care is owed to a **trespasser**, one who is on the premises without permission, either expressed or implied.

6.3.2.2. Proximate Cause

To establish the fact that one person's actions toward another were negligent and that this negligence caused damage to another person or that person's property, the negligent act and the damage must be tied together. The negligent act is then the proximate cause of loss.

The **proximate cause** of a loss is an action that, in a natural and continuous sequence, produced the loss. This sequence is unbroken by any other factors or events, and the loss would not have occurred without the proximate cause.

When an independent action breaks the chain of causation and sets in motion a new chain of events, this **intervening cause** becomes the proximate cause.

Here is an example. Farmer Jones has a grain silo that is blown over in a windstorm. Five weeks later, he allows his neighbor's cattle to feed on the water-soaked grain that was left lying on the ground. Seventeen cows contract an intestinal ailment as a result and die.

In this case, the windstorm was the proximate cause of the loss to the silo but not the cattle. Farmer Jones's intervening negligent act (allowing the cattle to eat water-soaked grain) was the proximate cause of the loss to the cattle.

At times, additional events may occur between the proximate cause of the loss and the loss itself, but these events occur as a chain reaction, with no other causal element interrupting the sequence.

Consider this example. Linde Gas and Electric Company had a small fire in a control unit. This fire caused a short in the electrical wiring, which made a machine stop operating. Because this machine regulated another machine, the second machine ran out of control and flipped a flywheel off its shaft, which badly damaged adjacent machinery. In this case, the fire is the proximate cause of the damage to the machinery because it started the chain reaction and there were no intervening causes.

6.3.2.3. Damages

The final factor used to establish negligence is that another party suffered **damages**. If no one was adversely affected by an individual's actions, there is no finding of negligence.

6.4. DEFENSES AGAINST NEGLIGENCE

6.4.1. Contributory and Comparative Negligence

Traditionally, to establish liability an individual must show that the other party was negligent and that the individual did not contribute to the loss through any negligence on his own part. So if a person contributed to his own damages in any way, another party cannot be held liable for them. Some states retain this system, ruling out liability when there has been **contributory negligence**.

In other jurisdictions, this doctrine has been softened to some degree by **comparative negligence** laws, which allow a finding of liability to be made even when both parties have contributed to the loss, with an award based on the extent of each party's negligence.

6.4.2. Other Defenses Against Negligence

In some states, a doctrine known as **assumption of risk** may apply. Assumption of risk applies when a person knowingly exposes himself to danger or injury. When a person assumes this risk, the person may be prevented from recovering from a negligent party. This doctrine is frequently associated with injuries incurred by spectators at sporting events.

Intervening cause—when an independent event affects the chain of events—may also serve as a defense against liability.

Another defense can be found in the **statutes of limitations** enacted in various states. Such laws provide that certain types of lawsuits must be filed within a specified time of the occurrence to be valid under the law.

Exercise 6.B

Identify the defense to negligence that may apply in each of the situations described.

1. Marilyn wants to sue her neighbor for a back injury she suffered 15 years ago when she slipped and fell on her neighbor's icy steps.

   ____

   ____

2. While attending a baseball game, Mario is hit in the head by a foul ball. Mario decides to sue the team's owner. ____________________

   ____

3. Philip, a detective, is rushing to the scene of a crime where other officers have captured an armed robber. On the way, he makes a wrong turn down a one-way street and smashes head-on into a car, injuring four people. The injured passengers sue the armed robber.

   ____

   ____

Exercise answers can be found at the end of the Unit 6 answers and rationale.

6.5. ABSOLUTE/STRICT LIABILITY

Earlier, we said that negligence had to be present to hold someone legally liable for an action. There are some exceptions, however. **Absolute liability** is imposed by law on those participating in certain activities that are considered especially hazardous. Individuals involved in such operations may be held liable for the damages of another, even though the individual was not negligent. Absolute liability is most frequently applied to activities involving dangerous materials, hazardous operations, or dangerous animals.

Another term that is sometimes used for absolute liability is **strict liability**. Strict liability is usually used in reference to products liability.

Suppose Larry keeps seven boa constrictors in a trailer for use in his nightclub act. Despite precautions, one of the reptiles escapes and seriously injures a child. Larry may not have been negligent, but he could still be held responsible by virtue of absolute liability.

6.6. VICARIOUS LIABILITY

There are times when a person may be held responsible for the negligent acts of another person. This is called **vicarious liability**, or **imputed liability**.

A very common form of vicarious liability involves the relationship between an employer and an employee. Often, the negligence of an employee can be imputed (charged) to an employer because the employer has control over the employee. For example, a pizza delivery driver may negligently cause an accident that injures two pedestrians. The employer becomes responsible for the negligence because the employee was driving a company vehicle and the accident occurred on company time.

6.7. LIABILITY INSURANCE

6.7.1. Third-Party Losses

Liability losses are known in the insurance business as **third-party losses**. The insured is the first party. The insurance company legally representing or defending the insured is the second party. The third party is the person who suffered the injury or damage. (Property losses are considered **first-party** losses. The insured is the first party .)

Third Party Losses

Exercise 6.C

Herb, who has liability coverage with Acme Insurance, is playing ball with his daughter and hits a line drive through the living room window of a neighbor, Maureen.

1. The first party is____.
2. The second party is ______________________________________.
3. The third party is____.

Exercise answers can be found at the end of the Unit 6 answers and rationales.

6.7.2. Damages: Compensatory and Punitive

The financial consequences of a liability loss can be devastating. If an individual is liable for the loss of another, the courts may require the individual to pay **damages** (monetary compensation) to the injured party. A number of different types of damages can be awarded.

Compensatory damages reimburse the injured party only for losses that were actually sustained. There are two types of compensatory damages: **special** and **general**.

Special damages include all direct and specific expenses involved in a particular loss, such as medical expenses, lost wages, funeral expenses, and the cost to repair or replace damaged property. General damages compensate for such things as pain and suffering and disfigurement. General damages also include mental anguish and loss of companionship.

If the courts feel that the individual acted wantonly or willfully in causing the injured party's damages, it may award **punitive**, or **exemplary**, **damages**. Punitive damages are intended to punish the defendant and make an example of him to discourage others from behaving the same way.

Exercise 6.D

Pat is driving too fast on an icy highway when he loses control of his car and collides head on with Ed. Ed's car is totaled in the accident, and he suffers a broken spine and pelvis, which causes him to miss two months of work.

1. Which of Ed's losses would be considered special damages?

   ____

2. Ed also claims damages for pain and suffering arising out of his injuries. These would be considered (special/general) ______________ damages.
3. Assume that Pat was intoxicated and driving over 100 miles per hour when the accident occurred. In addition to compensatory damages, Pat might also be required to pay ______________________________.

Exercise answers can be found at the end of the Unit 6 answers and rationales.

6.7.3. Purpose of Liability Insurance

Now that you've seen the potential consequences of a liability loss, the question becomes, "How can I protect myself against financial loss due to liability claims?" The answer is liability insurance, which protects an insured from financial loss arising out of liability claims by transferring the burden of financial loss from the insured to the insurance company.

6.7.4. Insuring Agreement

6.7.4.1. Coverages

Most liability policies agree to pay on behalf of the insured all sums for which the insured becomes legally liable to pay as damages because of bodily injury and property damage.

Terms are always defined in the policy, but in general, **bodily injury (BI)** means injury, sickness, disease, and death arising out of injury, sickness or disease. **Property damage (PD)** means damage to or destruction of property, including loss of use of the property. Some liability policies also cover the insured's liability for **personal injury (PI)**, such as slander, libel, false arrest, and invasion of privacy. (In the insurance business, "bodily injury" and "personal injury" have different meanings and are not used interchangeably.)

Exercise 6.E

For each of the following examples, decide whether the loss in italics is bodily injury **(BI)**, property damage **(PD)**, or personal injury **(PI)** according to the definitions you just learned.

____ 1. A truck veers off the road and jackknifes, *killing 70 cows that were being transported*.

____ 2. Tom's car is hit by another vehicle that runs a red light, causing extensive damage to Tom's car. Tom has to *rent a replacement car at $30 per day while his own car is being fixed*.

____ 3. Mary's dog breaks his chain and *bites a child. The child requires stitches to close the wound*.

____ 4. Grayson's Deli fails to refrigerate its potato salad properly. A customer who orders a double helping *develops food poisoning and dies the next day*.

____ 5. Christina's son *breaks all the windows in a neighbor's basement* as a Halloween prank.

____ 6. Martin *tells a reporter that his neighbor is an ex-convict. The reporter publishes this information, which is later found to be false*.

Exercise answers can be found at the end of the Unit 6 answers and rationales.

Note that the insured must be directly liable for the damage before the company will pay damages on the insured's behalf. Earlier, we said that an insured could be found legally liable in a court of law. However, if the insurance company believes its insured was negligent, it is common practice to settle the claim out of court.

6.7.4.2. Defense Costs

In addition to paying for bodily injury or property damage, liability policies promise to defend the insured in any suit seeking BI or PD damages, even if the charges are groundless or false. Defense costs are paid in addition to payments for claims.

The insurer pays for the defense, but its duty to defend ends once the amount it pays for damages equals the policy limit.

6.7.4.3. Prejudgment Interest

A court will sometimes award a third-party interest on an award for damages to compensate for the interest the third party might have earned if the party had received compensation at the time of injury or damage rather than at the time of judgment. Most liability policies cover this **prejudgment interest**. Some policies cover it along with the actual damages, up to the policy limits. Other policies may include it as a supplementary, or additional payment that is not subject to the limit of liability.

6.7.4.4. Supplementary Payments

Liability policies also provide certain **supplementary payments** that are paid in addition to the policy's regular limit of liability. These coverages vary from one type of liability policy to another, but in general they include:

- defense costs;
- expenses incurred in the investigation of a claim;
- premiums for certain types of bonds, such as bail bonds, appeal bonds, and release of attachment bonds;
- first aid to others at the time of an accident;
- reasonable expenses incurred by the insured at the company's request in the investigation or defense of a claim;
- loss of earnings (such as when the insured is required to miss work for court appearances);
- prejudgment interest (when it is not included as a part of damages); and
- postjudgment interest (interest accruing on the judgment after an award has been made but before payment is made by the company).

Suppose James has a liability policy with a $10,000 policy limit and a supplementary payments section that covers up to $250 for lost wages. A neighbor is injured because of James's negligence and files a lawsuit against him. The neighbor wins the suit, and a $10,000 judgment is awarded against James. In addition, James loses $250 in wages when he missed work to appear in court for the lawsuit. James's insurance company will pay $10,250. Supplementary payments are paid in addition to the policy's limit of liability, so the company will pay the $10,000 judgment and the $250 for lost wages.

6.7.4.5. Policy Limits and Restoration of Limits

Although the purpose of liability insurance is to protect the insured from financial loss by shifting the burden of payment from the insured to the company, there is a limit beyond which the company will not go. The maximum amount the company will pay on behalf of the insured is stated in the **policy limits**.

The policy may stipulate separate limits for BI and PD (**split limits**), or there may be one limit that applies to both BI and PD (**single** or **combined single limit**).

In general, these limits apply **per occurrence**. The word *occurrence* can mean either a loss that occurs at a specific time and place, such as when a person trips over a toy, or a loss that occurs over time, as when fumes escaping from an activity on the insured premises eventually damage the paint on a neighboring house.

Some liability coverage limits apply **per accident**, an older and more restrictive term that limits covered losses to those that occur at a specific time and place. But you need to be careful here. Some policies use the term *accident* because it's a more familiar word. But they define it so it means the same as *occurrence*. Only a careful inspection of the policy will determine how it should be interpreted.

Some liability policies have a **per person** limit that states how much will be paid for injury to any one person in an occurrence or accident. Others also have an **aggregate limit**. This is a limit that applies to all losses occurring within any one policy period.

With the exception of the aggregate limit, most policy limits are **restored** after payment of a loss. Suppose the insured's liability policy has a $50,000 aggregate limit and a $1,000 per occurrence limit. If the insured has a $500 covered loss, it will be subtracted from the aggregate limit. However, the full $1,000 per occurrence limit will be available for other covered losses that occur during the policy period as long as the aggregate limit has not been exhausted.

Exercise 6.F

An insured has a $15,000 per occurrence limit and a $25,000 aggregate limit. The insured has the following covered losses in a single policy year. How much would the policy pay for each of these losses?

1. January 6: $20,000 $____________
2. February 14: $3,000 $____________
3. April 9: $1,500 $____________
4. September 14: $6,000 $____________
5. November 2: $500 $____________

Exercise answers can be found at the end of the Unit 6 answers and rationales.

6.7.5. Exclusions

All liability policies contain certain exclusions. We'll examine these in detail when we look at specific policies, but we'll mention some common exclusions here. In general, there is no coverage for:

- damage to property owned by the insured;
- damage to property in the insured's care, custody, or control;
- bodily injury to an insured;
- losses covered under workers' compensation laws;
- losses covered under nuclear energy liability policies; and
- injuries or damages caused intentionally by the insured.

6.7.6. Conditions

6.7.6.1. Duties After Loss

A number of conditions are commonly found in liability policies, many of which we've already discussed, such as cancellation, assignment and misrepresentation, and concealment and fraud.

The duties after loss condition has some unique requirements in liability policies. The insured must notify the insurance company in writing of all losses. In addition, the insured is required to forward all applicable demands, notices, or summonses and give any necessary assistance to the case, such as testifying as required. The insured cannot voluntarily assume any liability or make any restitution to another party without the knowledge and consent of the insurer.

6.7.6.2. Other Insurance

Like property policies, liability policies contain other insurance clauses. In addition to the methods we've already discussed for handling other insurance, liability policies may provide for **contribution by equal shares**.

Under contribution by equal shares, all insurers pay equal amounts, up to the limit of the policy having the smallest limit. Then that company, having paid its policy limit, stops paying, and the other companies share the remainder of the loss. This continues until each company has paid its policy limit or the loss is paid in full.

Here's an example. The insured's $24,000 liability loss is covered by two policies—one issued by Company XYZ with a $5,000 limit and one issued by Company PDQ with a $25,000 limit. XYZ pays $5,000, and PDQ pays $19,000 ($5,000 + $14,000). If the loss had been $4,000, XYZ would pay $2,000 and PDQ would pay $2,000.

UNIT TEST

1. Which of the following are examples of liability losses?
   A. Ronald allows his large dog to run loose. One day the dog bites a child while the child is playing in her own yard.
   B. During a severe storm, a limb from a well-tended tree in Sandra's yard breaks and falls into Shirley's yard, damaging a swing set.
   C. Thomas's son leaves a toy truck on the front walk. The mail carrier trips over it and breaks her leg.

2. Failure to use the care that is required to protect others from the unreasonable chance of harm is
   A. proximate cause
   B. negligence
   C. a criminal act
   D. an intervening cause

3. All of the following must be present to establish negligence EXCEPT
   A. proximate cause
   B. legal duty owed and breach of duty
   C. damages
   D. willful action

4. An action that, in a natural and continuous sequence, produces a loss is the
   A. hazard
   B. proximate cause
   C. appraisal point
   D. exposure

5. Liability that is imposed as a matter of law without regard to negligence is
   A. vicarious liability
   B. absolute liability
   C. breach liability
   D. proximate liability

6. Liability that an insured incurs because of the actions of others, such as employees, is
   A. vicarious liability
   B. absolute liability
   C. breach liability
   D. proximate liability

7. Liability losses are known as
   A. first-party losses
   B. second-party losses
   C. third-party losses

8. Liability policies usually pay damages for the insured's liability for
   A. bodily injury
   B. property damage
   C. personal injury
   D. intentional torts

9. Supplementary payments are
   A. paid in addition to the policy's liability limit
   B. deducted from the policy's liability limit

10. An aggregate limit is the most a company will pay
    A. for any one event
    B. over the policy year
    C. for any one person or item of property

11. Theresa, a spectator at a baseball game, is injured when an errant ball hits her in the head. She sues the stadium owners for negligence. Which of the following defenses against negligence will the owners probably use?
    A. Assumption of risk
    B. Comparative negligence
    C. Contributory negligence
    D. Statute of limitations

12. Which of the following illustrates the concept of contributory negligence?
    A. Martin buys a tanning bed for his home. Although he follows the manufacturer's directions to the letter, he is severely burned after spending 5 minutes in the bed.
    B. Jane goes to a hair salon to have her hair colored. The hairdresser mixes the color improperly and dyes Jane's hair purple.
    C. Rosa is injured when her car is struck from behind while she is stopped at a red light.
    D. Ben turns a corner too fast and strikes Reba's car, which is illegally parked in a fire lane.

13. Lee sues Pat for injuries sustained in an auto accident. During the trial, it is determined that Lee's negligence contributed to the loss. Under comparative negligence laws
    A. Lee cannot recover any damages from Pat
    B. Lee's damages will be reduced to the extent of her own liability for the loss
    C. Lee can recover the full amount of the loss from Pat

14. What type of compensatory damages reimburse the injured party for direct, specific expenses involved in the loss?
    A. Special
    B. General

15. Damages that are awarded to punish the defendant and deter others from behaving the same way are called
    A. punitive damages
    B. general damages

16. Which of the following might be included as a *supplementary payment* in a liability policy?
    A. Premium for a bail or appeal bond
    B. Reasonable investigation expenses the insured incurs at the company's request
    C. First aid costs
    D. Judgment against the insured for bodily injury liability

17. Curt fails to clean the ice off his driveway after a major storm. The mail carrier slides on the ice but does not fall or otherwise injure himself. Could the mail carrier claim negligence against Curt?
    ( ) Yes ( )No

    Explain your answer.______________________________
    ____

18. The insured is sued by a neighbor, who claims she suffered a back injury when she tripped over a skateboard left on the insured's driveway. The insured knows the neighbor has had a bad back for many years; furthermore, her family doesn't even own a skateboard. Will her insurance company pay to defend this case in court?
    ( ) Yes ( ) No

19. An insured is found liable for a $100,000 bodily injury claim as a result of a car accident. Her insurance company incurred $25,000 in expenses defending the insured against the suit. The insured's auto policy limit is $100,000. How much will the insurance company pay for the bodily injury?
    A. $75,000
    B. $100,000

20. Brandon's auto policy has a $50,000 BI limit and a $25,000 PD limit. This is an example of a (split/single) ________________ limit policy.

21. The insured's valuable Ming vase is shattered when a neighbor carelessly knocks it off a shelf. Could the insured recover for this loss under her own liability policy?
    ( ) Yes ( ) No
    Explain your answer. ______________________________
    ____
    ____

22. The insured is furious with her neighbors for playing their music too loud, so she breaks all the windows in their house with a sledgehammer. If the neighbors sue, will the insured be covered for this loss under her liability policy? ( ) Yes ( ) No
    Explain your answer.______________________________

ANSWERS AND RATIONALES TO UNIT TEST

1. **A and C.** A liability loss occurs when a person is responsible, or liable, for loss to another person or another person's property and is required to make financial restitution.

2. **B.** Negligence is the lack of reasonable care that is required to protect others from the unreasonable chance of harm.

3. **D.** Negligence is the lack of reasonable care that is required to protect others from the unreasonable chance of harm. The factors used to establish negligence are legal duty owed, breach of legal duty owed, proximate cause, and damages.

4. **B.** Proximate cause is one of the elements required to establish a charge of negligence. It is an action that, in a natural and continuous sequence, produces a loss.

5. **B.** Absolute liability is imposed by law on those participating in certain activities that are considered to be especially hazardous. Individuals involved in such activities may be held liable for the damages of another, even though the individual was not negligent.

6. **A.** Vicarious liability is liability that a person or business incurs because of the actions of others, such as family members or employees.

7. **C.** Liability losses are called third-party losses. The insured is the first party. The insurance company representing the insured is the second party. The person who sustained the injury or damage is the third party.

8. **A, B, and C.** Most liability policies agree to pay on behalf of the insured all sums for which the insured becomes legally liable to pay as damages because of bodily injury or property damage. Some liability policies also cover the insured's liability for personal injury, such as slander, libel, false arrest, and invasion of privacy. Liability insurance generally provides no protection for the insured against liability arising out of intentional torts.

9. **A.** Liability policies provide certain supplementary payments that are paid in addition to the policy's regular limit of liability. Defense costs, postjudgment interest, and premiums for certain types of bonds are examples of coverages that are usually included as supplementary payments.

10. **B.** An aggregate limit is a limit that applies to all losses occurring within any one policy period. An aggregate limit is not restored after payment of a loss.

11. **A.** Assumption of risk applies when a person knowingly exposes himself to danger or injury. When a person assumes this risk, he may be prevented from recovering from a negligent party. This doctrine is frequently associated with injuries incurred by spectators at sporting events.

12. **D.** In this case, both parties contributed to the accident—Ben by driving too fast and Reba by illegally parking her car. In the other examples, the injured party's own negligence did not contribute to the loss.

13. **B.** Under a comparative negligence law, a finding of liability may be made even when both parties have contributed to the loss, with an award based on the extent of each party's negligence.

14. **A.** Special damages include all direct and specific expenses involved in a particular loss, such as medical expenses, lost wages, funeral expenses, and the cost to repair or replace damaged property.

15. **A.** If a court feels that an individual acted wantonly or willfully in causing the injured party's damages, it may award punitive, or exemplary, damages. Punitive damages are intended to punish the defendant and make an example out of him to discourage others from behaving the same way.

16. **A, B, and C.** A judgment against the insured for bodily injury liability would be covered under the policy's liability coverage (assuming the loss is not excluded).

17. **No.** He did not suffer damages, which is one of the elements required to establish negligence.

18. **Yes.** Liability policies promise to defend the insured in any suit seeking BI or PD damages, even if the charges are groundless or false.

19. **B.** Defense costs are paid in addition to the policy limit and will not reduce the amount paid under the policy for a claim.

20. **Split.** A split limit policy has separate limits for BI and PD.

21. **No.** Liability policies exclude damage to property owned by the insured.

22. **No.** Liability policies exclude damages that are caused intentionally by the insured.

UNIT 6 EXERCISE ANSWERS

Exercise 6.A

1. A and C

Exercise 6.B

1. Statute of limitations
2. Assumption of risk
3. Intervening cause

Exercise 6.C

1. Herb
2. Acme Insurance
3. Maureen

Exercise 6.D

1. Medical bills, replacement of the auto, and lost wages
2. General
3. Punitive damages

Exercise 6.E

1. **PD**
2. **PD**
3. **BI**
4. **BI**
5. **PD**
6. **PI**

Exercise 6.F

1. $15,000 (per occurrence limit)
2. $3,000
3. $1,500
4. $5,500 (remainder of aggregate limit)
5. $0 (aggregate limit exhausted)

UNIT

7

Dwelling Insurance

7.1. LEARNING OBJECTIVES

After completing Unit 7—Dwelling Insurance, you will be able to do the following:

- Identify the main differences between a dwelling policy and a homeowners policy
- Describe the types of buildings eligible for a dwelling policy and who is insured under the policy
- Describe what is covered under the four basic coverages provided by all dwelling forms
- Identify the perils automatically covered by the basic dwelling form and the additional perils provided by the extended coverage perils
- Explain how vandalism and malicious mischief coverage is added to the DP-1
- Identify the other coverages provided by the DP-1
- Identify situations and perils that are excluded under the dwelling policy
- Explain how the loss conditions in the dwelling policy apply
- Compare and contrast the DP-1, DP-2, and DP-3 in terms of the covered perils, basic policy coverages, other coverages, and valuation provisions
- Describe the coverage provided by the broad theft coverage and personal liability and medical payments to others endorsements
- Explain the purpose of the automatic increase in insurance and dwelling under construction endorsements

7.2. THE DWELLING POLICY

7.2.1. Introduction

The **dwelling policy** provides protection for individuals and families against loss to their dwelling and personal property. If you're already familiar with the homeowners policy, which also covers dwellings and personal property, you may wonder what the difference is between the two policies. We'll have an opportunity to look at both forms in detail, but two key differences are:

- the dwelling policy provides more limited property coverage than the homeowners policy; and
- the unendorsed dwelling policy provides property coverage only, while the homeowners policy provides a package of property and liability coverages.

There are three separate dwelling policy forms: the basic form, the broad form, and the special form, each providing a higher level of coverage than the last.

In this course, we'll focus on the dwelling 2002 policy issued by the Insurance Services Office (ISO).

7.2.2. Eligibility, Insureds

To be covered under a dwelling policy, a dwelling may have up to five boarders and up to four apartments. It may be a townhouse or a row house. The dwelling does not have to be occupied by the owner, and it may be under construction.

A dwelling policy may also be used to insure a mobile home meeting certain qualifications, including that it be permanently located. Mobile homes may only be covered under the basic form.

Dwelling policies may be used to insure homes that do not qualify for homeowners insurance. For example, the owner of a home that is rented to tenants could not insure the home under a homeowners policy but could insure it under a dwelling policy. Dwelling policies are also frequently used to insure vacation homes.

Eligible dwelling property does not have to be exclusively residential. Certain incidental business and professional occupancies are allowed. These operations must be conducted by the insured, provide service rather than sales, and involve no more than two people working on the premises at any one time. Examples of permitted occupancies include beauty parlors, photography studios, and professional offices.

The dwelling policy covers the named insured and the insured's spouse, as long as the spouse lives in the same household as the insured.

7.3. BASIC FORM (DP-1)

7.3.1. Basic Policy Coverages

We'll begin our discussion with the dwelling basic form, which is also known as the **DP-1** and **DP 00 01**. The basic form provides the following coverages:

- Coverage A—dwelling
- Coverage B—other structures
- Coverage C—personal property
- Coverage D—fair rental value

Although all four coverages are preprinted in the policy form, the insured does not have to purchase each one. For example, an insured who owns an unfurnished house that she rents to others might choose to purchase only Coverage A—dwelling and Coverage D—fair rental value.

Coverage A—Dwelling; Coverage B—Other Structures

Coverage A—dwelling covers the dwelling, structures attached to the dwelling, materials and supplies for use in the construction or repair of the dwelling or other structures at the location, and building or outdoor equipment used to service the premises.

Coverage B—other structures insures buildings on the premises that are separated from the dwelling by a clear space or connected only by a fence, utility line, or similar connection. The building may not be used for commercial, manufacturing, or farming purposes. However, structures that contain commercial, manufacturing, or farming property that is owned by the insured or a tenant of the dwelling are covered as long as the structure is not used to store gaseous or liquid fuel. Grave markers, including mausoleums, are not covered.

Coverage C—Personal Property

Coverage C—personal property covers the insured's personal property that is at the described location and is usual to the dwelling occupancy. Personal property belonging to the insured's guests or servants may be covered at the insured's request. The following items of personal property are not covered:

- Money, securities, manuscripts, bullion, currency, accounts, deeds, and evidences of debt
- Bank notes, coins, gold other than goldware, letters of credit, medals, personal records, platinum, silver other than silverware, tickets, and stamps
- Books of account, drawings and other paper records, electronic data processing tapes, wires, records, discs, and other software media (does not apply to blank recording or storage media or prerecorded media)

- Credit cards and fund transfer cards
- Animals, birds, and fish
- Aircraft
- Motor vehicles, other than motorized equipment used to maintain the premises
- Boats, other than rowboats and canoes
- Hovercraft and parts (*hovercraft* refers to self-propelled motorized ground effect vehicles, such as air cushion vehicles and flarecraft)
- Water or steam (under the earlier forms, it could be argued that water became the insured's personal property after it passed through the insured's water meter; this exclusion makes the intent of the policy clear)
- Grave markers, including mausoleums
- Electronic fund transfer cards or access devices used to deposit, withdraw, or transfer funds
- Scrip, stored value cards, and smart cards
- Data stored in computers and related equipment

Coverage is also available for property moved from the described location to another residence of the insured within the same state. The amount of insurance that applies is divided between the described location and the new location, according to the proportion of property at each location. This coverage is called automatic removal.

Coverage D—fair rental value is available if a covered property loss to the dwelling or other structure makes the building uninhabitable and the insured cannot collect the rent he would have been able to receive if the loss had not occurred. Twenty percent of the insurance on the dwelling is available for this coverage. If a civil authority prohibits use of the insured property because a covered peril damaged a neighboring location, payments are limited to a maximum of two weeks.

7.3.2. Perils Insured Against

The only perils that are automatically covered under the basic form are as follows:

Fire

Lightning

Internal Explosion

An internal explosion is an explosion that occurs in a covered building or in a building containing covered personal property. Typical losses covered would include the explosion of a furnace, stove, or hot water heater. Steam explosions are excluded if the equipment is owned, leased, or operated by the insured.

7.3.3. Extended Coverage (EC) Perils

Although only fire, lightning, and internal explosion are covered automatically, the insured has some additional options with the basic form. The insured may opt to be covered against a list of additional perils that are sometimes called the extended coverage, or EC, perils.

These perils are already printed in the DP-1 form. However, no coverage applies unless the insured pays the additional premium and the declarations indicate that the insured has selected the extended coverage perils, which includes the following items.

Extended Coverage Perils

Riot
Explosion
Vehicles
Smoke
Hail
Civil Commotion
Aircraft
Windstorm
Volcanic Eruption

The explosion peril in the extended coverage perils replaces the internal explosion peril that is automatically part of every dwelling policy. The explosion peril encompasses both internal explosions and other types of explosions, such as an explosion at a neighboring location.

Damage to the interior of a building from windstorm or hail is only covered if wind or hail first makes an opening that allows these elements to enter the building. Awnings, signs, and antennas outside a building are not covered against wind or hail damage.

The vehicles peril does not apply to damage caused by a vehicle owned or operated by the insured or a resident of the household. It also does not include vehicle damage to fences, driveways, and walks.

Smoke damage from fireplaces or from agricultural smudging or industrial operations is not covered. The smoke peril covers damage caused by **puffback**—the release of soot, smoke, vapor, or fumes from a furnace, boiler, or similar equipment.

The insured can also obtain coverage for **vandalism and malicious mischief (V&MM)** by paying an additional premium and indicating this coverage in the declarations. This coverage must be purchased in conjunction with the extended coverage perils. Vandalism and malicious mischief coverage does not cover:

- damage to glass parts of a building other than glass building blocks;
- losses by theft (does not apply to building damage caused by burglars); or
- vandalism to a building that has been vacant for more than 60 consecutive days.

7.3.4. Other Coverages

In addition to insuring against the listed perils, the dwelling basic form provides certain **other coverages**.

- **Other structures** provides that up to 10% of the Coverage A limit may be used to cover losses to other structures. (The term *appurtenant structures* may also be used to describe other structures.)
- **Debris removal** pays for the expense of removing debris resulting from a loss that is covered by the policy.
- **Property removed** covers loss to property that occurs while the property is being removed to protect it from a covered peril. (This is not the same as automatic removal, which extends personal property coverage to property moved to another residence.) In the basic form, property removed is covered for five days.
- **Reasonable repairs** pays for the reasonable costs to make necessary repairs to protect property from further damage following a covered loss.
- **Improvements, alterations, and additions** provides coverage for insureds who are tenants for improvements or alterations to the dwelling made at the tenant's expense. Up to 10% of the Coverage C limit is available for this coverage.
- **Fire department service charge** pays up to $500 for fire department charges incurred when the fire department is called to save or protect covered property from a peril insured against. No deductible applies to this coverage.
- **Worldwide coverage** provides 10% of the Coverage C limit for personal property while it is located anywhere in the world. An example is clothing the insured takes on vacation.

- **Rental value** provides 20% of the Coverage A limit for loss of fair rental value, payable at 1/12 of the 20% limit for each month the described location is unfit for its normal use.

Other structures and rental value are not really other coverages, since they are considered basic policy coverages. They are listed again in this section to provide additional information about how the coverages apply.

Exercise 7.A

Indicate which other coverage would apply in each of the following situations. Assume the insured's DP-1 includes extended coverage perils.

1. The fire department was called to put out a fire that started in the insured's home. The department charged the insured $250 for its services.

   ____

2. An explosion damaged a wall of the insured's garage. The insured paid to have the wall boarded up to protect the inside of the garage from additional damage.

   ____

3. When lightning struck the insured's roof, it left shingles scattered all over the lawn. The insured had to pay to have the shingles removed.

   ____

4. A fire that started in the insured's bedroom threatened to spread through the entire house. Before it got out of control, the insured managed to carry several pieces of furniture to the backyard. In the commotion created by the arrival of the fire department, someone stole the insured's favorite chair.

   ____

Exercise answers can be found at the end of the Unit 7 answers and rationales.

7.3.5. Exclusions

The basic form excludes the following:

- Losses resulting from ordinances or laws that require the insured to test for, monitor, clean up, or otherwise respond to pollutants or that require more elaborate or expensive reconstruction or demolition than was used in the original structure (replacing a dwelling's regular glass with safety glass is covered)
- Losses resulting from earth movement, including mudslides, sinkholes, and subsidence; does not apply to direct loss by fire or explosion resulting from earth movement
- Water damage in general, including flooding, water backing up into a building, and water leaking or seeping from below the ground; also

excluded is water or water-borne material that is discharged from a sump pump or related equipment

- Losses due to power interruption that occurs away from the insured location
- The insured's failure to save and preserve property after a loss, or to protect it from loss
- War
- Nuclear hazard
- Losses caused by the insured or by someone else at the insured's direction
- Destruction, confiscation, or seizure of property by the **government or a public authority**

7.3.6. Conditions

The dwelling policy contains many of the property insurance conditions we described in an earlier unit. There are also several conditions concerning how losses will be paid.

- The **loss settlement** condition states that covered property losses are valued at actual cash value but are not to exceed the amount necessary to repair or replace.
- The **our option** condition gives the insurer the right to repair or replace damaged property with material or property of like kind and quality within 30 days of receiving the insured's statement of loss.
- The **deductible** clause states that only the amount of loss over the deductible will be paid, up to the limit of liability.
- The **pair or set** condition states that in the case of a loss to an item that is part of a pair or set, the insurance company is not obligated to pay the value of the entire set. The company may either repair or replace part of the set or pay the difference between the actual cash value of the property before and after the loss.
- The **loss payment** condition states that the loss will be paid within 30 days after reaching an agreement with the insured.
- The **other insurance** condition states that if a loss is also covered by other insurance, the insurance company will pay only its proportion of the loss.
- The **recovered property** condition states that if the insured or insurer recovers property on which the insurer has made loss payment, the other party must be notified. The insured may have the property returned, in which case the loss payment will be adjusted, or allow the company to have it.

7.4. BROAD FORM (DP-2) AND SPECIAL FORM (DP-3)

7.4.1. Covered Perils—Broad Form

Now that you're familiar with the DP-1, we'll study the other dwelling forms. Our discussion will focus primarily on the differences between these forms and the DP-1.

Like the basic form, the broad form (DP-2, DP 00 02) is a named peril policy that lists the perils that dwellings, other structures, and personal property are insured against. The broad form automatically covers all of the standard and optional perils available on the basic form—fire, lightning, the extended coverage perils, and vandalism and malicious mischief. It also broadens some perils covered under the basic form and adds additional perils:

- Damage to covered property caused by burglars (does not apply to theft of property)
- Weight of ice, snow, or sleet
- Falling objects
- Freezing of plumbing, heating, air conditioning, or automatic fire protective sprinkler systems and household appliances (insured must use reasonable care to maintain heat in the building or shut off the water supply and drain all systems and appliances)
- Sudden and accidental tearing apart, cracking, or burning of steam or hot water heating, air conditioning, or automatic fire protective sprinkler systems and water heaters
- Sudden and accidental damage from artificially generated electrical current (does not include damage to a tube, transistor, or similar electrical component)
- Accidental discharge of water or steam at the described location from within a plumbing, heating, air conditioning, or automatic fire protective sprinkler system or household appliance

The weight of ice, snow, or sleet peril does not cover damage to awnings, fences, patios, pavement, swimming pools, foundations, retaining walls, bulkheads, piers, wharves, or docks.

The falling objects peril does not include damage to awnings, fences, outdoor equipment, or outdoor radio and television antennas, including their lead-in wires, masts, and towers. Damage to a building's interior or its contents is covered only if the falling object first damages the roof or an exterior wall.

The accidental discharge or overflow peril does not include continuous or repeated leakage or seepage, freezing, or damage to the system or appliance itself.

The burglars and accidental discharge perils are not covered if the building has been vacant for more than 60 consecutive days.

The broad form also expands coverage for two perils.

- The **vehicles** peril covers damage to fences, driveways, and walks when the vehicle is driven by someone who is *not* a resident of the insured's household. It also covers damage to other types of property when the vehicle is driven by an insured or a resident of the insured's household.
- The **smoke** peril includes loss caused by fireplace smoke.

Earlier, you learned that the DP-1 covers fire or explosion that results from earth movement. The DP-2 and the DP-3, which you will study in a moment, also cover breakage of glass or safety glazing material that is part of a building, storm door, or storm window that results from earth movement.

Exercise 7.B

1. Which of the following losses would be covered under the DP-2?
   A. Smoke from a nearby factory damaged the insured's home.
   B. After a blizzard, the roof on the insured's home collapsed from the weight of the snow.
   C. A streetlight in the alley behind the insured's house fell down in a windstorm and crushed a storage shed in the insured's back yard.
   D. The insured's neighbor lost control of his vehicle and knocked down the insured's fence.

Exercise answers can be found at the end of the Unit 7 answers and rationales.

7.4.2. Covered Perils—Special Form

The special form (DP-3, DP 00 03) provides open peril coverage on the dwelling and other structures, insuring against all risks of direct physical loss that are not specifically excluded in the policy. Personal property is covered on a named peril basis—the same perils listed in the DP-2.

Under Coverages A and B, the special form excludes:

- all property, losses, and perils not covered due to limitations of the general exclusions (as described earlier in relation to the basic form) and the insuring agreement;
- any loss involving collapse, other than as provided in the other coverages section;
- freezing of a plumbing, heating, air conditioning, or automatic fire protective sprinkler system or a household appliance, or overflow due to freezing, unless reasonable care was taken to maintain heat in the building or to shut off the water supply and drain the systems and appliances;

- freezing, thawing, pressure, or weight of water or ice to fences, pavement, patios, swimming pools, foundations, retaining walls, bulkheads, piers, wharves, or docks;
- theft in or to a dwelling or structure under construction, or theft of any property that is not part of a covered building or structure;
- damage by wind, hail, ice, snow, or sleet to outdoor radio and television antennas and aerials, including their lead-in wires, masts, or towers, and damage by these same perils to lawns, trees, shrubs, or plants;
- vandalism, malicious mischief, theft, and attempted theft if the dwelling has been vacant for more than 60 consecutive days at the time of loss;
- constant or repeated seepage or leakage of water or steam over time from a plumbing, heating, air conditioning, or fire protective sprinkler system or from a household appliance;
- gradual and expected losses, such as wear and tear, deterioration, inherent vice, latent defect, mechanical breakdown, smog, rust, corrosion, mold, wet or dry rot, and smoke from agricultural smudging or industrial operations;
- discharge, dispersal, seepage, migration, release, or escape of pollutants such as smoke, vapor, soot, fumes, acids, alkalis, chemicals, and waste;
- settling, shrinking, bulging, or expansion, including resulting cracking of pavements, foundations, walls, floors, roofs, or ceilings; and
- loss caused by birds, vermin, insects, and domestic animals.

If a loss that is not otherwise excluded involves water damage from a plumbing, heating, air conditioning, or fire protective sprinkler system or household appliance, the policy covers the loss caused by water and the cost of tearing out and replacing any part of a building necessary to repair the system or appliance. Loss to the system or appliance itself is not covered.

7.4.3. Basic Policy Coverages

All three dwelling forms provide these basic policy coverages:

- Coverage A—dwelling
- Coverage B—other structures
- Coverage C—personal property
- Coverage D—fair rental value

The DP-2 and DP-3 also include Coverage E—additional living expense. Coverage E pays for additional living expenses the insured incurs after a covered loss, including reasonable motel, dining, laundry, and transportation expenses. These are covered for the time needed to repair or replace the damaged property or become settled elsewhere in permanent quarters. If a civil authority prohibits use of the insured property because a covered peril damaged a neighboring location, payments are limited to a maximum of two weeks. (Note that this coverage can be added to the DP-1 by endorsement.)

7.4.4. Other Coverages

The DP-2 and DP-3 include some other coverages that are not contained in the DP-1.

Trees, shrubs, and other plants pays up to 5% of the Coverage A limit for damage to trees, shrubs, plants, or lawns caused by a specified list of perils. The policy will not pay more than $500 for damage to any one tree, shrub, or plant.

Collapse pays for the collapse of the dwelling caused by a specified list of perils. To be considered a collapse, the loss must involve the building or part of the building abruptly falling down or caving in, after which the building or part of the building cannot be occupied. Collapse that results from hidden decay or hidden insect or vermin damage is not covered if the insured knew about the damage before the building collapsed.

Glass or safety glazing material pays for the breakage of glass or safety glazing material and damage to covered property caused by glass breakage.

The **ordinance or law** coverage allows payment of up to 10% of the Coverage A limit of liability for the increased cost to repair or rebuild a dwelling or other structure to conform with applicable building and land use codes.

In the DP-2 and DP-3, property removed is covered for 30 days. In the DP-1, it is covered for only 5 days.

7.4.5. Replacement Cost Coverage

Both the DP-2 and the DP-3 settle losses to personal property at actual cash value. Losses to the dwelling and other structures, however, are paid on a replacement cost basis, with no deduction for depreciation, as long as the insured carries insurance equal to 80% or more of the full replacement cost of the building at the time of the loss.

Suppose an insured's home has a replacement value of $100,000. To have the home restored or replaced at replacement cost, the insured must have insurance equal to or greater than 80% of $100,000, or $80,000.

If the insured does not carry enough insurance to qualify for replacement cost coverage, the insured will be paid the larger of:

- the actual cash value of the loss, or;
- a proportion of the replacement cost.

Of course, the insured can never receive more than the policy limit.

Proportional replacement cost is calculated by dividing the amount of insurance the insured carries by the amount he is required to carry to qualify for replacement cost coverage. The figure that results is multiplied by the amount of the loss to determine the amount of reimbursement. Here is how it looks as a formula:

$$\frac{\text{Insurance carried}}{\text{Insurance required}} \times \text{amount of loss} = \text{amount of reimbursement.}$$

Suppose an insured's home has a replacement value of $100,000. This insured has $60,000 in coverage instead of the $80,000 needed to qualify for replacement cost coverage. The insured has a $16,000 loss. Using the proportional method, reimbursement would be:

$$\frac{\$60{,}000}{\$80{,}000} = .75\ (3/4).$$

$$.75 \times \$16{,}000 = \$12{,}000.$$

Exercise 7.C

An insured has a dwelling broad form with a $40,000 limit of liability. The home has a replacement value of $100,000.

1. How much insurance should the insured carry to obtain full replacement cost coverage for loss to the dwelling? $_________
2. The insured has a loss that has a replacement cost of $30,000. Will the company pay the full replacement cost? ___________
3. For what proportion of the full replacement cost could the insurance company be liable? $____________
4. Depreciation to the damaged portion of the home was $16,000. What is the actual cash value of the loss? $________________
5. How much will the insured be paid? $_______________
6. The insured also had a loss to personal property inside the home. On what basis will this loss be reimbursed? ______________________

Exercise answers can be found at the end of the Unit 7 answers and rationales.

7.5. DWELLING FORMS COMPARISON

This concludes our discussion of the dwelling forms. Before you go on to the next section, study the following comparison charts.

Basic Policy Coverages

Coverage	DP-1	DP-2	DP-3
Coverage A—Dwelling	X	X	X
Coverage B—Other Structures	X	X	X
Coverage C—Personal Property	X	X	X
Coverage D—Fair Rental Value	X	X	X
Coverage E—Additional Living Expense	By endorsement	X	X

Other Coverages

Other Coverage	DP-1	DP-2	DP-3
Other Structures*	X	X	X
Debris Removal	X	X	X
Improvements, Alterations, Additions	X	X	X
Worldwide Coverage	X	X	X
Rental Value*	X	X	X
Fire Department Service Charge	X	X	X
Reasonable Repairs	X	X	X
Property Removed	X	X	X
Trees, Shrubs And Other Plants		X	X
Collapse		X	X
Glass Or Safety Glazing Material		X	X
Ordinance or Law		X	X

*Listed as both a basic policy coverage and an Other Coverage

Perils Insured Against

Peril	DP-1	DP-2	DP-3	
			Dwelling	Personal Property
Fire	X	X	Open peril***	X
Lightning	X	X		X
Internal Explosion	X	N/A		N/A
Riot	X*	X		X
Explosion	X*	X		X
Vehicles	X*	X		X
Civil Commotion	X*	X		X
Smoke	X*	X		X
Hail	X*	X		X
Aircraft	X*	X		X
Windstorm	X*	X		X
Volcanic Eruption	X*	X		X
V&MM	X**	X		X
Burglars		X		X
Weight Of Ice, Snow, Sleet		X		X
Discharge Of Water Or Steam		X		X
Falling Objects		X		X
Freezing		X		X
Sudden Tearing, Cracking, Burning		X		X
Electrical Current		X		X
Fireplace Smoke		X		X

*Extended Coverage perils available for separate premium
** Available for separate premium
***Risks of loss not otherwise excluded are covered

Replacement Cost Coverages

	DP-1	DP-2	DP-3
Dwelling, Other Structures		X	X
Personal Property			

7.6. DWELLING POLICY ENDORSEMENTS

7.6.1. Broad Theft Coverage

The **broad theft coverage endorsement** adds coverage for theft of personal property to the dwelling policy. It may be written for an owner-occupied dwelling or an apartment occupied by a tenant who is the named insured.

The endorsement covers theft, attempted theft and vandalism, and malicious mischief as a result of theft or attempted theft. V&MM is not covered if the dwelling is vacant for more than 60 consecutive days immediately before the loss.

Property may be covered while on or off the premises. Separate limits of liability apply for on- and off-premises coverage, and off-premises coverage is available only if on-premises coverage is written.

The following property is not covered:

- Animals, birds, and fish
- Credit cards and fund transfer cards
- Property while it is in the mail
- Aircraft and parts, other than model or hobby aircraft
- Property held as a sample or for sale or delivery after sale
- Property separately described and specifically insured by other insurance
- Property of tenants, roomers, and boarders that are not related to an insured
- Business property of an insured or residence employee
- Property that is in the custody of a laundry, tailor, or cleaner (except for loss by burglary or robbery)
- Motor vehicles and their equipment (does not apply to vehicles used to service the location or to assist those with disabilities)

Special limits of liability apply to the following classes of property:

- $200 for money or related property, coins, and precious metals
- $1,500 for securities, manuscripts, and other valuable paper property
- $1,500 for watercraft, including trailers and equipment
- $1,500 for trailers not used with watercraft
- $1,500 for jewelry, watches, furs, and precious and semiprecious stones
- $2,500 for firearms
- $2,500 for silverware, goldware, or pewterware

The insured is required to notify the police when a theft loss occurs.

7.6.2. Personal Liability and Medical Payments to Others

7.6.2.1. Coverages

The insured may purchase **personal liability and medical payments to others** coverage as an endorsement to the dwelling policy or as a separate policy. These coverages are very similar to those provided in the liability section of the homeowners policy, which will be examined later in the course.

Coverage L—personal liability provides coverage for damages that the insured becomes legally obligated to pay because of an occurrence to which the coverage applies that causes bodily injury or property damage. The insurer will also defend the insured against such claims at its own expense, even if the suit is groundless or fraudulent. The policy limit is $100,000.

Under **Coverage M—medical payments to others**, the insurer will pay all necessary medical expenses incurred within three years of an accident that causes bodily injury. This coverage applies to injuries sustained while the injured party is:

- on the insured location with the insured's permission; or
- off the insured location if the injury arises out of a condition
  - on the insured location,
  - caused by the activities of the insured, or
  - caused by an animal in the insured's care.

There is a limit of $1,000 per person under this coverage. The insured does not have to be legally liable for coverage to apply. Coverage does not apply to any injury sustained by the insured or the insured's family members.

Exercise 7.D

The insured has a dwelling policy with the personal liability and medical payments to others endorsement attached. During a party at the insured's home, there is a small explosion. Several guests and the insured are injured. The explosion is later found to have been caused by carelessly stored household chemicals.

1. Coverage M of the personal liability and medical payments to others endorsement would pay for
   A. the guests' medical expenses
   B. the insured's medical expenses
   C. both 1 and 2
2. Suppose one of the guests ultimately had medical bills of $6,000. If the insured was legally liable for the explosion, would any section of the endorsed policy pay the full amount of these bills?
   A. Yes—Coverage M
   B. Yes—Coverage L
   C. No

Exercise answers can be found at the end of the Unit 7 answers and rationales.

7.6.2.2. Additional Coverages

Personal liability and medical payments to others coverage also includes three additional coverages: claim expenses, first aid to others, and damage to property of others. Losses under these coverages are paid in addition to the limit of liability.

Covered claim expenses include:

- defense costs;
- court costs charged against an insured in any suit the insurer defends;
- premiums on bonds that do not exceed the Coverage L limit and that are required in a suit defended by the insurer;
- reasonable expenses incurred by the insured at the insurer's request while assisting in the claim investigation or defense, including up to $50 per day for lost earnings; and
- postjudgment interest.

Expenses for first aid to others are covered when they are incurred by the insured for bodily injury to others that is covered by the policy.

If the insured causes damage to the property of others, the policy will provide replacement cost coverage of up to $500 per occurrence.

7.6.2.3. Exclusions

Bodily injury or property damage arising out of the following are excluded under both Coverage L and Coverage M:

- War
- Losses that are expected or intended by the insured
- Business pursuits or the rendering of or failure to render professional services
- Transmission of a communicable disease by an insured
- Sexual molestation, corporal punishment, or physical or mental abuse
- Use, sale, or possession of controlled substances other than the legitimate use of prescription drugs
- Rental of a premises that would not be eligible for coverage under the policy
- A premises owned by or rented to the insured or rented by the insured to others that is not considered an insured location
- Ownership, maintenance, use, loading, or unloading of most types of watercraft, aircraft, or vehicles

Suppose a visitor at the insured's home steals a bottle of painkillers that were prescribed for the insured while she recovered from surgery. The visitor dies after she accidentally overdoses on the pills. The visitor's family members sue the insured for damages. This loss would be covered under the insured's personal liability and medical payments coverage because the exclusion for bodily injury arising out of the possession of controlled substances does not apply to the legitimate use of prescription drugs.

Additional exclusions that apply only to Coverage L include liability:

- for damage to property owned by an insured;
- for damage to property rented to, occupied or used by, or in the care of an insured (unless the loss is caused by fire, smoke, or explosion);
- for losses that would be covered under a workers' compensation or similar law;
- for loss assessments charged against the insured as a member of an association, corporation, or community of property owners;
- assumed under most contracts or agreements; and
- for injury to the insured or any relative or minor who resides in the same household.

Coverage M does not apply to bodily injury:

- to a residence employee that occurs off the insured location and does not arise out of or in the course of work the employee performs for the insured;
- due to any nuclear hazard; or
- to any person other than a residence employee who regularly resides on any part of the insured location.

7.6.3. Other Endorsements

Other endorsements that may be used with the dwelling policy include:

- **automatic increase in insurance:** provides an annual increase in the Coverage A amount of 4%, 6%, or 8%; and
- **dwelling under construction:** when the intended occupant of a dwelling under construction is the named insured, this endorsement is attached to the dwelling policy to provide coverage. The limit of liability that applies at any given time is a percentage of the policy limit based on the value of the partially completed home. The available policy limit increases as construction of the home progresses.

UNIT TEST

1. Compared to the homeowners policy, the dwelling policy provides (broader/more limited) ________________________ property coverage.

2. Which of the following could be covered under a dwelling policy?
   A. Mobile home not permanently located
   B. Home under construction
   C. Townhouse
   D. Home rented to another person
   E. Five-unit apartment building

3. Which of the following coverages are contained in an unendorsed dwelling policy?
   A. Dwelling
   B. Other structures
   C. Liability
   D. Personal property
   E. Fair rental value
   F. Medical payments to others

4. Which of the following items of personal property would be covered under a dwelling policy?
   A. Motorcycle
   B. Poodle
   C. Pool table
   D. Sailboat

5. A DP-1 automatically provides coverage for
   A. fire
   B. lightning
   C. extended coverage perils
   D. internal explosion
   E. vandalism and malicious mischief

6. Under the DP-1, the insured may opt to have property covered against
   A. fire, lightning, and internal explosion
   B. all of the perils described in A plus the extended coverage perils
   C. all of the perils described in A plus the extended coverage perils and vandalism and malicious mischief
   D. any of the above

7. The DP-2 insures against fire, lightning, and which of the following?
   A. The extended coverage perils, V&MM, and additional perils
   B. The extended coverage perils only
   C. V&MM only

8. The DP-3 provides
   A. basic coverage for the dwelling and broad coverage for personal property
   B. broad coverage for the dwelling and basic coverage for personal property
   C. open peril coverage for the dwelling and broad coverage for personal property
   D. open peril coverage for both the dwelling and personal property

9. Which of the following other coverages are included in all dwelling forms?
   A. Collapse
   B. Fire department service charge
   C. Debris removal
   D. Reasonable repairs
   E. Trees, shrubs, and other plants
   F. Property removed
   G. Glass or safety glazing material

10. Under which of the dwelling forms may the insured be reimbursed for the replacement cost when the dwelling is destroyed?
    A. All dwelling forms
    B. DP-1 only
    C. DP-2 and DP-3
    D. DP-3 only

11. The insured has a DP-3 covering a home that has a replacement value of $100,000. The insured carries $60,000 of insurance. Following a loss, it is determined that it would cost $12,000 to replace the damaged portion of the home. How much could the insured collect, assuming the ACV of the loss is $6,000?
    A. $6,000
    B. $9,000
    C. $12,000
    D. Nothing

12. Which dwelling forms pay losses to dwellings and other structures on an actual cash value basis?
    A. DP-1
    B. DP-2
    C. DP-3

13. Which dwelling forms pay losses to personal property on an actual cash value basis?
    A. DP-1
    B. DP-2
    C. DP-3

14. Which of the following would be covered under Coverage A or Coverage B of the dwelling policy?
    A. A storage shed 100 feet in back of the insured's dwelling where she keeps various yard tools
    B. A detached garage that has been altered to house a manufacturing operation
    C. A stack of lumber placed at the edge of the insured's property that will be used to construct a boat shed
    D. A water softener and water heater located in the insured's attached garage

15. Which of the following losses would be excluded under the DP-1?
    A. While the insured is on vacation, a power failure that occurs away from the insured's home causes the electricity to go off in the insured's neighborhood for 10 hours. As a result, large amounts of food stored in a freezer are ruined.
    B. When Languid Lake overflows, the first story of the insured's home is flooded, causing extensive damage.
    C. Following a fire, the insured suffers an additional loss because a city ordinance requires that he replace his frame dwelling with more expensive fire-resistant materials.
    D. An earthquake causes a fire that destroys the insured's home.

16. The Johnsons' home is covered by the DP-3. When a fire damages the home, they are forced to stay at a motel for a month while repairs are made. What coverage would reimburse them for these expenses? ______________________________

    ____

    ____

17. Damage to covered property caused by glass breakage is
    A. covered in all dwelling forms
    B. excluded in all dwelling forms
    C. covered in the DP-2 and DP-3 but not the DP-1

18. Myrtle has a dwelling policy with broad theft coverage for on and off her premises. Which of the following theft losses would be covered?
    A. A $400 handgun taken from a bureau in her home
    B. A $9,000 fur coat taken from the cleaners where she had stored it for the summer
    C. Two credit cards taken from her desk in her home
    D. A CD player removed from the dashboard of her car that was parked in her garage

19. Giselle's home is covered by the DP-3 with the personal liability and medical payments to others endorsement. When a visitor at Giselle's home is injured, Giselle calls an ambulance to provide immediate first aid and transport the visitor to the emergency room. In addition to $800 in medical expenses, the ambulance service bills Giselle $250. The insured's medical payments to others limit is $1,000. How much would the insurer pay for this loss? $________

20. The insured rents tables and chairs for a neighborhood picnic she is hosting in her backyard. While setting up one of the tables, the insured accidentally breaks off one of its legs. If the insured were found liable for this damage, would Coverage L of the personal liability and medical payments to others coverage pay for the loss?
( ) Yes ( ) No
Why or why not?________________________________
____

21. A home under construction is insured by the dwelling policy with the dwelling under construction endorsement attached. The policy limit is $100,000. Is this amount of coverage available during the entire policy period?
( ) Yes ( ) No
Explain your answer.
____
____

ANSWERS AND RATIONALES TO UNIT TEST

1. More limited. The dwelling policy provides more limited property coverage than the homeowners policy. The unendorsed dwelling policy provides property coverage only, while the homeowners policy provides both property and liability coverage.

2. **B, C and D.** To be eligible, a mobile home must be permanently located. An apartment building may not contain more than four units.

3. **A, B, D, and E.** A dwelling policy automatically includes coverage for the dwelling, other structures, personal property, and fair rental value. Liability and medical payments coverage may be added by endorsement.

4. **C.** Animals, motor vehicles, and most types of boats are excluded under Coverage C.

5. **A, B, and D.** The only perils that are automatically covered under the DP-1 are fire, lightning, and internal explosion.

6. **D.** Under the DP-1, coverage for the extended coverage perils and vandalism and malicious mischief is optional. Coverage for fire, lightning, and internal explosion is automatically provided.

7. **A.** The DP-2 automatically covers all of the standard and optional perils available on the basic form: fire, lightning, the extended coverage perils, and vandalism and malicious mischief.

8. **C.** The DP-3 is also called the special form. It provides named peril coverage for personal property and open peril coverage for the dwelling and other structures.

9. **B, C, D, and F.** The other coverages listed in the other answer choices are included in the DP-2 and DP-3 but not the DP-1.

10. **C.** The DP-2 and DP-3 pay losses to the dwelling and other structures on a replacement cost basis. Under the DP-1, losses are paid on an actual cash value basis.

11. **B.** To qualify for replacement cost coverage, the insured must carry insurance equal to 80% of the replacement cost of the building. Since the insured does not carry enough insurance, the loss will be paid at proportional replacement cost or actual cash value, whichever is larger. In this case, proportional replacement cost ($9,000) is larger than ACV ($6,000).

12. **A.** The DP-1 pays losses to dwellings and other structures on an actual cash value basis. The DP-2 and DP-3 pay losses to dwellings and other structures on a replacement cost basis.

13. **A, B, and C.** All of the dwelling forms pay losses to personal property on an actual cash value basis.

14. **A, C, and D.** A detached garage that is used for commercial, manufacturing, or farming purposes may not be covered under a dwelling policy.

15. **A, B, and C.** Loss by fire that results from an earthquake is covered.

16. **Coverage E—additional living expense.** The DP-2 and DP-3 include Coverage E—additional living expense. It pays for additional living expenses the insured incurs after a covered loss, including reasonable motel, dining, laundry, and transportation expenses. These are covered for the time needed to repair or replace the damaged property or become settled elsewhere in permanent quarters.

17. **C.** The glass or safety glazing material other coverage pays for breakage of glass or safety glazing material and damage to covered property caused by glass breakage. It is included in the DP-2 and DP-3 but not the DP-1.

18. **A.** Credit cards, motor vehicles and their equipment, and property in the custody of a cleaner are all excluded under the broad theft coverage endorsement.

19. **$1,050.** First aid expenses are paid in addition to the limit of liability.

20. **No.** Liability for damage to property rented to the insured is not covered.

21. **No.** The limit of liability that applies at any given time is a percentage of the policy limit based on the value of the partially completed home.

UNIT 7 EXERCISE ANSWERS

Exercise 7.A

1. Fire department service charge
2. Reasonable repairs
3. Debris removal
4. Property removal

Exercise 7.B

1. B, C, and D

Exercise 7.C

1. $80,000
2. No
3. $15,000 ($40,000/$80,000 × $30,000)
4. $14,000 ($30,000 – $16,000)
5. $15,000
6. Actual cash value

Exercise 7.D

1. **A**
2. **B**

UNIT

8

Homeowners Insurance

8.1. LEARNING OBJECTIVES

After completing Unit 8—Homeowners Insurance, you will be able to do the following:

- Describe the types of buildings eligible for a homeowners policy and who is insured under the policy
- Compare and contrast the extent and scope of property coverage provided by the HO-2, HO-3, HO-4, HO-5, HO-6, and HO-8
- Describe what is covered under the four Section I coverages included in all homeowners forms
- Identify personal property that is excluded under the homeowners policy
- Describe the classes of personal property that have special limits of liability under the homeowners form and the amount of coverage provided for that property
- Identify the Section I additional coverages provided by all homeowners forms
- Describe the Section I additional coverages found only in selected coverage forms
- Compare and contrast the perils covered under basic, broad, and special coverage
- Identify situations and perils excluded under Section I of the homeowners policy
- Determine whether a property loss would be paid on an actual cash value or replacement cost basis
- For each homeowners form, use the amount of primary insurance to determine the policy limits for the Section I coverages
- Describe the types of losses covered under the Section II coverages
- Identify situations and perils that are excluded under both Section II coverages
- Describe exclusions that apply only to personal liability coverage or only to medical payments to others coverage
- Identify the additional coverages provided under Section II
- Explain how other insurance affects loss payments under Coverage E
- Describe the circumstances under which the insurer may cancel or nonrenew the policy and the number of days' notice that must be provided to the insured
- Explain the purpose of the following endorsements: personal property replacement cost, permitted incidental occupancies, earthquake, home

day care coverage, watercraft, business pursuits, limited fungi, wet or dry rot or bacteria coverage, and personal injury

8.2. THE HOMEOWNERS POLICY

8.2.1. Introduction

Just as companies that issue both property and casualty insurance policies are called multiline companies, policies that contain both property and casualty coverages in a single contract are called **multiline policies** or **package policies**. The **homeowners policy** is a multiline policy because it provides property and liability insurance in a single policy.

By obtaining property and liability coverage in one policy, the insured is more likely to avoid gaps in coverage and the overlapping of coverages that often happen when several monoline policies are purchased instead of a package policy. It also is advantageous to the insurance company because it means fewer contracts and records, simplified billing systems, and fewer duplicate services. These savings mean the price will be lower than the cost of separate policies offering equivalent coverage.

In this course, we'll focus on the homeowners 2000 policy issued by ISO.

8.2.2. Eligibility, Insureds

Not every person or every house is eligible for coverage under a homeowners policy. The rules are stricter than those that apply to the dwelling policy.

- The named insured must be the owner-occupant of the dwelling or condominium or a renter who maintains a residential occupancy.
- The home cannot contain more than four families; one additional family or two roomers or boarders are allowed per family.
- The insured cannot purchase coverage for personal property only unless the insured is a renter.
- The dwelling must be used exclusively as a residence, except for certain *incidental occupancies* such as offices, professional or private schools, or studios.
- Farms may not be covered under a homeowners policy; mobile homes are eligible if the mobile home endorsement is attached.
- Dwellings under construction and secondary or seasonal residences are eligible.
- Homes being purchased on an installment contract or occupied under a trustee or life estate arrangement are eligible.

Insureds under the homeowners policy include the named insured and residents of the same household, provided they are relatives or are under age 21 and in the care of the insured or a resident relative.

8.2.3. Extent and Scope of Homeowners Coverage

The homeowners policy is divided into two sections: Section I provides property insurance, and Section II provides liability and medical payments insurance.

Just as there are several dwelling forms that provide increasing levels of coverage, there are different homeowners forms that vary in extent of coverage: HO-2, HO-3, HO-4, HO-5, HO-6, and HO-8. Each of these forms provides identical liability coverage. The property coverage varies with the homeowners form selected.

The HO-2 (HO 00 02), or broad form, provides broad coverage for the dwelling and personal property. The covered perils are similar to those covered by the DP-1 with the extended coverage perils and V&MM coverage. Breakage of glass and theft are also covered. In addition, it broadens certain perils and adds others.

The HO-3 (HO 00 03), or special form, provides open peril coverage for loss to the dwelling and other structures. It provides broad coverage for personal property, which is identical to the HO-2's coverage of personal property.

The HO-4 (HO 00 04), or contents broad form, insures tenants—people who do not own the building where they reside. It provides broad coverage for personal property only that is similar to the HO-2's and HO-3's broad coverage of personal property, and no coverage for the dwelling.

The HO-5 (HO 00 05), or comprehensive form, provides open peril coverage for both the dwelling and other structures and personal property.

The HO-6 (HO 00 06), or unit-owners form, provides broad coverage on the personal property of condominium owners, similar to that provided under the HO-2, HO-3, and HO-4. It provides very limited dwelling coverage.

The HO-8 (HO 00 08), or modified coverage form, is designed for older homes with replacement values that may far exceed their market values. It provides basic coverage on the dwelling and personal property similar to the DP-1 with the extended coverage perils and V&MM coverage, but it also includes certain restrictions on valuation of losses. In many areas, the HO-8 is no longer available.

Another Homeowners form, the HO-1 basic form, was discontinued when the Homeowners 2000 policy was released. The HO-1 had the fewest covered perils and the most coverage restrictions.

Exercise 8.A

Fill in each blank with the word **basic, broad, open peril,** or **no.**

1. The HO-2 provides ____________________ coverage on the dwelling and __________________________ coverage on personal property.
2. The HO-3 provides ____________________ coverage on the dwelling and _______________________ coverage on personal property.
3. The HO-4 provides ____________________ coverage on the dwelling and ________________________ coverage on personal property.
4. The HO-6 provides ________________________ coverage on personal property.
5. The HO-8 provides ____________________ coverage on the dwelling and _______________________ coverage on personal property.

Exercise answers can be found at the end of the Unit 8 answers and rationales.

8.3. SECTION I—PROPERTY

8.3.1. Coverage A—Dwelling and Coverage B—Other Structures

Four separate property coverages are provided by the homeowners policy under Section I:

- Coverage A—dwelling
- Coverage B—other structures
- Coverage C—personal property
- Coverage D—loss of use

Coverage A—dwelling covers the dwelling and structures attached to the dwelling as well as materials and supplies for repair and construction of those structures if they are located on or next to the residence premises (the dwelling listed in the declarations).

Coverage B—other structures covers buildings on the described premises that are separated from the dwelling by clear space.

Neither the dwelling nor other structures may be used for business purposes, except for the incidental occupancies mentioned earlier. An other structure rented to someone other than tenants of the dwelling is also excluded unless the other structure is rented as a private garage.

Neither Coverage A nor Coverage B is included in the HO-4 because renters and tenants can insure only their personal property. The HO-6, or unit-owners form, includes limited Coverage A for:

- alterations, appliances, fixtures, and improvements that are part of the building containing the residence premises;
- items of real property pertaining solely to the residence premises;
- property that is the insured's responsibility under a condo association agreement; and
- structures other than the residence premises owned solely by the insured at the location of the residence premises.

The standard Coverage A limit for the HO-6 is $1,000.

8.3.2. Coverage C—Personal Property

Coverage C—personal property provides coverage for personal property owned or used by an insured while it is anywhere in the world. At the insured's request, coverage will also apply to property owned by others while in the part of the residence premises occupied by the insured or to the property of a guest or residence employee while in any residence occupied by the insured.

Coverage C—Personal Property

Property normally kept at a residence other than the residence premises shown in the declarations is covered for up to 10% of the Coverage C limit or $1,000, whichever is greater. However, this restriction does not apply to property being moved from the residence premises to a new principal residence. In this situation, full coverage applies for 30 days from the start of the move. Another exception applies when personal property is moved from the residence premises because the residence is being repaired or is unfit to live in. In this case, the personal property has full coverage while it is at the temporary residence.

Certain classes of property are specifically excluded from coverage:

- Animals, birds, or fish
- Motorized vehicles or aircraft, including equipment and accessories
- Property of boarders
- Property in an apartment held for rental by the insured
- Paper or electronic records containing business data, except for prerecorded programs available on the retail market
- Property rented to others off the residence premises
- Credit cards
- Hovercraft and parts (hovercraft are self-propelled motorized ground effect vehicles such as air cushion vehicles and flarecraft)
- Water or steam (under earlier versions of the homeowners policy, it could be argued that water became the insured's personal property after it passed through the insured's water meter; this exclusion makes the intent of the policy clear)

8.3.2.1. Special Limits of Liability

Certain classes of personal property have special limits of liability that are lower than the overall policy limits that apply to personal property. These coverage restrictions are designed to encourage insureds with personal property of especially high value or of a hard-to-value nature to insure this property on a specific basis. You'll learn about the forms used to insure this property later in the course.

Personal Property with Special Limits of Liability

Coverage Limit	Property
$200	Money or related property, coins and precious metals (does not apply to tableware)
$1,500	Securities, manuscripts and other valuable paper property (includes the cost to research, replace or restore the information from the lost or damaged property)
$1,500	Watercraft, including trailers and equipment
$1,500	Trailers not used with watercraft
$2,500	Property on the residence premises used for business purposes
$500	Property away from the residence premises used for business purposes
$1,500	Electronic apparatus while it is in, on or away from a motor vehicle (such as a car phone or portable CD player) provided the apparatus can be operated by both the vehicle's power and other power sources
$1,500	Electronic apparatus and accessories used primarily for business while away from the residence premises and not in or on a motor vehicle

For the following classes of personal property, the special limits apply only to theft losses:

Personal Property with Special Limits for Theft Losses Only

Coverage Limit	Property
$1,500	Jewelry, watches, furs, and precious and semi-precious stones
$2,500	Silverware, goldware or pewterware
$2,500	Firearms

Exercise 8.B

1. Which of the following losses would be completely covered if the loss were for the full value of the property described?
   A. A $900 computer the insured uses for her in-home secretarial service
   B. $250 worth of coins from the insured's coin collection
   C. Theft of a handgun collection valued at $1,900
   D. $2,000 worth of sound equipment the insured uses in her car and her home
   E. Theft of a $5,000 diamond and amethyst bracelet
   F. An $800 silver set
   G. A $3,000 boat

Exercise answers can be found at the end of the Unit 8 answers and rationales.

8.3.3. Coverage D—Loss of Use

Coverage D—loss of use provides two types of coverage. First, if a covered property loss makes the residence premises uninhabitable, the policy will cover additional living expenses related to maintaining the insured's normal standard of living.

Second, if a covered loss to the insured's property makes a part of the residence premises uninhabitable that is rented to others or held for rental by the insured, the policy will cover the loss of fair rental value, less any expenses that are not required while the premises is uninhabitable.

Exercise 8.C

For each of the following examples, write in which coverage applies: Coverage A, Coverage B, Coverage C, Coverage D, or none. Assume that all personal property belongs to the insured.

1. Lumber lying next to the house that will be used to construct a sun porch ______
2. Factory-installed car stereo ______
3. Detached garage ______
4. Tools stored in the garage ______
5. Rent lost from half of the insured's duplex when a fire leaves it uninhabitable ______
6. Puppy ______
7. Suitcase that is damaged in a storm while the insured is in London on business ______
8. Home where a silversmithing business is conducted in the basement ______
9. College thesis ______
10. Motel bill incurred when a covered loss to the home forces the insured to move out of the house for two weeks ______
11. Rowboat ______
12. Motorcycle ______
13. Wristwatch that is damaged in an explosion at the factory where it has been sent for repair ______

Exercise answers can be found at the end of the Unit 8 answers and rationales.

8.3.4. Additional Coverages

8.3.4.1. In All Homeowners Forms

In addition to the four coverages just discussed, the homeowners form contains certain additional coverages. The following additional coverages are included in all homeowners forms. Except where specifically noted, coverage is included in the policy limit.

- **Debris Removal:** Pays expenses to remove debris from covered property if a covered peril caused the loss and ash or other particles from a volcanic eruption caused direct loss to covered property. Under specified conditions, it also covers removal of fallen trees from the residence premises. For coverage to apply, the tree must have damaged a covered structure, be blocking access to a driveway, or be blocking access to a ramp designed for a handicapped person. Removal expense is permitted for the insured's trees only if the trees are felled by windstorm or hail or the weight of ice, snow, or sleet. Removal expense is permitted for a neighbor's trees only if the trees were felled by a peril insured against under Coverage C.

Except for fallen trees, debris removal is included in the policy limit; however, up to an additional 5% of that limit may be applicable. No matter how many trees fall, a maximum of $1,000 is available for tree debris removal for one occurrence, with a maximum of $500 per tree.

- **Reasonable Repairs:** Pays the reasonable costs incurred by the insured for repairs necessary to protect covered property from further loss after being damaged by a covered peril.
- **Trees, Shrubs, and Other Plants:** Covers trees, shrubs, and plants on the residence premises for loss by fire, lightning, explosion, riot, aircraft, vehicles not owned or operated by a resident, theft, and vandalism or malicious mischief. Coverage is limited to 5% of the Coverage A limit or a maximum of $500 for any one tree, shrub, or plant. (In the HO-4 and HO-6, the limit is 10% of the Coverage C limit or a maximum of $500 for any one tree, shrub, or plant.)
- **Fire Department Service Charge:** Pays up to $500 when the fire department is called to save or protect covered property from a covered peril. No deductible applies to this coverage. This coverage is not available for property located within the limits of the city furnishing the fire department service.
- **Property Removed:** Covers property against direct loss from any peril while being removed from a premises endangered by a covered peril and for up to 30 days while removed.
- **Credit Card, Electronic Fund Transfer Card or Access Device, Forgery, and Counterfeit Money:** Pays up to $500 for the insured's legal obligation to pay losses resulting from:

  — theft or unauthorized use of these cards;

  — forgery or alteration of the insured's checks; or

  — the insured's acceptance in good faith of counterfeit money.

  Coverage does not apply to loss arising out of business use or the dishonesty of an insured. No deductible applies to this coverage.
- **Loss Assessment:** Pays up to $1,000 for the insured's share of a loss assessment charged against the insured during the policy period, by either a corporation or association of property owners, as a result of direct loss to the property owned by all members collectively and caused by a covered peril. For instance, this coverage might pay a condominium owner's assessment for repair of a community clubhouse that was damaged by lightning. The deductible applies only once, regardless of the number of assessments in a single occurrence.
- **Glass or Safety Glazing Material:** Covers the breakage of glass that is a part of a building, including windows and storm doors.

8.3.4.2. In Selected Homeowners Forms

Other additional coverages are only contained in certain homeowners forms. The following table describes these additional coverages and the forms in which they are included. Except where specifically noted, coverage is included in the policy limit.

Additional Coverages Found In Selected Homeowners Forms

Additional Coverage	Forms	Description of Coverage
Collapse	■ HO-2 ■ HO-3 ■ HO-4 ■ HO-5 ■ HO-6	Pays for direct physical loss to covered property involving collapse of a building caused by a covered peril or one of the additional perils listed for this Additional Coverage.
Landlord's Furnishings	■ HO-2 ■ HO-3 ■ HO-5	Provides coverage of up to $2,500 for loss to appliances, carpeting, and other household furnishings in each apartment on the residence premises regularly rented or held for rental to others by an insured, caused by the perils specifically listed under this coverage in the policy.
Building Additions and Alterations	■ HO-4	Covers fixtures, installations and improvements made or acquired at the insured's expense. Coverage is limited to 10% of the Coverage C amount.
Grave Markers	■ HO-2 ■ HO-3 ■ HO-4 ■ HO-5 ■ HO-6	Provides up to $5,000 for damage to grave markers and mausoleums caused by a peril covered under Coverage C
Ordinance or Law Coverage	■ HO-2 ■ HO-3 ■ HO-4 ■ HO-5 ■ HO-6	Pays up to 10% of the Coverage A limit for the increased cost to repair or rebuild a dwelling or other structure to conform with applicable building or land use codes. This coverage is provided as an additional amount of insurance.

8.3.5. Perils Insured Against

8.3.5.1. Basic Named Perils

The number and breadth of the perils insured against by each of the homeowners forms is the major distinction among the forms. At the base are the perils that are provided in all homeowners forms.

These basic perils include:

Fire

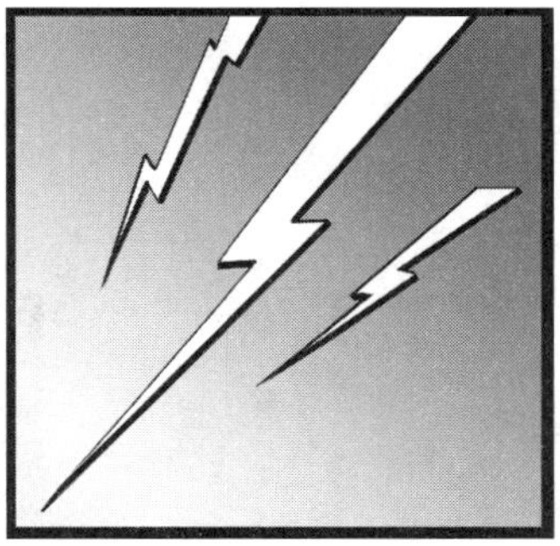

Lightning

Windstorm or Hail

Explosion

Riot or Civil Commotion

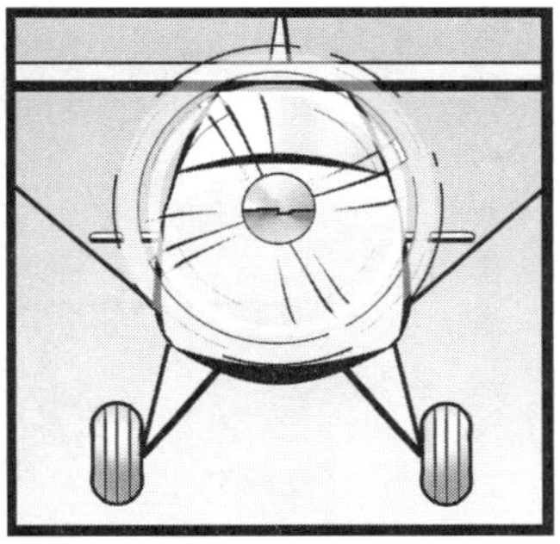

Aircraft

Vehicles

Smoke

Vandalism & Malicious Mischief

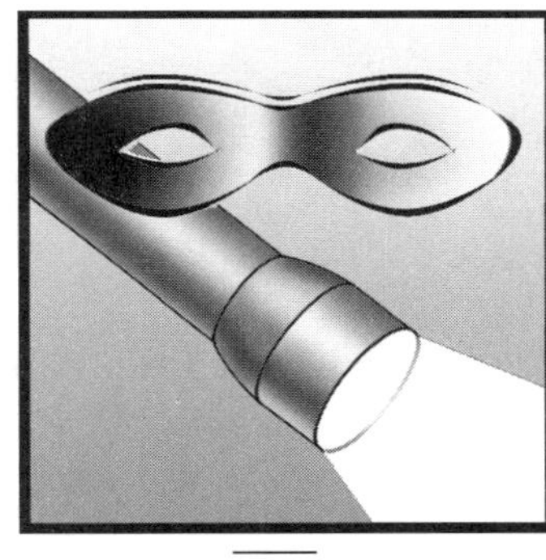

Theft

Volcanic Eruption

Interior damage from windstorm or hail is only covered if the wind or hail first makes an opening in the building. Watercraft, outboard motors, and related equipment are covered only while inside fully enclosed buildings.

Vehicle damage caused by a vehicle owned or operated by any resident of the residence premises is not covered.

Smoke from fireplaces, agricultural smudging, or industrial operations is not covered. The smoke peril also covers **puffback**—the release of soot, smoke, vapor, or fumes from a furnace, boiler, or similar equipment.

Vandalism or malicious mischief losses to property on the residence premises are not covered if the dwelling has been vacant for 60 or more consecutive days.

The theft peril includes loss of property from a known place when it is likely that the property has been stolen. It also includes attempted theft. It does not include:

Theft by the insured

Theft from a dwelling under construction

Theft from a portion of the premises that the insured rents out

Theft of watercraft or equipment, trailers or campers while off the premises

Mysterious disappearance (vanishing of property with no explanation)

The HO-8 only insures against the basic perils.

8.3.5.2. Broad Named Perils

The HO-2 adds some additional perils and expands the definitions of several others. The additional broad named perils are:

- falling objects;
- weight of ice, snow, or sleet;
- accidental discharge or overflow of water or steam from within appliances or plumbing or related systems (does not include discharge or overflow of water from a sump);

- sudden and accidental rupture of a heating, air conditioning, fire protective sprinkler, or hot water heating system;
- freezing of plumbing or related systems; and
- sudden and accidental damage from artificially generated electrical current.

In addition, the HO-2 expands coverage for two perils.

- The **vehicles** peril includes loss to a fence, driveway, or walk caused by a vehicle owned or operated by a person who lives in the insured household.
- The **smoke** peril includes loss caused by fireplace smoke.

The weight of ice, snow, or sleet peril does not cover damage to awnings, fences, patios, pavement, swimming pools, foundations, retaining walls, bulkheads, piers, wharves, or docks.

Damage to a building's interior or contents by a falling object is covered only if the falling object first damages the roof or an exterior wall.

Damage to a tube, transistor, or similar electrical component by artificially generated electrical current is not covered.

The freezing of plumbing or related systems peril does not cover losses that occur while the residence is unoccupied unless the insured has made an effort to maintain heat in the house or has shut off the water supply and drained the system and appliances of water.

Exercise 8.D

1. The insured's roof is damaged when it is struck by lightning. Which homeowners form(s) would cover this loss?

   A. HO-2
   B. HO-2 and HO-8

2. A hot water heater malfunctions and explodes, damaging the walls and floor in the insured's garage. Which homeowners form(s) would cover this loss?

   A. HO-2
   B. HO-2 and HO-8

3. The insured's fireplace spews smoke into his living room, damaging the curtains and furniture. Which homeowners form(s) would cover this loss?

   A. HO-2
   B. HO-2 and HO-8

Exercise answers can be found at the end of the Unit 8 answers and rationales.

The HO-4 insures personal property against the same perils covered under the HO-2. (Remember, there is no Coverage A or Coverage B in the HO-4.)

The HO-6 insures personal property against these same perils, with one exception. In the HO-6, the accidental discharge or overflow of water or steam peril includes coverage for the costs to tear out and replace any part of the building necessary to repair the system or appliance from which the water or steam escaped. (Earlier, we discussed the limited Coverage A available under the HO-6.)

8.3.5.3. Special Form Coverage

The HO-3, or special form, provides open peril coverage for the dwelling and other structures, insuring against all risks of direct physical loss that are not specifically excluded in the policy. Personal property is covered on a named peril basis for the same perils insured under the HO-2.

Under Coverages A and B, the HO-3 excludes:

- any loss involving collapse, other than as provided in the other coverages section;
- freezing of a plumbing, heating, air conditioning, or automatic fire protective sprinkler system or a household appliance, or overflow due to freezing while the dwelling is vacant, unoccupied, or under construction, unless reasonable care was taken to maintain heat in the building or to shut off the water supply and drain the systems and appliances;
- freezing, thawing, pressure, or weight of water or ice to fences, pavement, patios, swimming pools, foundations, retaining walls, bulkheads, piers, wharves, or docks;
- theft in or to a dwelling or structure under construction, including theft of materials and supplies used in construction;
- vandalism and malicious mischief when the dwelling was vacant for more than 60 consecutive days at the time of loss (does not apply to dwellings under construction);
- gradual and expected losses, such as wear and tear, deterioration, inherent vice, latent defect, mechanical breakdown, smog, rust, corrosion, mold, wet or dry rot, and smoke from agricultural smudging or industrial operations;
- discharge, dispersal, seepage, migration, release, or escape of pollutants such as smoke, vapor, soot, fumes, acids, alkalis, chemicals, and waste (does not apply when caused by a peril covered under Coverage C);
- settling, shrinking, bulging, or expansion, including resulting cracking of pavement, foundations, walls, floors, roofs, or ceilings; and
- loss caused by birds, vermin, insects, and animals owned by the insured.

If a loss that is not otherwise excluded involves water damage from a plumbing, heating, air conditioning, or fire protective sprinkler system or household appliance, the policy covers the loss caused by water and the cost of tearing out and replacing any part of a building necessary to repair the system or appliance. Loss to the system or appliance itself is not covered.

8.3.5.4. Comprehensive Coverage

Comprehensive coverage insures the dwelling, other structures, and personal property against loss by the package of special perils. In effect, form HO-5 provides coverage for personal property on the same basis as Coverages A and B on form HO-3, with only minor variations.

On HO-5, the coverage for theft of personal property is slightly broader than it is on HO-3. Although the special sublimits of coverage for theft of jewelry, watches, furs, precious stones, silverware, goldware, pewterware, and firearms remain the same, the comprehensive form says that these limits apply to "loss by theft, misplacing, or losing." HO-5 is the only homeowners policy insuring these personal property items against loss by "mysterious disappearance."

Certain fragile personal items, such as eyeglasses, glassware, statues, bric-a-brac, and porcelain items, are too delicate to be considered for all-risk coverage. HO-5 limits the coverage for these items to losses caused by the specific perils of fire, lightning, EC, V&MM, theft, collapse of a building, water risks that are not excluded, and sudden or accidental tearing, cracking, burning, or bulging of a steam or hot water heating system, air conditioning, or fire sprinkler system, or an appliance for heating water.

If any excluded loss is followed by a loss that is not excluded, the comprehensive form does cover the additional loss.

8.3.6. Exclusions

All homeowners forms contain exclusions that apply to the property coverages we've just discussed. They exclude losses due to:

- enforcement of law or ordinance regulating construction, repair, or demolition;
- earth movement, including earthquake and mine subsidence;
- water damage, including flooding and overflow from a sump pump;
- power interruption that takes place off the residence premises;
- the insured's failure to save and preserve property after a loss, or to protect it from loss;
- war;
- nuclear hazard;
- losses caused intentionally by the insured or by someone else at the insured's direction; and
- destruction, confiscation, or seizure of property by the government or a public authority.

8.3.7. Conditions

The homeowners policy contains many of the conditions we've already discussed regarding the insurer's and the insured's responsibilities under the policy, including duties after loss, mortgage condition, pair or set, appraisal, and other insurance.

The loss settlement condition is similar to the one found in the dwelling broad and special forms examined in an earlier unit. Losses to the following are paid at actual cash value, but not more than the cost to repair or replace them:

- Personal property
- Awnings, carpeting, appliances, outdoor antennas, and outdoor equipment
- Structures that are not buildings

Losses to the dwelling and other structures are paid at replacement cost as long as the insured carries an amount of insurance equal to or greater than 80% of the building's replacement cost. If the insured carries less than 80% of replacement cost, the insured will be paid the actual cash value of the loss or a proportion of the replacement cost, whichever is greater. (Of course, the insured can never receive more than the policy limit.) The formula used to determine proportional replacement cost is:

$$\frac{\text{Insurance carried}}{\text{Insurance required}} \times \text{amount of loss} = \text{amount of reimbursement.}$$

In addition, replacement cost is only available if the actual repair or replacement is complete, whichever is applicable, unless the amount payable is less than a specified amount. The insured cannot collect a check for what the replacement amount would have been and then not actually replace the items or repair the damaged property. The insurance company may initially pay the insured an amount based on the actual cash value of the damaged personal property that is covered under the loss. Once the insured has actually replaced those covered items (the policy typically has a designated time period that specifies how long the insured has to do this) and produced the necessary receipts, however, the insurance company will then reimburse them for the difference. If the insured chooses not to replace the covered items, the actual cash value of the property is all they will receive. A policy will not pay beyond the policy limits.

8.3.8. Limits of Liability, Deductible

Because the homeowners policy is a package policy, the policy requires a specific minimum limit of liability for each of the major property coverages, which is based on the primary amount of insurance selected by the insured. For all forms except the HO-4 and HO-6, the primary amount of insurance is Coverage A. For the HO-4 and HO-6, the primary amount of insurance is Coverage C. The following tables show how these limits of liability are determined:

Homeowners 3, Homeowners 2, Homeowners 5, and Homeowners 8

Section I Coverage	How Policy limit is Calculated
A	Primary Limit
B	**One Or Two Family Dwelling:** 10% of Coverage A limit **Three Or Four Family Dwelling:** 5% of Coverage A limit
C	**One Or Two Family Dwelling:** 50% of Coverage A limit **Three Family Dwelling:** 30% of Coverage A limit **Four Family Dwelling:** 25% of Coverage A limit
D	**Homeowners 8**: 10% of Coverage A limit **Homeowners, 2, 3 and 5**: 30% Of Coverage A limit

Homeowners 4 and Homeowners 6

Section I Coverage	How Policy Limit is Calculated
A	Not applicable (except for $1,000 Coverage A limit in HO-6)
B	Not applicable
C	Primary limit
D	**Homeowners 6**: 50% of Coverage C **Homeowners 4**: 30% of Coverage C

These limits are provided as separate amounts of insurance. Suppose the insured's single-family home is insured under an HO-3 with a Coverage A limit of $100,000. If the house and its contents were totally destroyed by a covered loss, the insured would receive $100,000 for the house and $50,000 for the contents (subject to any deductibles, special limits, and other policy conditions that might apply).

The homeowners form also provides for a deductible that applies to coverage under Section I. Typical deductibles are $500, $1,000, or $2,500; other deductible amounts may also be available.

Exercise 8.E

1. The insured has an HO-3 that covers his single-family home for $80,000. What limits would apply to each of the Section I coverages?
   A. Coverage A $__________
   B. Coverage B $__________
   C. Coverage C $__________
   D. Coverage D $__________

2. The insured has an HO-6 that covers her personal property for $30,000. What limits would apply to each of the Section I coverages?
   A. Coverage A $____________
   B. Coverage B $___________
   C. Coverage C $__________
   D. Coverage D $__________

Exercise answers can be found at the end of the Unit 8 answers and rationales.

8.4. SECTION II—LIABILITY

Now that we've reviewed the Section I property coverages, we'll turn our attention to Section II, the liability portion of the homeowners policy.

Individuals face many direct and indirect exposures to liability. A homeowner may be held liable for damages arising from his home or yard, as when a visitor slips and falls on a freshly waxed floor or a dead tree falls on and crushes a neighbor's bicycle. An individual can also be held liable for the actions of his children and pets, as when a five-year-old breaks all the windows in a neighbor's garage or the family dog bites the mail carrier. Finally, an individual may be held liable for damages arising out of personal activities away from the home, such as when an individual opens an umbrella in the crowded stands at a football game, accidentally poking it in the eye of another sports fan.

Remember, Section II is the same in all homeowners forms.

8.4.1. Coverage E—Personal Liability

There are two major coverages provided under Section II of the homeowners policy:

- Coverage E—personal liability
- Coverage F—medical payments to others

Coverage E—personal liability covers damages that the insured becomes legally obligated to pay because of bodily injury or property damage caused by an occurrence to which coverage applies. As used in the homeowners policy:

- **bodily injury** means bodily harm, sickness, or disease, including required care, loss of services, and death; and
- **property damage** means physical injury to or destruction of tangible property, including loss of use.

In general, Coverage E applies to liability for bodily injury or property damage arising out of insureds' personal, nonbusiness activities that occur anywhere. Coverage E also applies to liability for bodily injury or property damage arising from **insured locations**. These include:

- the premises described in the declarations;
- residences newly acquired during the policy period;
- locations where an insured is temporarily residing;
- locations an insured is renting for nonbusiness use;
- vacant land owned or rented by the insured;
- the insured's land on which a residence is being built; and
- cemetery plots or burial vaults.

The policy also states that the insurance company will provide a defense for the insured at the insurer's expense, even when the charges are groundless. The insurer's duty to defend ends once the amount it pays for damages reaches the policy limit.

The standard liability limit provided for all BI or PD arising out of any one occurrence is $100,000. This includes any prejudgment interest awarded on any amount of a judgment the insurer is obligated to pay.

8.4.2. Coverage F—Medical Payments to Others

Coverage F—medical payments to others pays all necessary medical expenses incurred within three years of an accident that causes bodily injury. This coverage applies to injuries:

- sustained while the injured party is **on an insured location** with any insured's permission; or
- sustained while the injured party is **off the insured location** if the injury arises out of a condition
  - — on the insured location,
  - — or the ways immediately adjoining the insured location,
  - — caused by the activities of an insured,

- — caused by any residence employee in the course of employment, or
- — caused by an animal owned by or in the care of any insured.

Injury to the named insured or regular residents, other than resident employees, is not covered under Coverage F. For this reason, Coverage F is sometimes called *guest medical.*

Notice that there is no requirement under Coverage F that the insured be legally liable for the injuries. Coverage F covers injuries to others that occur on the insured's premises or result from the insured's activities, whether the insured is liable or not.

Coverage F has a limit of $1,000 per person per accident.

Exercise 8.F

1. Which of the following would be covered under Coverage F—medical payments to others?
   A. The insured's maid hurt her back when she fell down the stairs while cleaning the carpet.
   B. The insured agrees to watch a neighbor's dog. While walking the dog around the block, the dog breaks free and bites a small child.
   C. The insured allows several neighborhood children to use his front yard for a football field. One child is cut after running into a barbed wire fence.
   D. The insured's dog bites the insured's toddler.
   E. While attempting to break into the insured's house, a burglar fell off a ladder and broke his arm.

Exercise answers can be found at the end of the Unit 8 answers and rationales.

8.4.3. Exclusions

There are some important exclusions that apply to Coverages E and F, including:

- liability for injury or damage that is expected or intended by the insured;
- BI or PD arising out of business pursuits or the rendering of or failure to render professional services;
- BI or PD arising out of the rental of any part of the premises, except for the rental of part of an insured location as a residence;
- liability arising out of ownership, maintenance, use, loading, or unloading of aircraft, watercraft, and motor vehicles;
- liability arising out of war and war-like acts, such as insurrection and rebellion;

- liability arising out of the transmission of a communicable disease by an insured;
- liability arising out of sexual molestation, corporal punishment, or physical or mental abuse; and
- liability arising out of the use, sale, manufacture, delivery, transfer, or possession of a controlled substance (does not apply to the legitimate use of prescription drugs).

There are some exceptions to the exclusion for liability arising out of the use of watercraft:

- Watercraft that are not sailing vessels and are powered by inboard or inboard-outdrive motors or engines that
  - — have 50 horsepower or less and are not owned by the insured, or
  - — have more than 50 horsepower and are not owned by or rented to an insured
- Watercraft that are not sailing vessels and are powered by one or more outboard engines or motors with
  - — 25 total horsepower or less,
  - — more than 25 total horsepower if the engines or motors are not owned by the insured, or
  - — more than 25 total horsepower and owned by the insured if the insured acquired the engines or motors during the policy period *or* owned the engines or motors prior to the policy period and either listed them on the declarations or asked the insurer to provide insurance on them within 45 days of their acquisition
- Sailing vessels that are
  - — less than 26 feet long, or
  - — more than 26 feet long but not owned by or rented to an insured
- Watercraft that are in storage

Additional exclusions that apply only to Coverage E include exclusion of liability:

- for any loss assessment charged against the insured as a member of an association, corporation, or community of property owners;
- assumed under a contract or agreement, except contracts that relate directly to the insured location or contracts where the liability of others is assumed prior to an occurrence;
- for property damage to property owned by, used by, or in the care of the insured; and
- for BI or PD for which the insured is covered under a nuclear energy liability policy.

These exclusions apply only to Coverage F:

- BI to a residence employee that occurs off the insured location and does not arise out of or in the course of work the employee performs for the insured
- BI due to nuclear reaction, radiation, or radioactive contamination, including any consequential injuries

8.4.4. Additional Coverages

Section II of the homeowners policy also provides the following additional coverages:

- **Claim Expenses:** Reimburses the insured for:
  - — defense costs,
  - — premiums for bonds required in a suit the insurer defends,
  - — postjudgment interest, and
  - — reasonable expenses incurred by the insured at the company's request, including loss of earnings of up to $250 per day

These expenses are paid in addition to the limit of liability. So if an insured had a $100,000 liability limit and a $100,000 judgment against him, the insurance company would pay the judgment plus claim expenses.

- **First Aid Expenses:** Reimburses the insured for expenses the insured incurs for first aid to others at the time of an accident. These expenses are included in the policy limit.
- **Damage to Property of Others:** Pays up to $1,000 per occurrence for property damaged or destroyed by the insured, *without regard to legal liability*. Covers the insured's "moral obligation" to pay for damage to property that the insured may have borrowed or rented. Property owned by any insured is excluded, but unlike under Coverage E, other property in an insured's care, custody, or control is covered. When a loss is also payable under Section I of the homeowners policy, this additional coverage applies on an excess basis.
- **Loss Assessment:** Pays up to $1,000 of the insured's share of any loss assessment charged against the insured during the policy period by a corporation or association of property owners when the assessment is made as a result of an occurrence to which Section II applies, or as a result of liability for the act of a director, officer, or trustee acting in that capacity for the homeowners.

8.4.5. Conditions

8.4.5.1. Section II

Section II of the homeowners policy contains many of the conditions we've already discussed, including an **other insurance** condition. In the homeowners policy, Coverage E is considered excess insurance over other insurance, except for liability insurance specifically written to be excess over the limits of liability that apply to the homeowners policy.

Exercise 8.G

1. Suppose the insured has a $75,000 liability loss that is covered under his homeowners policy and another liability policy. The homeowners liability limit is $100,000; the other policy's limit is $50,000. The other liability policy is *not* written to be excess over the homeowners policy. How much would the homeowners policy pay for this loss?
   A. $25,000
   B. $50,000
   C. $75,000
   D. $100,000

Exercise answers can be found at the end of the Unit 8 answers and rationales.

8.4.5.2. Section I and Section II

In addition to the conditions that apply separately to Sections I and II of the homeowners policy, there are general conditions that apply to both sections. These conditions include policy changes, assignment, concealment or fraud, liberalization, subrogation, policy period, and cancellation.

Under the cancellation condition, the insurance company may cancel for any reason with 10 days' written notice to the insured during the first 60 days of a policy term. After that, the company may only cancel for the following reasons:

- Material misrepresentation by the insured (30 days' notice required)
- Substantial change in risk insured (30 days' notice required)
- Nonpayment of premium (10 days' notice required)

The insurance company retains the right of nonrenewal, with 30 days' written notice to the insured required.

While this is the condition that appears in the standard policy, some state laws may require different cancellation procedures for policies issued in those states.

8.5. HOMEOWNERS ENDORSEMENTS

8.5.1. Section I Endorsements

The homeowners policy is designed for use by the average homeowner. Many homeowners, however, have special needs. To meet these needs, there are numerous endorsements that can be attached to the homeowners policy to modify coverage under Section I or Section II.

The **scheduled personal property** endorsement provides a separate schedule of insurance for one or more of nine major categories of valuable property.

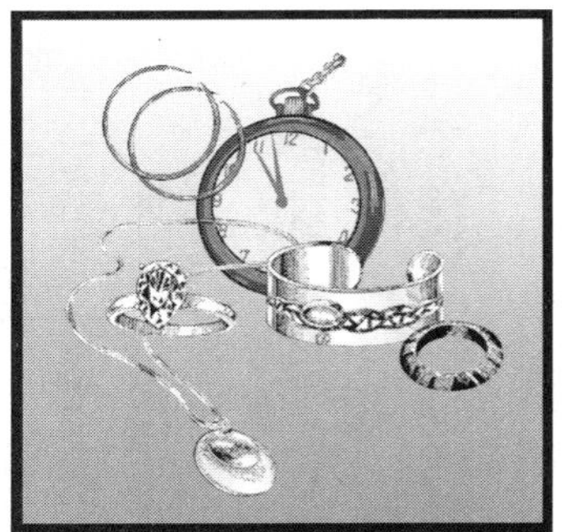

Jewelry

Furs and fur-trimmed garments

Cameras, projectors, films, and equipment

Musical instruments

Silverware

Golfer's equipment

Fine arts

Postage stamps

Rare and current coins

Many of these items represent property that has only a limited amount of coverage under the homeowners policy. The endorsement allows the insured to separately schedule one or more of these major categories of property with a separate amount of insurance for each category scheduled. After the insured schedules items of personal property on this endorsement, the property is not subject to the coverage limitations that apply to unscheduled personal property under the homeowners policy. In addition, coverage is provided on an open peril basis with no deductible, even if the endorsement is attached to a named perils homeowners policy. Depending on the type of property scheduled, losses may be paid on an actual cash value, market value, repair or replacement cost, or value basis. If the insured and the insurer do not agree on the amount of loss, either party may make a written request for an appraisal of the loss. When this occurs, the insured will select and pay a competent and impartial appraiser; the insurer will select and pay a competent impartial appraiser. The two appraisers will select an umpire. Each appraiser will state the amount of loss. If the appraisers do not agree, they will submit their statements to the umpire. The insured and insurer will equally share any appraisal expenses and the expense of the umpire. Agreement by the umpire and either of the appraisers will be binding.

The **personal property replacement cost** endorsement provides that the policy will reimburse losses to personal property on a replacement cost basis, rather than actual cash value, in the same way that homeowners forms reimburse loss to dwellings and other structures. Some property is excluded, such as obsolete articles, antiques, fine arts, and paintings that cannot be easily replaced.

The **permitted incidental occupancies** endorsement overrides the exclusions under the homeowners forms that apply to the insured's business activities conducted on the residence premises. For instance, this endorsement eliminates the Coverage B exclusion for using an other structure for business purposes. It also eliminates the $2,500 limit for business property on the residence premises with regard to furniture, supplies, and equipment used in the business listed in the endorsement. It also eliminates the Section II exclusion of liability and medical payments coverage in connection with business pursuits for the described business.

None of the homeowners forms covers earthquake. To add earthquake as a covered peril, the insured must purchase an earthquake endorsement.

Finally, the insured may purchase the **home day care coverage** endorsement to extend homeowners coverage to this type of business. The premium for this coverage is based on the number of children the insured cares for.

8.5.2. Section II Endorsements

There are also a number of homeowners endorsements that affect Section II.

Remember that the homeowners forms provide only limited liability coverage for watercraft. With the **watercraft** endorsement, an insured can purchase coverage for:

- watercraft up to 26 feet long powered by outboard engines or motors exceeding 25 horsepower;

- watercraft powered by inboard or inboard-outdrive engines or motors; and
- sailboats more than 26 feet long.

An unendorsed homeowners policy provides no coverage for liability arising out of business-related perils, other than for permitted incidental occupancies. The **business pursuits** endorsement provides liability coverage for a business conducted away from the residence premises.

The homeowners policy provides no protection against personal injuries such as libel, slander, false arrest, invasion of privacy, or malicious prosecution. The **personal injury** endorsement modifies the definition of bodily injury to include personal injury.

8.5.3. Limited Fungi, Wet or Dry Rot, or Bacteria Coverage

This endorsement adds coverage to the property or liability sections of the policy for property damage and liability losses arising out of fungi, wet or dry rot, or bacteria. It is used only with the HO-3 and HO-5. The limits for the coverages are scheduled in the endorsement.

Fungi are defined as any type or form of fungus, including mold or mildew. Under Section II, the definition does not include fungi that are on or part of a good or product intended for consumption. Bacteria and wet or dry rot are not defined.

For purposes of simplification, we will use the word *mold* in this section.

Under Section I, this coverage is added to the additional coverages section. It states that the amount shown in the schedule is the most the insurer will pay for:

- all loss payable under Section I caused by mold;
- cost to remove mold from covered property; and
- cost to tear out and replace any part of the building or other covered property as needed to gain access to the mold.

Coverage only applies if the loss or costs resulted from a covered peril that occurred during the policy period. The insured must have used all reasonable means to save and preserve the property from further damage when the covered loss occurred.

The amount shown in the schedule is the most the insurer will pay for losses under this additional coverage, regardless of the number of locations insured or the number of claims made. This coverage does not increase the policy limit that applies to the damaged covered property.

Under Section II, the limit of liability condition is modified to state that the insurer's total liability under Coverage E for all damages arising directly or indirectly out of the actual, alleged, or threatened contact with mold will not be more than the sublimit for this coverage shown in the schedule. The sublimit does not increase the Coverage E limit and applies separately to each consecutive annual period.

8.6. HOMEOWNERS FORMS COMPARISON

The following charts compare the features of the different homeowners forms.

Property Coverage Provided by the Homeowners Forms

	HO-2		HO-3		HO-4		HO-5		HO-6		HO-8	
	Dwelling	Personal Property	Dwelling	Personal Property	Dwelling	Personal Property	Dwelling	Personal Property	Dwelling*	Personal Property	Dwelling	Personal Property
Special			✔				✔	✔				
Broad	✔	✔		✔		✔				✔		
Basic											✔	✔

*Provides only limited dwelling coverage

Perils Insured Against

		HO-3			HO-5			
Peril	HO-2	Dwelling	Personal Property	HO-4	Dwelling	Personal Property	HO-6	HO-8
Fire	✔	Open Peril*	✔	✔	Open Peril*	Open Peril*	✔	✔
Lightning	✔		✔	✔			✔	✔
Windstorm or Hail	✔		✔	✔			✔	✔
Explosion	✔		✔	✔			✔	✔
Riot or Civil Commotion	✔		✔	✔			✔	✔
Aircraft	✔		✔	✔			✔	✔
Vehicles	✔		✔	✔			✔	✔**
Smoke	✔		✔	✔			✔	✔***
Vandalism & Malicious Mischief	✔		✔	✔			✔	✔
Theft	✔		✔	✔			✔	✔
Volcanic Eruption	✔		✔	✔			✔	✔
Falling Objects	✔		✔	✔			✔	
Weight of Ice, Snow, or Sleet	✔		✔	✔			✔	
Discharge of Water or Steam	✔		✔	✔			✔****	
Sudden, Accidental Rupture	✔		✔	✔			✔	
Freezing of Plumbing and Related Systems	✔		✔	✔			✔	
Artificially Generated Electrical Current	✔		✔	✔			✔	

*Risks of loss not otherwise excluded are covered

**Does not include losses to fences, driveways, or walks caused by vehicles owned or operated by residents of insured household

***Does not include damage from fireplace smoke

****Includes costs to tear out and replace area of the building to repair system or appliance

UNIT TEST

1. A homeowner who wants the maximum protection for her home and personal property should purchase the
   A. HO-2
   B. HO-3
   C. HO-4
   D. HO-5

2. Which homeowners form should someone who lives in an apartment purchase to cover his personal property?
   A. HO-3
   B. HO-4
   C. HO-6
   D. HO-8

3. Which homeowners form provides broad coverage for both the dwelling and its contents?
   A. HO-2
   B. HO-3
   C. HO-6
   D. HO-8

4. Which of the following could be covered by an unendorsed homeowners policy?
   A. Mobile home
   B. Home rented to another person
   C. Home occupied by the insured and two boarders
   D. Home owned and occupied by the insured

5. In the homeowners forms
   A. the property coverage varies in each form
   B. the property coverage is the same in each form
   C. the liability coverage varies in each form
   D. the liability coverage is the same in each form

6. Which of the following perils are covered in all homeowners forms?
   A. Fire
   B. Theft
   C. Volcanic eruption
   D. Weight of ice, snow, or sleet
   E. Falling objects
   F. Smoke
   G. Accidental discharge or overflow of water or steam
   H. Freezing of plumbing systems

7. The collapse additional coverage is included in which homeowners form(s)?
   A. HO-2 and HO-3
   B. HO-4 only
   C. All forms except the HO-8
   D. All forms

8. Which of the following classes of personal property have special limits under the homeowners policy?
   A. Animals, birds, and fish
   B. Money
   C. Watercraft
   D. Property of boarders
   E. Furniture
   F. Kitchen appliances
   G. Clothing
   H. Valuable papers
   I. Trailers

9. Under the homeowners policy, which of the following classes of personal property have special limits for theft losses but not for other types of losses?
   A. Money
   B. Firearms
   C. Silverware
   D. Jewelry
   E. Property used for business purposes
   F. Watercraft

10. Under an unendorsed homeowners policy, losses to the dwelling and other structures are paid on (an actual cash value/a replacement cost) ______________________ basis.

11. Under all homeowners forms except the HO-5, losses to personal property are paid on (an actual cash value/a replacement cost) ______________ basis.

12. Which of the following statements concerning medical payments to others coverage are CORRECT?
    A. Injury to an insured is not covered.
    B. The insured does not have to be legally liable for coverage to be available.
    C. Injuries that occur off the insured location are never covered.

13. Which of the following statements concerning personal liability coverage are CORRECT?
    A. It covers damages the insured becomes legally obligated to pay because of BI or PD.
    B. The insurer will not defend liability claims brought against the insured that are groundless or false.
    C. It applies to the insured's personal, nonbusiness activities that occur anywhere.

14. Identify the homeowners endorsement used to provide each of the following coverages.
    A. Liability coverage for a business that is conducted away from the residence premises ______________________
    B. Coverage for losses arising out of libel and slander ______________________
    C. Replacement cost coverage for losses to personal property______________________
    D. Scheduled coverage for certain classes of personal property______________________

15. The insured would have liability coverage under the homeowners policy while operating which of the following boats? (Assume there are no endorsements attached to the policy.)
    A. 8-foot boat with a 25 horsepower inboard-outdrive motor not owned by the insured
    B. 42-foot sailboat with no auxiliary power owned by the insured
    C. 15-foot boat powered by a 50 horsepower outboard motor that was purchased by the insured before the policy inception date and not reported to the insurer
    D. 8-foot boat with a 25 horsepower inboard motor rented by the insured

16. Which of the following would be covered under Coverage A or Coverage B of the homeowners policy?
    A. A greenhouse attached to the porch of the insured's home
    B. A guest cottage on the insured's estate
    C. The insured's ranch-style home
    D. A barn rented to a neighbor to use as a retail arts and crafts store
    E. A stack of lumber at the edge of the insured's property that will be used to construct a boat shed
    F. A detached shed rented to a neighbor as a private garage for an antique auto
    G. The insured's poolside cabana

17. Which of these statements about Coverage C of the homeowners policy are CORRECT?
    A. It only covers the insured's personal property while it is at the residence premises.
    B. At the insured's request, coverage applies to a guest's property while the guest is in the insured's residence.
    C. Property normally kept at a residence other than the residence premises is covered for 10% of the Coverage C limit or $1,000, whichever is greater.
    D. There is no coverage for property being moved from the residence premises to a new principal residence.

18. A hose on a washing machine in the insured's condominium comes loose and leaks water all over the floor. The repair person has to tear out part of the wall to fix the defective hose. The insured's HO-6 would cover
    A. the water damage to the floor
    B. the cost to repair the damaged wall
    C. both A and B

19. Which of the following losses would be excluded under all of the homeowners forms?
    A. Earthquake damage to a home
    B. Flood damage to a home
    C. Accidental and sudden discharge of water from a plumbing system
    D. An area power failure that shuts down the insured's refrigerator for 12 hours while he is on vacation, causing meat to spoil

20. A person is injured on the insured's premises and sues for the cost of nursing care required during the recovery period. Could the insured's liability for these expenses be covered under Coverage E of the homeowners policy?
    ( ) Yes ( ) No

21. The insured damaged a neighbor's tool shed when a tree he was cutting down in his yard fell on the neighbor's shed. Not only does the neighbor have to repair the shed, but he must find temporary storage for the garden equipment he stored in the shed. Could the insured's liability for these expenses be covered under Coverage E of the Homeowners policy?
    ( ) Yes ( ) No

22. What is the standard liability limit for Coverage E?
    A. $100,000 aggregate
    B. $100,000 per occurrence

23. Which of the following would be excluded under Section II of the homeowners policy?
    A. The insured has been feuding with her neighbor for years. One night, she hooks a rope from the front bumper of the neighbor's car to her neighbor's porch railing. When the neighbor drives away, the front porch rail is ripped free of the porch, causing extensive damage.
    B. The insured attorney meets with clients in his home. He is later sued for giving erroneous advice.
    C. The insured owns a private plane. A friend injures her finger when the insured closes the door on it.
    D. All of the above

24. A homeowners policy has been in force 30 days, and the company discovers the insured has misrepresented certain material facts. The insurer wants to cancel the policy. Under what circumstances may it do so?
    A. The company must wait until the policy has been in force for 60 days before it may cancel.
    B. The company must give the insured 30 days' written notice of cancellation.
    C. The company must give the insured 10 days' written notice of cancellation.
    D. Under no circumstances; a policy cannot be canceled because of material misrepresentation by the insured.

ANSWERS AND RATIONALES TO UNIT TEST

1. **D.** The HO-5, the comprehensive form, provides open peril coverage for dwellings, other structures, and personal property.

2. **B.** The HO-4 is designed for tenants. It provides broad coverage for personal property and no coverage for the dwelling.

3. **A.** The HO-3 provides open peril coverage for the dwelling and named peril coverage for personal property. The HO-8 provides basic coverage for the dwelling and personal property. The HO-6 offers limited coverage for the dwelling and broad coverage on personal property.

4. **C and D.** Up to two boarders per family are allowed if the home is also occupied by the insured. An endorsement is required to insure a mobile home under a homeowners policy. The insured must live in the dwelling to qualify for homeowners coverage.

5. **A and D.** The liability coverage is identical in all of the homeowners forms. The property coverage varies with the homeowners form selected.

6. **A, B, C, and F.** These are examples of basic perils covered under all homeowners forms.

7. **C.** The collapse additional coverage is included in all of the homeowners forms except the HO-8.

8. **B, C, H, and I.** Animals, birds, fish, and property of boarders are excluded. The items listed in the other answer choices are covered with no special limits of liability.

9. **B, C, and D.** The following classes of property have special limits for theft losses but not for other types of losses: jewelry, watches, furs, and precious and semiprecious stones; silverware, goldware, or pewterware; and firearms.

10. A replacement cost. Losses to the dwelling and other structures are paid on a replacement cost basis.

11. An actual cash value. In all homeowners forms except the HO-5, personal property losses are paid at actual cash value. The HO-5 provides replacement cost coverage for personal property.

12. **A and B.** Injuries to the named insured or regular residents other than resident employees are not covered. Injuries sustained while the injured party is off the insured location are covered if certain conditions are met. There is no requirement under Coverage F that the insured be legally liable for the injuries.

13. **A and C.** The insurance company will provide a defense for the insured at the insurer's expense, even when the charges are groundless.

14. **A.** Business pursuits. This endorsement provides liability coverage for a business conducted away from the residence premises.

    B. Personal injury. This endorsement modifies the definition of bodily injury to include personal injury.

    C. Personal property replacement cost. This endorsement adds replacement cost coverage for personal property.

    D. Scheduled personal property. This endorsement provides open peril scheduled coverage for nine optional classes of property.

15. **A and D**. The policy makes some exceptions to the exclusion for liability arising out of the use of watercraft. In these examples, the boats meet the policy's requirements for engine size and ownership.

16. **A, B, C, E, F, and G**. Dwellings and other structures may not be used for business purposes except for permitted incidental occupancies. An other structure rented to someone other than tenants of the dwelling is excluded unless the other structure is rented as a private garage.

17. **B and C**. Personal property is covered while it is away from the residence premises. When property is being moved to a new principal residence, full coverage applies for 30 days from the start of the move. Coverage for property belonging to an insured's guest or residence employee is available on request, but is not automatically provided.

18. **C.** In the HO-6, the accidental discharge or overflow of water or steam peril includes coverage for the costs to tear out and replace any part of the building necessary to repair the system or appliance from which the water or steam escaped.

19. **A, B, and D**. Accidental and sudden discharge of water from a plumbing system is covered in all forms except the HO-8.

20. **Yes**. The definition of bodily injury includes required care, loss of services, and death.

21. **Yes**. The definition of property damage includes loss of use.

22. **B.** The standard liability limited provided for all BI or PD arising out of any one occurrence is $100,000.

23. **D.** Choice A is excluded because the damage was expected or intended by the insured. Choice B is excluded because the loss arose from the rendering of professional services. Choice C is excluded because the injury arose out of the ownership of aircraft.

24. **C.** The insurance company may cancel a policy for any reason with 10 days' written notice to the insured during the first 60 days of a policy term.

UNIT 8 EXERCISE ANSWERS

Exercise 8.A

1. Broad, broad
2. Open peril, broad
3. No, broad
4. Broad
5. Basic, basic

Exercise 8.B

1. A, C, and F—the value of the item exceeds the specified limit in the other examples

Exercise 8.C

1. Coverage A
2. None
3. Coverage B
4. Coverage C
5. Coverage D
6. None
7. Coverage C
8. None
9. Coverage C
10. Coverage D
11. Coverage C
12. None
13. Coverage C

Exercise 8.D

1. **B**
2 **A**
3. **A**

Exercise 8.E

1. A. $80,000 B. $8,000 C. $40,000 D. $24,000
2. A. $1000 B. $0 C. $30,000 D. $15,000

Exercise 8.F

1. A, B, and C

Exercise 8.G

1. **A**

UNIT

9

Personal Auto Insurance

9.1. LEARNING OBJECTIVES

After completing Unit 9—Personal Auto Insurance, you will be able to do the following:

- Describe the policy's eligibility requirements for individuals and vehicles
- Explain how the following terms are defined in the personal auto policy: you/your, family member, bodily injury, occupying, property damage, covered auto, temporary substitute auto, and nonowned auto
- Explain how coverage for newly acquired autos applies under the four personal auto policy coverages
- For liability, medical payments to others, and uninsured motorists coverage, describe the purpose of the coverage, the conditions that must be met for a loss to be covered, who is considered an insured, losses that would be excluded, how the limits of liability apply, and how other insurance affects loss payments
- Identify expenses that are covered under the supplementary payments section of Part A—liability coverage
- Explain the purpose of the financial responsibility and out-of-state coverage provisions in Part A—liability coverage
- Compare and contrast the losses covered under collision and other than collision coverage
- Explain the provisions of transportation expenses coverage
- Describe important conditions that apply to the policy, including the insured's duties after loss, subrogation, and termination
- Explain the purpose of underinsured motorists coverage
- Explain the purpose of the following endorsements: joint ownership coverage, towing and labor costs, miscellaneous type vehicle, extended nonowned coverage for named individual, optional limits transportation expenses coverage, and named nonowner coverage
- Explain how a no-fault insurance plan affects auto liability insurance
- Describe the purpose of an assigned risk plan for auto insurance

9.2. INTRODUCTION

There are two major automobile exposures for which individuals seek protection. First, people want to be protected against their **liability** in case they injure someone or damage someone else's property through the use of their automobile. Second, people want protection for damage to their own automobile in case the auto is damaged in an accident or suffers other types of damage, such as fire or theft.

Because the homeowners form specifically excludes auto exposures, they must be covered separately, through a policy called the **personal auto policy (PAP)**. Because the PAP contains property and liability coverage, it is considered a package policy. In this course, we'll study the 2005 personal auto policy issued by ISO.

9.3. ORGANIZATION AND ELIGIBILITY

The personal auto policy consists of a **declarations page** and a **policy form**. The policy form contains four separate coverages, each with its own insuring agreement, exclusions, and conditions. They are as follows:

- Part A—liability coverage
- Part B—medical payments coverage
- Part C—uninsured motorists coverage
- Part D—coverage for damage to your auto (physical damage)

Many personal auto policies are written to include all of the available coverages, but the insured does not have to purchase each one. Part A—liability coverage may be written alone or with any of the other coverages. Medical payments coverage, Part B, is optional, but it may only be written if the policy includes liability coverage. Part C—uninsured motorists coverage may only be written in conjunction with liability coverage and is subject to other laws that vary from state to state. It is mandatory in some states; in others the insured may reject the coverage in writing. Either or both of the coverages under Part D (collision and other than collision) may be written alone or with liability coverage.

The personal auto policy can be issued to an individual or a married couple residing in the same household.

9.4. DEFINITIONS

The **definitions** section of the personal auto policy defines certain key terms used in the policy. These terms help clarify the intent of various coverages and conditions, as you will see throughout this unit.

The policy uses the words *you* and *your* to refer to the **named insured** shown in the declarations and the insured's spouse. The spouse must reside in the same household as the insured. However, if a separation occurs during the policy period or before the effective date of the policy, the spouse is still considered an insured for the least of:

- 90 days;
- the effective date of a new policy listing the spouse as a named insured; or
- the end of the policy period.

A **family member** is any person related to the named insured who is a resident of the insured's household. This includes those related by blood, marriage, or adoption and includes a ward or foster child.

Bodily injury means bodily harm, sickness, or disease, including death, that results from any of these.

Occupying means:

- in a vehicle;
- upon a vehicle; or
- getting into, onto, out of, or off of a vehicle.

Property damage means physical injury to, destruction of, or loss of use of tangible property.

The named insured's **covered auto** includes the following:

- Any vehicle listed in the declarations. Vehicles eligible to be listed include **private passenger autos,** which are four-wheel motor vehicles and pickup trucks and vans that are under a certain weight and are not used for business purposes. (Farming and ranching are not considered businesses.) The vehicles must be owned or leased under a long-term contract of six months or more.
- Any private passenger auto, pickup, or van the named insured acquires during the policy period.
- Any **trailer** owned by the named insured. This includes farm wagons or implements while towed by a vehicle listed in the declarations.
- Any auto or trailer not owned by the named insured that is being used as a temporary substitute for a vehicle shown in the declarations that is out of use because of breakdown, repair, servicing, loss, or destruction.

Earlier, we said that newly acquired autos qualify as covered autos. Coverage for newly acquired autos applies as follows.

TAKE NOTE

For Liability, Medical Payments, and Uninsured Motorists Coverage

If the newly acquired auto replaces one listed in the declarations, the new auto automatically has the broadest coverage provided for any vehicle already listed in the declarations.

If the new auto does not replace one that is already insured, the insured must request coverage within 14 days after acquiring the auto.

TAKE NOTE

For Physical Damage Coverage

For physical damage coverage, it doesn't matter if the new auto is a replacement or additional auto. If the insured already has at least one vehicle insured for physical damage under the policy, coverage begins on the date the auto is acquired as long as the insured requests coverage within 14 days after acquiring the auto. The new auto will then automatically have the broadest coverage provided for any vehicle already listed in the declarations.

If the insured does not already have physical damage coverage on an auto, coverage must be requested within 4 days after acquiring the auto. If a loss occurs in the time before the insured requests coverage, a $500 deductible applies.

If an insured requests coverage after any of the reporting periods specified in the policy have elapsed, coverage begins at the time coverage is requested. This is true for additional and replacement autos.

Suppose Jose sells his small pickup truck and buys a new sports car. The pickup truck had full coverage under a personal auto policy. Because the sports car is a replacement for the pickup, it automatically has liability coverage under the personal auto policy.

9.5. PART A—LIABILITY COVERAGE

9.5.1. Coverage

Part A—liability coverage covers damages for bodily injury or property damage that an insured becomes legally responsible for because of an auto accident.

There are several important concepts here. First, the policy only protects those who are considered insureds. We'll look at who is an insured under Part A of the policy in a moment. Second, coverage applies only to damages for which the insured is legally responsible. Finally, the damages must involve bodily injury or property damage and result from an auto accident.

The policy promises to settle or defend any claim or suit asking for such damages and promises to pay any defense costs incurred by the company. However, the duty to settle or defend ends when the limit of liability has been exhausted. Defense costs are paid in addition to the limit of insurance. There is no duty to settle or defend claims for BI or PD that are not covered under the policy.

Exercise 9.A

What are the three conditions that must be met for a loss to be covered under Part A—liability coverage?

1. ____________________
2. ____________________
3. ____________________

Exercise answers can be found at the end of the Unit 9 answers and rationales.

9.5.2. Who Is an Insured

Now let's look at who is considered an insured under Part A of the personal auto policy. Although there are some exceptions we'll cover later, in general the policy considers the following to be insureds:

- The named insured and members of the insured's family while using any auto
- Anyone using the insured's car with the insured's permission or the reasonable belief that he is entitled to do so
- Other people or organizations to the extent that they share liability with an insured
- Other persons or organizations for their liability arising out of an accident involving any auto or trailer used by the insured or a family member (does not apply if the auto or trailer is owned by the person or organization in question)

Let's take a closer look at each of these groups.

The named insured, the insured's spouse, or any family member is an insured for the ownership, maintenance, or use of any auto or trailer. Suppose the named insured's 16-year-old son borrows a neighbor's car and causes an accident. The son is considered an insured for liability coverage under the named insured's personal auto policy.

Any person using the named insured's covered auto with the insured's permission or the reasonable belief that he is entitled to do so is also covered for liability insurance. For instance, a neighbor would be insured under the policy if he had an accident while driving the named insured's car but would not be covered under the named insured's policy while driving his own vehicle.

The policy also insures any person or organization who is legally responsible for the acts or omissions of anyone insured under Part A of the policy that result in an auto accident involving a covered auto. This is an example of vicarious liability.

In addition, the policy insures any person or organization who is legally responsible for the acts or omissions of a named insured or family member that result in an accident involving any auto or trailer. The person or organization is not covered, however, if it owns or hires the auto or trailer.

Here's an example: Dave is on his way to a business luncheon in his own car when he hits Randall's car. Because Dave was on company business when the accident occurred, Randall sues Dave and his employer, Rock Oil, for damages. Under these circumstances, Dave's personal auto policy also covers Rock Oil's liability.

If Dave were driving a company-owned car when the accident occurred, his personal auto policy would not cover Rock Oil's liability. No coverage applies when the organization owns or rents the vehicle involved in the accident.

9.5.3. Supplementary Payments

Like other liability policies, the liability portion of the personal auto policy contains a supplementary payments section. Amounts paid under this section do not reduce the policy limit. Supplementary payments include:

- up to $250 for the cost of bail bonds;
- premiums on appeal bonds or bonds to release attachments;
- postjudgment interest (prejudgment interest is included as part of the liability limit);
- up to $200 per day for loss of earnings because of attendance at hearings or trials at the company's request; and
- other reasonable expenses incurred by the insured at the company's request.

9.5.4. Exclusions

There are a number of important exclusions that help define coverage under the liability section of the personal auto policy. Excluded are:

- BI or PD caused intentionally by the insured;
- damage to property owned or being transported by the insured;
- damage to property rented to, used by, or in the care of the insured;
- BI to an insured's employees (these losses are covered under workers' compensation);
- liability arising out of an insured's ownership or operation of a vehicle used as a public or livery conveyance, such as a taxi (this exclusion does not apply to a share-the-expense carpool);
- liability arising while the insured auto is being used in an auto business;
- use of a vehicle without permission (does not apply to family members using covered autos owned by the insured);
- BI or PD for which an insured is covered under a nuclear energy liability policy;
- motorized vehicles with fewer than four wheels or designed for use off public roads (does not apply to nonowned golf carts);
- vehicles other than covered autos owned by the named insured or furnished for the named insured's regular use;
- vehicles other than covered autos that are owned by family members or furnished for their regular use (does not apply to the named insured); and
- vehicles used in prearranged racing or speed contests.

Exercise 9.B

1. Which of the following losses would be excluded under Part A of the personal auto policy?
   A. Theresa uses her car as a taxicab. One evening, she hits a parked car while pulling into a parking place to pick up a passenger.
   B. Because the newspaper carrier never delivers the morning paper on time, Bryce deliberately runs over the boy's bicycle while it is parked at the edge of Bryce's driveway.
   C. Jerry's teenage son backs into his car with one of the other family autos, damaging both autos.
   D. While riding his motorcycle through the neighborhood, Herman hits a parked car, damaging the car's bumper and grille.
   E. Bill is the named insured. His 18-year-old son Jeff, who lives at home, has been furnished a van by the pizza restaurant that employs him. One day, while driving the van off duty, Jeff strikes and injures a pedestrian.

Exercise answers can be found at the end of the Unit 9 answers and rationales.

9.5.5. Limits of Liability

The Part A limit of liability is the most the company will pay for all damages resulting from any one auto accident, regardless of the number of insureds, claims filed, vehicles or premiums listed in the declarations, or vehicles involved in the accident.

Liability coverage is provided on a split limits basis. The limits are usually expressed as a series of three numbers, such as 25/50/25. This means that the policy will pay:

- $25,000 **per person** for bodily injury;
- $50,000 **per accident** for bodily injury; and
- $25,000 **per accident** for property damage.

The policy also states that a person cannot collect duplicate payments for a loss that is covered under Part A and another coverage in the personal auto policy or under any underinsured motorists coverage provided by the policy. (You'll learn about underinsured motorists coverage later in this unit.)

Assume the named insured's personal auto policy has limits of 100/300/100 for Part A. After an accident, there is a $250,000 judgment against him for injuries to one person. In this case, the policy will pay $100,000 (the policy limit for BI to one person).

9.5.6. Financial Responsibility

An important provision under Part A of the personal auto policy deals with financial responsibility laws.

Almost all states have financial responsibility laws that require each driver to prove that he can pay for bodily injury or property damage liability losses arising out of auto accidents. A driver normally meets this requirement by purchasing an auto insurance policy with limits of liability that meet the limits required by that state's law.

This provision states that the insurance company can certify the policy as proof of future financial responsibility. When it does, the policy will automatically reflect any changes in the state's financial responsibility laws.

9.5.7. Out-of-State Coverage

Vehicles are usually driven in more than one state, and the personal auto policy provides for such situations. The **out-of-state coverage** provision modifies the personal auto policy to meet other states' financial responsibility requirements and other state laws concerning out-of-state drivers when the covered auto is being driven in that state.

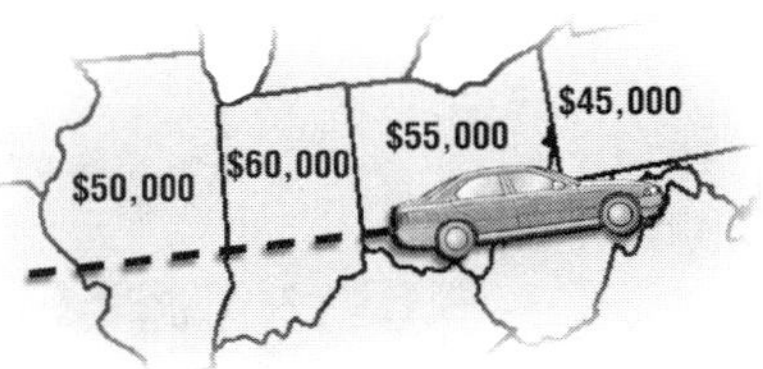

9.5.8. Other Insurance

The **other insurance clause** for liability coverage states that the company will pay only its share of a loss that is also covered by other insurance. The company's share is the proportion that its policy limit bears to the total of all applicable limits. However, any insurance the company provides for a vehicle that is not owned by the insured, including vehicles used as temporary substitute autos, will be considered excess to other insurance.

Suppose the named insured has an accident in her car and is liable for damages of $60,000. She has a personal auto policy with a $50,000 single liability limit and other applicable liability insurance of $25,000. The personal auto policy would pay $40,000 for this loss (50,000 ÷ 75,000 × 60,000 = 40,000).

9.6. PART B—MEDICAL PAYMENTS COVERAGE

9.6.1. Coverage, Who Is an Insured

Part B—medical payments coverage provides protection for the named insured, family members, and passengers in the named insured's auto for injuries received in an accident, regardless of who was at fault. It is not a form of liability coverage for injuries sustained by passengers in another auto involved in an accident with the insured.

Part B covers reasonable expenses for necessary medical and funeral services incurred within three years of the date of the accident.

Insureds for medical payments coverage include:

- the named insured and any family member
  - while occupying a motor vehicle designed for use on public roads or a trailer, or
  - when struck by a vehicle designed for use on public roads or a trailer; and
- any other person while occupying the named insured's covered auto.

Suppose the named insured ran a red light while driving his covered auto and hit another vehicle. The occupants of the car he hit were badly injured. The named insured, his daughter, and two of his daughter's friends were in the insured's auto and were also injured. Medical payments coverage would pay the medical bills for the named insured, his daughter, and her friends. It would not cover the medical bills of the other car's occupants.

9.6.2. Exclusions

Medical payments coverage is subject to some of the same exclusions as liability coverage. There is no coverage for injuries:

- sustained while occupying a motor vehicle with fewer than four wheels;
- sustained while using a covered auto as a public or livery conveyance;
- that would be covered under workers' compensation;
- sustained while occupying an uninsured auto **owned by the insured or furnished for his regular use;**
- sustained while occupying an uninsured auto **owned by a family member or furnished for the family member's regular use (does not apply to the named insured);**
- sustained while the insured is occupying a vehicle without the reasonable belief that he is entitled to do so (does not apply to family members using covered autos owned by the insured);
- sustained while occupying a vehicle that is being used in the insured's business;

- caused by war or nuclear hazard;
- sustained while occupying a vehicle located for use as a residence or premises; or
- sustained during prearranged racing or speed contests.

9.6.3. Limits of Liability, Other Insurance

Medical payments coverage has a single limit of liability that applies to all injuries sustained by each person injured in any one accident. Typical limits are $1,000, $2,000, $5,000, or $10,000.

A person cannot collect duplicate payments for a loss that is covered under Part B and another coverage in the personal auto policy or under any underinsured motorists coverage provided by the policy.

The other insurance condition for medical payments coverage is identical to the one for liability coverage.

Exercise 9.C

Noreen's personal auto policy has a $5,000 limit for medical payments coverage. Three women are injured in an accident while riding in Noreen's car. Determine how much each person will be paid under the policy.

	Total Medical Expenses	Amount paid by Policy
Melba	$2,000	1. $______________
Harriet	$4,000	2. $______________
Winifred	$7,500	3. $______________

Exercise answers can be found at the end of the Unit 9 answers and rationales.

9.7. PART C—UNINSURED MOTORISTS COVERAGE

9.7.1. Coverage

Part C of the personal auto policy provides **uninsured motorists (UM) coverage**. In most states, this coverage indemnifies the insured for bodily injury only as a result of an accident with a legally liable uninsured motorist. Only compensatory damages are covered; punitive damages are specifically excluded.

Some states offer property damage coverage in addition to bodily injury coverage. This is provided by adding an endorsement to the policy.

Before the insured can be indemnified under Part C, four conditions must be met.

- The loss must be caused by an auto accident and involve bodily injury (in most states).
- The loss must be sustained by an insured.
- The insured must be legally entitled to recover for BI damages.
- The other vehicle must meet the definition of an uninsured vehicle.

9.7.2. Definition of Uninsured Motor Vehicle

The policy defines an **uninsured motor vehicle** as one that:

- has no liability coverage at the time of the accident;
- has liability coverage but not enough to meet the state's financial responsibility requirement;
- is operated by a hit-and-run driver who cannot be identified who strikes an insured or a family member, the insured's covered auto, or any auto occupied by the insured or a family member; or
- has invalid liability coverage at the time of the accident because the insurer is insolvent or denies coverage.

This definition does not apply to a vehicle or equipment that is:

- owned by or furnished or available for the regular use of the insured or any family member;
- owned or operated by a self-insurer, except for an insolvent self-insurer;
- owned by a government unit or agency;
- operated on rails or crawler treads;
- designed for use off public roads; or
- located for use as a residence or premises.

Earlier, you learned that the out-of-state coverage provision automatically amends the policy limit to conform with other states' financial responsibility laws. Because of this provision, the part of the definition referencing policies with inadequate limits rarely applies to drivers insured under a personal auto policy. However, not all policies include an out-of-state coverage provision. This part of the definition is intended to protect insureds involved in accidents with drivers insured by such policies.

Keep in mind that for the purpose of this course (including related exam questions) we will ignore the impact of the out-of-state coverage provision on the definition of an uninsured motorist.

9.7.3. Who Is Insured

Insureds for uninsured motorists coverage include:

- the named insured and family members;

- anyone occupying the named insured's covered auto; and
- any person entitled to recover damages because of BI caused by an uninsured motorist to the named insured, family members, or passengers in the covered auto.

Examples include a parent who is entitled to recover for medical expenses incurred by a child or a spouse who is entitled to damages for loss of consortium (loss of a spouse's services).

9.7.4. Exclusions

Part C does not cover losses:

- for BI sustained by an insured while occupying or when struck by an auto that is owned by the insured but not insured for uninsured motorists coverage under the policy;
- for BI sustained by a family member while occupying or when struck by an auto owned by the named insured that has primary uninsured motorists coverage under another policy;
- that are settled without the insurer's consent if the settlement prejudices the insurer's right to subrogate against the uninsured driver;
- that occur when the auto is being used as a public or livery conveyance; or
- that occur while the insured is using an auto without the reasonable belief that he is entitled to do so (does not apply to family members using covered autos owned by the insured).

In some states, workers' compensation insurers and disability insurers may have the right to subrogate against a third party who has caused an injury. In the case of an injury caused by an uninsured motorist, this right could extend to making a claim under the injured party's uninsured motorists coverage. Such claims are specifically prohibited by the policy.

9.7.5. Limit of Liability

The limit of liability provision for Part C is similar to the one used for Part A. It also states that the insurance company will not:

- make duplicate payments for losses that were paid by or on behalf of the person who was responsible for the accident; or
- pay any part of a loss that could be covered under a workers' compensation or disability benefits law.

9.7.6. Other Insurance

The other insurance provision for uninsured motorists coverage is similar to the ones used for Parts A and B. One important difference is that the amount that the insured can be paid is limited to the highest single policy limit for uninsured motorists coverage. This prevents stacking coverage—adding the limits of coverage available to provide a higher coverage limit.

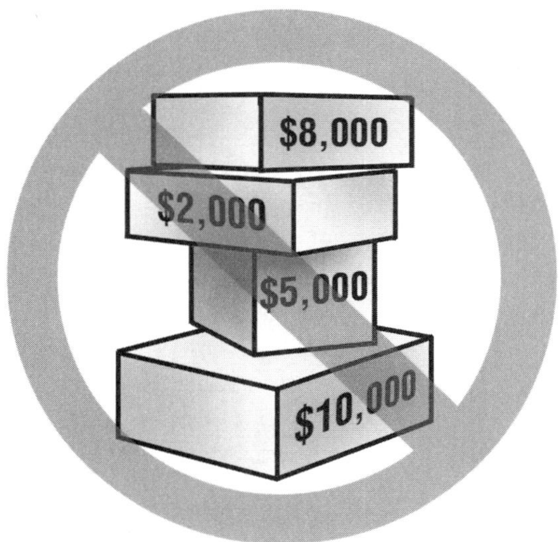

Suppose Imelda has two personal auto policies, both with a $200,000 limit of liability for uninsured motorists coverage. She is involved in a serious accident with an uninsured driver and incurs $350,000 in medical expenses. The maximum amount she could collect under both policies for this loss is $200,000.

9.7.7. Arbitration

Part C provides specific provisions on arbitration that come in to play when the insured and the insurance company do not agree whether the insured is entitled to uninsured motorists coverage or the amount of damages. This provision operates much like the arbitration clauses we discussed earlier.

9.8. PART D—COVERAGE FOR DAMAGE TO YOUR AUTO

9.8.1. Coverage

The liability section of the personal auto policy excludes damage to property owned by, rented to, used by, or in the care of the insured. Such coverage is provided under the Personal Auto policy by **Part D—coverage for damage to your auto**, commonly known as **physical damage coverage**.

Physical damage coverage pays for direct and accidental loss to the named insured's covered auto or any nonowned auto against loss caused by:

- collision; or
- other than collision (sometimes referred to as OTC or comprehensive). It does not cover any personal property in the vehicle.

Together, these two coverages provide what amounts to open peril coverage for damage to the named insured's auto. The named insured may purchase collision coverage only, other than collision coverage only, or both. Coverage may also vary by car. But only coverages for which a premium is shown in the declarations will apply.

In general, **collision** is defined as the impact of an auto covered by the policy with another object or vehicle, or the upset of a vehicle.

Other than collision coverage pays almost every other type of direct, accidental loss to the vehicle that is not specifically excluded by the policy. These perils are specifically listed in the policy as being other than collision losses:

- Missiles or falling objects
- Fire
- Theft or larceny
- Explosion or earthquake
- Windstorm
- Hail, water, or flood
- Malicious mischief or vandalism
- Riot or civil commotion
- Contact with a bird or animal
- Breakage of glass

If glass breakage is caused by collision, the insured has the option of having it treated as a collision loss. This eliminates a double deductible when glass breakage and other collision damage occur in the same accident.

Exercise 9.D

Label each of the following as a collision loss **(C)** or other than collision loss **(O).**

____ 1. An auto slides on ice, runs into a curb, and flips onto its side.

____ 2. A cow escapes from a farm and wanders onto the highway. A passing auto runs into the cow.

____ 3. An auto is stolen from a parking lot.

____ 4. An auto stops suddenly on the freeway, causing two motorists following it to crash into it in a chain reaction.

____ 5. A bird flies into the windshield of an auto.

____ 6. An auto is swept away in a flood.

Exercise answers can be found at the end of the Unit 9 answers and rationales.

If the named insured has a covered loss in a nonowned auto, the broadest coverage that applies to any of the insured's covered autos will apply to the nonowned auto. A **nonowned auto** is any private passenger auto, pickup truck, trailer, or van not owned by or available for the regular use of the named insured or a family member, such as a short-term rental car. Under physical damage coverage only, a temporary substitute auto is considered a nonowned auto instead of a covered auto.

9.8.2. Transportation Expenses

In addition to collision and other than collision coverage, Part D provides **transportation expenses coverage**. This coverage pays up to $20 per day, to a maximum of $600, for:

- transportation expenses incurred by the insured because of physical damage losses to the insured's covered auto; and
- loss of use expenses for which the insured becomes legally responsible because of loss to a nonowned auto.

Transportation expenses will be paid for collision and other than collision losses provided the insured has purchased these coverages.

For transportation expenses arising out of the total theft of the auto, there is a 48-hour waiting period before expenses will be paid. Coverage continues until the auto is returned to use or the company pays for its loss.

For other types of losses, there is a 24-hour waiting period. Coverage is limited to the period reasonably required to repair or replace the auto.

Exercise 9.E

1. Marla returns to a parking lot one evening to discover that her car is missing. The next morning, she rents a car to temporarily replace her stolen vehicle. She returns the car 10 days later when the insurance company pays for the stolen car. Her rental car expenses were $300 (10 days' rental at $30 per day). Her car is insured for other than collision coverage under the personal auto policy. How much of this bill will the insurance company pay? $______________
2. Rich rents a Ford Taurus on vacation. While en route from the airport, he makes a wrong turn onto a one-way street and hits another car head on. The car rental agency loses five days of rental fees while the Taurus undergoes repairs. Rich's pickup truck has collision coverage under the personal auto policy. Would his personal auto policy pay for the rental agency's loss of use of the Taurus? ( ) Yes ( ) No

Exercise answers can be found at the end of the Unit 9 answers and rationales.

9.8.3. Exclusions

Part D excludes losses:

- to an auto being used as a public or livery conveyance;
- due and confined to wear and tear, freezing, mechanical or electrical breakdown, or road damage to tires (does not apply when the damage results from the total theft of the auto);
- caused by war or nuclear perils;
- to electronic equipment that reproduces, receives, or transmits audio, visual, or data signals (does not apply to equipment that is permanently installed in the auto);
- to tapes, records, disks, and other media used with the electronic equipment described above;
- due to destruction or confiscation by government or civil authorities (does not apply to the interests of any loss payee in a covered auto);
- to a camper body, trailer, or motor home that is not listed in the declarations. This exclusion also applies to cooking, dining, plumbing, and refrigeration facilities used with these items. This exclusion does not apply to
  - — trailers and their facilities and equipment that are not owned by the insured, or
  - — trailers, camper bodies, and their facilities and equipment acquired during the policy period if coverage is requested within 14 days after acquisition;
- to a nonowned auto when used by the named insured or family member without a reasonable belief that he is entitled to do so;

- to awnings, cabanas, or equipment designed to create additional living space;
- to custom furnishings or equipment in a pickup or van (does not apply to caps, covers, or bedliners on pickup trucks);
- to radar or laser detection equipment;
- to nonowned autos being used by any person engaged in an auto business;
- to nonowned autos being used in any business (does not apply to the use of a private passenger auto or trailer by the named insured or family member);
- to any auto being used in a prearranged racing or speed contest; and
- to an auto rented by the named insured or a family member if the rental agency is prohibited from recovering from the insured or a family member under the provisions of state law or a rental agreement.

9.8.4. Other Provisions

Physical damage losses are reimbursed for actual cash value or the amount needed to repair or replace the property, whichever is less. If the insured and the insurance company do not agree on the amount that should be paid, the loss may be appraised. If the insurer pays for a loss in money, the payment will include the applicable sales tax for the damaged or stolen property.

The most the policy will pay for loss to a nonowned trailer is $1,500. Coverage for electronic equipment that is permanently installed in an area of the car that is not normally used by the manufacturer for this equipment is limited to $1,000.

Collision and other than collision coverage are usually written with a deductible that applies separately to each occurrence.

In the physical damage part of the personal auto policy, the other insurance condition is called **other sources of recovery**. It is essentially the same as the other insurance conditions in Part A and Part B, except that it states that the insurer will pay only its share of the loss if any other source of recovery, not just insurance, applies to the loss.

The **no benefit to bailee** condition states that a bailee cannot benefit from the insurance policy if a loss occurs to the car while it is in the bailee's possession. Examples of bailees are repair shop owners and employees of parking garages.

9.9. PARTS E AND F—CONDITIONS

Parts E and F of the personal auto policy list conditions that apply to the policy as a whole. **Part E—duties after an accident or loss** details the duties of insureds following a loss. They are similar to the duties required under other property and liability policies.

Note that under uninsured motorists coverage, the insured is required to notify the police promptly if a hit-and-run driver is involved. Under physical damage coverage, the insured must take reasonable steps after a loss to protect a covered auto and its equipment from further damage. Reasonable expenses required to do so will be reimbursed. In addition, the police must be notified if the car is stolen. Finally, the insurance company must be permitted to inspect or appraise the property before its repair or disposal following a loss.

Part F—general provisions establishes conditions for the coverage and describes the duties and obligations of the insured and insurer.

The policy applies only to accidents and losses that occur during the **policy period** shown in the declarations and within the **policy territory**. The coverage territory includes the United States, its territories and possessions, Puerto Rico, and Canada. Covered autos are also insured while being transported between territorial ports.

Legal action against the insurer may not be taken by an insured until all policy terms have been complied with. Under Part A, legal action may not be taken against the insurer until it agrees in writing that an insured has an obligation to pay, or unless the amount of such an obligation has been established by judgment after a trial. No person or organization may take action against the insurer to determine whether an insured is liable for a loss.

Policy terms may not be changed or waived except by written endorsement. Any premium adjustment due to a change will take effect as of the date of change. If the policy form is revised to provide broader coverage without additional charge, all policyholders will automatically and immediately benefit from the broader coverage on the date the change is implemented in their state of residence.

The insurer has **subrogation** rights under all coverages except physical damage coverage against a person using a covered auto with a reasonable belief of being entitled to do so.

The **termination** provision describes conditions for cancellation and nonrenewal. The insured may cancel the policy at any time by returning the policy or providing advance written notice of the desired cancellation date. The insurer must provide advance written notice of cancellation or nonrenewal. At least 10 days' notice must be given if the policy is being canceled for nonpayment of premium or if cancellation occurs during the first 60 days of an initial policy term (a new policy that has not been renewed or continued). At least 20 days' notice must be given in all other cases.

Once a policy has been in effect for 60 days, or after it has been renewed or continued, the insurer may only cancel for the following reasons:

- Nonpayment of premium
- Material misrepresentation in obtaining the policy
- A regular operator of the vehicle has had his driver's license suspended or revoked

Nonrenewal requires at least 20 days' advance notice.

9.10. UNDERINSURED MOTORISTS COVERAGE

Earlier, we stated that a vehicle with liability insurance in an amount equal to or greater than the state's financial responsibility limit is not considered an uninsured vehicle under uninsured motorists coverage. This financial responsibility limit, however, often falls far short of fully reimbursing the insured for a loss. **Underinsured motorists coverage** fills this gap. In general terms, underinsured motorists coverage pays the difference between the insured's actual damages for bodily injury and the amount of liability insurance carried by the driver who was at fault, up to the limits of the insured's underinsured motorists coverage.

Underinsured motorists coverage is subject to state law, being mandatory in some states and optional in others. It is added to the personal auto policy by endorsement.

Suppose the insured, who carries $100,000 of underinsured motorists coverage, is involved in an auto accident. The other driver, who was at fault, carries the state's required limit of $50,000 of auto liability insurance. The named insured's damages for bodily injury are $65,000. The insured's underinsured motorists coverage will pay $15,000 for this loss ($65,000 less the $50,000 limit of the at-fault driver's liability policy).

9.11. PERSONAL AUTO POLICY ENDORSEMENTS

Although the personal auto policy provides broad coverage for an individual's auto exposures, some insureds may have additional coverage needs that can be met by adding an endorsement to the policy.

Earlier, we stated that a personal auto policy can be issued to an individual or a married couple who live in the same household. When the **joint ownership coverage** endorsement is attached, the policy can be issued to two or more people who live in the same household or two or more people who are related in another way besides being spouses.

The **towing and labor costs** endorsement reimburses the insured for the cost of having a vehicle towed. The basic coverage limit is $25 for combined towing and labor costs each time a covered auto is disabled. Higher limits are usually available. Labor must be performed at the place of disablement: work performed after the vehicle is taken to a garage is not covered.

The **miscellaneous type vehicle** endorsement may be added to the personal auto policy to provide coverage for motorcycles, mopeds, and recreational vehicles such as motor homes and golf carts. (Some companies issue specialized policies to cover these vehicles rather than endorsing the standard policy.)

The **extended nonowned coverage—vehicles furnished or available for regular use** endorsement expands the extensive coverage automatically provided under the personal auto policy for the insured and the family while driving cars other than the insured's covered autos. It eliminates most exclusions applicable to autos that are furnished or available for the regular use of the named insured or family members.

Part D of the personal auto policy pays up to $20 per day to a maximum of $600 for transportation expenses when a covered auto is out of service due to a covered loss. The **optional limits transportation expenses coverage** endorsement allows the insured to select the daily and maximum limits of coverage provided for transportation and loss of use expenses for scheduled and nonowned autos. The limits selected are shown in the declarations.

The **excess electronic equipment** endorsement has two purposes. It allows the insured to:

- add coverage for tapes, records, and disks used with electronic media; and
- increase the limit of insurance for electronic equipment that is permanently installed in an area of the auto not normally used for installing this equipment.

The **named nonowner coverage** endorsement may be issued to someone who does not own an automobile but drives borrowed or rented autos. It might be used to provide coverage for an individual who drives a corporate-owned auto furnished for his use by an employer. Although the individual would have coverage while driving the company car under the company's auto policy, there would be no coverage for any other auto the insured might regularly or occasionally drive. This endorsement to the personal auto policy provides such coverage. If the insured acquires a private passenger auto, pickup, panel truck, or van during the policy period, the endorsement will automatically cover it for 14 days if no other insurance applies.

9.12. NO-FAULT INSURANCE

You've learned that an insured's auto liability insurance pays only for losses that the insured is legally liable for. But in many cases, this traditional fault system has created a backlog in the courts and excessive costs—all to determine who is at fault.

In an attempt to deal with these problems, some states have adopted **no-fault laws**. Under these laws, an insured driver is reimbursed by his own insurance company for medical expenses and loss of wages, regardless of who was at fault in the auto accident. Subrogation from the other company is not allowed.

Suppose Samuel's car crosses the center line and strikes Mohammed's car head on. If this accident occurred in a state with a pure no-fault law, then Mohammed's insurance company would reimburse him for the injuries he sustained in the accident and Mohammed would be prevented from suing the other driver who normally would have been declared at fault. With pure no-fault, there is no reimbursement for pain and suffering losses.

But at this time, a pure no-fault plan does not exist in any state. What does exist is a variety of modified no-fault plans that allow one party to sue another if the injuries are severe or if medical expenses exceed a specified amount. For example, one state's no-fault law provides that one party may sue another for pain and suffering if the medical expenses exceed $2,000 or if there has been death, disfigurement, dismemberment, or a fracture.

To this point, we have not mentioned the impact of no-fault insurance as it relates to physical damage and medical payments coverage. That's because both of these coverages are already no fault.

No-fault plans are not standardized. If your state has a no-fault law, you need to learn how it works.

9.13. ASSIGNED RISK PLANS

It has become increasingly difficult for some drivers to obtain automobile insurance. This is partly because most of these drivers are not average drivers. Because of poor driving records, most companies will not accept them because their loss experience is much greater than the average driver's. However, it is in society's best interest to have all drivers insured so they can live up to their financial responsibilities when accidents do occur.

Assigned risk plans, or **automobile insurance plans**, are voluntary agreements between insurance companies licensed in a particular state. These companies agree to share the poor risks among themselves. Because these risks are randomly assigned to the participating companies, they are called assigned risks. Each company accepts its share of assigned risk drivers according to the size of the individual insurance company.

In most cases, drivers in the assigned risk plan only have to be issued BI and PD liability coverage in the minimum amount required by state law. In some states, physical damage and medical payments coverage may also be issued.

There are several other methods besides assigned risk plans used to provide insurance for drivers whose records exclude them from obtaining coverage through normal channels. For instance, one state operates its own insurance company to handle such drivers. You should become familiar with the type of plan used in your state.

UNIT TEST

1. List the four coverages contained in the personal auto policy.
   A. ______________________________
   ____
   B. ______________________________
   ____
   C. ______________________________
   ____
   D. ______________________________
   ____

2. Ned loses control of his car and hits a parked car. Which coverage of Ned's personal auto policy will pay for the damage to the parked car?
   A. Part A—liability coverage
   B. Part D—coverage for damage to your auto

3. Nusrut was injured when she lost control of her car and hit an embankment. Which part of her personal auto policy will cover her medical expenses?
   A. Part A—liability coverage
   B. Part B—medical payments coverage

4. Ma'Chelle was injured when she was struck by a car while walking across the street. The driver, who cannot be identified, left the scene of the accident. Would this loss be covered under Ma'Chelle's personal auto policy?
   A. Yes, it would be covered under Part C—uninsured motorists coverage.
   B. No.
   C. Yes, it would be covered under Part A—liability coverage.

5. During a windstorm, a tree limb fell on Tom's car and broke the windshield. Which coverage of his personal auto policy will cover the damage to his car?
   A. Collision coverage of Part D—coverage for damage to your auto
   B. Other than collision coverage of Part D—coverage for damage to your auto

6. Ann's auto was damaged when it was struck by another car whose driver ran a stop sign. Which part of Ann's personal auto policy will cover the damage to her car?
   A. Part A—liability coverage
   B. Collision coverage of Part D—coverage for damage to your auto
   C. Other than collision coverage of Part D—coverage for damage to your auto

7. Which of the following would be eligible for a personal auto policy?
   A. McGuffin's Linen Service Company
   B. Nancy Hardwicke
   C. John and Suzette Oglesby, a married couple who live together

8. Which of the following autos owned by the named insured could be covered under the personal auto policy?
   A. Pickup truck used on the insured's farm
   B. Station wagon
   C. Chevrolet sedan
   D. Panel truck used to make deliveries for the insured's small manufacturing operation
   E. Small trailer designed to be pulled by a car

9. If the named insured acquires a new car that does not replace a previously insured auto, what must the insured do to obtain liability coverage for the auto under her personal auto policy?
   A. Nothing—coverage is automatic
   B. Submit a new policy application
   C. Notify the company of the new car within 14 days of the purchase
   D. Notify the company immediately; no coverage applies until the company is notified

10. Which of the following could be covered under the liability section of a named insured's personal auto policy?
    A. Injuries a named insured receives in a car accident
    B. Injuries to a person struck by the named insured's auto
    C. Injuries to a member of the named insured's family who was a passenger in the named insured's car when it overturned

11. Which of the following have liability coverage under Marty's personal auto policy?
    A. Marty's wife, who resides with him
    B. Marty's 16-year-old son, who lives at home
    C. A neighbor who borrows Marty's car with Marty's permission
    D. A group of teenagers who steal Marty's car from a parking lot and take it for a joy ride

12. Medical payments coverage provides protection for all of the following EXCEPT
    A. the insured
    B. the insured's family
    C. passengers in the insured's vehicle
    D. occupants of a vehicle that is struck by the insured's vehicle

13. Which of the following could be considered an uninsured motorist?
    A. Motorist that has less insurance than is required by the state's financial responsibility law
    B. Driver whose insurance company is insolvent
    C. Motorist who has enough insurance to meet the state's financial responsibility law but not enough to fully reimburse the insured for his injuries
    D. Unidentified hit-and-run driver
    E. All of the above

14. Which of the following losses could be paid under uninsured motorists coverage? (Assume there are no endorsements attached to the policy.)
    A. Tabb, the insured, drives the wrong way down a one-way street and collides with another car. Tabb is seriously injured. The driver of the other car has no liability insurance.
    B. Barb, the insured, is hit by a drunk driver who is uninsured. She is not injured, but her car is totaled.
    C. Leslie, the insured, is injured when she is struck by a car that runs a red light. The driver has no liability insurance.
    D. Bernard, the insured, is on his way to work when his vehicle is rear-ended by a car that was following too closely. Bernard suffers a back injury. The driver of the other car carries the minimum amount of insurance required in the state.

15. Which of the following losses would be paid under the other than collision coverage of the personal auto policy?
    A. A radiator develops a leak after the car has 100,000 miles on it.
    B. The insured's car is stolen and never recovered.
    C. The insured's auto skids on icy pavement and flips over.
    D. The insured's auto is damaged when it is hit by another car that runs a red light.

16. Under a no-fault plan
    A. a court of law must determine that an insured is legally liable for an auto loss before the insurer will pay for bodily injury or property damage caused by the insured
    B. an insurance company reimburses its insured for auto losses regardless of who was at fault for the loss

17. An assigned risk plan covers
    A. insureds who are uninsurable in the standard market
    B. insureds who do not own their own autos
    C. insurance companies for losses involving government-owned automobiles
    D. insureds who cannot afford standard rates

18. Which of the following are considered family members under the personal auto policy?
    A. The insured's ex-husband, who lives in another state
    B. The insured's mother-in-law, who resides with the insured
    C. The insured's foster child

19. Jessica's personal auto policy has Part A limits of 10/20/10, which meets her state's financial responsibility requirement. The insurance company has certified Jessica's policy as proof of future financial responsibility. If the state raised its limits to 25/50/10, Jessica's liability limits (would/would not) __________ be raised to comply with the law.

20. Lisa's personal auto policy has a $20,000 Part A limit, which meets her state's financial responsibility requirement. While driving in another state, she causes an accident that results in $25,000 of bodily injury and property damage. That state's financial responsibility law requires drivers to carry $25,000 in liability coverage. How much will Lisa's insurance company pay for her loss?
    A. $20,000
    B. $25,000

21. Jamal owns two cars. One is insured under a personal auto policy. The other, which is older and has very little resale value, is not insured. While driving the older car, Jamal hits a telephone pole and is injured. Could he collect for his injuries under medical payments coverage? ( ) Yes ( ) No Explain your answer.

    ____
    ____
    ____

22. Susan is critically injured by a hit-and-run driver while she is driving her car on a work-related errand. Her medical expenses, which total $50,000, are paid in full by her employer's workers' compensation policy. Her injuries are also covered under her personal auto policy's uninsured motorists coverage. Assuming she carried a $100,000 limit for uninsured motorists coverage, how much would Susan be paid under the personal auto policy?
    A. $0
    B. $50,000
    C. $100,000

23. Under Part D of the personal auto policy, a temporary substitute auto is considered a (nonowned/covered) ____________________ auto.

24. Which of the following losses would be excluded under Part D?
    A. When the insured fails to pay his taxes, the IRS confiscates his car and sells it.
    B. The insured's car is stolen on a cold winter day. The thieves run down the battery and then abandon the car in a field. Before the car is discovered, the battery freezes and is ruined.
    C. The insured's cell phone that she sometimes carries in her car is damaged in a collision.
    D. Custom carpeting that the named insured added to his van is damaged in a flood.

ANSWERS AND RATIONALES TO UNIT TEST

1. The personal auto policy has four coverages: Part A—liability coverage, Part B—medical payments coverage, Part C—uninsured motorists coverage, and Part D—coverage for damage to your auto.

2. **A.** Because Ned was responsible for this loss, it is covered under his liability coverage. Part D—coverage for damage to your auto covers physical damage losses to the insured's car.

3. **B.** Part B—medical payments coverage provides protection for the named insured, family members, and passengers in the named insured's auto for injuries received in an accident, regardless of who was at fault.

4. **A.** A car operated by a hit-and-run driver who cannot be identified is considered an uninsured motor vehicle.

5. **B.** Damage caused by a falling object and breakage of glass are considered other than collision losses under Part D of the personal auto policy.

6. **B.** This would be considered a collision loss under Part D of the personal auto policy because it involves the impact of an auto covered by the policy with another vehicle. Part A—liability coverage would not cover damage to the insured's own car.

7. **B and C.** Choice A is not correct because the auto is owned by a business.

8. **A, B, C, and E.** Choice D is not correct because the auto is used for business purposes.

9. **C.** The personal auto policy considers newly acquired cars to be covered autos. How coverage applies depends on several factors, such as the policy coverage, whether the car is a replacement auto, and when the insurer is notified about the new car.

10. **B.** Part A—liability coverage covers damages for bodily injury or property damage that an insured becomes legally responsible for because of an auto accident. Injuries to the named insured or the insured's family members would be covered under Part B—medical payments coverage.

11. **A, B, and C.** Under Part A, the named insured, the insured's spouse, or any family member is insured for the ownership, maintenance, or use of any auto or trailer. A family member is any person related to the named insured who is a resident of the insured's household. An individual who uses a vehicle without permission is not covered under Part A unless that person is a family member using a covered auto owned by the insured.

12. **D.** Medical payments coverage provides protection for the named insured, family members, and passengers in the named insured's auto for injuries received in an accident, regardless of who was at fault. It is not a form of liability coverage for injuries sustained by passengers in another auto involved in an accident with the insured.

13. **A, B, and D.** Choice C is an example of an underinsured motorist.

14. **C.** Choice A is not correct because the uninsured driver was not liable for the accident. Choice B is not correct because the loss does not involve bodily injury. Choice D is not correct because the driver who caused the accident is not an uninsured motorist.

15. **B.** Choice A is not correct because mechanical breakdown is excluded by the policy. Choices C and D are not correct because they are collision losses.

16. **B.** Under a no-fault law, an insured driver is reimbursed by his own insurance company for medical expenses and loss of wages arising out of an auto accident, regardless of who was at fault for the accident.

17. **A.** Assigned risk plans insure motorists with poor driving records who are unacceptable risks for most insurance companies.

18. **B and C.** The personal auto policy defines a family member as any person related to the named insured who is a resident of the insured's household. This includes those related by blood, marriage, or adoption and includes a ward or foster child.

19. **Would.** The financial responsibility provision under Part A—liability coverage states that the insurance company can certify the policy as proof of future financial responsibility. When it does, the policy will automatically reflect any changes in the state's financial responsibility laws.

20. **B.** The out-of-state coverage provision would amend the policy to reflect the state's higher financial responsibility limit.

21. **No.** Medical payments coverage does not cover injuries sustained while the insured is occupying an uninsured auto that is owned by the insured or furnished for his regular use.

22. **A.** The Part C limit of liability provision states that the insurer will not pay any part of a loss that could be covered under a workers' compensation law.

23. **Nonowned.** Under physical damage coverage, a temporary substitute auto is considered to be a nonowned auto instead of a covered auto.

24. **A, C, and D.** Damage due to freezing is normally excluded under Part D. However, an exception is made when the damage results from the total theft of the auto.

UNIT 9 EXERCISE ANSWERS

Exercise 9.A

The answers may be listed in any order.

1. The person involved must be an insured.
2. The insured must be legally insured.
3. Damage must involve BI or PD and result from an auto accident.

Exercise 9.B

1. All choices A, B, C, D, and E

Exercise 9.C

1. $2,000
2. $4,000

3 $5,000

Exercise 9.D

1. C
2. O
3. O
4. C
5. O
6. O

Exercise 9.E

1. $160 (8 days × $20) 48 hour waiting period
2. Yes—Rich was legally responsible for the nonowned auto

UNIT

10

Miscellaneous Personal Insurance

10.1. LEARNING OBJECTIVES

After completing Unit 10—Miscellaneous Personal Insurance, you will be able to do the following:

- Describe the federal government's role in flood insurance
- Explain the basic eligibility requirements for flood insurance
- Identify the maximum limits available for buildings and contents under the emergency and regular flood insurance programs
- Describe other important aspects of the flood insurance program, including the type of losses covered, property not covered, deductible requirements, and how losses are paid
- Explain how the Write Your Own program for flood insurance works
- Describe required application procedures for flood coverage
- Explain how an insured can obtain earthquake coverage for a home and its contents
- Explain how an insured can obtain coverage for a mobile home, and the basic coverages available for a mobile home
- Describe the purpose of personal inland marine insurance and why an individual might need this coverage
- Explain how a personal inland marine policy is structured
- Describe the property covered by the personal articles form and how losses are settled under this form
- Explain how newly acquired property is covered under the personal articles form
- Describe the purpose of the personal property and personal dffects forms
- Explain how the limited watercraft coverage in a homeowners policy creates a need for separate personal watercraft policies
- Compare and contrast the basic coverages provided under boatowners/watercraft package policies, outboard motor and boat insurance, and personal yacht policies
- Describe the purpose of the following provisions in personal yacht policies: collision clause, water skiing clause, layup warranty, and navigational limits
- Explain the two purposes of personal umbrella insurance
- Explain why it is important to maintain underlying liability insurance for an umbrella policy, and how failing to do so affects loss payments under the umbrella
- Describe how the self-insured retention applies in an umbrella policy
- Explain the role of FAIR plans in providing property insurance

10.2. INTRODUCTION

Although the personal lines policies we've studied so far insure a number of personal loss exposures, they also exclude or limit coverage for certain exposures. For example, the dwelling and homeowners policies both exclude losses caused by floods, and the homeowners policy provides only limited coverage for watercraft and certain types of valuable personal property. In this unit, we'll study some specialized personal insurance policies that were developed to cover these exposures.

10.3. FLOOD INSURANCE

10.3.1. Eligibility

Flood insurance coverage was generally unavailable until the federal government became involved. In 1968, Congress created the **National Flood Insurance Program (NFIP)** to make flood insurance available to eligible communities through federal subsidization. The program is managed by the Federal Insurance Administration (FIA), which is a branch of the Federal Emergency Management Agency (FEMA).

In most cases, communities voluntarily apply for coverage through the NFIP. However, the government may also determine that a community is flood prone and require it to comply with federal flood program standards.

Almost any building that is walled and roofed, is principally above ground, and is fixed to a permanent site is eligible for coverage under a flood policy. The policy may cover a building, its contents, or both.

10.3.2. Coverage

There are two types of flood insurance programs available: emergency and regular. The emergency program goes into effect when the community applies to the NFIP and remains in effect until the government finalizes the flood insurance rates for that community. Under the emergency program, insureds may purchase limited amounts of flood insurance for buildings and contents at subsidized rates. After the regular program goes into effect, additional coverage may be purchased. The following table shows the maximum limits of flood insurance available for single-family residential homes.

Maximum Limits for Flood Insurance Coverage

	Emergency Program	Regular Program
Building	$35,000	$250,000
Contents (Personal Property)	$10,000	$100,000

Both building and contents coverage have deductibles. The standard deductible for each coverage is $1,000 under the emergency program and $500 under the regular program. The deductible applies separately to each building loss and each contents loss on a per occurrence basis. Higher deductibles are available.

The NFIP's policies cover described property against all direct loss by or from flood at the described location. Indirect financial loss or loss of use is not covered. Property is also covered at another place, either above ground or outside of the special flood hazard area, for 45 days when removed by the insured to protect it from flood. Personal property must be in a building or otherwise protected from the elements while it is removed from the described location.

Flood generally refers to the following.

An overflow of inland or tidal waters

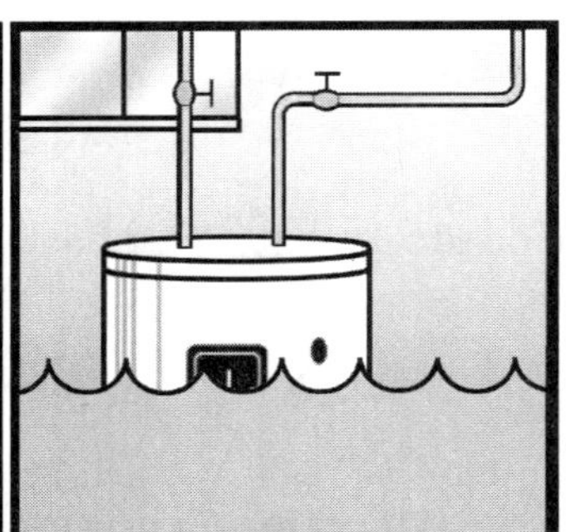

Unusual and rapid accumulation or runoff of surface water from any source, unless general flooding exists

Mudslides caused by accumulations of water on the ground or underground

Collapse of land as a result of excessive erosion due to flood

Sewer backup into a dwelling is not covered.

Exercise 10.A

1. When a nearby river floods and damages the insured's home, she is forced to live in a motel for a week while repairs are made. Are these additional living expenses covered under the NFIP policy?
( ) Yes ( ) No
Why or why not? ____
____

2. When a flood warning is issued for the insured's city, he loads as much personal property into his car as he can and heads to his sister's house in another state. He stores the belongings in his sister's garage until he is able to return home. Would this personal property be covered under the NFIP policy? ( ) Yes ( ) No
Why or why not? ____
____

Exercise answers can be found at the end of the Unit 10 answers and rationales.

10.3.3. Property Not Covered

Flood policies do not cover:

- accounts, bills, currency, deeds, evidences of debt, money, securities, bullion, and manuscripts;
- lawns, trees, shrubs, plants, growing crops, and livestock;
- aircraft, self-propelled vehicles, and motor vehicles;
- fences, retaining walls, outdoor swimming pools, bulkheads, wharves, piers, bridges, docks, and other open structures on or over water;
- underground structures and equipment, such as wells and septic tanks;
- newly constructed buildings that are in, on, or over water; or
- structures that are primarily containers, such as gas or liquid storage tanks (does not apply to silos, grain storage buildings, or their contents).

10.3.4. Other Provisions

Single-family dwellings (other than mobile homes) are the only buildings that may be insured on a replacement cost basis under a flood policy. Replacement cost coverage is automatically provided when the building is insured for at least 80% of its replacement value or for the maximum amount of insurance allowed by the flood program. All other losses are paid on an actual cash value basis.

Debris removal expenses are covered if the expenses plus the direct loss do not exceed the policy limit.

10.3.5. Write Your Own Program

NFIP policies may be sold by private insurance companies through the FIA's Write Your Own program. Under this system, the FIA sets rates, eligibility requirements, and coverage limitations. The participating insurer collects premiums and pays for losses out of these premiums. If the amount of losses exceeds the amount of premium collected, the FIA pays the difference. If the insurer collects more in premiums than it pays out in losses, the excess must be returned to the government.

10.3.6. Application Procedures

Applications for the NFIP must be completed in full and must be accompanied by payment in full of the gross policy premium for coverage to go into effect. Payment of partial deposit premiums is not permitted.

Coverage does not take effect until after a waiting period of 30 days following the date of application, with the following exceptions.

- There is no waiting period when the initial purchase of flood insurance is made in connection with a loan.
- When a community first enters the emergency or regular program, during the first 30 days policies take effect at 12:01 am on the day after the application and premium payment are mailed.
- When an existing flood policy is assigned to a property purchaser before the title is transferred, coverage takes effect on the date title is transferred.
- After a policy is in effect, requested changes in coverage take effect at 12:01 am on the fifth day after the date the request and premium payment are mailed.

During the waiting period, binders may not be issued to provide flood coverage.

10.4. EARTHQUAKE INSURANCE

The dwelling and homeowners policies do not cover the earthquake peril. Many insureds do not need this coverage; however, many companies are willing to offer earthquake insurance separately to insureds who want it, either as an endorsement to their dwelling or homeowners policy or as a separate policy.

Earthquake insurance generally covers damage to a structure, its contents, or both as the result of an earthquake. All earthquake shocks that occur within 72 hours constitute a single earthquake.

10.5. MOBILE HOME INSURANCE

Eligibility rules for the standard homeowners policy specifically exclude mobile homes. Although mobile homes share many characteristics of dwellings, they also have unique exposures: high susceptibility to wind and fire damage and exposure to loss by collision or upset while the unit is being transported. The dwelling policy can be used to provide property coverage for mobile homes, but only the basic form can be used and only mobile homes permanently placed on foundations are eligible. The HO-4 forms can be used to cover the contents of a mobile home but not the mobile home itself.

Many companies and rating organizations have developed a separate mobile home package policy. In addition, ISO has developed a mobile homeowners endorsement that can be attached to an HO-2 or HO-3 to modify coverage for mobile homeowners. Coverage is provided for:

The mobile home and all equipment and accessories originally built into the unit

Equipment, additions and appurtenant structures not originally included with the unit, such as shelters, cabanas, awnings, carports, and water pumps

Additional living expenses

Damage to the mobile home from collision or upset while it is in transit is available as an optional coverage. Up to 10% of the coverage on the mobile home can be extended to cover other structures.

Liability coverage is similar to Section II of the homeowners policy. Available discounts are also offered for alarm systems, fire prevention, sprinkler systems, and tie-downs.

10.6. PERSONAL INLAND MARINE INSURANCE

The homeowners policy can cover many of the risks to which an average household is exposed. But there are certain risks for which the insured will require additional coverage. The homeowners forms contain exclusions and limitations for certain types of property that are particularly susceptible to loss, difficult to value, or of extremely high value. In some cases, an individual who has no homeowners insurance may need coverage for personal property.

Broader coverage for personal property can be obtained through personal inland marine forms. Inland marine insurance originally developed from ocean marine insurance, which provides very broad coverage for property being transported over water. Inland marine insurance provides the same type of broad, flexible coverage for portable personal property. Because they provide coverage that moves with the property to protect it at various locations, inland marine forms are sometimes called *floaters*.

The three most commonly used personal inland marine forms are:

- personal articles;
- personal property; and
- personal effects.

To form a policy, the form must be attached to the **personal inland marine form**, a skeleton policy that contains basic conditions that apply to all personal inland marine coverages.

Personal inland marine floaters provide open peril coverage, although a few exclusions apply, such as:

- war;
- nuclear hazard;
- wear and tear;
- gradual deterioration;
- insects;
- vermin; and
- inherent vice (a condition or defect that exists within the property).

Like many other property policies, personal inland marine floaters contain a **pair or set** condition that states that the insurance company will not be liable for the entire value of a set when only a part of it is damaged. Inland marine floaters give the company two reimbursement options in this situation:

- Repair, replace, or restore the set
- Pay the insured the difference between the actual cash value of the full set and the actual cash value of the undamaged part

10.6.1. Personal Inland Marine Forms

10.6.1.1. Personal Articles Form

The **personal articles form** provides coverage for nine optional classes of personal property—the same nine categories covered under the homeowners scheduled personal property endorsement: jewelry, furs, cameras, musical instruments, silverware, golf equipment, fine arts, stamps, and coins. Generally, an appraisal is required when the personal articles form is issued to help develop an accurate description of covered property and to arrive at the value for which the property should be insured.

However, the personal articles form is not a valued policy. For purposes of loss settlement, the value is determined at the time of loss. In general, the company will reimburse the insured for the least of:

- actual cash value;
- cost to repair;
- cost to replace with a substantially identical item; or
- amount of insurance specified in the policy.

Another important feature of the personal articles form is that it provides automatic coverage for certain classes of newly acquired property when the property is in a category of property that is already insured. Automatic coverage is available for:

- jewelry;
- furs;
- cameras;
- musical instruments; and
- works of fine art.

For all property except fine art, coverage applies for 30 days; the property is covered for 25% of the applicable limit of insurance or $10,000, whichever is less. For fine art, coverage applies for 90 days and is provided for up to 25% of the applicable limit of insurance.

Coverage for newly acquired property ceases after the 30 or 90 days unless the insured notifies the insurance company about the property during this time.

Exercise 10.B

1. Millicent's jewelry collection is insured for $15,000 under a personal articles form. If she buys a new $5,000 tiara, how much coverage would it automatically have under the policy?
   A. None; newly acquired property is not covered.
   B. $3,750
   C. $5,000
   D. $10,000
2. For how long will the property have automatic coverage, assuming Millicent does not notify the insurance company about the property?
   A. 30 days
   B. 90 days
   C. Until the policy expiration date listed in the declarations

Exercise answers can be found at the end of the Unit 10 answers and rationales.

10.6.1.2. Personal Property Form

The **personal property form** provides open peril coverage on a blanket basis for most kinds of personal property found in a typical home. It is similar to the coverage provided for personal property under Coverage C in a homeowners policy endorsed to provide open peril coverage for personal property. The personal property floater is most often issued to condominium or apartment dwellers who cannot obtain this open peril coverage for personal property under the HO-4 or HO-6.

Property is divided into 13 basic categories (including an "all other personal property" category), and a separate limit of insurance is assigned to each category. Particularly valuable property can be scheduled separately.

10.6.1.3. Personal Effects Form

The **personal effects form** is designed for individuals and families who want to insure their personal belongings while traveling. Open peril coverage on an unscheduled basis is provided for the types of property usually carried by tourists, such as clothing, cameras, sports equipment, and souvenirs.

Specifically excluded are valuable papers, tickets, passports, currency, contact lenses, artificial limbs, and salesperson's samples. Property is excluded from coverage while on the insured's premises or while in storage. Insureds who travel frequently might carry this coverage on a permanent basis. Often, however, the coverage is taken out for a short term to cover a specific trip.

10.7. PERSONAL WATERCRAFT INSURANCE

10.7.1. Boatowners and Outboard Motor and Boat Policies

The homeowners policy provides only limited coverage for watercraft. Property coverage is subject to a special limit of $1,500, and coverage may be totally excluded for certain perils. Liability coverage is excluded for boats with motors of more than specified horsepower or boats of more than a specified length.

Insureds typically need more coverage for this exposure than that provided by the homeowners policy, particularly those who own larger or more powerful boats. This coverage can be provided through inland marine forms, ocean marine policies, or specialized policies.

Regardless of the type of coverage purchased, certain conditions and exclusions are almost always part of a personal watercraft policy. They stipulate that the craft must be used solely for private pleasure purposes and that coverage will not apply if the boat is hired out, chartered, or used to transport people or property for a fee. Coverage is usually excluded when the watercraft is being used in an official race or speed contest (unofficial events are not excluded).

Boatowners/watercraft package policies, developed by individual insurance companies, combine property, liability, and medical payments insurance on an open peril basis. They are used to insure boats under a specified length—such as 30 feet—or under a maximum dollar value, such as $25,000. Losses are usually paid on an actual cash value basis.

Outboard motor and boat insurance can be written to cover the physical damage exposure of boats. This insurance is commonly provided under open peril inland marine floaters. Outboard policies typically cover motors, motor boats, accessories, and trailers. Losses are usually paid on an actual cash value basis. Many provide a limited amount of coverage for collision damage to another vessel. When these policies are written, it is customary for the insured to have liability coverage under a homeowners policy or separate liability policy.

10.7.2. Personal Yacht Policies

Personal yacht policies are ocean marine forms that provide a package of property and liability coverages. Most inboard boats, sailboats with inboard auxiliary power, and large pleasure boats are insured under personal yacht policies. Smaller boats that are in good condition and have some value may also be covered under these policies.

When smaller vessels are insured on a personal yacht form, coverage is usually limited to property coverage on the hull, with or without coverage for a trailer. The liability exposure is usually covered under a homeowners or separate liability policy. Owners of larger vessels are more likely to purchase the complete package of yacht coverages, which includes:

- hull insurance (pays replacement cost for partial losses and on a valued basis for total losses);
- boat trailer insurance (pays on actual cash value basis);
- protection and indemnity (a form of bodily injury and property damage liability insurance);
- medical payments coverage; and
- federal longshore and harbor workers' compensation insurance (provides benefits for maritime workers).

Coverage is usually provided on an open peril basis.

Hull coverage on a yacht policy contains a collision clause, which covers the insured's liability for collision damage to other vessels. This is an additional amount of insurance, and it is equal to the amount of coverage written on the hull. Protection and indemnity (P&I) coverage for collision damage to another vessel begins after the insurance provided by the collision clause is exhausted.

A water skiing clause commonly excludes coverage for people skiing or otherwise being towed by the vessel until they are back on board or have landed safely.

The layup warranty applies when the yacht is located in a safe berth for storage and is not being used, such as during the winter months. It provides for a return of premium because of the reduced risk of loss.

Every yacht policy has navigational limits, a clause that defines an area in which the yacht is permitted to operate. Losses that occur outside these limits are not covered unless the insurer has granted permission for the insured to do so.

10.8. PERSONAL UMBRELLA INSURANCE

Some insureds need more extensive liability coverage than can be provided by personal lines policies. This need can be met through a **personal umbrella** policy, which has two important purposes:

- Provide additional liability insurance over and above the basic coverage provided by underlying liability insurance
- Cover some losses excluded by the underlying liability insurance

Coverage limits for a personal umbrella policy range from $1 million to $5 million.

10.8.1. Excess Liability Coverage

Let's examine how a personal umbrella provides excess liability coverage. Suppose an insured has the following liability coverage:

For a loss payable under the homeowners policy, the insured would have an additional $1 million of coverage after the $100,000 limit under the homeowners contract had been exhausted. On a $300,000 loss, the homeowners contract would pay $100,000 and the umbrella policy would pay $200,000. For a loss payable under the auto policy, this same personal umbrella policy would pay up to an additional $1 million, but only after the $100,000 limit of the underlying auto policy was used.

Because of the pivotal role played by the underlying policies, the insured must identify any underlying liability insurance to the insurer before an umbrella policy is issued. If the insured allows an underlying policy to lapse or be reduced in coverage, the insured is responsible for paying damages up to the underlying policy's limit before the umbrella policy takes over.

Suppose the insured has a homeowners policy with $200,000 in liability coverage and a $1 million umbrella policy. If the insured has a $100,000 liability loss payable under the homeowners policy, the homeowners policy will pay $100,000 and the umbrella will pay nothing because the loss is fully covered by the underlying insurance.

If this same insured has a $300,000 liability loss that would have been payable under the homeowners policy except the insured allowed the homeowners policy to lapse, the umbrella will pay $100,000. If the insured allows an underlying policy to lapse, he must pay damages up to the underlying policy's limit before the umbrella policy will pay.

10.8.2. Coverage for Excluded Losses

A personal umbrella may also cover losses that are excluded by the underlying policy. For this type of coverage, the insured must select a **retention limit**. Retention limits, which vary from $250 to $10,000, work like deductibles. They are sometimes referred to as *self-insured retentions* because they represent the amount of loss the insured must cover out of pocket. Self-insured retentions do not apply to losses that are covered under the underlying liability coverage.

Of course, even an umbrella policy has exclusions, such as intentional acts, liability covered under workers' compensation, and liability arising out of business pursuits. When a loss is excluded under both the underlying policy and the umbrella, no coverage is available.

10.9. FAIR PLANS

The extensive inner-city rioting that took place in the United States in the mid-1960s led to the withdrawal from those areas of much of the availability of property insurance. This made it very difficult for mortgage companies and lenders to operate in those areas and, thus, difficult for individuals to meet insurance requirements and remain in those areas. This compounded the downward trend of inner-city areas.

In response, the government acted in 1968 to provide riot insurance under a federal reinsurance plan. To obtain this insurance, states were required to develop plans through which inner-city property could be insured at reasonable rates. Such plans are called **Fair Access to Insurance Requirements**

(FAIR) plans. Although the original legislation under which the plans were created has been repealed, FAIR plans still exist in many states.

Although it is not a type of insurance policy, the FAIR plan addresses the issue of property insurance availability. Essentially, a FAIR plan makes insurance available to risks that were previously considered uninsurable because of environmental hazards. These are defined as conditions surrounding the property of an insured that might increase the chance of a loss but that are not within the control of the property owner or tenant occupying that property.

Under a FAIR plan, no application for insurance may be rejected simply because of environmental hazards that are beyond the insured's control, although the property may be subject to inspection before it is accepted in the plan.

UNIT TEST

1. What is the standard deductible under the regular program of the National Flood Insurance Program?
   A. $ 250
   B. $ 500
   C. $1,000

2. Which flood insurance coverage has a deductible?
   A. Building only
   B. Contents only
   C. Both building and contents

3. Who administers the NFIP?
   A. State insurance department
   B. Federal government
   C. Private insurance companies

4. What is the maximum amount of coverage that may be purchased under the emergency flood insurance program?
   A. $35,000 for buildings and $10,000 for contents
   B. $250,000 for buildings and $100,000 for contents
   C. $100,000 for buildings; contents coverage is not available under the emergency program
   D. $100,000 for contents; building coverage is not available under the emergency program

5. Coverage for earthquake losses is
   A. included in an unendorsed dwelling or homeowners policy
   B. provided by the federal government
   C. available by adding an endorsement to the dwelling or homeowners policy
   D. available by purchasing a separate policy

6. Mobile home policies
   A. include liability coverage that is similar to Section II of the homeowners policy
   B. may include collision coverage
   C. cover the mobile home unit but not its contents
   D. do not cover additional living expenses

7. Match the personal inland marine form listed in the left-hand column with its correct description in the right-hand column.

1) Personal articles form	____ A. Covers the insured's personal belongings while traveling
2) Personal property form	
3) Personal effects form	____ B. Provides open peril coverage for the same categories of property covered under the homeowners scheduled personal property endorsement
	____ C. Provides open peril coverage for the insured's personal property

8. Adequate coverage for large, powerful boats is provided by
   A. a homeowners policy
   B. a homeowners policy with the watercraft endorsement attached
   C. specialized personal watercraft policies, such as outboard motor and boat, boatowners, or personal yacht policies

9. A typical outboard motor and boat policy provides which of the following coverages?
   A. Liability
   B. Medical payments
   C. Physical damage
   D. All of the above

10. Assume the insured has the following liability insurance:

    A. Auto: $500,000
    B. Homeowners: $250,000
    C. Personal umbrella: $3 million with $2,000 retention limit

    A. The insured is liable for $600,000 in damages for a liability loss that would be covered under his auto policy.
       I. How much would the auto policy pay? $__________
       II. How much would the umbrella policy pay? $__________
       III. How much would the insured pay? $__________
    B. The insured is liable for a $10,000 loss that is excluded under the homeowners policy but not under the umbrella.
       I. How much would the homeowners policy pay? $__________
       II. How much would the umbrella policy pay? $__________
       III. How much would the insured pay? $__________
    C. The insured is liable for a $1 million liability loss stemming from an aviation accident. The insured has no underlying coverage for this type of loss, and the umbrella policy also excludes this type of loss.
       I. How much would the umbrella policy pay? $__________
       II. How much would the insured pay? $__________

11. Under the NFIP policy, losses to which of the following could be paid on a replacement cost basis?

    A. Personal property
    B. Single-family homes
    C. Mobile homes
    D. Both A and B

12. Unless an exception applies, coverage under an NFIP policy begins

    A. as soon as the gross policy premium is received
    B. 5 days after the application and premium payment are mailed
    C. 30 days after the date of application

13. Why would an insured need both homeowners insurance and personal inland marine insurance?
    ____
    ____
    ____

14. Why would an insured who does not have homeowners insurance purchase personal inland marine insurance? ____________________
    ____
    ____
    ____

15. The insured's stamp collection, which is insured under a personal articles floater for $5,000, is destroyed in a fire. The actual cash value of the stamps at the time of the loss is $4,000. How much will the insured receive for this loss, assuming that the stamps cannot be repaired or replaced?

    A. $4,000
    B. $5,000

16. Which of the following losses would be excluded under most yacht policies?

    A. Injury suffered by a passenger in a water skiing accident
    B. Collision damage to another boat for which the insured is liable
    C. Both A and B
    D. Neither A nor B

17. Under a FAIR plan, an insurance application (can/cannot) ______________ be rejected solely on the basis of environmental hazards that are beyond the insured's control.

ANSWERS AND RATIONALES TO UNIT TEST

1. **B.** The standard deductible is $500 under the regular program and $1,000 under the emergency program. Higher deductibles are available.

2. **C.** Both coverages require a deductible.

3. **B.** The federal government created the NFIP to make flood insurance available to eligible communities through federal subsidization. It is managed by the Federal Insurance Administration.

4. **A.** When the regular program goes into effect, additional coverage may be purchased: up to $250,000 for building coverage and up to $100,000 for contents.

5. **C and D**. The dwelling and homeowners policies do not cover the earthquake peril. This coverage is provided by adding an endorsement to the dwelling or homeowners policy or buying a separate policy.

6. **A and B**. Mobile home policies include coverage for contents and additional living expenses.

7. 3 A. 1 B. 2 C.
   The personal articles form provides scheduled coverage for nine optional classes of personal property: jewelry, furs, cameras, musical instruments, silverware, golf equipment, fine arts, stamp collections, and coin collections. The personal property form provides open peril coverage for personal property. The personal effects form covers an insured's personal belongings, such as baggage, while traveling.

8. **C.** The homeowners policy provides only limited coverage for watercraft. Property coverage is subject to a special limit of $1,500, and coverage may be totally excluded for certain perils. Liability coverage is excluded for boats with motors of more than specified horsepower or boats of more than a specified length. Insureds typically need more coverage for this exposure than that provided by the homeowners policy, particularly those who own larger or more powerful boats. This coverage can be provided through inland marine forms, ocean marine policies, or specialized policies.

9. **C.** This insurance is written to cover the physical damage exposure of boats. It is commonly provided under open peril inland marine floaters.

10. A. I. $500,000. Because the loss would be covered under the underlying auto policy, it would pay the full amount of the loss up to the policy limit.

II. $100,000. The umbrella policy would pay the amount of the loss not covered by the underlying auto policy.

III. $0. The retention limit only applies for losses that are excluded by the underlying policy.

B. I. $0. The loss is not covered under the underlying homeowners policy.

II. $8,000. This is the amount of the loss remaining after the retention limit is subtracted.

III. $2,000. Because the loss is excluded by the underlying policy, the insured would pay the $2,000 retention limit.

C. I. $0. There is no underlying policy that would cover this loss, and the loss is excluded under the umbrella.

II. $1 million. The insured would be responsible for the entire amount of the loss.

11. **B.** Single-family dwellings (other than mobile homes) are the only buildings that may be insured on a replacement cost basis under a flood policy. All other losses are paid on an actual cash value basis.

12. **C.** Unless an exception applies, coverage does not take effect until after a waiting period of 30 days following the date of application. Binders may not be issued during the waiting period to provide flood coverage.

13. The insured may own personal property that is not covered under the homeowners policy or is covered for a limited amount.

14. The insured may own personal property that he needs to insure.

15. **A.** Under a personal articles form, the value of the property is determined at the time of loss. In general, the company will reimburse the insured for the least of actual cash value, the cost to repair, the cost to replace with a substantially identical item, or the amount of insurance specified in the policy. In this example, the actual cash value is less than the policy limit.

16. **A.** The collision clause on a yacht policy covers the insured's liability for collision damage to other vehicles. The water skiing clause commonly excludes coverage for people skiing or otherwise being towed by the vessel until they are back on board or have landed safely.

17. Cannot. A FAIR plan makes insurance available to risks that may be considered uninsurable because of environmental hazards—conditions surrounding the property of an insured that might increase the chance of a loss but that are not within the control of the property owner or tenant. Under a FAIR plan, no application for insurance may be rejected simply because of environmental hazards beyond the insured's control.

UNIT 10 EXERCISE ANSWERS

Exercise 10.A

1. No. Loss of use is not covered.

2. Yes. Personal property is covered at another location when it is removed to protect it from flood. It must be in a building or otherwise protected from the elements while it is removed from the described location

Exercise 10.B

1. **B**

2. **A**

UNIT

11

The Commercial Package Policy

11.1. LEARNING OBJECTIVES

After completing Unit 11—The Commercial Package Policy, you will be able to do the following:

- Identify the advantages of purchasing a commercial package policy over buying separate monoline policies
- List the required components of a commercial package policy
- Define coverage part and interline endorsement
- Identify the information contained in the common policy declarations
- Explain why a first named insured is designated in a commercial package policy
- Describe the purpose of each of the common policy conditions

11.2. INTRODUCTION

Throughout the remainder of this course, we'll discuss insurance policies designed for businesses. Because businesses share many of the same exposures to risks as individuals do, you will find many similarities between personal and commercial forms. Businesses also have many unique exposures that require different policies or modifications to the coverages we've already discussed.

Just as families often choose the convenience of package policies such as the homeowners policy or personal auto policy, businesses often choose to purchase several different lines of coverage in a single policy.

One of the most important commercial packages is ISO's **commercial package policy (CPP)**. The CPP can be used to provide almost any commercial insurance the insured might need. Almost all commercial risks are eligible for coverage under the CPP.

Like all package policies, the CPP offers advantages to both the insured and the insurer. Repetitive information is eliminated, and the policy is easier to understand. Because of the economies an insurance company may realize when carrying several different lines of coverage for the same insured, the company is able to make package discounts to the insured, which provides further incentive for a package plan.

11.3. ELIGIBLE COVERAGES

The CPP can include almost any commercial coverage the insured might need, with the exception of ocean marine, workers' compensation, and aviation insurance. It can include:

- commercial property coverage;
- commercial general liability coverage;
- commercial auto coverage;

- commercial crime coverage;
- commercial inland marine coverage;
- boiler and machinery coverage;
- professional liability coverage;
- employment practices liability coverage;
- farm coverage;
- liquor liability coverage;
- pollution liability coverage; and
- capital assets program (output policy).

The following coverages are not eligible:

- Businessowners policy
- Risks eligible for the homeowners program
- Coverages excluded by state regulation

You'll learn more about each of these lines of insurance as you progress through the course.

Each line of insurance eligible for the CPP has its own **coverage part** consisting of a variety of mandatory and optional forms that are used to provide the coverage desired. The forms and endorsements available under each coverage part can be used to issue a policy covering a single line of insurance or combined to provide a commercial package policy. A commercial package policy consists of:

- common policy declarations;
- common policy conditions; and
- two or more coverage parts.

For instance, a commercial package policy might include both a commercial property coverage part and a commercial general liability coverage part.

A CPP might also contain **interline endorsements**—endorsements that may be used with more than one line of insurance. Some interline endorsements are mandatory, while others are optional.

Exercise 11.A

1. What two forms are always included in the CPP?

   A. ______________________________

   B. ______________________________

2. Which section of the CPP varies based on the lines of coverage included? ______________________

Exercise answers can be found at the end of the Unit 11 answers and rationales.

11.4. COMMON POLICY DECLARATIONS

Although we'll discuss the individual coverage parts of the CPP in subsequent units, in this unit we'll review the two general forms that are a part of every CPP and are also included in any monoline policy issued using CPP forms: the common policy declarations and the common policy conditions.

The **common policy declarations** contains information about who is insured, when he is insured, and for what lines. It includes:

- the name and mailing address of the named insured;
- the policy period, including the time and date coverage begins and ends;
- a description of the covered business;
- the coverage parts purchased and their premiums; and
- a list of forms applicable to all coverage parts.

11.5. COMMON POLICY CONDITIONS

The **common policy conditions** apply to all of the coverage parts contained in the CPP.

Under the common policy conditions, certain responsibilities and obligations are assigned to the **first named insured**—the person whose name is listed first in the declarations. It is necessary to specify the first named insured because the CPP may be issued to more than one named insured, such as business partners.

11.5.1. Cancellation

The **cancellation** condition sets forth the circumstances under which the policy may be canceled. The first named insured must cancel the policy in writing, and any premium refund due will be sent to the first named insured. This refund may be less than a pro rata refund to make up for the expense of issuing the contract.

If the insurance company cancels, it must mail a written notice to the last known address of the first named insured. Ten days' notice is required for cancellation for nonpayment of premium; 30 days' notice is required for cancellation for any other reason permitted by the policy. The premium is refunded to the first named insured on a pro rata basis.

Remember that although this is the cancellation condition that appears in the standard contract, some states may legislate unique cancellation rules for policies issued in those states.

Exercise 11.B

Under the standard contract, how many days' notice of cancellation is required when the policy is cancelled for

1. nonpayment of premium? _________ days
2. another reason permitted by the policy? _________ days

Exercise answers can be found at the end of the Unit 11 answers and rationales.

11.5.2. Changes, Premiums

Along with the right to cancel the policy, the first named insured has some other rights and responsibilities.

The **changes** condition states that only the first named insured is authorized to make changes in the terms of the policy with the consent of the insurance company. Terms can be amended or waived only by an endorsement issued by the insurer that is made a part of the policy.

The **premiums** condition states that the first named insured is responsible for the payment of all premiums and will receive any return premiums due.

11.5.3. Examination of Books and Records, Inspections and Surveys

The common policy conditions also give the insurance company the right to obtain information it needs to accurately rate the policy and provide the appropriate coverage.

The **examination of your books and records** condition states that the company may examine and audit the insured's books and records at any time during the policy period and for up to three years after the end of the policy period.

The **inspections and surveys** condition gives the company the right to make inspections or surveys of the insured business at any time. The company may choose to report on the conditions it finds and recommend changes. These inspections are related to insurability and premiums only and are not considered safety inspections. The insurer will not warrant that conditions are safe or healthful or comply with laws or regulations.

This condition does not apply to inspections performed to certify boilers, elevators, or pressure vessels under state or local laws.

11.5.4. Transfer of Rights and Duties

Finally, the **transfer of your rights and duties under this policy** condition states that insureds' rights and duties under the policy cannot be transferred without the written consent of the insurance company, except in the case of the death of a named insured. This is sometimes called the *assignment* clause, and it is a common feature of both personal and commercial lines policies.

If the named insured dies, his rights are transferred to the deceased's legal representative, but only while the representative is acting within the scope of the duties of the legal representative. Until a legal representative is appointed, anyone having proper temporary custody of the property will have the insured's rights and duties as they relate to the property.

UNIT TEST

1. Which of the following statements concerning the commercial package policy are CORRECT?
   A. Almost all commercial risks are eligible for coverage under the commercial package policy.
   B. The insured can choose a variety of eligible commercial coverages to tailor the package to fit his specific business insurance needs.
   C. It can only include property and liability coverage.
   D. A complete CPP includes common policy declarations, common policy conditions, and two or more coverage parts.
   E. It can include ocean marine and aviation insurance.

2. Which of the following coverages are eligible for the CPP?
   A. Businessowners policy
   B. Commercial property coverage
   C. Commercial crime coverage
   D. Workers' compensation coverage

3. Which of the following are contained in the common policy declarations?
   A. Conditions specifying the insured's duties following a loss
   B. The policy period
   C. The name and mailing address of the insured
   D. A list of perils insured against
   E. A description of the business being covered
   F. The insured's premium for each coverage part purchased

4. The common policy conditions apply to (all/selected) ________________ coverage parts included in a CPP.

5. The person whose name is listed first in the declarations and who is assigned certain responsibilities and obligations is the (first named/additional) ____________ insured.

6. Which of the following may cancel a commercial package policy?
   A. Any named insured
   B. Insurance company
   C. First named insured
   D. None of the above; once a policy is issued, it can never be canceled.

7. Under what circumstances does the insurance company allow the transfer of an insured's rights and duties under a CPP without the written permission of the insurance company?

   ____

   ____

   ____

ANSWERS AND RATIONALES TO UNIT TEST

1. **A, B, and D**. Other types of coverage besides property and liability may be included in a CPP. Ocean marine and aviation insurance are not eligible for the CPP.

2. **B and C**. Most commercial coverages are eligible for the CPP, with the exception of ocean marine, aviation, workers' compensation, and businessowners coverages.

3. **B, C, E, and F**. The common policy declarations contains information about who is insured, when he is insured, and for what lines. It includes the name and mailing address of the named insured, the policy period, a description of the covered business, the coverage parts purchased and their premiums, and a list of forms applicable to all coverage parts.

4. All. The common policy conditions are included in every CPP and every monoline policy issued using CPP forms. The common policy conditions apply to all of the coverage parts contained in the CPP.

5. First named. Under the common policy conditions, certain responsibilities and obligations are assigned to the first named insured—the person whose name is listed first in the declarations. It is necessary to specify the first named insured because the CPP may be issued to more than one named insured, such as business partners. The first named insured may cancel the policy and make changes to the policy with the consent of the insurance company. The first named insured is also responsible for paying all premiums and will receive any return premiums due.

6. **B and C**. Under the common policy conditions, certain responsibilities and obligations are assigned to the first named insured. One of these is cancellation of the policy. The insurance company may also cancel the policy under certain circumstances.

7. When the named insured dies, rights are transferred to the deceased's legal representative while acting within this scope.

UNIT 11 EXERCISE ANSWERS

Exercise 11.A

1. In any order: common policy conditions and common policy declarations
2. Coverages

Exercise 11.B

1. 10 days
2. 30 days

UNIT

12

The Businessowners Policy

12.1. LEARNING OBJECTIVES

After completing Unit 12—The Businessowners Policy, you will be able to do the following:

- Explain why an insured might choose a businessowners policy (BOP) instead of a commercial package policy
- Identify buildings and businesses that are eligible for a BOP
- Describe property covered under the businessowners property section's building and business personal property coverages
- Identify property that cannot be covered under the businessowners property section
- Describe the covered perils, additional coverages, coverage extensions, optional coverages, and exclusions in the BOP property section
- Describe the types of losses covered under the businessowners liability section
- Identify the supplementary payments included in the businessowners liability section
- Explain how the limits of insurance apply in the businessowners liability section
- Identify situations and perils that are excluded under the businessowners liability coverage
- Explain the purpose of the following endorsements: utility services—direct damage coverage, utility services—time element coverage, protective safeguards, and hired and nonowned auto liability
- Compare and contrast key features of the BOP and the CPP

12.2. INTRODUCTION

The **businessowners policy (BOP)** is a commercial package policy that provides property and liability insurance to certain types of small businesses. While the CPP allows the insured to choose the coverages to be included in the CPP, the businessowners policy prepackages a group of coverages desirable to small businesses.

Many companies have developed their own small businessowners-type package policy, but in this unit we'll focus on ISO's businessowners policy.

12.3. ELIGIBILITY, POLICY ORGANIZATION

12.3.1. Eligible Occupancies

The eligibility rules for the BOP are more stringent than those for the CPP, which can be used to cover almost any commercial risk. Specific rules of eligibility that deal with the size of buildings and the specific type of business involved determine what risks are eligible to be covered under a businessowners policy. The ideal BOP prospect is the small, well managed, one-location business with easily predicted coverage needs.

Only certain types of businesses are eligible under current ISO rules. They include certain wholesale, processing and service, restaurant, convenience store, and contracting risks. Eligible businesses are listed in the classification table of ISO's businessowners policy rules.

Unless otherwise noted, eligible risks may not exceed 25,000 square feet in total floor area or $3 million in annual gross sales at each location.

Occupancy	Comments
Apartments (Includes Residential Condominium Associations)	■ Any size building permitted ■ Permitted occupancies include offices, contractors and eligible wholesaler, mercantile, processing, and service occupancies ■ Building owner's business personal property in the building is covered
Condominium Commercial Unit-Owners	■ Business personal property of owners of condominium units used for eligible mercantile, wholesaler, processing, service, office, or contractor occupancies
Mercantile Risks	■ Only certain mercantile risks eligible ■ Both building and business personal property may be covered
Motels	■ Both building and business personal property may be covered ■ Building cannot exceed three stories; no limitation on floor area ■ Bars and cocktail lounges prohibited ■ Eligible restaurant occupancies permitted ■ Seasonal operations that are closed more than 30 consecutive days not eligible
Offices (Including Office Condominium Associations)	■ Building cannot exceed 6 stories in height or contain more than 100,000 square feet ■ Permitted occupancies include offices, contractors and eligible wholesaler, mercantile, processing, and service occupancies ■ Business personal property in offices that do not occupy more than 25,000 square feet in one building are eligible
Processing and Service Risks	■ Only certain processing and service risks eligible ■ No more than 25% of annual gross sales obtained from off-premises operations
Restaurants and Grills	■ Limited to 7,500 sq ft ■ Seating capacity of no more than 75 ■ Fast food restaurant is limited to max seating of 150 as long as there is no table service
Self-Storage Facilities	■ May not exceed two stories in height; no limitation on floor area ■ Facilities that permit cold storage or storage of industrial materials, pollutants, chemicals, or waste not eligible ■ Both building and business personal property may be covered
Wholesale Risks	■ Both building and business personal property may be covered ■ Only certain wholesale risks eligible ■ No more than 25% of annual gross sales derived from retail operations ■ No more than 25% of total floor area open to the public ■ Operations of manufacturers representatives or contractors not eligible

12.3.2. Ineligible Risks

Some classes of risks and certain property are specifically not eligible for the businessowners policy:

Ineligible Risk Categories

- Auto repair or service stations, unless incidental to another otherwise eligible class
- Auto, motor home, mobile home, and motorcycle dealers, unless incidental to another otherwise eligible class
- Banks, building and loan associations; savings and loan associations; credit unions; stockbrokers; and similar financial institutions
- Bars and pubs
- Buildings occupied wholly or partially for manufacturing
- Condominium associations other than office or residential condominiums
- Household personal property
- Insureds whose business operations involve one or more locations that are used for manufacturing
- One- or two-family dwellings, unless they are garden apartments where multiple units are grouped within a single area and are under common ownership, management and control
- Parking lots or garages, unless incidental to an otherwise eligible class
- Places of amusement

12.3.3. Organization

The businessowners policy includes the required property and liability coverages and policy conditions in one form, with certain required information about the insured in a separate declarations.

The policy declarations will show the policy number, name of insurer, name of producer, name and address of the named insured, and the policy period. Spaces are provided for a description of the business, the form of business, locations of described premises, and name and address of any mortgage holder. Limits of insurance will be shown for buildings and for business personal property. Any optional coverages the insured has selected will be indicated on the declarations, along with the limit of insurance for those coverages.

12.4. PROPERTY COVERAGE

The property coverage of the BOP includes two major coverages:

- Coverage A—buildings
- Coverage B—business personal property

A limit of insurance must be shown in the declarations for each type of property covered. For example, an insured who is a tenant would not require the building coverage.

12.4.1. Building Coverage

Building coverage applies to more than just the buildings and structures at the premises structure itself. Other items covered under the building coverage include:

- completed additions;
- permanently installed machinery and equipment;
- fixtures, including outdoor fixtures, such as lawnmowers, garden hoses, and snow removal equipment;
- personal property used to maintain or service buildings, structures, or the premises, including portable fire extinguishing equipment, outdoor furniture, floor coverings, and appliances used for refrigerating, ventilating, cooking, dishwashing, or laundering; and
- personal property furnished by the insured in apartments, rooms, or common areas that are rented to others.

The following items are also covered under the building coverage if no other insurance applies:

- Additions under construction
- Alterations and repairs to the buildings or structures
- Materials, equipment, supplies, and temporary structures that are on or within 100 feet of the premises and being used for additions, alterations, or repairs

12.4.2. Business Personal Property Coverage

There are five different classes of business personal property covered:

- Property owned and used by the insured in the business
- Property of others in the insured's care, custody, or control
- Tenants' improvements and betterments
- Leased personal property that the insured has a contractual responsibility to insure
- Exterior building glass

Property is covered when it is located at the described premises and in or on a building, in a vehicle, or in the open within 100 feet of the premises.

Tenants' improvements and betterments are fixtures, alterations, installations, or additions that tenants make to rented buildings in which they operate their businesses. For coverage to apply, these items must be permanently attached to the building, acquired or made at the insured's expense, and unable to be legally removed. Examples are when tenants have new carpeting or light fixtures installed.

Examples of leased personal property the insured has a contractual responsibility to insure include photocopiers and computer equipment leased under contracts that require the lessees to insure the leased property.

Exterior building glass is covered as business personal property for insureds who are tenants and do not have building coverage. The glass must be owned by the insured or in the insured's care, custody, or control.

12.4.3. Property Not Covered

The following property is not covered under the BOP:

Property Not Covered
■ Aircraft
■ Motor vehicles and other vehicles subject to motor vehicle registration
■ Land (including land on which the property is located), water, growing crops, and lawns
■ Contraband and property being illegally traded or transported
■ Outdoor fences, trees, shrubs, and plants*
■ Outdoor radio or television antennas, including satellite dishes, and their lead-in wiring, masts, or towers*
■ Money and securities*
■ Watercraft while afloat, including motors, equipment, and accessories
■ Outdoor signs not attached to buildings*
■ Accounts, bills, food stamps, other evidences of debt, accounts receivable, and valuable papers and records
■ Computers that are permanently installed or designed to be permanently installed in an aircraft, watercraft, motor truck, or other vehicle subject to motor vehicle registration
■ Electronic data*

*Except as covered under an optional coverage or coverage extension

12.4.4. Covered Causes of Loss

Property coverage in the BOP is provided on an **open peril** basis. This means that the policy covers any causes of loss that are not specifically excluded or limited. An endorsement can be added to the policy so that coverage is provided on a **named peril** basis, meaning that the policy covers only the causes of loss specifically named in the endorsement.

12.4.4.1. Limitations

The following limitations in the BOP exclude certain types of losses or cap the amount of particular coverages.

Damage to steam equipment such as boilers, pipes, engines, or turbines is not covered if the damage results from a condition that originates inside the equipment. There is coverage, however, for damage that results from explosions of gases or fuel inside the furnace of a fired vessel or within the flues or passages through which gases pass.

Damage to hot water boilers or other water heating equipment is not covered if the damage results from a condition that originates inside the equipment. There is coverage, however, for explosions.

There is no coverage for property that is missing for which no physical evidence exists to show what happened to it, such as shortage disclosed from an inventory. This limitation does not apply to money and securities when the money and securities optional coverage is added to the policy.

There is no coverage for property that has been transferred to someone or someplace outside the described premises and under unauthorized instructions.

The interior of a building is covered against damage from rain, snow, sand, sleet, ice, or dust only if the roof or walls are first damaged by a covered cause of loss that allows these elements to enter, or if the loss or damage is caused by or results from thawing of snow, sleet, or ice on the building.

Loss or damage to fragile articles that are broken is not covered unless the damage is caused by building glass breakage or the specified causes of loss named in the policy. Fragile articles include glassware, marbles, porcelains, statuary, and chinaware. The specified causes of loss are:

- fire;
- lightning;
- explosion;
- windstorm or hail;
- smoke;
- aircraft or vehicles;
- riot or civil commotion;
- vandalism;
- leakage from fire extinguishing equipment;
- sinkhole collapse;
- volcanic action;
- falling objects;
- weight of snow, ice, or sleet; and
- water damage.

This restriction does not apply to glass that is part of a building, containers of property held for sale, or photographic or scientific instrument lenses.

For the following types of property, the amount paid for **theft** losses is limited to $2,500:

- Furs, fur garments, and garments trimmed with fur
- Jewelry, watches, watch movements, jewels, pearls, precious and semi-precious stones, bullion, gold, silver, platinum, and other precious alloys or metals; does not apply to jewelry and watches worth $100 or less per item
- Patterns, dies, molds, and forms

12.4.4.2. Exclusions

The following are excluded in the BOP:

- Ordinance or law
- Earth movement (does not include a fire or explosion resulting from earth movement)
- Government action
- Nuclear hazard
- Failure of power or other utility services occurring away from the insured's premises (does not apply to loss or damage to computers and electronic media and records)
- War and military action
- Water, including flood, sewer backup, mudslides, or seepage of ground water (does not include fire, explosion, or sprinkler leakage resulting from water)
- Failure of computers to recognize a particular date or time, such as the year 2000
- Mold, wet rot, dry rot, and bacteria, except as provided as an additional coverage (does not apply when caused by fire or lightning)
- Artificially generated electrical current (loss or damage to computers from artificially generated electrical current is covered if the loss results from an occurrence that took place within 100 feet of the described premises, such as an interruption of electric power supply, power surge, blackout, or brownout)
- Delay, loss of use, or loss of market
- Smoke, vapor, or gas from agricultural smudging or industrial operations
- Explosion of any steam boilers, pipes, engines, or turbines
- Water, liquids, powder, or molten material that leaks or flows from any equipment other than fire protective systems as the result of freezing unless the insured has done his best to maintain heat in the building or has drained the equipment and shut off the supply

- Dishonest or criminal acts of the insured or his employees
- Voluntarily parting with property if induced to do so by fraud or a trick
- Rain, snow, ice, or sleet damage to personal property left in the open
- Any type of collapse other than as provided as an additional coverage under the policy
- Pollution (unless the release, discharge, or dispersal is caused by a specified cause of loss)
- Failure of an insured to use all reasonable means to save and preserve property from further damage at and after the loss
- Errors or omissions in programming, processing, or storing data or in any computer operations, or in processing or copying valuable papers and records
- Errors or deficiency in design, installation, testing, maintenance, modification, or repair of the insured's computer system, including electronic media and records
- Electrical or magnetic injury, disturbance, or erasure of electronic media and records, except as provided as a coverage extension under the policy
- Weather conditions that contribute to causing a loss
- Loss resulting from acts or decisions, or the failure to act or decide
- Faulty planning, development, design, specifications, workmanship, or repair
- Rust, corrosion, decay, deterioration, and hidden or latent defects
- Smog
- Settling, cracking, shrinking, or expansion
- Damage caused by insects, birds, rodents, or other animals
- Wear and tear
- Continuous or repeated seepage or leakage of water that occurs over 14 or more days

Exercise 12.A

1. Which of the following losses would be excluded under the businessowners policy?
   A. Loss caused when underground water seeps through the foundation of an insured's building
   B. Additional expense incurred when the insured's damaged building is required by a city ordinance to be completely torn down and rebuilt rather than repaired
   C. Loss caused by a power failure that occurs on the insured's premises
   D. Damage that occurs during a riot related to a civil war
   E. Loss caused when an insured's equipment breaks down and prevents the insured from earning income

Exercise answers can be found at the end of the Unit 12 answers and rationales.

12.4.5. Additional Coverages

Additional coverages provide coverage in specific situations. These coverages may have a separate limit of insurance or require that certain conditions be met for coverage to apply.

12.4.5.1. Debris Removal

The debris removal additional coverage pays for expenses to remove debris of covered property caused by a covered cause of loss during the policy period. Expenses will be paid only if the insured reports them to the insurance company in writing within 180 days of the date of loss. Costs to extract pollutants or remedy polluted land or water are not covered.

The most the insurer will pay for the total of the direct physical loss or damage and the debris removal expense is the limit of insurance applicable to the property that was damaged. Subject to this limit, the amount reimbursed for debris removal expenses is 25% of the amount paid for the direct physical loss plus the deductible applicable to that loss.

An additional $10,000 of insurance for each location in any one occurrence is available for debris removal under the following circumstances:

- The direct physical loss and the debris removal expense together exhaust the limit of insurance
- The maximum amount collectible for debris removal (25% of the loss plus the deductible) is not enough to cover the debris removal expense

If either of these conditions applies, the total payment for the direct physical loss and the debris removal expense may be up to—but cannot exceed—the policy limit plus $10,000.

12.4.5.2. Collapse

The collapse additional coverage applies only when very specific conditions are met.

The form defines *collapse* as an abrupt falling down or caving in of the building or part of the building that results in the building being unusable. This definition does not include a building that is in danger of collapsing or a building or part of a building that is still standing but has separated from another part of the structure or shows signs of instability such as bulging, cracking, leaning, or settling.

Collapse of a building or part of a building is covered only when it is caused by one of the specified causes of loss, building glass breakage, hidden decay, hidden insect or vermin damage, weight of people or personal property, weight of rain that collects on a roof, or use of defective materials or methods in construction, remodeling, or renovation if the collapse occurs during the course of the construction, remodeling, or renovation.

Collapse that results from hidden decay or hidden insect or vermin damage is not covered if the insured knew about the damage before the collapse occurred. If collapse occurs after construction, remodeling, or renovation is completed and is caused by a peril listed above, the loss or damage is covered even if the use of defective materials or methods contributed to the collapse.

Certain types of outdoor properties, even if they are otherwise covered under the policy, are covered for collapse only when they are damaged directly by a collapsed building. This includes awnings, gutters and downspouts, yard fixtures, outdoor swimming pools, piers, wharves and docks, beach or diving platforms or appurtenances, retaining walls, and walks, roadways, and other paved surfaces.

Under certain conditions, loss or damage that occurs when personal property falls down or caves in is covered even when there is no building collapse.

- The property must be inside a building.
- The collapse must result from one of the causes of loss listed above.
- The property that collapses must not be one of the items of outdoor property listed above.

The collapse additional coverage is subject to the limits of insurance. It does not provide an additional amount of insurance.

12.4.5.3. Business Income

Under the business income additional coverage, the insurance company will pay for loss of business income that occurs when the insured's business operations have to be suspended after a loss and income cannot be generated.

For coverage to apply, there must be direct physical loss or damage to property at the described premises. This includes personal property in a vehicle or in the open within 100 feet of the premises.

The loss must be caused by or result from a covered cause of loss. Payment is for loss during the period the property is being restored that occurs within 12 consecutive months after the date of the direct physical damage.

Also included in this additional coverage is extended business income coverage. This coverage extends the period for which business income loss will be paid under certain circumstances. The extended business income coverage begins after the insured's operations are resumed and continues until the insured is restored to the previous earning condition or for 30 consecutive days (or the number of days listed in the declarations) after operations could have been resumed.

This additional coverage is not subject to the limits of insurance.

12.4.5.4. Extra Expense

The extra expense additional coverage allows reimbursement for additional costs an insured incurs to avoid or minimize suspending business operations after a covered loss.

If an insured spends more money than would otherwise be required in order to reduce a loss, the insurance company will reimburse specified expenses during the period of restoration.

The insurance company will pay for extra expense that occurs within 12 consecutive months after the date of the direct physical loss or damage. This coverage is in addition to the insured's limits of insurance.

12.4.5.5. Increased Cost of Construction

The increased cost of construction additional coverage applies only to buildings insured on a replacement cost basis. If a covered cause of loss damages a covered building, the company will pay the additional costs required to comply with an ordinance or law in repairing the damage or replacing damaged parts. This additional coverage has a limit of $10,000.

If the building is repaired or replaced at the same premises or rebuilt at the insured's option at another premises, the most the company will pay is the increased cost of construction at the same premises. If the ordinance or law requires relocation, the most the company will pay is the increased cost of construction at the new premises.

The provisions of the ordinance or law exclusion do not apply to this additional coverage to the extent they conflict with this coverage.

12.4.5.6. Civil Authority

The civil authority additional coverage is available for losses that result from actions of civil authorities. Covered is business income an insured loses when a civil authority denies the insured access to the described premises because property not at the described premises was damaged by a covered cause of loss.

Coverage applies for a specified period. Coverage for business income begins 72 hours after the action by the civil authority and is effective for up to three consecutive weeks. Coverage for extra expenses begins immediately after the action by the civil authority and ends either three consecutive weeks after that action or when the business income coverage ends, whichever is later.

12.4.5.7. Forgery and Alteration

The forgery and alteration additional coverage applies to an insured's loss that results directly from someone forging or altering checks, drafts, and similar items made or drawn by or on the insured or the insured's agent.

If the insured is sued for refusing to pay any of these items because it has been forged or altered, and if the insured has the insurance company's written promise to defend the insured, the company will pay for any reasonable legal expenses the insured incurs in that defense. However, the most that will be paid for a loss, including legal expenses, is $2,500, unless a higher limit is shown in the declarations.

12.4.5.8. Business Income from Dependent Properties

This additional coverage covers loss of business income the insured sustains due to physical loss or damage at a dependent property from a covered cause of loss. A dependent property is a business that delivers materials or services to the insured, accepts the insured's products or services, manufactures products for delivery to the insured's customers, or attracts customers to the insured's business.

Coverage is limited to $5,000 unless a higher limit is shown in the declarations. Coverage begins 72 hours after the loss at the dependent property and continues until the date the damage should be repaired, rebuilt, or replaced with reasonable speed and similar quality. Coverage does not apply if the only property damaged at the dependent property is electronic data. The amount paid will be reduced to the extent the insured can resume operations, in whole or in part, by using another source of materials or outlet for its products.

12.4.5.9. Electronic Data

The electronic data additional coverage pays to replace or restore electronic data that have been destroyed or corrupted by a covered cause of loss. Electronic data means information, facts, or computer programs stored, created, used on, or transmitted to or from computer software, CD-ROMs, hard or floppy disks, or any other repositories of computer software used with electronically controlled equipment. It does not include the insured's stock of prepackaged software.

Also covered are viruses or other instructions introduced to a computer system or network designed to damage or destroy any part of its system or disrupt its normal operation. There is no coverage for loss or damage caused by or resulting from manipulation of a computer system by an employee or an entity retained by the insured to inspect, design, install, maintain, repair, or replace the system.

To the extent that electronic data are not replaced or restored, the loss will be valued at the cost of replacement of the media on which the data were stored with blank media that is substantially identical. The most that will be paid under this additional coverage is $10,000 for all loss or damage sustained in any one policy year, regardless of the number of losses or the number of premises, locations, or computer systems involved. If payment for one loss does not exhaust this limit, the balance is available for subsequent loss or damage sustained in, but not after, that policy year. An occurrence that begins in one policy year and continues or results in additional loss in a subsequent policy year will be treated as if all loss occurred in the year in which the occurrence began.

12.4.5.10. Limited Coverage for Fungi, Wet Rot, Dry Rot, and Bacteria

This additional coverage provides limited coverage for fungus (i.e., mold), wet rot, dry rot, or bacteria that result from a specified cause of loss other than fire or lightning. (Coverage for mold-related losses arising out of fire or lightning is provided elsewhere in the form.) The loss must occur during the policy period, and all reasonable means must have been used to save and preserve the property from further damage at the time of and after that occurrence. The insurer will pay for:

- direct physical loss or damage to covered property caused by mold, including the cost to remove it;
- costs to tear out and replace any part of the building or other property if needed to gain access to the mold; and
- cost of testing performed after removal, repair, replacement, or restoration of the damaged property is completed, provided there is a reason to believe that mold is present.

Coverage is limited to $15,000 for all loss or damage arising out of all occurrences that take place in a 12-month period, regardless of the number of claims. The 12-month period starts with the beginning of the present annual policy period. If a particular loss results in mold, the insurer will not pay more than a total of $15,000 even if it continues to be present or active or recurs in a later policy period. This additional coverage does not increase the applicable limit of insurance on covered property.

12.4.5.11. Other Additional Coverages

The money orders and counterfeit money additional coverage provides coverage for loss that results when an insured accepts these items in good faith and in exchange for merchandise, money, or services as part of normal business transactions. A $1,000 limit applies to this additional coverage.

The pollutant clean up and removal additional coverage does what the debris removal additional coverage does not do: it provides limited coverage for costs to extract pollutants from land or water at the insured's premises as a result of a covered cause of loss. Coverage applies only under specified circumstances; there is a $10,000 limit for each separate 12-month policy period. The insured must report expenses within 180 days after the date of loss.

The preservation of property additional coverage covers direct physical loss or damage from any cause of loss if the property has been removed to another location to preserve it from damage by a covered peril. Coverage applies while the property is being moved or while it is temporarily stored at another location, but only for 30 days after the property is first moved.

The fire department service charges additional coverage covers charges that might be levied because such liability was assumed by the insured under a contract or agreement before the loss or because these charges are required by local ordinance. Coverage applies when a fire department is called to save or protect covered property from a covered cause of loss. The standard limit for this coverage is $2,500, unless a different limit is shown in the declarations.

The water or other liquid, powder, or molten materials additional coverage covers damage to a building that indirectly results from the escape of these items. If the damage is otherwise covered, this additional coverage pays for necessary costs to tear out and replace any part of the building to repair damage to the system from which the material escaped. The policy will also cover repair or replacement of damaged parts of fire extinguishing equipment if the damage results in discharge of any substance from an automatic fire protection system or is directly caused by freezing. The cost to repair the defect that caused the loss or damage is not covered.

The glass expenses additional coverage covers expenses incurred to put up temporary plates or board up openings if repair or replacement of damaged glass is delayed. It also covers expenses required to remove or replace obstructions (other than window displays) when repairing or replacing glass that is part of a building.

The interruption of computer operations additional coverage extends the business income and extra expense coverages to include a suspension of operations caused by an interruption in computer operations caused by destruction or corruption of electronic data. The most that will be paid under this additional coverage is $10,000 for all loss or damage sustained in any one policy year, regardless of the number of losses or the number of premises, locations, or computer systems involved. If payment for one loss does not exhaust this limit, the balance is available for subsequent loss or damage sustained in, but not after, that policy year.

Finally, the fire extinguisher systems recharge expense additional coverage pays to recharge or replace the insured's fire extinguishers and fire extinguishing systems if they are discharged on or within 100 feet of the premises. It also covers loss or damage to covered property caused by the accidental discharge of chemicals from a fire extinguisher or fire extinguishing system. This coverage has a per occurrence limit of $5,000.

12.4.6. Coverage Extensions

Coverage extensions permit an insured to extend the insurance for other specified purposes. Unless otherwise provided, coverage extensions apply to property located in or on the building covered under the policy or to property located in the open or in a vehicle within 100 feet of the premises.

Under the newly acquired or constructed property coverage extension, if the insured acquires a building at another location or builds a new building on the described premises, the newly acquired or constructed buildings are covered under the policy's building coverage for up to $250,000 at each location. Business personal property coverage can be extended to property, including newly acquired property, at newly acquired or constructed buildings, or to newly acquired property at the described premises. Coverage for newly acquired business personal property is $100,000 at each location. Coverage applies for 30 days after the new premises or property is acquired or construction has begun on the new premises, until the policy expires or until the insured reports values to the insurance company, whichever occurs first.

Coverage may be extended to apply to the insured's covered property, other than money and securities, valuable papers and records, or accounts receivable, while it is in the course of transit or at a premises the insured does not own, lease, or operate. The most the policy will pay for loss or damage under this extension is $10,000.

Coverage may be extended to apply to outdoor property, including outdoor fences, signs not attached to buildings, trees, shrubs and plants, and radio and television antennas, including satellite dishes. Debris removal expense is also covered. Coverage applies only for loss by fire, explosion, aircraft, lightning, and riot or civil commotion. Coverage is limited to $2,500 and not more than $500 for any one tree, shrub, or plant.

Business personal property coverage may be extended to include personal effects owned by the insured and the insured's officers, partners, or employees. The most the company will pay under this extension is $2,500 at each insured premises.

If the insured has business personal property coverage, the valuable papers and records coverage extension can be used to cover the costs to research, replace, or restore information on lost or damaged valuable papers and electronic or magnetic records for which duplicates do not exist. It does not apply to property held as samples or for delivery after sale or to property in storage away from the premises shown in the declarations. There is a maximum limit of $10,000 at each described premises, unless a higher limit is shown in the declarations. For valuable papers and records not at the described premises, the limit is $5,000.

If the insured has business personal property coverage, the accounts receivable coverage extension may be used to cover amounts due from customers that the insured is unable to collect because of damage from a covered loss, interest charges on loans required to offset those amounts, excess collection expenses incurred because of the loss, and other reasonable expenses required to reestablish accounts receivable records. Limits are the same as those for the valuable papers and records coverage extension: $10,000 at the described premises and $5,000 for accounts receivable not at the described premises.

Exercise 12.B

1. During a storm, lightning destroyed a tree worth $1,000. Would the outdoor property coverage extension reimburse the insured for the entire loss? ( ) Yes ( ) No
2. A computer the insured sent out for repairs sustained $3,000 in damage while being transported in a service truck. Would the business personal property off premises coverage extension reimburse the insured for the entire loss? ( ) Yes ( ) No

Exercise answers can be found at the end of the Unit 12 answers and rationales.

12.4.7. Optional Coverages

A number of optional coverages are included in the businessowners policy, but they apply only if so designated in the declarations. Optional coverages usually require an additional premium.

12.4.7.1. Employee Dishonesty

Loss to business personal property and money and securities that results from dishonest acts of employees is covered by the employee dishonesty optional coverage. Coverage applies whether the employees act alone or in collusion with others, except the insured and partners of the insured. There is no coverage for loss where the only proof is an inventory or profit and loss computation.

Coverage for an employee is canceled immediately upon discovery by the insured or any partners, members, managers, officers, or directors not in collusion with the employee of any dishonest act committed by that employee before or after he was hired by the insured.

The amount shown in the declarations is the most that will be paid for all loss or damage in one occurrence, whether one or more people or acts are involved. Only loss that occurs during the policy period is covered. The insurance company will not pay for a covered loss that is discovered after one year from the end of the policy period. This is known as the discovery period.

Under certain circumstances, the insured has coverage under the employee dishonesty optional coverage of the current policy for losses that occurred during the previous policy period that would have been covered by that policy except that the discovery period expired. The following conditions must be met for the current policy to apply.

- The current policy must have become effective at the time the previous policy terminated.
- The current policy would have covered the loss had it been in effect when the loss occurred.

12.4.7.2. Mechanical Breakdown

Under this optional coverage, the insurance company will pay for direct damage to covered property caused by a sudden and accidental breakdown of an object, as defined by the policy, that damages the object so it needs to be repaired or replaced. The object may be one that is owned by the insured or is in the insured's care, custody, or control. It must be at the described premises.

The policy definition of *object* lists equipment in two main categories: certain boiler and pressure vessels and certain types of air conditioning units. The policy also defines exactly what is not considered an accident.

There is no coverage for accidents that occur while an object is being tested.

The insurance company may suspend this coverage by immediately mailing written notice to the insured if it is discovered that the object is in or is exposed to a dangerous condition. The insured will receive a pro rata refund of the premium.

12.4.7.3. Other Optional Coverages

The outdoor signs optional coverage provides coverage for direct physical loss or damage to all outdoor signs on the premises that are owned by or in the care, custody, or control of the insured. The limit of insurance for this optional coverage is specified in the declarations. When this optional coverage applies, all other references to outdoor signs in the policy no longer apply.

The money and securities optional coverage applies to loss of money and securities used in the insured's business as a result of theft, disappearance, or destruction. Coverage applies while the money and securities are:

- at a bank or savings institution;
- within the living quarters of the insured, a partner, or an employee who has custody of the property;
- at the described premises; or
- in transit between any of these places.

12.4.8. Limits of Insurance

The most the insurer will pay for loss or damage in any one occurrence is the applicable limit of insurance in the declarations. Each coverage shown in the declarations has its own limits, and the per occurrence rule applies separately to each.

Some coverages have internal or inside limits. These limits are stipulated in the limits of insurance provision and in various other sections of the policy, such as the covered property, additional coverages, and coverage extensions sections. An example is the $2,500 limit for the fire department service charge additional coverage.

A $1,000 per occurrence limit applies to outdoor signs attached to buildings. This provision also specifies that the limits applicable to the coverage extensions, the fire department service charge additional coverage, and the pollutant clean up and removal additional coverage are in addition to the policy's limits of insurance.

The businessowners policy also includes a provision that addresses inflation. A percentage selected by the insured from a number of options the insurance company offers is indicated in the declarations for the building coverage. Over the policy period, the limit of insurance gradually increases until it reaches the full amount by the end of the period.

The limit for business personal property will automatically increase by 25% to provide for seasonal variations, but only if the limit of insurance for business personal property coverage in the declarations is at least 100% of the insured's average monthly values during either the 12 months or the period the insured was in business before the loss, whichever is less.

12.4.9. Deductible

The standard deductible for property losses is $500.

A base deductible applies to all building and business personal property coverages, including both mandatory and optional coverages. No deductible applies to the fire department service charge, extra expense, business income, civil authority, and fire extinguisher systems recharge expense additional coverages.

A separate $500 deductible applies to the money and securities, employee dishonesty, and outdoor signs optional coverages. There is also a separate $500 deductible for the glass expenses additional coverage. These deductibles are not in addition to the base deductible.

12.5. LIABILITY AND MEDICAL EXPENSES COVERAGE

12.5.1. Liability Coverage

Business liability coverage covers the insured's legal liability that arises from bodily injury, property damage, and personal and advertising injury. Personal and advertising injury is injury, including consequential bodily injury, that arises out of any of the following offenses:

- False arrest, detention, or imprisonment
- Malicious prosecution
- Wrongful eviction from a place a person occupies, by or on behalf of its owner, landlord, or lessor
- Wrongful entry into a place a person occupies, by or on behalf of its owner, landlord, or lessor
- Invasion of the right of private occupancy of a place a person occupies, by or on behalf of its owner, landlord, or lessor

- Oral or written publication of material that slanders or libels a person or organization; disparages a person's or organization's goods, products, or services; or violates a person's right of privacy
- Use of another's advertising idea in the insured's advertisement
- Infringement of copyright, trade dress, or slogan

For a policy to cover any of the injuries or offenses we have described, the loss must take place in the coverage territory and occur during the policy period. The coverage territory for liability coverage is the following:

- The United States, its territories and possessions (e.g., Puerto Rico), and Canada
- International waters or airspace between the United States, its territories or possessions (e.g., Puerto Rico), and Canada
- All parts of the world if the injury or damage arises out of
    - goods or services normally made or sold by the insured in the United States, its territories and possessions (e.g., Puerto Rico), or Canada;
    - the activities of a person who is away from home on business in any of these places; or
    - personal and advertising injury offenses that take place through the Internet or similar electronic means of communication

Coverage also typically applies in all parts of the world if the insured's responsibility to pay damages is determined in a suit on the merits in the United States, its territories and possessions (e.g., Puerto Rico), or Canada or in a settlement to which the insurance company has agreed.

The insuring agreement also stipulates that losses of a continuing or ongoing nature that were—prior to the policy period—known to the insured or employees authorized to report losses are not covered.

Under liability coverage, the insurance company accepts the right and duty to defend suits that seek damages under the policy. The insurance company has the sole right to investigate and settle claims and resulting suits. However, when the limits of insurance are used up in paying judgments, settlements, or medical expenses, the insurance company's duty to defend ends.

12.5.2. Supplementary Payments

The businessowners policy includes the following supplementary payments. These payments do not reduce the policy limit:

Supplementary Payments
■ Expenses the insurance company incurs
■ Up to $250 for the cost of bail bonds related to violations that arise from vehicles to which bodily injury liability coverage applies
■ Cost of bonds to release attachments, up to the limit of insurance
■ Reasonable expenses the insured incurs at the insurance company's request to assist in investigating or defending a claim or suit, including $250 per day for lost earnings because of time off from work
■ Costs the insured is required to pay because of a suit
■ Prejudgment interest the insured is required to pay, unless the insurance company makes an offer to pay the limit of insurance, and then it will not pay prejudgment interest based on the period after that offer
■ Interest that accrues after a judgment and before it is paid, offered, or deposited in court

If certain conditions are met, the insurer will pay the defense costs for an **indemnitee**—a party who is not an insured who is under contract to provide goods or services to an insured—in addition to the policy's limit of liability and provide a defense for the indemnitee. Among the conditions that must be met for this coverage to apply are that the insured and the indemnitee must be named in the same lawsuit and the liability assumed by the insured must be covered by the policy.

12.5.3. Medical Expenses Coverage

The businessowners policy also covers specified medical expenses without regard to who is at fault. If other requirements are met, the policy will pay for medical expenses even if the insured would not have been legally liable for them or for the events that precipitated them. The policy will pay reasonable expenses for the following:

- First aid when an accident occurs
- Medical and surgical services
- Hospital services
- X-ray services
- Ambulance services
- Professional nursing services
- Dental services
- Funeral services

To be covered, the medical expenses must be necessary expenses that result from bodily injury that occurs on or next to premises the insured owns or rents, or injury that occurs because of the insured's business operations. The accident that causes the injury must occur in the coverage territory and during the policy period, and the medical expenses must be incurred and reported to the insurance company within one year after the accident.

Medical expenses coverage is intended to pay for such expenses incurred by the general public. Therefore, medical expenses will generally not be paid for the following:

- Any insured (does not include the insured's volunteer workers)
- Anyone hired to work for or on behalf of any insured or any insured's tenant
- A person who is injured on a part of the premises the insured owns or rents and that the injured person normally occupies
- A person (whether or not an employee of the insured) whose injury calls for benefits payable under a workers' compensation, disability, or similar law
- A person who is injured while taking part in athletics

12.5.4. Exclusions

For BI and PD liability losses, the businessowners policy excludes liability:

- arising out of expected or intended injury (does not apply to bodily injury that occurs when the insured uses reasonable force to protect persons or property);
- assumed under contracts or agreements (does not apply to contracts that meet the policy's definition of an insured contract or to liability the insured would have whether or not a contract or agreement existed);
- related to liquor, but only for insureds whose business is manufacturing, distributing, selling, serving, or furnishing alcoholic beverages;
- for obligations under workers' compensation, disability benefits, unemployment compensation, or similar laws;
- for BI to employees that arises out of and in the course of their employment with the insured;
- arising out of pollutants, including associated cleanup costs;
- arising out of the ownership, maintenance, and use of aircraft, autos, and watercraft;
- arising out of the use of mobile equipment in, or while practicing or preparing for, any prearranged race, speed or demolition contest, or any stunting activity;
- arising out of war or war-like acts;

- arising from rendering or failing to render professional services;
- for damage to property the insured owns, rents, or occupies, or property in the insured's care, custody, or control;
- for damage to the insured's product or the insured's own work;
- for damage to impaired property or to property that has not been physically injured arising out of a defect or deficiency in the insured's product or work, or a delay or failure to perform a contract or agreement;
- for losses, costs, or expenses incurred for the loss of use, withdrawal, recall, inspection, repair, replacement, adjustment, removal, or disposal of the insured's product, work, or impaired property;
- for business liability or medical expenses resulting from the hazardous properties of nuclear materials;
- for medical expenses that are included within the products-completed operations hazard, excluded under liability coverage or due to war and acts of war;
- arising out of loss or damage to electronic data; or
- arising out of violations of any law that prohibits or limits the distribution of material or information, including the federal Telephone Consumer Protection Act and CAN-SPAM Act.

The following exclusions apply specifically to personal and advertising injury losses. Not covered are personal and advertising injury:

- caused by or at the direction of the insured with the knowledge that the act would violate the rights of another and inflict personal and advertising injury;
- that arises out of oral or written publication of material that occurs by or at the insured's direction with the insured's knowledge that it is false;
- that arises out of oral or written publication of material that was first published before the beginning of the policy period;
- that arises out of a criminal act committed by or at the direction of any insured;
- for which an insured has assumed liability in a contract or agreement (does not apply to liability for damages the insured would have even if there were no contract or agreement);
- arising out of breach of contract (other than an implied contract to use another's advertising idea in the insured's advertisement, which is covered);
- arising out of the failure of goods, products, or services to conform with advertised quality or performance;
- arising out of a wrong description of the price of goods, products, or services;

- arising in connection with any actual, alleged, or threatened discharge, dispersal, seepage, or escape of pollutants as well as any requests to test for, clean up, contain, or otherwise respond to pollutants;
- committed by insureds in the business of advertising, broadcasting, publishing, telecasting, designing Websites, or providing Internet search, access, content, or service;
- arising out of an electronic chat room or bulletin board the insured hosts, owns, or controls;
- arising out of infringement of copyright, trademark, patent, trade secret, or other intellectual property rights;
- arising out of the unauthorized use of another's name or product in the insured's email address, domain name, or metatags; or
- arising out of a criminal act committed by or at the direction of the insured.

12.5.5. Who Is an Insured

Who is considered an insured under the businessowners policy depends on how the named insured is designated in the policy declarations: as an individual, partnership, or joint venture, limited liability company, or organization other than a partnership, joint venture, or limited liability company.

Who is an Insured

Designation	Who are Insureds	Restrictions
Individual	■ Named insured ■ Named insured's spouse	■ Only in connection with sole proprietorships
Partnership or joint venture	■ Named insured ■ Named insured's partners and their spouses ■ Named insured's members and their spouses	■ Members, partners and their spouses are insureds only in connection with conducting the business ■ Current or past partnerships or joint ventures not insureds unless designated in Declarations
Limited liability company	■ Named insured ■ Members ■ Managers	■ Members are insureds only in connection with conducting the business ■ Managers are insureds only in connection with their duties as managers ■ Current or past limited liability companies not insureds unless designated in Declarations
Organization other than partnership, joint venture or limited liability company	■ Named insured ■ Executive officers and directors ■ Stockholders	■ Executive officers and directors are insureds only in connection with conducting the business ■ Stockholders are insureds only in connection with liability as stockholders

Others that are considered insureds under the businessowners policy include:

- named insured's **employees** (other than executive officers and managers) when acting within the scope of their employment;
- organization or person (other than employees) while acting as insured's **real estate manager**; and
- if the named insured dies
  - — any person or organization that has **temporary custody of the deceased's property,** but only with regard to liability that arises out of maintenance or use of the property and only until a legal representative has been appointed, or
  - — insured's **legal representative** while acting within the scope of those duties.

12.5.6. Limits of Insurance

The limits shown in the policy's declarations are the most that will be paid under the circumstances described in the policy. These limits are the limits, no matter how many insureds, claims, suits, people, or organizations are involved.

The following chart illustrates the most the insurance company will pay under the businessowners policy in various circumstances:

Limits of Insurance

Limit Shown in the Declarations	Maximum Amount Payable for
Liability And Medical Expenses	Total of all damages that arise out of: ■ Bodily injury, property damage and medical expenses in one occurrence ■ Personal injury and advertising injury to one person or organization
Medical Expenses	Medical expenses for bodily injury to one person
Under Business Liability Coverage, Damage To Premises Rented To You	Property damage to premises the insured rents or occupies temporarily with the owner's permission that arises out of one fire or explosion

The policy also includes two separate aggregate limits: one for injury or damage under the products-completed operations hazard and another for all other injury, damage, or medical expenses except fire legal liability losses. Both of the aggregates are two times the limit shown in the declarations for liability and medical expenses coverage.

12.6. CONDITIONS

There are several sets of conditions in the businessowners policy. The conditions that apply to the entire policy are called the **common policy**

conditions. There are two sets of conditions for the property coverage: the property general conditions and the property loss conditions. The liability conditions are called the liability and medical expenses general conditions.

Most of these are standard conditions that appear in other commercial property and liability policies.

12.7. ENDORSEMENTS

12.7.1. Utility Services Endorsements—Direct Damage and Time Element

Endorsements for both the property and liability sections of the policy may be used to alter the coverage or to provide additional coverages.

The **utility services—direct damage coverage endorsement** covers loss or damage to property caused by an interruption in water, communication, or power supply service. For coverage to apply, the property must be scheduled for coverage on the endorsement and the service interruption must be caused by a covered cause of loss.

Here's an example of a loss that would be covered under this endorsement. The insured, a photographer, has her developing equipment insured under a businessowners policy with the utility services—direct damage endorsement. When an electrical transformer is struck by lightning, a power surge results that damages the equipment. The businessowners policy would cover this loss.

The **utility services—time element coverage endorsement** pays for loss of business income or extra expense if damage to certain utility services property located outside the covered building by a covered cause of loss results in an interruption of service to the described premises.

Exercise 12.C

1. The insured's restaurant was closed for two days when an earthquake damaged a water main and interrupted the restaurant's water service. Would the insured's business income loss be covered under the utility services—time element endorsement? ( ) Yes ( ) No Explain your answer. ______________________________
____
____

Exercise answers can be found at the end of the Unit 12 answers and rationale.

12.7.2. Protective Safeguards Endorsement

The **protective safeguards endorsement** requires the insured to maintain the protective devices or services listed on the endorsement on specified property as a condition of the policy. The protective safeguards are identified by the following symbols:

- P-1—automatic sprinkler system: any automatic fire protective system, including related supervisory services and connected sprinklers, pipes, pumps, and similar devices
- P-2—automatic fire alarm system: an automatic fire alarm system that protects the entire building and is connected to a central station or reports to a public or private fire alarm station
- P-3—security service: a security service with a guard that makes hourly rounds of the premises while the business is closed
- P-4—service contract: a privately owned fire department that provides fire protection service to the premises
- P-9—any other protective system described in the endorsement

The insurer will not pay for fire damage losses if the insured failed to keep the protective safeguard in working order or did not notify the insurer that the device was not working properly. When an automatic sprinkler system is shut off due to breakage, leakage, freezing, or opening of sprinkler heads, the insurer does not have to be notified if the system can be restored within 48 hours.

12.7.3. Hired Auto and Nonowned Auto Liability

The **hired auto and nonowned auto liability endorsement** covers the insured's liability for one or both of the following:

- Bodily injury or property damage that arises out of the maintenance or use of a hired auto by the insured or the insured's employees in the course of the insured's business
- Bodily injury or property damage that arises out of the use of any nonowned auto in the insured's business by any person

Hired autos are autos the insured leases, hires, or borrows, but not from employees or members of their households or any partners or executive officers of the insured. Nonowned autos are autos not owned, leased, or borrowed by the insured but used in the business.

These coverages are purchased separately and scheduled on the endorsement. The endorsement is available only when the insured has no other commercial auto insurance.

12.8. COMPARISON OF COMMERCIAL PACKAGE POLICY AND BUSINESSOWNERS POLICY

The following table summarizes the key differences between the commercial package policy and the businessowners policy:

Feature	Commercial Package Policy	Businessowners Policy
■ Eligibility	■ Almost all commercial risks	■ Small- to medium-sized businesses in limited occupancy classes ■ Insurer specifies limitations on size of building and specific type of business involved
■ Format Of Policy	■ Common Policy Declarations ■ Common Policy Conditions ■ Two or more coverage parts	■ Businessowners Common Policy Declarations ■ Businessowners Policy Form
■ Coverages	■ All eligible coverages selected separately	■ Prepackaged policy containing Property and Liability coverage

UNIT TEST

1. The largest office building risk that may be eligible for a businessowners policy is
   A. 3 stories and 50,000 square feet
   B. 3 stories and 75,000 square feet
   C. 6 stories and 75,000 square feet
   D. 6 stories and 100,000 square feet

2. In addition to maximum floor space, the businessowners eligibility rules limit eligible risks to a maximum of
   A. $750,000 in annual sales
   B. $1.5 million in annual sales
   C. $3 million in annual sales
   D. $5 million in annual sales

3. What are the two major property coverages provided under a businessowners policy?
   A. ______________________________
   B. ______________________________

4. Under the additional coverages of the businessowners property coverage, property removed to protect it from loss will be covered at another location for up to
   A. 5 days
   B. 10 days
   C. 20 days
   D. 30 days

5. The standard deductible for the BOP property coverage is
   A. $100
   B. $250
   C. $500

6. Mechanical breakdown coverage is
   A. not available in a BOP
   B. automatically provided in a BOP
   C. an optional BOP coverage that is activated by an entry in the declarations

7. Which one of the following coverages is NOT included in the businessowners policy?
   A. Bodily injury liability
   B. Property damage liability
   C. Medical expense
   D. Professional liability
   E. Personal and advertising injury liability

8. Which of the following would be covered under the building coverage of the businessowners policy?
   A. Restroom fixtures
   B. Photocopy machines
   C. Furnishings in the insured's private office
   D. Carpets and floor tiles

9. Which of the following would be covered under the business personal property coverage of the businessowners policy?
   A. Desks, filing cabinets, and other office equipment the insured uses in her business
   B. An enclosure around the front entry to a store that the insured tenant had built when he began leasing the building
   C. Cans of paint that are stacked near a newly constructed outer wall prior to painting the wall
   D. Fire extinguishers located at various places on the inside walls of the building

10. Which of the following losses would be covered under the property coverage of the businessowners policy?
    A. An insured moved inventory to another location to protect it from a tornado. Two days later, a sewer backup in the new location damaged that property.
    B. An explosion at the insured's business spewed toxic chemicals onto property belonging to another company. That company's owner sued the insured for the costs to clean up the chemicals.
    C. When a tornado damaged a nearby business, authorities closed off the area for one week to clean up the damage. The insured lost business income during that period.

11. Which of the following losses would be excluded under the property coverage of the BOP?
    A. An angry employee vandalized an insured's building.
    B. Termites damaged an insured's building.
    C. Pianos in an insured's warehouse were damaged by dryness during an extremely cold winter.
    D. An error in the design specifications for an insured's building resulted in the building's collapse 6 months after construction was completed.
    E. All of the above.

12. Which of the following are excluded under businessowners liability coverage?
    A. Damages the insured causes intentionally
    B. Pollution losses caused by the insured
    C. Liquor liability for those in the business of serving liquor
    D. Liability assumed under an insured contract
    E. The cost of recalling the insured's product because of a suspected safety hazard
    F. Damage to the insured's own work
    G. Liability for damage to property in the insured's custody

13. What two conditions must be met for a loss to be covered under the utility services—direct damage endorsement?
    A. ______________________________
    B. ______________________________

ANSWERS AND RATIONALES TO UNIT TEST

1. **D.** Office buildings that are no more than 6 stories high and contain no more than 100,000 square feet are eligible for the businessowners policy.

2. **C.** Certain types of wholesale, processing, and service businesses are eligible for the BOP as long as gross annual sales do not exceed $3 million.

3. The two primary coverages in the businessowners property section are buildings and business personal property.

4. **D.** The preservation of property additional coverage covers loss from any cause of loss to property that was removed from the insured location to protect it from damage by a covered peril. Coverage applies for up to 30 days after the property is first moved.

5. **C.** The standard deductible is $500.

6. **C.** Optional coverages are usually preprinted in the policy but apply only if they are designated in the declarations.

7. **D.** The businessowners liability coverage includes the following coverages: BI liability, PD liability, personal and advertising injury liability, and medical expense.

8. **A and D.** Property owned and used by the insured in the business, such as photocopy machines and furnishings in the insured's private office, would be covered under business personal property coverage.

9. **A and B.** Property owned and used by the insured in the business and tenants' improvements and betterments made at the tenant's expense that cannot be legally removed are covered under business personal property coverage. Materials that are on or within 100 feet of the premises being used for alterations, such as the cans of paint, are covered under building coverage. Personal property used to maintain or service the building, such as the fire extinguishers in, are also covered under building coverage.

10. **A and C.** The pollutant cleanup and removal additional coverage pays the costs to extract pollutants from the insured's premises, not property belonging to others.

11. **E.** All of these losses would be excluded under the businessowners property coverage.

12. **A, B, C, E, F, and G.** The exclusion for liability assumed under contract has some exceptions. One is liability assumed under an insured contract.

13. Two conditions must be met for a loss to be covered under the utility services—direct damage endorsement: the damaged property must be scheduled for coverage on the endorsement, and the service interruption must be caused by a covered cause of loss.

UNIT 12 EXERCISE ANSWERS

Exercise 12.A

1. A, B, D, and E

Exercise 12.B

1. No—Coverage is limited to $500

2. Yes

Exercise 12.C

1. No—The service interruption was caused by an earthquake which is not a covered cause of loss under the businessowner's policy

UNIT

13

Commercial Property Insurance

13.1. LEARNING OBJECTIVES

After completing Unit 13—Commercial Property Insurance, you will be able to do the following:

- Explain the purpose of commercial property insurance
- Describe the purpose of each component in a commercial property coverage part
- Summarize the provisions of the commercial property conditions form
- Identify property covered under the building and personal property coverage form's building coverage, business personal property coverage, and personal property of others coverage
- Describe property that is not covered under the building and personal property coverage form
- Describe the additional coverages, coverage extensions, and optional coverages available in the building and personal property coverage form
- Explain the purpose of the following building and personal property coverage form conditions: duties in the event of loss, loss payment, valuation, vacancy, mortgageholders, and coinsurance
- Describe the purpose of the builders risk coverage form and the property it covers
- Identify when coverage begins and ends under a builders risk coverage form
- Explain how the amount of coverage available under a builders risk coverage form is determined
- Compare and contrast the conditions found in the builders risk coverage form and the building and personal property coverage form
- Explain how the builders risk coverage form is affected when the builders risk reporting form is attached
- Identify the purpose of the condominium association coverage form and the condominium commercial unit-owners coverage form
- Compare and contrast the property covered under the condominium association coverage form and the condominium commercial unit-owners coverage form
- Explain how the business income forms define period of restoration and business income
- Describe the purpose of the business income coverage forms and the conditions that must be met for a loss to be covered
- Compare and contrast the extra expense and expenses to reduce loss coverages in the business income coverage forms

- Explain the purpose of the business income from dependent properties—broad form
- Explain how the following terms are defined in the business income from dependent properties form: contributing location, recipient location, manufacturing location, and leader location
- Explain why a business might need the extra expense coverage form instead of one of the business income coverage forms
- Describe how the policy limit under the extra expense coverage form applies during the period of restoration
- Summarize the coverage provided under the legal liability coverage form
- Compare and contrast the covered perils, exclusions, and additional coverages in the basic, broad, and special causes of loss forms
- Explain the limitations imposed on certain types of losses by the special causes of loss form
- Describe the perils covered under the earthquake and volcanic eruption endorsement and how it is used in a commercial property coverage part
- Describe the purpose of the following endorsements: value reporting form, peak season, ordinance or law coverage, and spoilage

13.2. COMMERCIAL PROPERTY COVERAGE PART

One important insurance need for businesses is the need for **property insurance**: insurance on real property such as office buildings, factories, and warehouses, and insurance on business personal property such as furniture, fixtures, machinery, and inventory. The most widely used means for providing the property insurance that businesses need is the **commercial property coverage part** of the commercial package policy.

The commercial property coverage part consists of a number of separate components that can be combined to provide the appropriate property coverage for a wide variety of commercial insureds. In addition to the common policy declarations and conditions, each commercial property coverage part must include:

- commercial property declarations form;
- commercial property conditions form;
- one or more commercial property coverage form;
- causes of loss form; and
- any mandatory endorsements.

We'll look briefly at each of these components before we study some of the individual components in more detail.

13.2.1. Commercial Property Declarations and Coverage Forms

The commercial property declarations form provides additional information about the premises to be insured and the specific forms that will apply. It also includes the name and addresses of any mortgage holders.

The commercial property coverage forms contain descriptions of the specific coverages being provided to the business. Each commercial property coverage form defines what property is covered, what property is not covered, how limits and deductibles apply, and what special conditions apply.

In this unit, you'll study the following coverage forms:

- Building and personal property
- Builders risk
- Condominium association
- Condominium commercial unit owners
- Business income with extra expense
- Business income without extra expense
- Extra expense
- Legal liability

13.2.2. Causes of Loss Forms

The **causes of loss forms** list the perils that the property is insured against. There are three separate causes of loss forms:

- Basic
- Broad
- Special

There are a variety of **endorsements** that can be added to the policy to modify coverage. Some endorsements are mandatory by law or when particular coverages are written.

13.2.3. Commercial Property Conditions Form

The **commercial property conditions form** includes conditions that apply specifically to the commercial property coverage forms.

The **control of property** condition states that an act of neglect of a person beyond the insured's direction or control will not affect the insurance. In addition, if the insured violates a condition of the policy with regard to a specific location, the insurance applicable to other locations will not be affected.

The **legal action against us** condition gives the insured two years from the date that direct physical loss occurred to bring an action against the insurer.

Such an action cannot be brought unless the insured has complied with all conditions of the policy.

The **other insurance** condition states that when there is other insurance written on the same basis, the policy pro rates with the other policies. If there is other insurance covering the same loss but subject to a different plan or coverage, the policy is excess over the other insurance.

The **policy period, coverage territory** condition states that a loss must occur during the policy period and in the coverage territory to be covered. The coverage territory is the United States, its territories and possessions, Puerto Rico, and Canada.

The **transfer of rights of recovery against others to us** condition gives the insurance company subrogation rights.

The **concealment or fraud** condition states that the commercial property coverage part is void if the insured intentionally conceals or misrepresents a material fact concerning the coverage part, the covered property, the insured's interest in covered property, or a claim.

If two or more of the policy's coverages apply to the same loss, the **insurance under two or more coverages** condition provides that the insurer will not pay more than the actual amount of loss or damage.

The **no benefit to bailee** condition prohibits a bailee from being reimbursed by the insured's commercial property insurance if the insured's property is damaged or destroyed while in the bailee's custody.

The **liberalization** condition states that any revision that broadens coverage without requiring additional premium will automatically apply to the coverage part if the revision is adopted by the insurer during the policy period or within 45 days of the policy's effective date.

13.3. BUILDING AND PERSONAL PROPERTY COVERAGE FORM

13.3.1. Property Covered

The most commonly purchased form, and the form that is the core of the commercial property coverage part, is the **building and personal property coverage form**. It covers buildings, the insured's business personal property, and the personal property of others located at the business premises. The insured may select coverage for one or more of these categories. Coverage is only provided for coverages that have a limit of insurance shown in the declarations.

In addition to the building itself, building coverage includes:

- completed additions;
- fixtures, including outdoor fixtures;
- permanently installed machinery and equipment;
- personal property used to maintain or service the premises, such as fire extinguishers;

- outdoor furniture, floor coverings, and certain appliances; and
- if not otherwise covered, additions under construction and alterations or repairs to the building, including materials, equipment, supplies, and temporary structures within 100 feet of the described premises.

Business personal property is covered while it is in the building, in the open, or in a vehicle within 100 feet of the premises. It includes:

- furniture;
- fixtures;
- machinery;
- equipment;
- stock;
- other owned personal property used in the business;
- the value of labor, parts, or services on the personal property of others;
- if the insured is a tenant, the improvements and betterments added by the insured; and
- leased personal property that the insured has a contractual responsibility to insure, unless it's otherwise covered.

Stock is the insured's merchandise. It includes items stored or offered for sale, raw materials for manufacturing, materials in the process of being manufactured, manufactured items, and supplies used in packaging and shipping.

Improvements and betterments are fixtures, alterations, installations, or additions that are made a part of a building that the insured tenant occupies but does not own, and which are acquired by or made at the expense of the insured but cannot legally be removed by the insured.

Personal property of others pays for damage to property of others in the insured's care, custody, or control, whether the insured is legally liable for that loss. The person who owns the property receives payment for the loss.

Exercise 13.A

Decide whether the examples below would be covered as business personal property **(BP)** or personal property of others **(PP).**

____ 1. The cost of repairs to an appliance left by a customer

____ 2. A television damaged while in the insured's shop for repairs

____ 3. Supplies sitting in the insured's truck at the loading dock directly behind the insured's plant

Exercise answers can be found at the end of the Unit 13 answers and rationales.

13.3.2. Property Not Covered

The following property is excluded from coverage:

- Money, accounts, food stamps, notes, securities, and related property (lottery tickets held for sale are not securities and are covered)
- Animals, unless they are boarded or held for sale
- Autos for sale
- Bridges, roads, walks, patios, and other paved surfaces
- Contraband (property being illegally transported or traded)
- Cost of excavations and other ground preparation
- Foundations of buildings, structures, machinery, or boilers if their foundation is below the basement level or below ground level if there is no basement
- Land, water, growing crops, and lawns
- Personal property while it is airborne or waterborne
- Bulkheads, pilings, piers, wharves, and docks
- Property covered under another policy in which it is more specifically described
- Retaining walls that are not a part of the building described in the declarations
- Underground pipes, flues, and drains
- The cost to replace or restore information contained in valuable papers or records, including those that exist as electronic data, except as provided in the coverage extensions
- Vehicles, including watercraft and aircraft, that are licensed for use on public roads or are principally operated away from the premises; this exclusion does not apply to
    - vehicles that are manufactured, processed, or warehoused by the insured,
    - vehicles, other than autos, that the insured holds for sale, or
    - rowboats or canoes out of water at the described premises.
- The following property while outside of buildings, except as provided in the coverage extensions
    - Grain, hay, straw, or other crops
    - Fences

- Antennas (including satellite dishes)
- Signs that are not attached to the building
- Trees, shrubs, and plants

- Electronic data, except as provided as an additional coverage

13.3.3. Additional Coverages

In addition to the basic coverages, the building and personal property coverage form provides some **additional coverages**.

Debris removal pays expenses to remove debris of covered property caused by or resulting from a covered cause of loss. It does not cover extraction of pollutants from land or water. It pays up to 25% of the amount paid for direct loss to covered property, plus the deductible. But if the actual debris removal expense exceeds the 25% limitation or if the sum of the direct loss and the debris removal expense exceeds the limit of insurance, the insurer will pay an additional $10,000 for debris removal expense.

Preservation of property pays for loss to property that was removed from the insured location to protect it from a peril insured against. Coverage only applies if the loss occurs within 30 days after the property was removed.

Fire department service charge pays up to $1,000 for a fire department service charge. This is paid in addition to the limit of insurance; no deductible applies.

Pollutant cleanup and removal covers the costs to extract pollutants from land or water at the insured's premises if the pollution was caused by a covered cause of loss. This coverage is subject to a $10,000 limit per policy period that applies in addition to the policy limit. The expenses must be reported to the insurer in writing within 180 days of the loss.

Suppose a tornado strikes the insured's business, resulting in $75,000 in damages to the building and $25,000 in debris removal expenses. The building is insured for $200,000 with a $5,000 deductible. The insured will receive $23,750 for the debris removal expenses (75,000 × 25% = 18,750; 18,750 + 5,000 = 23,750).

The **increased cost of construction** additional coverage covers the additional costs required to comply with building codes when a building is damaged by a covered cause of loss. It does not cover costs arising out of the enforcement of any ordinance or law that:

- requires demolition, repair, replacement, reconstruction, remodeling, or remediation of property due to the presence of mold; or
- requires the insured to test for, clean up, remove, or otherwise respond to or assess the effects of mold.

The coverage is only available for buildings insured on a replacement cost basis. The maximum amount payable is the lesser of 5% of the amount the building is insured for or $10,000.

The **electronic data** additional coverage pays to replace or restore electronic data that have been destroyed or corrupted by a covered cause of loss.

Electronic data means information, facts, or computer programs stored, created, used on, or transmitted to or from computer software, CD-ROMs, hard or floppy disks, or any other repositories of computer software used with electronically controlled equipment. It does not include the insured's stock of prepackaged software.

In general, the covered causes of loss include those in the applicable causes of loss forms, plus collapse. Also covered are viruses or other instructions introduced to a computer system or network designed to damage or destroy any part of its system or disrupt its normal operation. There is no coverage for loss or damage caused by or resulting from manipulation of a computer system by an employee or an entity retained by the insured to inspect, design, install, maintain, repair, or replace the system.

To the extent that electronic data are not replaced or restored, the loss will be valued at the cost of replacement of the media on which the data were stored with blank media that is substantially identical. The most that will be paid under this additional coverage is $2,500 for all loss or damage sustained in any one policy year, regardless of the number of losses or the number of premises, locations, or computer systems involved. If payment for one loss does not exhaust this limit, the balance is available for subsequent loss or damage sustained in, but not after, that policy year. An occurrence that begins in one policy year and continues or results in additional loss in a subsequent policy year will be treated as if all loss occurred in the year in which the occurrence began.

13.3.4. Coverage Extensions

There are also certain coverage extensions that apply, but only if the insured has agreed to meet an 80% or higher coinsurance requirement or has purchased a reporting form (more on these later). These coverage extensions provide additional limits of insurance.

The **newly acquired or constructed property** coverage extension applies to Coverage A and Coverage B. Up to $250,000 for each new building may be extended for up to 30 days to cover new buildings being constructed at the same location, and buildings newly acquired at other locations that are intended for use as a warehouse or a use similar to that of the building described in the declarations. Business personal property insurance may be extended for up to 30 days to cover business personal property located at newly acquired locations (other than fairs, trade shows, or exhibitions) and newly acquired or constructed buildings at the location described in the declarations. This business personal property may be insured property or newly acquired property. The maximum amount payable is $100,000 at each building.

Personal effects and property of others provides up to $2,500 of coverage for personal effects of the named insured, partners, and employees (excluding loss from theft) and personal property of others. This coverage extension is available even if the insured has not purchased personal property of others coverage, as long as the coinsurance requirement is met.

Valuable papers and records—other than electronic data pays up to $2,500 to replace or restore information on damaged valuable papers and records.

Property off-premises extends up to $10,000 in coverage for covered property that is away from the described premises. Coverage is provided while the property is:

- temporarily at a location the insured does not own, lease, or operate;
- in storage at a location the insured leases; or
- at a fair, trade show, or exhibition.

Property is not covered while it is in or on a vehicle or in the care of a salesperson, except while the salesperson is at a fair, trade show, or exhibition.

Outdoor property extends a limited amount of coverage to fences, antennas, satellite dishes, signs, trees, plants, and shrubs. The maximum payable is $1,000, with a $250 limit applying to any one tree, plant, or shrub.

Another coverage extension is for **nonowned detached trailers**. Trucking companies that make deliveries to businesses sometimes leave the trailer for the insured to unload and return later to pick up the empty trailer. Some businesses also use rented trailers as storage facilities. In both cases, the insured is usually responsible for damage to the trailer while it is on the premises. This coverage extension applies to such losses.

The trailer must be in the insured's care, custody, or control at a premises described in the declarations, and the insured must be contractually obligated to pay for damage to the trailer. There is no coverage for damage that occurs while the trailer is attached to a vehicle or while it is being hitched or unhitched from a vehicle.

The limit is $5,000 unless a higher limit is shown in the declarations.

13.3.5. Conditions

In addition to the conditions listed in the common policy conditions and commercial property conditions forms, there are also several important conditions listed in the building and personal property coverage form.

The **duties in the event of loss** condition states that after a loss, the insured must:

- notify the insurer about the loss or damage as soon as possible; the insured must provide a description of the property involved and describe how, when, and where the loss or damage occurred;
- notify the police if a law may have been broken;
- take reasonable steps to protect the covered property from further damage and keep a record of expenses incurred to protect the property; if possible, the insured should set the damaged property aside for examination;
- provide a complete inventory at the insurer's request;
- allow the insurer to inspect the property, examine books and records, and take samples of the property at its request;

- testify under oath with regard to the claim if requested by the insurer; and
- send a signed, sworn statement of loss within 60 days of the insurance company's request.

The **loss payment** condition states that the insurance company will give the insured notice of how it intends to settle the loss within 30 days after it receives the insured's sworn statement of loss. As long as the insured has complied with all of the terms of the coverage part and has reached agreement with the company on the amount of the loss, the insurer will pay the loss within 30 days after it receives the sworn statement of loss.

The **valuation** condition describes how losses will be settled. Most losses are paid at **actual cash value**. However, if the coinsurance conditions are met and costs are $2,500 or less, the policy will pay the cost of building repair or replacement without taking depreciation into account.

Stock already sold is valued at its net selling price.

Glass is valued at the cost of replacement with safety glazing material if this is required by law.

Valuable papers and records are valued at the cost of blank materials needed to reproduce the lost records and labor to transcribe or copy the records.

Tenants improvements and betterments are valued at actual cash value if the insured-tenant makes the repairs promptly or at a proportion of the original cost of the improvements if the repairs are not made promptly. If someone besides the insured, such as the building owner, pays for repairs, the insurer will pay nothing for the loss.

The **vacancy** condition states that if a building has been vacant for more than 60 consecutive days before the loss, the insurer will not pay for loss due to vandalism, water damage, theft or attempted theft, building glass breakage, or sprinkler leakage (unless the system has been protected against freezing). In addition, any amount that would otherwise be paid for a covered loss will be reduced 15%. Note that buildings under construction are not considered vacant.

The **mortgageholders** condition promises to pay losses to any mortgageholders named in the declarations as their interest may appear. This condition protects the interest of mortgageholders by promising advance notice of cancellation. The insurer must provide 10 days' written notice if it cancels for nonpayment of premium and 30 days' notice if it cancels for any other reason allowed by the policy. If the insurer decides not to renew, it must give the mortgageholder at least 10 days' advance written notice.

The **coinsurance** condition states that when the insured's amount of coverage at the time of loss does not meet the required coinsurance percentage, the company reduces the payment it would otherwise make in the same proportion as the insurance carried bears to the insurance required.

The standard deductible is $500.

Exercise 13.B

1. An explosion damages a building that has been vacant for 90 days. The amount of loss is $50,000; the limit of insurance is $100,000. How much will the insurer pay? (Ignore any deductible that might apply.)
   A. $42,500
   B. $50,000
   C. $85,000
   D. Nothing—all losses to vacant buildings are excluded.

Exercise answers can be found at the end of the Unit 13 answers and rationales.

13.3.6. Optional Coverages

The building and personal property coverage form also provides three optional coverages that must be listed in the declarations to be activated. An additional premium is charged for each optional coverage selected.

Agreed value coverage suspends the coinsurance requirement for the covered property designated and substitutes an agreement to cover any loss in the same proportion that the limit of insurance carried bears to the stated value. The insured is required to submit a form stipulating the value of the property.

If the agreed value on an item is stated to be $50,000 and the limit is $50,000, then any loss is covered in full. If the limit carried was only $25,000, then only 50% of any loss would be covered. (The standard coinsurance clause would pay the proportion of the loss that the limits carried bear to the value at the time of loss, rather than the agreed value.)

When the insured selects **inflation guard coverage**, the insured and the insurance company agree on one of several percentages that will apply annually to the limits of insurance. For example, if 8% is selected, the total limits of insurance will gradually increase on a pro rata basis until, at the end of the year, the available limit is 8% higher than the limits shown initially. The coverage form includes a precise formula for determining the amount of increase at any given time during the policy period.

Replacement cost coverage overrides actual cash value in the valuation condition by agreeing to pay for loss or damage to covered property on a replacement cost basis, with the exception of certain property listed in the declarations. Replacement cost coverage is subject to the same coinsurance provisions as the standard ACV valuation.

13.4. BUILDERS RISK COVERAGE FORM

13.4.1. Property Covered

Another form that can be added to the commercial property coverage part is the builders risk coverage form. This form covers commercial, residential, or farm buildings that are under construction. Coverage begins:

- on the date construction begins if the building does not have a basement; or
- on the date construction starts above the lowest basement floor if there is a basement.

Coverage is written for one year but ceases whenever any of the following occur:

- The property is accepted by the purchaser
- 90 days have elapsed since construction was completed
- The building is occupied or put to its intended use
- The insured's interest in the property ceases
- The insured abandons the construction with no intention of completing it

Coverage includes both the building under construction and its foundation. Fixtures, machinery, equipment used to service the building, and the insured's building materials and supplies can be covered if they will become a permanent part of the building and are within 100 feet of the building.

In addition, coverage may be extended to cover building materials and supplies owned by others but in the insured's care, custody, or control, provided they are within 100 feet of the described building. The most that will be paid under this extension is $5,000.

The following property is not covered:

- Land or water
- Lawns, trees, shrubs, or plants when outside of buildings
- Radio and television antennas when outside of buildings, including lead-in wiring, masts, or towers
- Signs when outside of buildings and not attached to buildings (attached signs are covered)

13.4.2. Amount of Coverage Available

The amount of coverage available under the builders risk coverage form is determined in accordance with the anticipated completed value of the building under construction.

The insurance company agrees to pay the actual cash value of the loss; however, it will not pay a greater share of any loss than the proportion that the limit of insurance bears to the value of the building on the date of completion. This is stipulated in the need for adequate insurance condition. Consider this example: the value of a building on its date of completion is $200,000. The limit of insurance carried is $100,000, with a $500 deductible. The amount of loss is $80,000. The company will pay $39,500. Here's how we calculated this figure:

$100,000 ÷ $200,000 = .50;
$80,000 × .50 = $40,000;
$40,000 – $500 = $39,500.

Exercise 13.C

1. The value of a building upon completion is $250,000. The limit of insurance carried is $150,000, with a $250 deductible. The amount of loss is $30,000. How much will the insurance company pay? $__________

Exercise answers can be found at the end of the Unit 13 answers and rationales.

13.4.3. Miscellaneous Conditions

The builders risk coverage form includes most of the same conditions found on the building and personal property coverage form, with the following variations.

- There is no vacancy provision because buildings under construction are not considered vacant.
- There is a clause stating that all property is valued at ACV at the time of loss. Since actual cash value is paid for all losses, the form does not include options for replacement cost, agreed value, or inflationary adjustment.
- There is no coinsurance condition (the need for adequate insurance condition serves essentially the same purpose by penalizing insureds who do not have the required amount of insurance when a loss occurs).

13.4.4. Builders Risk Reporting Form

The **builders risk reporting form** provides another option with regard to the amount of insurance that must be carried. When this form is attached to the builders risk coverage form, the insured is allowed to purchase a smaller amount of insurance that gradually increases as the value of the building under construction increases. This form requires a report of value that must be filed with the insurer each month. The insurance company will not pay more for any loss than the proportion the values last reported before the loss bears to the actual cash value of the covered property on the effective date of the last report.

13.5. CONDOMINIUM COVERAGE FORMS

There are two condominium forms available under the commercial property coverage part.

The **condominium association coverage form** insures a condominium association against direct physical loss or damage to:

- buildings;
- business personal property; and
- personal property of others in the care, custody, or control of the association while it is at the premises.

It can be used to insure the condominium associations of residential or commercial condominiums. Again, the perils insured against are contained in the causes of loss forms you'll study later in the unit.

The definition of *building* is extended to cover items such as permanently installed machinery and equipment. It will also cover outdoor fixtures that are a part of the building as well as other specifically named personal property. In general, however, the definition of *building* does not include personal property owned, used, or controlled by a unit owner. Business personal property includes only property owned by the association or owned indivisibly by all unit owners.

The **condominium commercial unit-owners coverage form**, as its name implies, is designed for the owner of a condominium. It covers the condominium's contents and is available only for the owner of a commercial condominium. (Residential condo owners can obtain contents coverage with an HO-6.) It covers the unit owner's business personal property and the personal property of others in the insured's care, custody, or control. It does not cover buildings; this coverage is typically provided under the condominium association coverage form issued to the association.

In case both the association and unit-owners forms apply to a specific loss, the association form's coverage is primary.

Exercise 13.D

1. The condominium association coverage form is used to insure
   A. personal property belonging to the owners of residential condominiums
   B. residential or commercial condominium associations against loss or damage to buildings, business personal property, and personal property of others in the association's control
   C. the contents of a commercial condominium
2. The condominium commercial unit-owners coverage form is used to insure
   A. personal property belonging to the owners of residential condominiums
   B. residential or commercial condominium associations against loss or damage to buildings, business personal property, and personal property of others in the association's control
   C. the contents of a commercial condominium

Exercise answers can be found at the end of the Unit 13 answers and rationales.

13.6. BUSINESS INCOME COVERAGE FORMS

13.6.1. Coverages

The **business income coverage forms** pay for loss of income that the insured sustains due to a direct physical loss from a peril insured against that forces the insured to suspend operations during the period of restoration. The period of restoration begins on the date of the direct physical loss and ends on the date on which the property can be repaired, rebuilt, or replaced with reasonable speed. **Suspension** means a slowdown or cessation of the insured's business activities.

The type of coverage provided under the business income forms is known as **time element coverage**, since it provides coverage for the loss of business income over a period that results from direct physical loss. Business income includes net income that would have been earned if the loss had not occurred and the costs of continuing normal operations, including payroll.

For loss of business income to be covered, the suspension of operations must result from direct physical loss to property at the described premises caused by a peril insured against in the causes of loss form.

There are two business income forms: business income with extra expense and business income without extra expense.

Extra expense is a coverage that reimburses the insured for expenses incurred to keep a business going after a loss caused by a covered peril.

The **business income with extra expense coverage form** includes an extra expense coverage that reimburses the insured for money spent to avoid or minimize a business shutdown. It covers only expenses the insured would not have incurred if the property had not been damaged.

The **business income without extra expense coverage form** replaces the extra expense coverage with an **expenses to reduce loss coverage** that covers expenses the insured incurs to reduce loss, up to the amount the loss is reduced.

With either of the business income forms, the insured may select:

- business income coverage, including rental value coverage;
- business income coverage, other than rental value coverage; or
- rental value coverage only.

Rental value includes the total anticipated rental income from a tenant occupancy, all amounts that are legal obligations of the tenant and would otherwise be the insured's obligations, and fair rental value of any part of the premises occupied by the insured.

Like the other commercial property forms we've discussed, the business income coverage forms contain a coinsurance clause. Coinsurance applies to business income coverage but not to extra expense coverage.

13.6.2. Additional Coverages

Both business income forms contain certain additional coverages. One such coverage is extended business income. This pays for loss of business income, even after operations have been resumed, until the business has been restored, but for no more than 30 days from the date business is resumed.

The **order of civil authority** coverage pays business income and extra expense losses incurred when a civil authority prohibits access to the described premises because property other than the described premises was damaged by a covered cause of loss. Both business income and extra expense losses are paid for up to three consecutive weeks. Payment for business income losses begins 72 hours after the action by the civil authority.

The **alterations and new buildings** coverage pays business income and extra expense losses incurred when a covered cause of loss damages a new building or an alteration or addition to a new building. Also covered is damage to machinery, equipment, supplies, or building materials on or within 100 feet of the described premises if these items are being used in construction, alterations, or additions or are incidental to the occupancy of new buildings. If the loss delays the start of the insured's operations, the period of restoration under this coverage begins on the date operations would have begun if the loss had not occurred.

13.6.3. Optional Coverages

There are also several optional coverages included in the business income coverage forms.

The **extended period of indemnity** option gives the insured extended business income coverage for the number of days stated in the declarations, rather than the 30 days allowed by the extended business income additional coverage.

The **maximum period of indemnity** optional coverage limits reimbursement for extra expenses or loss of business income to no more than the amount of loss incurred during the first 120 days following the direct loss.

The **monthly limit of indemnity** optional coverage allows the insured to establish the amount of reimbursement for loss of business income during each 30-day period. The insured selects a fraction that is multiplied by the limit of insurance to determine the maximum that could be paid for each 30 days.

The coinsurance condition that applies to the business income coverage forms is waived when either the maximum period of indemnity or monthly limit of indemnity coverages are selected by the insured.

The insured may also select the **agreed value** optional coverage. This coverage requires the insured to submit a business income report/worksheet every 12 months that shows financial data for the 12 months prior to the submission as well as estimated data for the 12 months following. As long as a new worksheet is submitted every 12 months, the coinsurance clause will not apply. Instead, the insured is expected to carry insurance to value, or the agreed value established by the worksheets. If the insured fails to file the required financial data, the coinsurance clause is reactivated.

Exercise 13.E

Select the appropriate optional coverage for each of the examples listed below.

1. The insured wants to limit the amount of reimbursement available in each 30-day period. ______________________
2. The insured wants to limit reimbursement to 120 days following direct physical loss. ______________________
3. The insured wants to bypass the coinsurance condition and instead meet a requirement that insurance be carried to the value established by periodic financial reports. ______________________
4. The insured wants to purchase extended business income coverage for longer than the 30-day period allowed by the extended business income additional coverage. ______________________

Exercise answers can be found at the end of the Unit 13 answers and rationales.

13.6.4. Business Income from Dependent Properties—Broad Form

The **business income from dependent properties—broad form** is a variation on the business income forms. It provides coverage for the following.

- Insureds who depend on another business as their sole supply of merchandise or raw materials may suffer a loss if their supplier is forced to cut back or eliminate shipments because of a direct physical loss. The business income from dependent properties—broad form protects the insured against loss due to loss at such a **contributing location.**

- Insureds who depend on a particular business as the primary buyer for their products are covered under this form if direct physical loss at such a **recipient location** causes the insured's earnings to suffer.
- Insureds may depend on a manufacturer to deliver certain products or components to the insured's customers under a sales contract. Should the **manufacturing location** be unable to fulfill the contract because of direct physical loss, insureds may suffer a loss of income that can be covered under this form.
- Insureds may depend on another business to attract customers to their own business. Loss to such a **leader location** may cause insureds to suffer a loss of earnings that can be covered under this form.

Exercise 13.F

The insureds in each of the following cases rely on certain dependent properties. Identify each type as a contributing location **(C),** recipient location **(R)**, manufacturing location **(M),** or leader location **(L).**

____ 1. An insured operates an ice cream parlor in a recently developed commercial area and relies on the proximity of a toy store that is part of a nationwide chain to attract many of the shop's customers.

____ 2. An insured has invented a radically different computer, which another company manufactures for delivery to the insured's customers.

____ 3. An insured has developed a very successful pharmaceutical business that serves nursing homes and depends on a particular drug producer to supply orders quickly.

____ 4. A group of insureds are in the business of handcrafting one-of-a-kind articles that are sold primarily to one large retailer.

Exercise answers can be found at the end of the Unit 13 answers and rationales.

13.7. EXTRA EXPENSE AND LEGAL LIABILITY COVERAGE FORMS

Although one of the business income coverage forms includes extra expense coverage to help minimize or prevent a suspension of business, some insureds simply cannot accept such a suspension. Instead, they will do whatever is required to avoid a shutdown. For these insureds, the need is not to protect lost income but to cover the extra expenses needed to continue operations at any cost. Examples are public utilities, newspapers, dairies, and other businesses where, if the business shut down, there would be a great hardship on customers or lost business would likely never be regained.

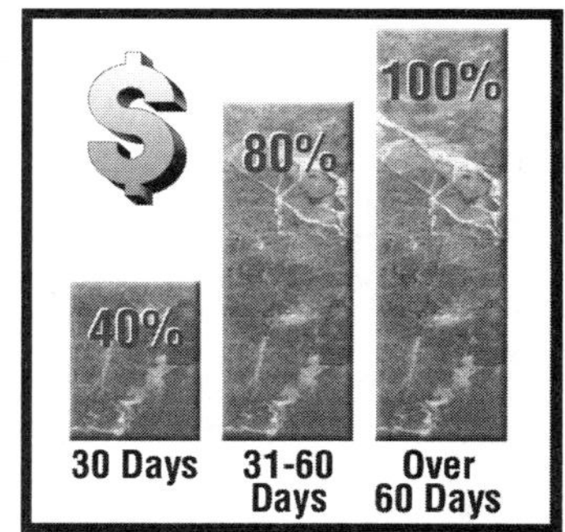

This type of risk needs the **extra expense coverage form**, which provides no reimbursement for lost business income but concentrates on reimbursing the insured for extra expenses incurred to remain in operation. The extra expense coverage form is a time element coverage.

Limits are applied to recovery depending on the period of restoration. For instance, limits might be stated in the declarations as 40%/80%/100%. This means that if the restoration period was:

- **30 days or less,** 40% of the full amount of insurance would be paid;
- **31–60 days**, 80% of the full amount of insurance would be paid; or
- **over 60 days**, 100% of the full amount of insurance would be paid.

Earlier, you learned that the building and personal property coverage form covers damage to property of others in the insured's care, custody, or control, whether the insured is legally liable for that loss. The legal liability coverage form also covers damage to property of others while in the insured's control, but only if the insured is legally liable for the damage.

An insured may choose this form to obtain a lower rate because it covers fewer types of losses. Payment is made on behalf of the insured. Coverage may apply to exposures arising from the insured's occupancy of another's building or from having custody of the property of others, such as customers' goods.

13.8. CAUSES OF LOSS FORMS

13.8.1. Basic

In addition to one or more coverage forms, the commercial property coverage part requires a **causes of loss form**. While the coverage forms explain what property is covered and what coverages are provided, the causes of loss form states what perils are insured against. It also lists specific exclusions. There are three causes of loss forms: basic, broad, and special.

The **causes of loss—basic form** is a named perils form that lists 11 covered perils:

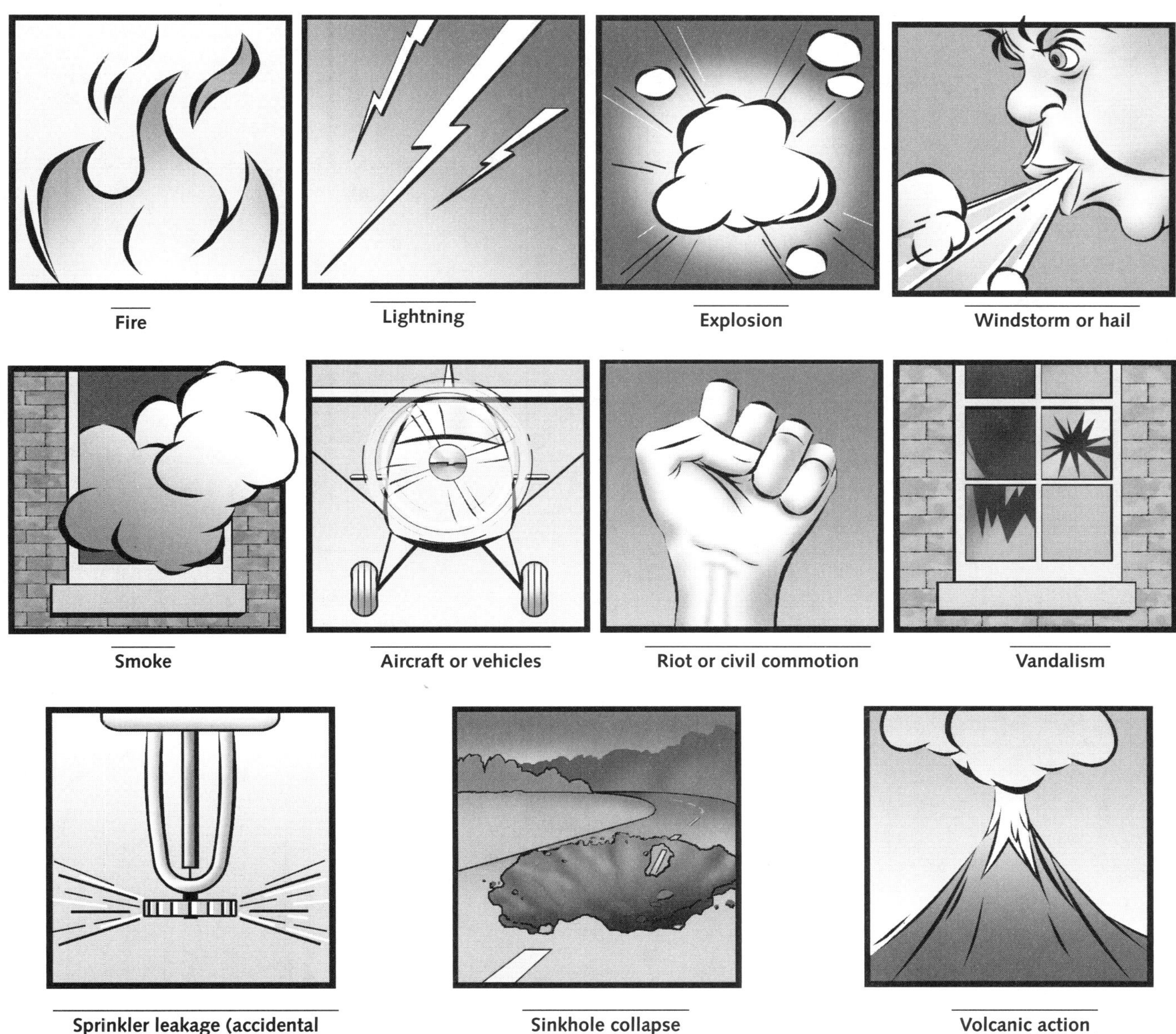

Smoke from agricultural smudging or industrial operations is not covered.

The windstorm or hail peril does not include damage caused by frost, cold weather, snow, sleet, or ice other than hail. Damage to the interior of a building or its contents is covered only when the wind or hail first creates an opening in the walls or roof.

The explosion peril includes explosion of gasses or fuel within the furnace or flues of any fired vessel.

Vehicle damage caused by vehicles the named insured owns or operates in the course of the insured's business is not covered.

Volcanic action includes airborne volcanic blast or shockwaves, ash, dust, particulate matter, and lava flow. Removal of ash, dust, and particulate matter is not covered if it does not cause direct physical loss to the described premises.

The exclusions include:

- fungus, wet rot, dry rot, and bacteria (except as provided as an additional coverage); does not apply when they result from fire or lightning;
- ordinance or law;
- earth movement (does not include a fire or explosion resulting from earth movement);
- government action;
- nuclear hazard;
- failure of power or other utility services occurring away from the insured's premises;
- war and military action;
- water, including flood, sewer backup, mudslides, or seepage of ground water;
- artificially generated current;
- rupture or bursting of water pipes (other than automatic sprinklers);
- leakage or discharge of water or steam resulting from breaking of water or steam system or appliance (does not apply to automatic sprinklers), including continuous or repeated seepage or leakage or the presence or condensation of humidity, moisture, or vapor that occurs over 14 days or more;
- explosions of steam boilers, pipes, engines, or turbines; and
- mechanical breakdown.

13.8.1.1. Additional Coverage—Limited Coverage for Fungus, Wet Rot, Dry Rot, and Bacteria

The basic form also includes the **limited coverage for fungus, wet rot, dry rot, and bacteria additional coverage**. Fungus is defined as any type or form of fungus, including mold or mildew, and any mycotoxins, spores, scents, or byproducts produced or released by fungi. For purposes of simplification, we will use the word *mold* in this section.

This additional coverage provides limited coverage for mold that results from a covered cause of loss other than fire or lightning. (Coverage for mold-related losses arising out of fire or lightning is provided elsewhere in the form.) The loss must occur during the policy period, and all reasonable means must have been used to save and preserve the property from further damage at the time of and after that occurrence. The insurer will pay for:

- direct physical loss or damage to covered property caused by mold, including the cost to remove it;
- costs to tear out and replace any part of the building or other property if needed to gain access to the mold; and
- cost of testing performed after removal, repair, replacement, or restoration of the damaged property is completed, provided there is a reason to believe that mold is present.

Coverage is limited to $15,000 for all loss or damage arising out of all occurrences of covered causes of loss that take place in a 12-month period, regardless of the number of claims. The 12-month period starts with the beginning of the present annual policy period. If a particular loss results in mold, the insurer will not pay more than a total of $15,000 even if it continues to be present or active or recurs in a later policy period. This additional coverage does not increase the applicable limit of insurance on covered property.

13.8.2. Broad

The **causes of loss—broad form** covers all of the perils listed in the basic form and:

- falling objects (does not cover damage to interior property unless the exterior of the building is damaged first);
- weight of snow, ice, or sleet; and
- water damage (accidental discharge or leakage of water or steam as a result of the cracking or breaking of a water or steam system or appliance).

Coverage also includes the cost of tearing out or replacing any part of a building to repair damage to the system from which the water or steam escaped, and costs to repair the system itself. Not covered are the costs to repair any defect that caused the loss, loss from continuous seepage over 14 days or more, or loss caused by freezing unless proper precautions were taken to prevent freezing.

13.8.2.1. Collapse Additional Coverage

The broad form contains the limited mold coverage additional coverage and another additional coverage for collapse. **Collapse** is defined as an abrupt falling down or caving in of the building or part of the building that results in the building being unusable. This definition does not include a building that is in danger of collapsing or a building or part of a building that is still standing but has separated from another part of the structure or shows signs of instability such as bulging, cracking, leaning, or settling.

Collapse of a building, part of a building, or a building that contains covered property is covered only when it is caused by one of the specified broad form perils or any of the following additional perils:

- Breakage of glass
- Hidden decay
- Hidden insect or vermin damage
- Weight of people or personal property
- Weight of rain that collects on a roof
- Use of defective material or methods in construction, remodeling, or renovation if the collapse occurs while the construction, remodeling, or renovation is in progress

Collapse that results from hidden decay or hidden insect or vermin damage is not covered if the insured knew about the damage before the collapse occurred. If collapse occurs after construction, remodeling, or renovation is completed and is caused by a covered peril, the loss or damage is covered even if the use of defective materials or methods contributed to the collapse.

The following types of outdoor properties, even if they are otherwise covered under the policy, are covered for collapse only when they are damaged directly by a collapsed building:

- Outdoor radio or television antennas, including satellite dishes, and their lead-in wiring, masts, or towers
- Awnings, gutters, and downspouts
- Yard fixtures
- Outdoor swimming pools
- Fences
- Piers, wharves, and docks
- Beach or diving platforms or appurtenances
- Retaining walls
- Walks, roadways, and other paved surfaces

Under certain conditions, loss or damage that occurs when personal property falls down or caves in is covered even when there is no building collapse.

- The property must be inside a building.
- The collapse must result from one of the specified causes of loss.
- The property that collapses must not be one of the items of outdoor property described above.

Also, coverage does not apply if marring or scratching is the only damage that results from the collapse. Settling, shrinkage, expansion, cracking, bulging, leaning, sagging, or bending is not considered to be collapse.

The collapse additional coverage does not increase the limits of insurance provided by the coverage part.

13.8.3. Special

The **causes of loss—special form** covers any direct physical loss not specifically excluded or limited in the form. In other words, it provides open perils coverage. Because of this, the list of exclusions is more extensive and detailed than in the other causes of loss forms you've studied. In addition to some of the exclusions contained in the other forms, such as earth movement, war, and nuclear hazard, the special form excludes:

- wear and tear;
- rust, corrosion, fungus, decay, deterioration, and hidden or latent defects;
- smog;
- pollutants (unless the release, discharge, or dispersal is caused by a specified cause of loss);
- settling, cracking, shrinking, or expansion;
- damage caused by insects, birds, rodents, or other animals;
- mechanical breakdown;
- explosion of steam boilers, pipes, and engines;
- dishonest or criminal acts of the insured or the insured's employees;
- voluntary parting with property if induced to do so by fraud or a trick;
- rain, snow, ice, or sleet damage to personal property that is not in a building;
- loss resulting from acts or decisions, or the failure to act or decide;
- collapse (other than that specifically included under the collapse additional coverage); and
- faulty planning, development, design, specifications, workmanship, or repair.

Both the limited mold coverage and the collapse additional coverages are included in the special form.

13.8.3.1. Limitations

The special causes of loss form imposes limitations on coverage for certain types of losses.

The special form covers theft, but coverage for various classes of property is limited to the following amounts:

- $2,500 for furs, fur garments, and garments trimmed with fur
- $2,500 for jewelry, watches, jewels, pearls, precious and semi-precious stones, gold, silver, and platinum (does not apply to jewelry and watches worth less than $100 per item)
- $2,500 for patterns, dies, molds, and forms
- $250 for stamps, tickets, lottery tickets held for sale, and letters of credit

The following property is covered only if the loss is caused by a specified cause of loss (the same as the broad form perils) or breakage of building glass:

- Valuable papers and records, abstracts, drawings, and data processing, recording, or storage media
- Animals, and then only if killed or if it is necessary to destroy them
- Breakage of fragile articles, such as statuary, marble, chinaware, and porcelain
- Building machinery, tools, and equipment that the insured owns or is entrusted with while away from the premises

Exercise 13.G

1. A furrier's inventory is insured under a building and personal property coverage form for $500,000. An individual ran into the store and poured acid over a fur coat valued at $3,500. Will the insured receive the full amount of this loss if she has the special causes of loss form?
   () Yes () No
2. If instead the customer took a $5,000 coat without paying for it, what is the maximum amount the insured would receive?
   $_________________

Exercise answers can be found at the end of the Unit 13 answers and rationales.

13.8.4. Causes of Loss—Earthquake and Volcanic Eruption

None of the causes of loss forms covers earthquake or volcanic eruption. An insured can obtain coverage for these perils by adding the earthquake and volcanic eruption endorsement to the policy. This endorsement must be used in conjunction with one of the causes of loss forms.

Volcanic eruption means the eruption, explosion, or effusion (pouring forth) of a volcano. All earthquake shocks or volcanic eruptions that occur within any 168-hour period constitute a single earthquake or volcanic eruption. The expiration of the policy does not reduce the 168-hour period.

An insured may choose to limit coverage to sprinkler leakage caused by an earthquake or volcanic eruption and not cover other losses resulting from these perils. This is indicated by entering earthquake—sprinkler leakage only in the policy declarations. The 168-hour time period for earthquake shocks and volcanic eruptions also applies to this optional coverage.

13.8.5. Comparison of Causes of Loss

The following chart summarizes the perils covered by the basic, broad, and special causes of loss forms and the earthquake and volcanic eruption endorsement.

Perils Insured Against

Peril	Basic	Broad	Special	Earthquake and Volcanic Eruption Endorsement*
			Open Peril**	
Fire	√	√		
Lightning	√	√		
Explosion	√	√		
Windstorm Or Hail	√	√		
Smoke	√	√		
Aircraft Or Vehicles	√	√		
Riot Or Civil Commotion	√	√		
Vandalism	√	√		
Sprinkler Leakage	√	√		
Sinkhole Collapse	√	√		
Volcanic Action	√	√		
Limited Mold Coverage***	√	√	√	
Falling Objects		√		
Weight Of Snow, Ice, Sleet		√		
Water Damage		√		
Collapse***		√	√	
Earthquake				√
Volcanic Eruption				√

*Must be used in conjunction with Basic, Broad or Special Causes Of Loss form
**Risks of loss not otherwise excluded are covered
***Additional coverage

13.9. ENDORSEMENTS

13.9.1. Value Reporting Endorsements

There are several endorsements that can be added to the commercial property coverage part.

Some businesses may insure property for which values fluctuate regularly, or property that is moved from one location to another from time to time. For these insureds, the **value reporting form** is used to provide coverage based on actual values at certain locations at specific times. The insured purchases a somewhat higher amount of insurance than he thinks will be needed, then reports actual values at each location on a regular basis, paying premium on the basis of these reports at the end of the policy period based on average exposures. Coverage amounts are also adjusted accordingly, reducing the risk that the insured will be underinsured or overinsured at any one location. Property that can be covered by the value reporting form includes business personal property, stock, and the personal property of others.

A variation of the reporting form is the **peak season endorsement** that allows the insured to carry increased coverage during certain seasons of the year when inventory or other covered property is higher than usual.

13.9.2. Ordinance or Law Coverage Endorsement

The ordinance or law policy exclusion prohibits payment for increased costs due to building regulations or demolition laws. The **ordinance or law coverage endorsement** offsets this exclusion by providing coverage when an insured's loss is increased because of such laws.

Both demolition costs and increased construction costs are covered if they are required or regulated by law or ordinance. Loss in value of the undamaged portion of the building as a consequence of enforcement of such an ordinance or law is also covered. However, the endorsement does not cover costs resulting from the enforcement of laws regarding pollutants, such as laws concerning pollution cleanup or removal.

13.9.3. Spoilage Endorsement

The **spoilage endorsement** may be added to the building and personal property and condominium commercial unit-owners coverage forms to provide coverage for the insured's perishable stock—personal property that must be maintained under controlled conditions to protect it from loss or damage.

UNIT TEST

1. List **all** of the components required in a commercial property coverage part.

   A. ______________________________

   B. ______________________________

   C. ______________________________

   D. ______________________________

   E. ______________________________

   F. ______________________________

   G. ______________________________

2. Match the commercial property coverage form listed in the left-hand column with its correct definition in the right-hand column.

1. Building and personal property	____ A. Covers buildings under construction
2. Builders risk	____ B. Covers the insured for liability arising out of negligent damage to the property of others in the care, custody, or control of the insured
3. Condominium association	____ C. Reimburses the insured for extra expenses required to avoid a suspension of business and continue operations
4. Extra expense	____ D. Covers buildings, the insured's business personal property, and the personal property of others located at the business premises
5. Legal liability	____ E. Insures a condominium association against direct physical loss or damage to buildings, business personal property, and personal property of others in the care, custody, or control of the association while it is at the premises

3. Which of the following perils are covered in the causes of loss—basic form?
   A. Collapse
   B. Explosion
   C. Volcanic eruption
   D. Nuclear hazard
   E. Weight of snow, ice, or sleet
   F. Smoke

4. Under the earthquake and volcanic eruption endorsement, all earthquake shocks or volcanic eruptions that occur within a certain number of hours constitute a single earthquake or volcanic eruption. What is that period?
   A. 24 hours
   B. 40 hours
   C. 72 hours
   D. 168 hours

5. Which causes of loss form provides open peril coverage?
   A. Basic
   B. Broad
   C. Special
   D. Both basic and broad

6. Loss caused by sprinkler leakage is covered under which commercial property causes of loss forms?
   A. Basic
   B. Broad
   C. Special
   D. All of the above

7. Which commercial property causes of loss forms cover collapse?
   A. Basic
   B. Broad
   C. Special
   D. All of the above

8. Which commercial property coverage endorsement would be appropriate for an insured
   A. whose property values fluctuate regularly?
   ____
   ____
   B. that needs coverage for its perishable stock?
   ____
   ____
   C. that wants coverage for increased costs due to building regulations or demolition laws?
   ____
   ____

9. List the three types of coverages provided by the building and personal property coverage form.
   A. ______________________________
   ____
   ____
   B. ______________________________
   ____
   ____
   C. ______________________________
   ____
   ____

10. Which of the following would be covered under the building coverage of the building and personal property coverage form?
    A. Inventory stored at the insured's warehouse
    B. An addition to the insured's store on which construction has just begun
    C. Fire extinguishers located in the insured's factory

11. The insured's business sustains $25,000 damage in a fire. The fire department that was called to the scene billed the insured $1,000. The business is insured under the building and personal property coverage form for $500,000 with a $5,000 deductible. How much will the insurance company pay for this loss?
    A. $20,000
    B. $21,000
    C. $26,000

12. Which of the following property would be excluded under the building and personal property coverage form?
    A. Lawn
    B. Driveway
    C. Private company jet
    D. Animals held for sale
    E. Cost of excavation
    F. Vehicles manufactured by the insured

13. The insured buys an office building next door to her insured business. Is the new building covered under her existing building and personal property coverage form?
    A. No. The insured must purchase a separate policy for the new building.
    B. Yes. Up to $250,000 coverage is available under the newly acquired or constructed property coverage extension.

14. For a loss to be covered under the personal effects and property of others coverage extension in the building and personal property coverage form, the insured must
    A. meet the coinsurance requirement
    B. have purchased coverage for personal property of others
    C. Both A and B

15. According to the loss payment condition in the building and personal property coverage form, if the insured has complied with all of the terms of the coverage part and has reached agreement with the company on the amount of the loss, the insurer will pay the loss
    A. as soon as possible after it receives the sworn statement of loss
    B. within 30 days after it receives the sworn statement of loss

16. When are losses under the building and personal property coverage form paid at replacement or repair cost?
    A. Always
    B. Never
    C. If the insured meets the coinsurance requirements and costs are $2,500 or less

17. Which of the following have special loss valuation requirements under the building and personal property coverage form?
    A. Buildings
    B. Furniture and fixtures
    C. Glass
    D. Valuable papers and records
    E. Exterior signs

18. Which of the following losses would be excluded under the building and personal property coverage form if the insured building was vacant for more than 60 days before the loss occurred?
    A. Attempted theft
    B. Sprinkler leakage when the insured had protected the system against freezing
    C. Vandalism
    D. Glass breakage

19. Which of the following would be covered under the builders risk coverage form?
    A. Building under construction
    B. Foundation of the building under construction
    C. Fixtures, machinery, and equipment used to service the building if they will become a permanent part of the building and are located within 100 feet of the building
    D. All of the above

20. A partially constructed duplex is destroyed in a fire. Would the amount paid under the builders risk coverage form be reduced because the duplex was vacant at the time of the loss?
    ( ) Yes ( ) No Why or why not?

    ____
    ____
    ____
    ____
    ____

21. What is included in the definition of business income?

    ____
    ____

22. Which business income coverage form covers expenses the insured incurs to reduce loss?

____

____

____

23. Which business income coverage form covers money spent to avoid or minimize a business shutdown?

____

____

____

24. Why would some insureds select extra expense coverage instead of business income coverage?

____

____

____

25. The limit of insurance on the insured's extra expense coverage form is $200,000, with percentages of 40%/80%/100% shown in the declarations. What is the maximum amount the insured could receive when the period of restoration is

A. less than 30 days? $________
B. between 31 and 60 days? $__________
C. more than 60 days? $_________

26. The insured's business is covered under a building and personal property coverage form with the broad causes of loss form. Years of water damage from a leaky foundation have caused the basement walls in the insured's building to bulge. The building is still standing and being used in the insured's business operations. Would the costs to repair these walls be covered under the collapse additional coverage? ( ) Yes ( ) No
Why or why not?

____

____

____

____

27. Which of the following perils/additional coverages are included in the causes of loss—broad form?

A. Collapse
B. Weight of ice, snow, or sleet
C. War
D. Nuclear hazard
E. Falling objects
F. Water damage

ANSWERS AND RATIONALES TO UNIT TEST

1. A commercial property coverage part must include the following components: common policy declarations, common policy conditions, commercial property declarations, commercial property conditions, one or more commercial property coverage forms, causes of loss form, and any mandatory endorsements.

2. 2 A. 5 B. 4 C. 1 D. 3 E.
The building and personal property coverage form covers buildings, the insured's business personal property, and the personal property of others located at the business premises. The builders risk coverage form covers buildings under construction. The condominium association coverage form insures a condominium association against direct physical loss or damage to buildings, business personal property, and personal property of others in the care, custody, or control of the association while it is located at the premises. The extra expense coverage form reimburses the insured for extra expenses required to avoid a suspension of business and continue operations. The legal liability coverage form covers the insured for liability arising out of negligent damage to the property of others in the care, custody, or control of the insured.

3. **B and F**. Coverage for collapse is provided as an additional coverage in the broad and special causes of loss forms. Volcanic eruption is covered under the earthquake and volcanic eruption endorsement. (The other causes of loss forms cover volcanic action, which is not the same thing as volcanic eruption.) Loss arising out of a nuclear hazard is excluded under all causes of loss forms. Loss from the weight of snow, ice, or sleet is included in the broad and special causes of loss forms.

4. **D.** Under this endorsement, all earthquake shocks or volcanic eruptions that occur within any 168-hour period constitute a single earthquake or volcanic eruption.

5. **C.** The basic and broad causes of loss forms are named peril forms.

6. **D.** All of the causes of loss forms cover sprinkler leakage.

7. **B and C**. Collapse is not covered under the basic causes of loss form.

8. **A.** Value reporting endorsement. This endorsement provides coverage based on the actual values of property at certain locations at specific times.

   B. Spoilage endorsement. This endorsement is used with the building and personal property and condominium commercial unit-owners coverage forms. It adds coverage for the insured's perishable stock—personal property that must be maintained under controlled conditions to protect it from loss or damage.

   C. Ordinance or law coverage endorsement. This endorsement provides coverage for demolition costs and increased construction costs required or regulated by law or ordinance.

9. Under the building and personal property coverage form, the insured may select one or more of the following coverages: building, business personal property, and personal property of others.

10. **B and C**. Inventory would be covered under business personal property coverage.

11. **B.** Fire department service charges are paid in addition to the limit of insurance, with no deductible.

12. **A, B, C, and E**. Animals are not excluded if they are boarded or held for sale. The vehicles exclusion does not apply to vehicles manufactured by the insured.

13. **B.** The newly acquired or constructed property coverage extension covers new buildings that are being built on the described premises and buildings the insured acquires. The most that will be paid under this coverage extension is $250,000 per building.

14. **A.** The personal effects and property of others coverage extension is available even if the insured has not purchased personal property of others coverage, as long as the coinsurance requirement is met.

15. **B.** If the insured complies with all of the terms of the coverage part and has reached agreement with the company on the amount of the loss, the insurer will pay the loss within 30 days after it receives the sworn statement of loss.

16. **C.** Most losses are paid at actual cash value. However, if the coinsurance conditions are met and costs are $2,500 or less, the policy will pay the cost of building repair or replacement without taking depreciation into account.

17. **C and D**. Stock, glass, valuable papers and records, and tenants' improvements and betterments all have special valuation requirements.

18. **A, C, and D.** Damage in a vacant building due to sprinkler leakage is covered if the system was protected against freezing.

19. **D.** The builders risk coverage form covers the building under construction and its foundation. Fixtures, machinery, equipment used to service the building, and the insured's building materials and supplies can be covered if they will become a permanent part of the building and are within 100 feet of the building.

20. No. The builders risk coverage form does not have a vacancy condition because buildings under construction are not considered vacant.

21. The definition of business income includes net income that would have been earned if the loss had not occurred and the cost of continuing normal operations.

22. The business income without extra expense coverage form covers expenses the insured incurs to reduce loss.

23. The business income with extra expense coverage form covers money spent to avoid or minimize a business shutdown.

24. Some insureds would select extra expense coverage instead of business income coverage because the nature of some businesses requires that they spend whatever amounts are necessary to keep the business operating and avoid a shutdown.

25. **A.** $80,000. Limits are applied to recovery depending on the length of the period of restoration. These limits are expressed as percentages in the declarations. Since the period of restoration was less than 30 days, the first percentage (40%) would apply. The most the insured will receive is 40% of the limit, or $80,000.

B. $160,000. Limits are applied to recovery depending on the length of the period of restoration. These limits are expressed as percentages in the declarations. Since the period of restoration was between 31 and 60 days, the second percentage (80%) would apply. The most the insured will receive is 80% of the limit, or $160,000.

C. $200,000. Limits are applied to recovery depending on the length of the period of restoration. These limits are expressed as percentages in the declarations. Since the period of restoration was more than 60 days, the last percentage (100%) would apply. The insured will receive the full policy limit.

26. No. This building is not in a state of collapse as it is defined in the causes of loss form.

27. **A, B, E, and F**. War and nuclear hazard are excluded in all of the causes of loss forms.

UNIT 13 EXERCISE ANSWERS

Exercise 13.A

1. **BP**
2. **PP**
3. **BP**

Exercise 13.B

1. **A** $42,500—The amount payable is reduced 15%

   $50,000 × 15% = $7,500

   $50,000 – $7,500 = $42,500

Exercise 13.C

1. $17,750

   ($150,000/$250,000=.60

   $30,000 × .60=$18,000

   $18,000 – $250=$17,750)

Exercise 13.D

1. **B**
2. **C**

Exercise 13.E

1. Monthly limit of indemnity
2. Maximum period of indemnity
3. Agreed value
4. Extended period of indemnity

Exercise 13.F

1. **L**
2. **M**
3. **C**
4. **R**

Exercise 13.G

1. Yes—The $2,500 limit only applies to theft losses
2. $2,500

UNIT

14

Ocean and Inland Marine Insurance

14.1. LEARNING OBJECTIVES

After completing Unit 14—Ocean and Inland Marine Insurance, you will be able to do the following:

- Identify the four categories of ocean marine insurance and the type of coverage provided under each category
- Describe the perils covered under ocean marine insurance
- Define perils of the sea, jettison, barratry, and average
- Explain the difference between a general average loss and a particular average loss
- Define the implied warranties associated with ocean marine insurance
- Describe the purpose of the nationwide definition
- Identify the categories included in the nationwide definition and the insurance coverages used to cover these risks
- Explain the difference between a filed inland marine form and a nonfiled inland marine form
- Identify the commercial inland marine forms that may be included in the commercial package policy
- Identify the required components of a commercial inland marine coverage part
- Summarize the provisions of the commercial inland marine conditions
- Describe the following provisions in the mail coverage form, including property covered and where coverage applies, property that is only covered if sent by registered mail, when coverage begins and ends, and how losses are valued
- Describe the provisions in the physicians and surgeons equipment coverage form, including property covered and where coverage applies, situations and perils that are excluded, and protective safeguards condition
- Describe property that can and cannot be covered under the theatrical property coverage form and situations and perils that are excluded
- Describe the provisions of the film coverage form, including property that can and cannot be covered, losses that are excluded, how losses are valued, when coverage under the form ends, how the coverage territory differs from typical insurance policies, and requirements for maintaining records and reporting information that the insured uses to determine the premium
- Identify property that can be covered under the commercial articles coverage form, where coverage applies, and how additional acquired property is covered

- Describe the provisions of the accounts receivable coverage form, including types of losses covered, exclusions, how losses are valued when the exact amount of loss cannot be determined, and requirements for storing records
- Describe the provisions of the valuable papers and records coverage form, including types of losses covered, how coverage is provided for property away from the premises, exclusions, how losses are valued, and requirements for storing papers and records
- Identify property that can be covered under the signs coverage form and losses that are excluded
- Describe the provisions of the jewelers block coverage form, including property that can and cannot be covered, optional show windows and money coverages, exclusions, how losses are valued, protective safeguards condition, and requirements for taking inventory and maintaining business records
- Describe the provisions of the floor plan coverage form, including property covered, who may be insured under the form, when coverage ends, exclusions, requirement for maintaining inventory records, purpose of the transit coverage in the event of cancellation condition, how policy provisions apply when coverage is written on a dual-interest basis, and requirements for reporting information used to determine premium
- Describe the provisions of the equipment dealers coverage form, including property that can and cannot be covered, exclusions, coverage for debris removal and pollutant cleanup and removal, protective safeguards condition, requirement for maintaining inventory records, and how losses are valued
- Describe the following provisions of the camera and musical instrument dealers coverage form: property that can and cannot be covered, exclusions, and how losses are valued
- Identify the filed commercial inland marine coverage forms that cover one or more of the following: collapse of a building, damage to a building from theft or attempted theft, and removal of property to protect it from loss
- Compare and contrast the annual transit policy and the trip transit policy
- Compare and contrast the various motor truck cargo policies
- Describe the purpose of the following types of nonfiled inland marine forms: bailee's customer policies, equipment floaters, business floaters, and dealers policies

14.2. OCEAN MARINE INSURANCE

Marine insurance is a type of property insurance that protects property wherever it is, on land or sea. There are two types of marine insurance: ocean marine and inland marine.

We'll begin by studying **ocean marine insurance**, which covers cargo and ships in transit over sea. It is one of the oldest types of insurance and one of the first to provide open-peril coverage for the insured's property. There are no standardized forms.

14.2.1. Hull, Cargo, Freight, and Protection and Indemnity Coverage

There are four categories of ocean marine insurance.

Hull insurance provides **physical damage coverage** for the ship itself while in transit on oceans, rivers, and lakes. Coverage may be obtained for a single vessel or an entire fleet. Limited **liability insurance** may also be included through the **running down clause,** which protects the owner if he is held liable for the negligent operation of the vessel in damaging another ship.

Cargo insurance covers goods while they are in transit over water. Through the use of the **warehouse to warehouse clause,** coverage is also extended to include coverage from the property's point of origination to its point of destination. This includes not only ocean travel but also any incidental journey by land. For instance, the inland trip from the warehouse to the shipping dock would be covered. Coverage may be purchased on a **trip** or **voyage basis** or may be purchased as **open cargo.** An insured who frequently ships cargoes, such as an importer or exporter, would arrange for open cargo coverage.

Freight insurance protects the insured against the loss of shipping costs. This coverage can be written separately or included with hull insurance or cargo insurance, depending on how the shipping costs are handled. When shipping is prepaid by the owner of the cargo, the owner would lose the shipping charges if the cargo is lost. In these cases, it is common for the owner to purchase freight coverage along with the cargo insurance. Alternately, if the freight is not prepaid and the cargo is lost, it is the shipper or vessel owner who would stand to lose. A ship owner may protect against this loss by adding freight insurance to the hull coverage.

Finally, **protection and indemnity insurance (P&I)** provides marine **liability** insurance. P&I protects against liability for:

- job-related injuries to sailors;
- injuries to stevedores, longshore workers, or harbor workers;
- damage to cargo through negligence;
- damage to other property not caused by collision; and
- damage to other property or another boat resulting from collision.

Exercise 14.A

Match the type of ocean marine insurance listed in the left-hand column with the description of the coverage it provides in the right-hand column.

_____ 1. Hull	A. Covers the ship itself while in transit over water
_____ 2. Cargo	B. Covers goods being shipped overseas
_____ 3. Freight	C. Covers watercraft liability exposures
_____ 4. Protection and indemnity	D. Covers loss of shipping costs

Exercise answers can be found in the end of the Unit 14 answers and rationales.

14.2.2. Characteristics of Ocean Marine Insurance

To fully understand ocean marine insurance, you need a thorough understanding of the terminology and practices that are a part of the shipping industry and the marine trade—a task that goes beyond the scope of this course. We can, however, introduce you to a few of the more important characteristics of ocean marine insurance.

Ocean marine insurance can be issued on a named-peril or open-peril basis. Waterborne properties are subject to a wide variety of perils, such as fire, explosion, pilferage, contact with other cargo, and leakage or damage by ship sweat. They are also subject to a group of perils known as **perils of the sea.** These perils, which often result from stormy weather, include:

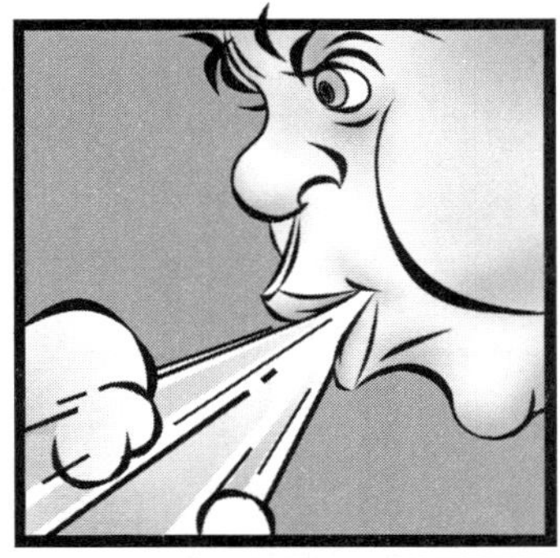

Unusual wind or wave action

Stranding

Lightning

Collision

Sinking

Another peril covered under ocean marine contracts is **jettison.** Jettison is a voluntary action to rid the ship of cargo to prevent further peril. Jettison is permitted if the action is taken to save the remaining property. The loss incurred by sacrificing a portion of the cargo will be reimbursed.

Another peril unique to ocean marine forms is called **barratry.** Barratry refers to illegal acts committed willfully by the ship's master or crew for the purpose of damaging the ship or its cargo. It includes hijacking, abandonment, or embezzlement.

Exercise 14.B

Identify each of the following as examples of perils of the sea, jettison or barratry.

1. When a ship becomes stranded on a reef near a remote island, the ship's master decides to throw several thousand pounds of cargo overboard to lighten the load.

   ____

2. When a ship filled with valuable ores disappears, its owner assumes it has been lost at sea. Much later, the surprised owner is informed by international police that the crew was arrested for smuggling the ship and its cargo onto a South Pacific island.

   ____

3. A ship capsizes and sinks when it is struck by a tidal wave.

   ____

Exercise answers can be found at the end of the Unit 14 answers and rationales.

In marine insurance, the term used to indicate a partial loss is *average*. Jettison is known as a **general average loss**. This means that partial loss resulting from a sacrifice of cargo to save remaining property is shared by all other property owners, including the owners of the ship. Each owner shares in the general average loss in proportion to the total property interest, regardless of which owner's property was actually jettisoned. There are three requirements that must be met in order for the law of general average to apply.

- There must be a common danger in which all participate (vessel, cargo, and crew) and for which the danger is imminent and apparently inevitable—except by voluntarily incurring the loss of a portion of the whole to save the remainder.
- There must be a voluntary jettison of some portion of the joint concern with the purpose of transferring the peril from the whole to a particular portion of the whole.
- The attempt to avoid the imminent common danger or peril must be successful.

Any other partial loss that does not arise from a general sacrifice of property is known as a **particular average loss.** There is no distribution of the loss among all property owners for particular average; instead, each owner bears whatever loss his own property sustained.

Because of the far-ranging travels of ships and their cargoes, ocean marine insurers are particularly dependent on implied warranties. **Implied warranties** are not written into the policy but carry the same weight as those that are written. Breach of an implied warranty can void the contract. These warranties include:

- **seaworthiness**, which means that the vessel must be fit for the voyage, must not be overloaded, and must have a competent crew;
- **conditions of cargo**, which means that the cargo must be warranted to be sound and packed properly;
- **legality**, which means that the trip must involve a lawful enterprise; and
- **no deviation in voyage**, which means that the ship must follow an agreed route, with no changes in destination and no untoward delays.

14.3. INLAND MARINE INSURANCE

Inland marine insurance first developed as an extension of ocean marine insurance to provide coverage for cargo that travels over land instead of by sea. From there, however, inland marine insurance branched out to provide very broad coverage on a wide variety of portable property in addition to the coverage it continues to provide for cargo in transit.

14.3.1. Nationwide Definition

To help identify the kinds of risks that are eligible for either Ocean or inland marine insurance, the insurance industry developed the **nationwide definition.** The definition lists six categories of eligible marine risks:

- Imports
- Exports
- Domestic shipments
- Instrumentalities of transportation or communication
- Personal property floater risks
- Commercial property floater risks

The first two categories, imports and exports, are covered by ocean marine insurance. Personal property floater risks are covered by personal inland marine insurance, which we studied in an earlier unit. The three remaining categories represent risks eligible for commercial inland marine insurance:

- Domestic shipments
- Instrumentalities of transportation or communication
- Commercial property floater risks

Exercise 14.C

For each of the categories of risks that are eligible for marine insurance, note whether they can be covered by ocean marine insurance **(O),** personal inland marine insurance **(P),** or commercial inland marine insurance **(C).**

____ 1. Imports

____ 2. Exports

____ 3. Domestic shipments

____ 4. Instrumentalities of transportation or communication

____ 5. Personal property floater risks

____ 6. Commercial property floater risks

Exercise answers can be found at the end of the Unit 14 answers and rationales.

A wide variety of seemingly unrelated risks falls into the categories eligible for commercial inland marine coverage. Usually, the characteristic that makes them eligible is an element of portability, although there are exceptions. As a general rule, inland marine insurance does not cover stationary property, such as real estate, furniture, fixtures, or merchandise while it is being manufactured.

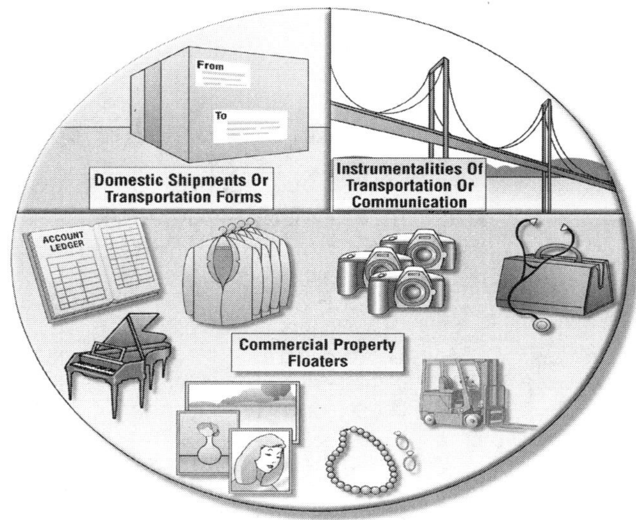

Domestic shipments are covered through a variety of inland marine Transportation forms that cover property being transported.

Instrumentalities of transportation or communication include forms that cover property related to transportation or communication, such as bridges, pipelines, and television towers.

Commercial property floater risks embrace a number of subcategories of inland marine forms, including bailee's customer forms, equipment forms, business floaters, and dealers policies.

14.3.2. Filed and Nonfiled Forms

Because inland marine insurance can cover such a wide variety of mobile property, there is no one standard policy. Instead, each type of property requires a unique policy form, with each company preparing its own contracts. The only exception is filed (controlled) classes of inland marine insurance that can be written under the commercial inland marine coverage part of the Commercial package policy. They include these coverage forms:

Mail

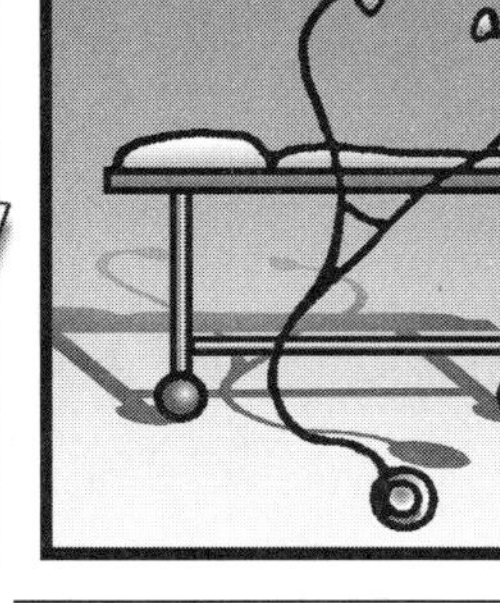

Physicians And Surgeons Equipment

Theatrical Property

Film

Commercial Articles

Accounts Receivable

Valuable Papers And Records

Signs

Jewelers Block

Floor Plan

Equipment Dealers

Camera and Musical Instrument Dealers

Nonstandardized forms for other inland marine coverages not specifically listed are known as **nonfiled classes** or **nonfiled** forms.

14.4. FILED FORMS

14.4.1. Commercial Inland Marine Coverage Part

We'll begin by looking at filed forms — those that may be written under the commercial package policy (CPP).

The commercial inland marine coverage part requires the following forms in addition to the common policy declarations and the common policy conditions:

- Commercial inland marine declarations form
- Commercial inland marine conditions form
- One or more of the 12 filed coverage forms we listed earlier

When inland marine coverage is issued as a monoline policy, the commercial inland marine declarations form may be combined with the common policy declarations to form a single declarations form.

All of the filed coverage forms provide open-peril coverage that is typical of inland marine coverages. Nonfiled forms may be written on a named-peril or open-peril basis.

14.4.2. Commercial Inland Marine Conditions

The commercial inland marine conditions are divided into two sections: **loss conditions** and **general conditions.** Many of the conditions are similar to those contained in other policies, such as abandonment, pairs, sets or parts, appraisal, and no benefit to bailee.

The insured's duties in the event of loss are similar to what is found in other property forms. The insured must:

- notify the police if a law may have been broken;
- give the insurer prompt notice of the loss and describe the property involved;
- give the insurer a description of how, when, and where the loss occurred as soon as possible;
- take reasonable steps to protect the property from further damage, set damaged property aside if feasible, and keep a record of expenses related to the loss;
- make no statement that assumes any obligation or admits any liability without the insurer's consent;
- permit the insurer to inspect the property and records proving loss;
- submit under oath to questioning if requested;
- send a signed, sworn statement of loss within 60 days after it is requested by the insurer;

- promptly send the insurer any legal papers or notices concerning the loss; and
- cooperate with the investigation or settlement of the claim.

The **other insurance** condition states that if the insured has other insurance that is written on the same basis as the commercial inland marine form, the commercial inland marine form pays on a pro rata basis. If the other coverage is not written on the same basis, commercial inland marine coverage is excess over any other insurance that applies to the loss, regardless of whether the insured can collect under the other insurance.

The **reinstatement of limit after loss** condition provides that the limit of insurance will not be reduced by payment of any claim, except for a total loss of a scheduled item. When this occurs, the insurer will refund the unearned premium on that item.

Losses are valued on an actual cash-value basis or the cost to restore or replace the property, whichever is less. The property's value is determined at the time of the loss.

14.4.3. Mail Coverage Form

In this section, we'll look at each of the filed commercial inland marine coverage forms. Then, we'll look at some of the key nonfiled forms written in the industry. The first coverage form we'll talk about falls into the domestic shipments (transportation forms) category of the nationwide definition.

The **mail coverage form** provides open-peril coverage against loss to property in transit by registered mail, first class mail, certified mail, or express mail. Covered property includes bonds, stock certificates, certificates of deposit and other securities, stamps, money orders, checks, and other documents and papers of value except food stamps, unsold travelers checks, and money. When sent by registered mail, covered property also includes bullion, platinum and other precious metals, jewelry, watches, precious and semiprecious stones, unsold travelers checks, food stamps, and money.

Property is covered while it is in the care, custody, and control of a government postal service and while in transit by a common carrier or messenger to and from a government post office. Property is covered until it is delivered to the address shown on the package or returned to the sender in the event of nondelivery.

If the value of any mailing was not recorded properly because of error or oversight, the insurer will pay the actual value of the property in the event of loss if promptly notified after discovery of the error or oversight. However, if the value of property in any one shipping exceeds the limit of insurance, the insurer will pay only the proportion of a loss that the limit of insurance bears to the actual value.

In the event of loss, the value of covered property is its actual value, but not less than its market value, on the date of mailing. Coverage is always written on a reporting basis, with reports required within 30 days after the end of each reporting period.

14.4.4. Physicians and Surgeons Equipment Coverage Form

There are no filed forms that fall under the **instrumentalities of transportation and communication** category of the nationwide definition. The remaining filed forms all fall within the final category of the nationwide definition: **commercial property floater risks.** As we've already mentioned, this category can be further divided into several subcategories. We'll look first at the **equipment floater** subcategory.

The **physicians and surgeons equipment coverage form** covers medical and dental instruments on and off the premises, as well as furniture and fixtures at the office and the insured's interest in improvements and betterments. Medical and dental equipment of others used by the insured is also covered at the insured's option. Radium is not covered.

The form provides open peril coverage, with the following exclusions:

- Government action
- Nuclear hazard
- War and military action
- Marring, scratching, or exposure to light
- Breakage of tubes, bulbs, lamps, or articles made primarily of glass (does not apply to lenses)
- Delay, loss of use, loss of market, or any consequential loss
- Dishonest or criminal acts committed by the insured, the insured's employees, or anyone else with an interest in the property or to whom the property is entrusted (does not apply to carriers for hire or acts of destruction by employees)
- Artificially generated current that creates a short circuit or other electric disturbance within an article covered by the policy
- Voluntarily parting with property if induced to do so by a fraudulent scheme, trick, or false pretense
- Unauthorized instructions to transfer property to another person or place
- Neglect of an insured to protect property at the time of loss or after a loss
- Weather conditions
- Acts or decisions, or the failure to act or decide, of any person, group, or government body
- Faulty, inadequate, or defective planning, zoning, workmanship, repair, construction, materials, or maintenance
- Wear and tear, inherent vice, hidden or latent defect, or gradual deterioration

- Mechanical breakdown
- Insects, vermin, or rodents
- Corrosion, rust, dampness, cold, or heat

The physicians and surgeons equipment coverage form also covers collapse of a building or structure when it is caused by one of the perils specified in the form and damage caused by theft or attempted theft to the building.

The insured must maintain any protective safeguards (such as a security service or automatic fire alarm system) that were in effect at the beginning of the policy period. If the insured fails to keep these safeguards in working condition and in operation when the business is closed, coverage at that location is suspended until the protective safeguards are back in operation.

Exercise 14.D

1. What happens if the insured fails to maintain a protective safeguard that was in effect at the beginning of the policy period?
   A. Coverage at that location is suspended until the protective safeguard is back in operation.
   B. Coverage is canceled immediately.
   C. Coverage is suspended for 30 days.

Exercise answers can be found at the end of the Unit 14 answers and rationales.

14.4.5. Theatrical Property Coverage Form

Another equipment floater, the **theatrical property coverage form,** covers scenery, props, and costumes used by a theater group in a specific production identified in the declarations. Also covered is theatrical property in the insured's care, custody, or control or on which the insured has made partial payments. The form does not cover the following:

- Buildings or their improvements and betterments
- Vehicles (unless actually used on the stage in the covered production)
- Jewelry with precious or semiprecious stones, metals, or alloys
- Accounts, bills, currency, deeds, money, securities, and admission tickets
- Animals
- Contraband
- Property being illegally transported or traded

The form provides open-peril coverage and contains many of the exclusions we've described in relation to other commercial inland marine forms. In addition, the form excludes:

- theft from an unlocked, unattended vehicle;
- unexplained disappearance; and
- shortage found upon taking inventory.

Collapse of a building or structure is also covered when it is caused by one of the perils specified in the form.

14.4.6. Film Coverage Form

The **film coverage form** is also considered an equipment floater. It provides open-peril coverage for exposed motion picture film, soundtracks, video tapes, and magnetic tapes that are used in the production scheduled in the declarations and that the insured owns or has in his custody or control. It does not cover cut-outs, unused footage, positive prints or films, or library stock.

In addition to the exclusions found in all commercial inland marine forms, the film coverage form excludes loss resulting from the following:

- Deterioration, atmospheric dampness, or changes in temperature
- Exposure of negative film to light
- Use of developing chemicals
- Developing, cutting or printing of film, or other laboratory work
- Electric or magnetic injury, disturbance, or erasure of electronic recordings or video tape (does not apply to damage caused by lightning)

Collapse coverage is included.

Covered property is valued on the basis of the cost of reproducing the lost or damaged property plus any reduction in value of undamaged parts of a production. The cost of the story, scenario, music rights, continuity, permanent sets, owned wardrobes, and props are not considered when valuing the property. The insured must use any means available to recreate the damaged property to reduce the amount of loss. Payment cannot exceed the value of the covered production as shown in the insured's books.

Property is covered until the full quota of positive prints or films is completed, the insured's interest in the property ends, or the policy expires or is canceled, whichever occurs first.

The coverage territory includes the United States and its territories and possessions, Puerto Rico, and Canada. Property is also covered when it is located within 50 miles of these areas.

The insured is required to keep accurate business records and retain them for at least three years after the policy ends. The insured must also send the insurer a written report for each production when it is no longer covered under the policy. The report must include the actual cost, overhead expenses, and other expenses of the completed production and a list of each studio, laboratory, vault, and cutting room used and the period the policy covered property at these locations. The actual premium charged is based on this report, using the rates in effect at the time the coverage began. The premium is adjusted to reflect any difference between the actual premium owed and the premium paid.

14.4.7. Commercial Articles Coverage Form

The final coverage form in the equipment floater subcategory is the **commercial articles coverage form**. It covers the interests of the owner of commercial cameras, musical instruments, and related equipment and similar property of others that is in the insured's care, custody, or control.

The form provides open-peril coverage, with essentially the same exclusions as in other commercial inland marine forms. Property is covered worldwide. It also covers collapse.

Additional acquired property is automatically covered for up to 30 days if it is a type of property already covered by the form. In the event of loss, the insurer will pay the lesser of 25% of the policy limit, or $10,000. The insured is required to report any additional acquired property within 30 days and pay any additional premium required. If not reported, coverage automatically ends after 30 days.

14.4.8. Accounts Receivable Coverage Form

There are three business floaters that fall within the commercial property floater risk category of the nationwide definition.

The **accounts receivable coverage form** reimburses the insured for amounts that can't be collected from customers because of damage to the company's accounts receivable records. It also covers extra collection expenses and interest on any loans the insured must obtain to stay in business while collections are impaired. Accounts receivable records in storage away from the premises are not covered.

In addition to the usual exclusions, the accounts receivable coverage form does not cover loss resulting from the following:

- Alteration, falsification, concealment, or destruction of accounts receivable records done to conceal wrongful acts
- Bookkeeping, accounting, or billing errors or omissions
- Electrical or magnetic injury, disturbance or erasure of electronic recordings caused by
  - programming errors or faulty machine instructions,
  - faulty installation or maintenance of data processing equipment or components,
  - an occurrence that takes place more than 100 feet from the insured's premises, or
  - interruption of electrical power supply, power surge, blackout, or brownout that occurs more than 100 feet from the insured's premises

Any loss that requires an audit of records or inventory computation to prove its existence is not covered.

Exercise 14.E

1. The insured's accounting records are destroyed in a fire. Which of these losses would be covered under the insured's accounts receivable coverage form?
   A. Bill payments the insured cannot collect from customers because of damage to the records
   B. Interest on a short-term loan the insured obtains to stay in business while collections are impaired
   C. Fees charged by the collection agency the insured hires to collect payments
   D. All of the above

Exercise answers can be found at the end of the Unit 14 answers and rationales.

In addition to the collapse coverage provided by other commercial inland marine forms, the accounts receivable coverage form covers loss of records when removed from the premises to protect them from imminent loss. Removal coverage applies only if the insured gives written notice of the removal within 10 days.

If the insured cannot accurately establish the amount of accounts receivable outstanding at the time of loss, the average monthly amounts receivable for the preceding 12-month period will be used. That amount is then adjusted for normal fluctuations in the amount receivable or demonstrated variance from the average for the month in which the loss occurred. The following will be subtracted from the total amount of accounts receivable:

- The amount of accounts for which there is no loss
- The amount of accounts that the insured is able to reestablish and collect
- An amount to allow for probable bad debts that the insured is normally unable to collect
- Unearned interest and service charges

To the extent that any loss is paid by the insurer, any later recovery of amounts receivable must be returned to the insurer. Recoveries in excess of the amount paid by the insurer do not have to be returned.

The insured must keep all accounts receivable records in receptacles described in the declarations when the business is closed and when the records are not in use.

14.4.9. Valuable Papers and Records Coverage Form

Another form in the business floaters category is the **valuable papers and records coverage form**, which reimburses the insured for the cost of replacing damaged items, such as manuscripts, films, maps, drawings, deeds, and books that belong to the insured or are in the insured's care, custody, or control. Money and securities are not covered.

The collapse and removal coverages previously described in this section are included. The form also pays up to $5,000 for loss to covered property while it is away from the premises unless a higher limit is specified in the declarations.

Important exclusions include errors or omissions in processing or copying and electrical or magnetic injury, disturbance, or erasure of electronic recordings.

The value of each item of property that is specifically declared and described in the declarations is the applicable limit for that item. If property is recovered after the loss is settled, the insured may choose to have the property returned, with an adjustment made to the amount already paid.

The insured must keep all valuable papers and records in receptacles described in the declarations when the business is closed and when the records are not in use.

14.4.10. Signs Coverage Form

The final form in the business floaters category is the **signs coverage form,** which insures businesses against loss to neon, fluorescent, automatic, or mechanical electric signs and lights. The form covers the insured's signs and similar property of others in the insured's care, custody, or control.

Breakage during transportation or during installation, repairing, or dismantling is not covered. Also excluded is artificially generated current that creates a short circuit or other electric disturbance within a covered item.

The standard collapse coverage is included.

14.4.11. Jewelers Block Coverage Form

There are several filed forms in the dealers policy subcategory of commercial property floater risks. These policies represent an exception to the general rule of mobile property. Although dealers do need occasional coverage for property away from the premises, their primary coverage need is for damage to merchandise while on the business premises.

The first dealers policy we'll cover is the **jewelers block coverage form,** which covers:

- the insured's stock in trade, which includes jewelry, precious and semiprecious stones, precious metals and alloys, and other stock used in the business;
- property that is sold but not delivered;
- similar property of others *who are not in the jewelry trade* in the insured's care, custody, or control; and
- similar property of others *in the jewelry trade* in the insured's care, custody, or control, but only to the extent of the insured's legal liability for the property or the amount of money actually advanced by the insured.

The form does not cover property:

- sold under a deferred sales payment agreement after it leaves the insured's premises;
- at an exhibition promoted or financially assisted by a trade association or public authority;
- exhibited in showcases or show windows away from the premises;
- while being worn by the insured, an employee or a family member of either (does not apply to watches worn solely for purposes of adjustment); or
- in transit by
  - — mail (unless sent by registered mail),
  - — express carriers, railroads, or waterborne or air carriers (does not apply to property accompanied by a passenger and transported by passenger parcel or baggage services), or
  - — motor carriers (does not apply to shipments by a carrier operating exclusively as a merchant's parcel delivery service, by an armored car service or by parcel transportation or baggage services of passenger bus lines).

The jewelers block coverage form contains two optional coverages. **Show windows coverage** covers theft of stock from a show window when the window is cut or smashed. **Money coverage** covers theft of money from locked safes or vaults on the insured's premises. The form also covers collapse of a building or structure when it is caused by one of the perils specified in the form and damage caused by theft or attempted theft to the building.

In addition to the exclusions common to commercial inland marine forms, the jewelers block coverage form excludes:

- water damage to property at the insured's premises;
- theft from any vehicle unless the insured, an employee, or other person whose only duty is to attend the vehicle is actually in or on the vehicle when the theft occurs (does not apply to property in the custody of the post office or other carriers);
- unexplained disappearance;
- shortage found upon taking inventory;
- shortage of property claimed to have been shipped when the package is received in good condition with the seals unbroken;
- dishonest or criminal acts committed by the insured, the insured's employees, or anyone else to whom the property is entrusted;
- insufficient or defective packing; and
- breakage of fragile articles.

In the event of loss, the value of the property is determined at the time of loss and is the lesser of:

- actual cash value;
- cost to restore the property to its condition immediately before the loss;
- cost to replace the property; or
- the lowest figure listed in the insured's inventories, stock books, stock papers, or lists existing at the time of loss.

Antique or historical value is not considered in the value of the property.

The insured must maintain any protective safeguards (such as a security service or automatic fire alarm system) that were in effect at the beginning of the policy period. If the insured fails to keep these safeguards in working condition and in operation when the business is closed, coverage at that location is suspended until the protective safeguards are back in operation.

The insured must take a physical inventory at least once every 12 months and maintain detailed records of inventory, purchases, sales, property of others, and property off premises. These records must be retained for three years after the policy ends.

14.4.12. Floor Plan Coverage Form

Another type of inland marine Dealers policy is the **floor plan coverage form.** It covers stock that is subject to a floor plan arrangement, in which a dealer borrows money from a lender with which to pay for merchandise. This encumbered merchandise can then be insured under a floor plan policy. Coverage may be written to cover the interest of the dealer, the lending institution, or both. Property is not covered after the insured's interest in it ceases or after it is sold, delivered, or otherwise disposed of.

Excluded are:

- water damage to property at the insured's premises;
- bankruptcy, foreclosure, or similar proceedings;
- artificially generated current that creates a short circuit or other electrical disturbance within an article covered by the policy;
- breakage of glass or other fragile articles; and
- damage to property in the open caused by rain, hail, sleet, snow, or freezing.

Collapse coverage is included.

The condition regarding maintaining inventory records discussed previously in this section also applies to the floor plan coverage form.

A number of conditions appear in the floor plan coverage form that are not included in the other commercial inland marine forms. The **transit coverage in the event of cancellation** condition states that if the policy is canceled, property already in transit will be covered until it reaches its destination.

When coverage is written on a dual-interest basis, the policy provisions are binding on all parties. However, the protection given a secured lender will not be impaired by failure of another party to comply with policy provisions if the secured lender diligently tried to comply with all provisions.

Coverage is written on a reporting basis. The insured must file reports of values within 30 days after the end of each month. Premiums will be computed according to monthly rates. The insurer is not liable for loss in excess of the amount of insurance written, even if reported values exceed the limit of insurance.

If the insured has not filed any report at the time of a loss, the insurer is liable for only 90% of the limit of insurance written. If the insured fails to make a report when required, the insurer is liable for only the amount last reported. The penalty for underreporting values is a proportional reduction in recovery for a loss. Coverage is rerated at each anniversary. The insured must furnish information required for rerating purposes within 30 days after each anniversary.

14.4.13. Equipment Dealers Coverage Form

The **equipment dealers coverage form** is used to cover dealers of mobile equipment and construction equipment. It covers the dealer's stock in trade, consisting primarily of mobile agricultural equipment and construction equipment. It also covers property of others in the dealer's care, custody, or control. It does not cover:

- automobiles, trucks, motorcycles, aircraft, and watercraft;
- money, securities, accounts, and bills;
- property in the course of manufacture;
- property that is leased, rented, or sold, including property sold under a deferred payment sales agreement;
- furniture, fixtures, office supplies, improvements and betterments, machinery, tools, patterns, dies, molds, and models; or
- property of others described in the declarations.

Important exclusions include:

- water damage to property at the premises;
- unexplained disappearance;
- shortages found upon taking inventory; and
- artificially generated current that creates a short circuit or electrical disturbance within an article covered by the policy.

The form includes collapse coverage and covers damage caused by theft or attempted theft to the building.

Debris removal coverage pays expenses to remove the debris of covered property that is damaged by a covered cause of loss, subject to a limit of 25% of the amount paid for the direct physical loss plus the amount of the deductible. However, if the amount of the debris removal expenses and the direct loss exceeds the limit of insurance, or if the total debris removal expense exceeds the 25% limitation, the insurer will pay up to an additional $10,000 for debris removal costs. The expenses must be reported to the insurer within 180 days of the date of loss.

Pollutant cleanup and removal coverage pays expenses to extract pollutants from land or water if the release or discharge of the pollutants resulted from a covered cause of loss that occurred during the policy period. The most the insurer will pay is $10,000 for all such expenses arising during each separate 12-month period of coverage under the policy. The expenses must be reported to the insurer within 180 days of the date of loss.

The conditions regarding protective safeguards and maintaining inventory records discussed earlier also apply to the equipment dealers coverage form.

The value of unsold property is the lesser of actual cash value, the cost to restore the property, or the cost to replace it. Property that is sold but not delivered is valued at its net selling price after all allowances and discounts. The value of property of others in the insured's care, custody, or control is the lesser of the amount for which the insured is liable or actual cash value. The value of the insured's labor and materials is considered both cases.

Exercise 14.F

Name two coverages in the equipment dealers coverage form that are not included in the other commercial inland marine forms you've studied.

1. ______________________________

2. ______________________________

Exercise answers can be found at the end of the Unit 14 answers and rationales.

14.4.14. Camera and Musical Instrument Dealers Coverage Form

The final form in the dealers category is the **camera and musical instrument dealers coverage form.** It covers the insured's stock in trade as well as customer property in the insured's care, custody, or control, such as an instrument or camera that is being repaired, cleaned, or adjusted. It does not cover:

- property that has been sold and delivered to customers, including property sold under a deferred payment sales agreement;
- money, securities, accounts, or bills;
- furniture, fixtures, office supplies, improvements and betterments, machinery, patterns, molds, and models; or
- property that is in the mail (does not apply to property sent by registered or government insured mail).

Excluded are:

- earthquake damage to property at the insured's premises;
- water damage to property at the insured's premises;
- theft from an unattended, unlocked vehicle with no visible signs of forced entry;
- marring and scratching;
- exposure to light;
- breakage of tubes, bulbs, lamps, or items made largely of glass (except lenses);
- unexplained disappearance;
- shortage found upon taking inventory; and
- artificially generated current that creates a short circuit or other electrical disturbance within an item covered under the policy.

Collapse and theft damage coverages are included. The conditions concerning protective safeguards and maintaining inventory records also apply to this form.

Losses to unsold property, sold property, and property of others are valued on the same basis as the equipment dealers coverage form. For negatives, positives, or prints, their value is the cost of unexposed film or developing paper, including labor and materials.

14.5. NONFILED FORMS

14.5.1. Domestic Shipments

Now that you're familiar with some popular filed inland marine forms, we'll turn our attention to **nonfiled forms**—that is, those that cannot be included in the commercial package policy.

The domestic shipments category of the nationwide definition includes a number of nonfiled inland marine transportation forms that provide coverage for shipments traveling by truck, train, air, or mail. We've already mentioned the filed mail coverage form and the nonfiled parcel post policy.

Businesses that ship or receive merchandise need coverage against loss to their cargoes while they are in transit. Common carriers—that is, those who hold themselves out to the public to ship goods—must accept a certain amount of liability for losses to cargo. (These obligations are set forth in the **bill of lading**, which must be issued to each business for whom the carrier ships goods.) However, there are many losses for which the carrier is not responsible. Even when the carrier is liable for loss to cargo in its custody, reimbursement of the loss may be uncertain. The various inland marine transportation forms were developed to cover this exposure.

The **annual transit policy** protects the shipper or receiver of goods against loss to goods in transit. Coverage is available on a named-peril basis, protecting against such losses as fire, windstorm, collision, and theft, or on an open-peril basis. The policy covers all of the insured's incoming or outgoing shipments during the year.

The **trip transit policy** is similar to the annual transit policy. However, it is used to insure single shipments of goods for companies that have only occasional shipments to insure. Coverage extends from the time and point of origination to the time and point of destination.

The nonfiled **motor truck cargo policy** covers cargo while it is being transported in a truck. It protects the carrier, instead of the shipper, for liability for loss to domestic shipments in transit. The carrier has a responsibility to deliver goods entrusted to it unharmed. There are only a few things, such as **acts of God** (e.g., floods and tornadoes) or the shipper's own neglect (e.g., poor packing), for which the carrier is not liable. This form is sometimes called the **motor truck cargo—truckers form.**

A variation of motor truck cargo insurance provides coverage known as **owner's goods on owner's trucks** to companies that transport their own goods. It provides direct damage coverage instead of liability coverage. This form may also be called the **motor truck cargo—shipper's form** or the **motor truck cargo—owner's form**. Some companies issue a **motor truck cargo—combination form** that provides both liability coverage for the shipment of another's goods and direct damage coverage for the shipment of the insured's own goods on its own trucks.

Exercise 14.G

Match the inland marine transportation form listed in the left-hand column with its correct description in the right-hand column.

_____ 1. Annual transit policy	A. Insures single shipments of goods
_____ 2. Trip transit policy	B. Protects all of the insured's incoming or outgoing shipments during the year against loss while in transit
_____ 3. Motor truck cargo policy	C. Provides direct damage coverage for a company's goods while transported on the company's trucks
_____ 4. Motor truck cargo—Shipper's policy	D. Insures a truck carrier for its liability for loss to cargo in transit

Exercise answers can be found at the end of the Unit 14 answers and rationales.

14.5.2. Instrumentalities of Transportation and Communication

The next category of the nationwide definition, **instrumentalities of transportation and communication**, includes forms covering such property as bridges, tunnels, oil pipelines, loading docks, and radio and TV towers.

Although this property itself is not portable, it is directly connected with transportation and is subject to many of the same perils as property in transit.

14.5.3. Commercial Property Floater Risks

14.5.3.1. Bailee's Customer Policies

There are a number of nonfiled forms that fall under the commercial property floater risk category of the nationwide definition. **Bailee's policies** are a subcategory for which there are no filed forms but for which there are several important nonfiled forms.

Bailment is the delivery of property by the owner to someone else to be held for some special purpose and then to be returned to the owner. An example of bailment is leaving your shoes at the repair shop to have them reheeled. The **bailee** is the one who receives the property; the one who owns the property is called the **bailor.**

Just as carriers have a responsibility for the safety of property in their custody, bailees also have a responsibility for property in their custody. If the property is damaged through the bailee's own fault, the bailee will be liable to the customer for damage. Even when the property is damaged in a fire or some other disaster that is not the bailee's fault, the customer will expect to get the property back undamaged or be compensated for the loss. To retain the goodwill of the customer, the bailee will probably reimburse the customer. The **bailee's customer policy** reimburses the insured for damage to a customer's property that is in the insured's care, regardless of whether the insured is liable for the damage, as long as the damage resulted from a covered peril.

There are several different bailee's customer policies available that are tailored to specific businesses, such as the **cleaners, dyers, and laundries policy.** One unique peril covered by this form is **confusion of goods**, which covers the loss that can occur when the resulting damage from another loss has made it impossible to identify which garments belong to a particular customer.

14.5.3.2. Equipment Floaters

There are a number of nonfiled equipment floaters, one of the most important of which is the contractors equipment floater.

The **contractors equipment floater** covers the heavy machinery, equipment, and tools a customer needs to conduct business. It covers the contractor on an open-peril or named-peril basis for loss to all types of tools, machinery, and equipment owned, rented, or borrowed by the insured. The property is protected from loss caused by fire, landslide, theft, and other perils while it is on the job site, on the way to and from a job site, and in temporary storage. Neither the commercial property nor the commercial auto policies provide the extensive coverage that can be obtained under the contractors equipment floater.

14.5.3.3. Business Floaters

We've already discussed several filed business floaters. There are also two nonfiled forms in this subcategory of commercial property floater risks.

A firm selling refrigeration systems, elevators, or other pieces of large equipment may have a great deal of property on location awaiting or in the process of installation. Such installation and final testing can take months, even years. The **installation policy** is an inland marine coverage that insures against loss to machinery, equipment, building materials, and supplies in transit to or being used with or during the course of installation, testing, building, renovating, or repair. It can be issued to cover the interest of the owner, the seller, or the contractor.

The **electronic data processing equipment floater** provides open-peril coverage for computer hardware, software, and data that is owned by the insured or in the insured's care, custody, or control. Property in transit is covered. Optional breakdown coverage insures against damage to the equipment caused by mechanical breakdown, electrical disturbances, and temperature changes. Extra expense and business interruption coverage is also included.

14.5.3.4. Dealers Policies

In addition to the filed dealers policies we've covered, nonfiled policies can be written for a number of dealers, including art, stamp, coin, and antique dealers. These policies are generally written on an open-peril basis and cover property on the premises, off the premises, and while in transit, provided certain conditions are met.

UNIT TEST

1. List the appropriate category of ocean marine insurance for each of the following examples.
   A. The insured wants coverage for her interest in a commercial freighter.

   ____

   B. The insured wants coverage for liability he might incur if the ship he owns goes down with a shipper's cargo.

   ____

   C. The owner of a large banana plantation wants insurance to cover against damage to the fruit while it is being shipped to the United States.

   ____

   D. A ship owner who has prepaid the costs of shipping cargo wants insurance to reimburse for the loss of shipping costs if the cargo is destroyed while it is en route.

   ____

2. A voluntary action to rid the ship of cargo to prevent further damage is called
   A. jettison
   B. particular average
   C. barratry
   D. general average

3. General average losses are
   A. borne by each property owner whose cargo sustains damage
   B. shared by all property owners, including the owners of the ship

4. What is the nationwide definition?

   ____

5. Which of these categories of risks are eligible for commercial inland marine insurance?
   A. Imports
   B. Personal property floater risks
   C. Domestic shipments
   D. Commercial property floater risks
   E. Exports
   F. Instrumentalities of transportation or communication

6. Which of the following commercial inland marine coverage forms can be included in the commercial package policy?
   A. Film
   B. Floor plan
   C. Parcel post
   D. Annual transit
   E. Physicians and surgeons equipment
   F. Accounts receivable
   G. Bailee's customer
   H. Equipment dealers

7. The motor truck cargo policy
   A. insures a truck carrier for liability arising out of the transportation of cargo
   B. covers any loss to cargo in transit, regardless of whether the carrier is liable for damage
   C. insures the shipper for all incoming or outgoing shipments during the policy term
   D. provides coverage for a shipper on a single shipment of goods

8. A bailee's customer policy covers
   A. only the bailee's legal liability for damage to customers' property
   B. the bailee for loss to customers' property, regardless of liability
   C. the bailor for damage to property left in the custody of another

9. Which of the following actions represents a breach of an implied warranty?
   A. The insured has arranged to carry a large shipment of cocaine in addition to the cargo he has declared to the insurer.
   B. The shipowner knows a vessel needs to be repaired but decides to try to make one more passage before having the repairs made. He knows there is insurance if the ship has any trouble.
   C. The ship master orders the crew to jettison a large part of the ship's cargo to lighten the load and prevent the ship from sinking.

10. Which of the following forms must be included in a commercial inland marine coverage part?
    A. One or more of the 12 filed coverage forms
    B. Commercial inland marine conditions form
    C. Commercial inland marine declarations form
    D. Common policy conditions and declarations
    E. One nonfiled coverage form

11. If the insurance company requests a proof of loss on a commercial inland marine claim, the insured must submit it within
    A. 10 days
    B. 30 days
    C. 60 days

12. A loss is covered under a commercial inland marine form and another policy. Both policies are written on the same basis. The commercial inland marine form will
    A. not pay anything on the loss
    B. pay on a pro rata basis
    C. pay on an excess basis

13. Which of these statements about the mail coverage form are CORRECT?
    A. It covers bonds, securities and checks when they are sent by first class mail or certified mail.
    B. Food stamps and money are always excluded under the policy.
    C. Property is covered on a named-peril basis.
    D. Losses are valued on the basis of the property's actual value, but not less than its market value, on the date of mailing.

14. Which of the following can be covered under the physicians and surgeons equipment coverage form?
    A. Medical instruments that are on the premises
    B. Dental instruments that are off the premises
    C. Radium
    D. All of the above

15. Which of the following coverages are included in the physicians and surgeons equipment coverage form?
    A. Collapse
    B. Theft damage to buildings
    C. Both A and B

16. Which of the following losses could be covered under the theatrical property coverage form?
    A. Theft of costumes from an unlocked vehicle
    B. Damage to a vehicle used as a prop in the production
    C. Destruction of admission tickets for the production in a fire
    D. All of the above

17. Which of the following property could be covered under the film coverage form?
    A. Positive prints
    B. Motion picture film
    C. Soundtrack
    D. Unused footage

18. The insured removes accounting records from her business to protect them from loss. Are the records covered under the accounts receivable coverage form while away from the premises?
    A. No
    B. Yes, if the insured notifies the insurer within 10 days

19. Burglars stole $500 out of a car wash's cash register. Would this loss be covered under the valuable papers and records coverage form?
    A. Yes
    B. No

20. Which of these losses would be covered under the signs coverage form?
    A. The electric sign above the insured's business is destroyed when it is blown down in a thunderstorm.
    B. The insured's neon sign is damaged when vandals throw rocks at it.
    C. A power surge blows out several tubes in the insured's fluorescent sign.
    D. All of the above.

21. The jewelers block coverage form would cover a jeweler's stock in trade while it is
    A. on exhibit at a trade show
    B. being worn by the insured's spouse
    C. in transit by registered mail

22. Which of these losses would be covered under the jewelers block coverage form, assuming the insured has purchased all available optional coverages?
    A. Theft of money from a locked vault on the insured's premises
    B. Theft of money from an unlocked vault on the insured's premises
    C. Theft of covered property from an unattended auto
    D. Theft of items on display in a show window when the window is smashed

23. Under the jewelers block coverage form, the insured is required to
    A. take a physical inventory at least once every 12 months
    B. maintain business records for three years after the policy expires
    C. Both A and B

24. How often is the insured required to submit reports of values under the floor plan coverage form?
    A. Quarterly
    B. Monthly
    C. Annually
    D. Weekly

25. Which of the following businesses could be insured under an equipment dealers coverage form?
    A. A business that sells covers and tops for boats
    B. A business that sells and repairs tractor parts
    C. A business that sells construction equipment

26. Which of these losses would be covered under the camera and musical instrument dealers coverage form?
    A. When the insured plugs in an electric guitar to demonstrate it for a customer, there is a short circuit that damages the guitar's wiring.
    B. A clerk drops a camera when arranging digital cameras in a show window. The lens shatters.
    C. Both A and B.
    D. Neither A nor B.

27. The electronic data processing equipment floater
    A. covers computer hardware, but not software or data
    B. covers property in transit
    C. does not cover computer equipment that is in the insured's care, custody, or control
    D. may contain breakdown coverage

28. The installation floater covers property while it is
    A. at the insured's premises
    B. in transit to an installation site
    C. being tested
    D. being installed

ANSWERS AND RATIONALES TO UNIT TEST

1. **A.** Hull insurance. ocean marine hull insurance provides coverage for physical damage to the ship.
   B. Protection and indemnity insurance. Ocean marine protection and indemnity insurance covers a variety of types of liability, such as damage to cargo through negligence and damage to other property or another boat resulting from collision.
   C. Cargo insurance. Ocean marine cargo insurance covers goods while they are in transit over water.
   D. Freight insurance. Ocean marine freight insurance protects the insured against the loss of shipping costs.

2. **A.** Jettison is a voluntary action to rid the ship of cargo to prevent further peril. Jettison is permitted if the action is taken to save the remaining property. The loss incurred by sacrificing a portion of the cargo will be reimbursed.

3. **B.** In Marine insurance, the term used to indicate a partial loss is average. A general average loss is one in which a partial loss resulting from a sacrifice of cargo to save remaining property is shared by all other property owners, including the owner of the ship. Each owner shares in the general average loss in proportion to his or her total property interest.

4. The nationwide definition was developed to identify the kinds of risks that are eligible for either ocean or inland marine insurance.

5. **C**, **D** and **F** are correct. Imports and exports are covered under ocean marine insurance. Personal property floater risks are covered by personal inland marine insurance.

6. **A**, **B**, **E**, **F**, and **H** are correct. Filed classes of inland marine insurance can be written under the commercial inland marine coverage part of the commercial package policy. They include the following coverage forms: mail, physicians and surgeons equipment, theatrical property, film, commercial articles, accounts receivable, valuable papers and records, signs, jewelers block, floor plan, equipment dealers, and camera and musical instrument dealers.

7. **A** This form protects the carrier, instead of the shipper, for liability for loss to domestic shipments in transit.

8. **B.** A bailee's customer policy reimburses the insured for damage to a customer's property that is in his care, regardless of whether the insured is liable for the damage, as long as the damage resulted from a covered peril.

9. **A** and **B** are correct. Implied warranties are an important concept in ocean marine insurance. They are not written into the policy but carry the same weight as those that are written. Breach of an implied warranty can void the contract. These warranties include seaworthiness (i.e., the vessel must be fit for the voyage, must not be overloaded, and must have a competent crew), conditions of cargo (i.e., the cargo must be warranted to be sound and packed properly), legality (i.e., the trip must involve a lawful enterprise), and no deviation in voyage (i.e., the ship must follow an agreed route, with no changes in destination and no untoward delays).

10. **A**, **B**, **C**, and **D** are correct. Nonfiled forms cannot be included in a CPP.

11. **C.** The commercial inland marine conditions form states that the insured must send a signed, sworn statement of loss within 60 days after the insurer requests it.

12. **B.** The other insurance condition in the commercial inland marine conditions form states that if the insured has other insurance that is written on the same basis as the commercial inland marine form, the commercial inland marine form pays on a pro rata basis. If the other coverage is not written on the same basis, commercial inland marine coverage is excess over any other insurance that applies to the loss, regardless of whether the insured can collect under the other insurance.

13. **A** and **D** are correct. The mail coverage form provides open-peril coverage against loss to property in transit by registered mail, first class mail, certified mail, or express mail. Food stamps and money may be covered when sent by registered mail.

14. **A** and **B** are correct. This form covers medical and dental instruments on and off the premises, furniture and fixtures at the office and the insured's interest in improvements and betterments. Radium is not covered.

15. **C.** The physicians and surgeons equipment coverage form covers collapse of a building or structure when it is caused by one of the perils specified in the form and damage caused by theft or attempted theft to the building.

16. **B.** Vehicles are covered if they are actually used on the stage in the covered production. Admission tickets are not covered property. Loss by theft from an unlocked, unattended vehicle is excluded.

17. **B** and **C** are correct. The film coverage form covers exposed motion picture film, soundtracks, video tapes, and magnetic tapes used in the production scheduled in the declarations and that the insured owns or has in his custody or control. It does not cover cut-outs, unused footage, positive prints or films, or library stock.

18. **B.** The accounts receivable coverage form covers loss of records when removed from the premises to protect them from imminent loss. Removal coverage applies only if the insured gives written notice of the removal within 10 days.

19. No. Money and securities are not covered under this form.

20. **A** and **B** are correct. Loss caused by artificially generated current that creates a short circuit or other electrical disturbance within a covered item is not covered.

21. **C.** A jeweler's stock in trade is not covered while it is in transit by mail unless it is sent by registered mail. Such property is also not covered while being worn by a family member or at an exhibition promoted or financially assisted by a trade association.

22. **A** and **D** are correct. The show windows optional coverage covers theft of stock from a show window when the window is cut or smashed. Money coverage covers theft of money from locked safes or vaults on the insured's premises. Theft from any vehicle is excluded unless the insured, an employee, or other person whose only duty is to attend the vehicle is actually in or on the vehicle when the theft occurs.

23. **C.** The jewelers block coverage form requires the insured to take a physical inventory at least once every 12 months and maintain detailed records of inventory, purchases, sales, property of others, and property off premises. These records must be retained for three years after the policy ends.

24. **B.** Coverage under the floor plan form is written on a reporting basis. The insured must file reports of values within 30 days after the end of each month.

25. **B** and **C** are correct. The equipment dealers coverage form covers mobile equipment and construction equipment dealers. It covers the insured's stock in trade as well as customer property in the insured's care, custody, or control. Watercraft is not covered under the form.

26. **B.** This form excludes loss arising out of artificially generated current that creates a short circuit or other electrical disturbance within an item covered under the policy.

27. **B** and **D** are correct. The electronic data processing equipment floater provides open-peril coverage for computer hardware, software, and data that is owned by the insured or in the insured's care, custody, or control. Property in transit is covered. Optional breakdown coverage insures against damage to the equipment caused by mechanical breakdown, electrical disturbances, and temperature changes.

28. **B**, **C**, and **D** are correct. An installation policy covers loss to machinery, equipment, building materials, and supplies in transit to or being used with or during the course of installation, testing, building, renovating, or repair.

UNIT 14 EXERCISE ANSWERS

Exercise 14.A

1. **A**
2. **B**
3. **D**
4. **C**

Exercise 14.B

1. Jettison
2. Barratry
3. Perils of the sea

Exercise 14.C

1. **O**
2. **O**
3. **C**
4. **C**
5. **P**
6. **C**

Exercise 14.D

1. **A**

Exercise 14.E

1. **D**

Exercise 14.F

These answers can occur in any order.

1. Debris removal
2. Pollutant cleanup and removal

Exercise 14.G

1. **B**
2. **A**
3. **D**
4. **C**

15

Commercial General Liability Insurance

15.1. LEARNING OBJECTIVES

After completing Unit 15—Commercial General Liability Insurance, you will be able to do the following:

- Define common business liability exposures and identify those that are covered under commercial general liability (CGL) insurance
- List the required components of a CGL coverage part
- Compare and contrast the coverage triggers in occurrence and claims-made CGL forms
- Describe the purpose of a retroactive date
- Compare and contrast the features of the 60-day basic extended reporting period, five-year basic extended reporting period, and supplemental extended reporting period
- Explain how the following terms are defined in the CGL forms: auto, mobile equipment, insured's product, insured's work, impaired property, coverage territory, loading or unloading, pollutants, products-completed operations hazard, leased worker, temporary worker, employee, and volunteer worker
- For each of the three coverages included in the CGL form, describe the types of losses covered, the conditions that must be met for a loss to be covered, and situations and perils that are excluded
- Identify expenses that are covered under the supplementary payments section
- Explain how an insured may be designated in the declarations and how this designation affects who is considered an insured under the policy
- Describe the circumstances under which a newly acquired organization may be considered a named insured
- Explain how the various coverage limits and sublimits in the CGL apply
- Describe the provisions of these conditions: insured's duties after loss, nonrenewal, other insurance, and claim information
- Explain how the pollution liability coverage extension endorsement affects policy coverage
- Describe the purpose of the liquor liability and owners and contractors protective liability coverage forms
- Compare and contrast the pollution liability coverage forms

15.2. BUSINESS LIABILITY EXPOSURES

15.2.1. Premises and Operations Exposure

Commercial general liability (CGL) insurance covers business liability exposures. **Business liability** is liability that arises out of the conduct of a business. A business has a number of liability exposures, one of the most important of which is its **premises and operations exposure**—that is, liability arising out of the business location or the activities of the business. This includes liability for bodily injury, property damage, and personal and advertising injury. **Personal and advertising injury** includes such things as slander, libel, copyright infringement, invasion of privacy, false arrest, wrongful entry onto another's premises, and malicious prosecution.

One example of the premises and operations liability exposure is a claim against Sandle Appliances for injuries a customer suffers when she slips and falls on a newly waxed floor inside the store. Another example is a claim against Breckenridge Manufacturers for libelous statements made about a competitor's products.

15.2.2. Products-Completed Operations Exposure

A business may also be exposed to liability by defects in its **products or completed operations**. Examples of this exposure include a claim against Hooks Bakery for injury resulting from the sale of spoiled cream puffs and a claim against Magic Carpets Inc. for injury that results when a customer steps on a carpet tack left behind by Magic's workers.

15.2.3. Indirect/Contingent Liability Exposure

A business may not only be held liable for its own actions, but in certain cases, may be held liable for the actions of others. A business may have **indirect** or **contingent liability** for the actions of its employees, agents, contractors, or subcontractors. An example is a claim against First National Bank when a passerby is injured at the construction site of a new bank branch being built by Rolland Construction Company. This liability exposure is sometimes called **owners and contractors protective**.

15.2.4. Exposures Covered by Commercial General Liability Insurance

There are other types of liability exposures faced by businesses, including:

- work-related injuries to employees;
- pollution;
- contractual agreements in which the insured assumes liability; and
- ownership, maintenance or use of autos, watercraft, and aircraft.

However, because of the unique nature of these liability exposures, they are either excluded outright from the commercial general liability policy or may be covered only in certain circumstances or for limited amounts. More complete protection for these liability exposures is available under contracts specifically designed to cover them.

A business's liability for the premises and operations exposure, products-completed operations exposure and indirect/contingent liability exposure can all be covered by the **commercial general liability (CGL) policy**.

15.3. COMMERCIAL GENERAL LIABILITY COVERAGE PART

The commercial general liability policy may be included in the CPP or issued as a stand-alone policy. The coverage provided by the liability section of the businessowners policy is similar to that provided by the CGL.

A commercial general liability coverage part must include the following:

- Common policy declarations
- Common policy conditions
- CGL declarations
- One or more CGL coverage forms
- Any mandatory endorsements

15.4. OCCURRENCE AND CLAIMS-MADE FORMS

15.4.1. Occurrence Form

There are two primary CGL coverage forms: the **occurrence form** and the **claims-made form**. Although the two forms contain basically the same coverages, exclusions, and conditions, they differ in how coverage under the form is activated, or "triggered."

Traditionally, liability policies have been written on an occurrence basis. Coverage under the **occurrence form** is triggered by damage or injury that occurs during the policy period.

Suppose Joe is injured when a small piece of steel from the defective motor of a Niftycare lawnmower hits him in the eye. Provided the claim is otherwise covered, Niftycare's occurrence policy that was in effect at the time the injury occurred will apply to the loss, whether Joe makes his claim against Niftycare during the policy period or years later. There is coverage for any covered occurrence that happens during the policy period, even if the claim is made after the policy expires.

Suppose that on April 7, 2005, a ladder on which Brian is standing falls apart. He lands on his back and complains of some slight pain, but nothing major. Because the injury seems so slight, Brian does not file a claim for the injury. In 2007, however, he experiences recurring back pain and consults a physician, who decides the problem is a result of the 2005 injury. Brian files a claim against the manufacturer of the defective ladder, Newstep Ladder Company. Newstep had an occurrence CGL with Company A from 2000–2006; it took out a new occurrence CGL with Company B in 2007. Company A would pay for Brian's injury.

15.4.2. Claims-Made Form

The occurrence form is suitable for many insureds, but for others, it is not the best choice.

Consider an individual who owns and renovates rental properties. From 1961–1971, he painted his properties with a lead-based paint made by a well-known manufacturer. In 1998, he is diagnosed as having developed lead poisoning from exposure to the lead-based paint. This individual may be able to recover damages from the paint manufacturer under all of the occurrence policies in effect between 1961 and 1971. This insurance may be interpreted in several ways as to how it should be paid, and the insurance companies may not have set aside adequate reserves to take care of such long-range exposures since there is no way of adequately predicting such losses. The claims-made form was developed to address these types of considerations.

Coverage under the **claims-made form** is triggered when a claim is first made against the insured during the policy period, even if the actual injury or damage occurred at another time. This means that if Joe from our earlier example files a claim against Niftycare, it will be covered under the policy in effect when the claim is filed, rather than the policy in effect when the injury occurred. Under the claims-made form, claims filed during the policy period are covered, even when the occurrence took place prior to the effective date of the policy.

15.4.2.1. Retroactive Date

Although we have said that a claim made during the policy period is covered by a claims-made form even if the injury did not occur during that period, there may be some date before which a claims-made policy will not pay. This is known as the **retroactive date**, and it provides some measure of protection against previous losses that may have occurred before the claims-made form was written.

The retroactive date is listed in the CGL Declarations. The insured has three options for the retroactive date:

- Use the same date as the policy effective date
- Use an earlier date than the policy effective date
- Use no retroactive date

Exercise 15.A

1. Suppose a claims-made form has an effective date of 1/1/08, an expiration date of 12/31/08 and a retroactive date of 1/1/06. Which of the following would be covered?
   A. A claim filed 10/1/08 for a covered loss that occurred 6/1/06
   B. A claim filed 6/15/08 for a covered loss that occurred 5/15/07
   C. A claim filed 1/1/09 for a covered loss that occurred 12/1/08
   D. A claim filed 3/20/08 for a covered loss that occurred 12/3/05
   E. A claim filed 11/1/09 for a covered loss that occurred 2/14/06

Exercise answers can be found at the end of the Unit 15 answers and rationales.

A producer must be careful when selling a new CGL to avoid creating a coverage gap (a period during which the insured is without coverage). For instance, if the expiring policy is a claims-made form and it is being replaced with another claims-made form, the retroactive date of the new policy should be the same as the old one to avoid a coverage gap .

Advancing the retroactive date can also create a coverage gap. To avoid this situation, the rules by which claims-made CGL coverage is governed require that the insured give written consent to advancing the retroactive date, and even with the insured's consent, the retroactive date may be advanced only for one of the following reasons.

- A different insurance company is writing the new policy.
- A substantive change in the insured's operations has resulted in a greater exposure to loss.
- The insured did not provide the insurer with information the insured knew or should have known that would have been material to the insurance company's decision to accept the risk, or the insured did not provide information requested by the insurance company.
- The insured requests that the retroactive date be advanced.

15.4.2.2. Extended Reporting Periods: Basic and Supplemental

A gap can also occur when a claims-made policy is replaced by an occurrence form. However, a special feature built into the claims-made form, called the extended reporting period, can help close potential coverage gaps.

Extended reporting periods (ERPs) provide coverage for claims made after the policy's expiration date. The policy provides an extended reporting period if:

- the claims-made form is canceled or not renewed;
- the insurer renews or replaces the form with insurance that has a retroactive date later than the date shown in the declarations of the current form; or
- the insurer renews or replaces the form with an occurrence form.

Once an extended reporting period is in effect, it cannot be canceled.

A **basic extended reporting period** of either 60 days or five years is available automatically and free of charge under specified conditions.

Let's first consider the 60-day basic ERP. When a claims-made policy is terminated, a 60-day basic ERP automatically becomes available. The insured does not have to apply for it, and no premium is charged. It provides automatic coverage for any valid claim made during the 60 days after the policy expires, as long as the incident occurred between the expiring policy's retroactive date and its expiration date.

Now, suppose the insured is aware of an event that took place before the claims-made policy expired but suspects that claims may first come in after the 60-day basic ERP. The insured has up to 60 days following policy expiration to report the occurrence or offense to the insurer. In this case, the five-year basic ERP automatically applies. Claims for damages arising from the reported occurrence can be brought any time during the five-year period.

A **supplemental extended reporting period endorsement** is also available. It provides an unlimited extension of the reporting period, although the event causing the claim must still occur between the retroactive date and the policy expiration date. This ERP takes effect at the end of either the 60-day or five-year ERP, whichever applies. The insured must request this endorsement and pay an additional premium.

Exercise 15.B

True or false?

1. The supplemental ERP endorsement extends the policy period of a claims-made form for an unlimited amount of time.
   ( ) True ( ) False
2. The supplemental ERP takes effect at the end of either the 60-day or five-year basic ERP, whichever applies. ( ) True ( ) False
3. An event does not have to occur between the retroactive date and the policy expiration date to be covered under a claims-made CGL that has the supplemental ERP endorsement attached.
   ( ) True ( ) False
4. The insured must request the supplemental ERP endorsement and pay an additional premium for it. ( ) True ( ) False

Exercise answers can be found at the end of the Unit 15 answers and rationales.

15.5. DEFINITIONS

Both versions of the CGL forms contain a definitions section that helps clarify the intent of various coverages and conditions. This section is identical in both the occurrence and claims-made forms.

An **auto** is a land motor vehicle, trailer, or semitrailer, including any attached machinery or equipment, that is:

- designed for travel on public roads; or
- subject to compulsory or financial responsibility laws or other motor vehicle laws.

It does not include mobile equipment.

Mobile equipment means any of the following types of land vehicles, including any attached machinery or equipment:

- Bulldozers, farm machinery, forklifts, and other vehicles designed for use principally off public roads
- Vehicles maintained for use solely on or next to premises the insured owns or rents
- Vehicles that travel on crawler treads
- Vehicles, self-propelled or not, maintained primarily to provide mobility to permanently mounted power cranes, shovels, loaders, diggers, or drills, or road construction or resurfacing equipment such as graders, scrapers, or rollers
- Vehicles that are not self-propelled and are maintained primarily to provide mobility to permanently attached equipment such as air compressors, pumps, and generators, or cherry pickers and similar devices used to raise or lower workers

- Any vehicle that does not fit any of the above descriptions and is maintained primarily for purposes other than the transportation of persons or cargo

Certain self-propelled vehicles are not mobile equipment and are considered autos:

- Self-propelled vehicles with permanently attached equipment designed primarily for snow removal, road maintenance (other than construction or resurfacing), or street cleaning
- Cherry pickers and similar devices that are mounted on automobile or truck chassis and used to raise or lower workers
- Self-propelled vehicles with attached air compressors, pumps or generators

Land vehicles that are subject to compulsory or financial responsibility laws or other motor vehicle insurance laws are considered autos, not mobile equipment.

The **insured's product** means any goods or products, other than real property, that are manufactured, sold, handled, distributed, or disposed of by the insured, others trading under the insured's name, or a person or organization whose business or assets the insured has acquired. It also includes:

- containers, materials, parts, or equipment furnished in connection with the product;
- warranties or representations made at any time with respect to the fitness, quality, durability, or performance of any part of the product; and
- the providing of or failure to provide warnings or instructions.

The **insured's work** means work or operations performed by or on behalf of the insured, and materials, parts, or equipment furnished in connection with such work or operations. It also includes warranties or representations made at any time with respect to the fitness, quality, durability, or performance of the insured's work and the providing of or failure to provide warnings or instructions.

Impaired property means tangible property other than the insured's product or the insured's work that cannot be used or is less useful because:

- it incorporates the insured's product or work that is known or thought to be defective, deficient, inadequate, or dangerous; or
- the insured failed to fulfill the terms of a contract or agreement.

The property is impaired only if it can be restored to use by repair, replacement, adjustment, or removal of the insured's product or work, or by the insured fulfilling the terms of the contract or agreement.

Coverage territory usually means the described territory of the United States of America, including its territories and possessions, Puerto Rico, and Canada. It also means international waters or airspace if the injury or damage does not occur in the course of travel or transportation to or from any place not included in the described territory.

When the insured is determined to be responsible for damages in a lawsuit in the described territory, or in a settlement the insurer agrees to, the coverage territory includes all parts of the world if injury or damage arises out of:

- goods or products made or sold in the described territory;
- activities of a person whose home is in the described territory, but who is for a short time out of the described territory on business for the insured; or
- personal and advertising offenses that take place through the Internet.

Loading or unloading means handling of property:

- after it is accepted for movement into or onto an aircraft, watercraft, or auto;
- while it is in or on an aircraft, watercraft, or auto; or
- while it is being moved from an aircraft, watercraft or auto to the place where it is finally delivered.

It does not include the movement of property by a mechanical device, other than a hand truck, that is not attached to the aircraft, watercraft, or auto.

Pollutants means any solid, liquid, gaseous, or thermal irritant or contaminant, including smoke, vapor, soot, fumes, acids, alkalis, chemicals, and waste. Waste includes materials to be recycled, reconditioned or reclaimed.

The **products-completed operations hazard** includes all BI and PD occurring away from the premises owned or rented by the insured, and arising out of the insured's product or work, other than products that are still in the insured's physical possession and work that has not yet been completed or abandoned. Until the insured actually transfers products to others or completes work, liability exposures do not fall within the products-completed operations hazard.

A **leased worker** means a person leased to the named insured by a labor leasing firm under an agreement between the insured and labor leasing firm to perform duties related to the conduct of the insured's business.

A **temporary worker** is a person who is furnished to the insured to substitute for a permanent employee on leave, or to meet seasonal or short-term workload conditions.

The definition of **employee** includes leased workers, but not temporary workers.

A **volunteer worker** is a person who is not an employee, who donates his time and who is not paid by the insured or anyone else for work performed. A volunteer worker acts at the direction of the insured to perform duties determined by the insured.

15.6. COVERAGE A—BODILY INJURY AND PROPERTY DAMAGE LIABILITY

15.6.1. Coverage

The CGL forms provide three coverages:

- Coverage A—bodily injury and property damage liability
- Coverage B—personal and advertising injury liability
- Coverage C—medical payments

Coverage A—bodily injury and property damage liability pays those sums the insured becomes legally obligated to pay as damages because of bodily injury or property damage to which the insurance applies. To be covered, the BI or PD must be caused by an **occurrence**, which is defined in the CGL as an accident, including continuous or repeated exposure to the same general harmful conditions.

Remember that the occurrence form covers only BI or PD that occurs during the policy period. The insuring agreement of the occurrence form also stipulates that losses of a continuing or ongoing nature that were—prior to the policy period—known to the insured or employees authorized to report losses are not covered. The claims-made form covers BI or PD that occurred on or after the retroactive date, if any, and for which a claim for damages is first made against the insured during the policy period. A claim is considered to have been made when notice of claim is received and recorded by any insured or by the insurer, whichever comes first.

In addition to paying those sums the insured is legally obligated to pay, the company has the right and duty to defend an insured against any suit alleging liability for damages to which the policy applies.

15.6.2. Exclusions

There are a number of important exclusions that apply to Coverage A, including liability:

- arising out of intentional injury;
- the insured assumes under a contract or agreement;
- for those in the alcoholic beverage business, any liability imposed by law concerning alcoholic beverages;
- for work-related injuries covered under workers' compensation or employer's liability laws;
- for most pollution losses that result in bodily injury, property damage, or clean-up costs; or
- resulting from the maintenance, operation or use of aircraft, autos, or watercraft, except as specified in the policy.

The exclusion for liability assumed under contract has some important exceptions. Liability that the insured would have incurred even without assuming it under contract and liability assumed under **insured,** or **incidental, contracts** is covered. Insured contracts include leases, sidetrack agreements, easement agreements, contracts with municipalities required by ordinance, elevator maintenance agreements, and contracts relating to the insured's business under which the insured assumes another's liability.

As part of an insured contract, the insured may also assume liability for any defense costs incurred by or for a third party. These costs are considered covered damages if they are related to a loss that is insured by the policy. Since these costs are classified as covered damages, they will reduce the policy's limit of liability. Later, you'll learn that the insurer will sometimes pay these costs in addition to the policy's limit of liability.

Exercise 15.C

What two types of contractual liability are covered under the CGL?

1. ______________________________
2. ______________________________

Exercise answers can be found at the end of the Unit 15 answers and rationales.

Also excluded under Coverage A is liability:

- arising out of the transportation of mobile equipment by auto or the use of mobile equipment in any prearranged racing or related activity, or while practicing or preparing for such an activity;
- arising out of war or warlike acts;
- for damage to property owned, rented, or occupied by the insured or in the insured's care, custody, or control (does not apply to property and its contents for premises rented to the insured for seven consecutive days or less);
- for damage to the insured's own product arising out of the product itself;
- for damage to the insured's own work;
- for claims based on
  - — defects, deficiencies, inadequacies, or dangerous conditions in the insured's products or work, and
  - — delays or failures to properly perform contracts;
- related to recall of the insured's products or work because of a known or suspected defect;
- for bodily injury arising out of personal and advertising injury;

- arising out of loss or damage to electronic data; and
- arising out of violations of any law that prohibits or limits the distribution of material or information, including the federal Telephone Consumer Protection Act and CAN-SPAM Act.

An exception to certain exclusions under Coverage A protects the insured against legal liability for negligent acts that result in fire damage to a premises rented to the insured or temporarily occupied by the insured with the owner's permission.

15.7. COVERAGE B—PERSONAL AND ADVERTISING INJURY LIABILITY

15.7.1. Coverage

Coverage B provides **personal and advertising injury liability** coverage, which covers liability arising out of such offenses as libel or slander. Like Coverage A, personal and advertising injury liability coverage may be offered on either an occurrence or claims-made basis.

15.7.2. Exclusions

Liability arising out of any of the following is excluded under Coverage B:

- Knowingly inflicting injury that violates the rights of another
- Oral or written publication of material that the insured knows is false, but publishes anyway
- Material that was published before the effective date of the policy
- Criminal acts committed by or at the direction of the insured
- Assumed under contract, except for liability the insured would have incurred even without assuming it under contract
- Breach of contract
- Failure of goods, products, or services to conform with advertised quality or performance
- Incorrect price descriptions of goods, products, or services
- Any offense committed by an insured who is involved in the business of advertising, publishing, broadcasting, telecasting, or designing or determining content of Websites for others
- Infringement of copyright, patent, trademark, trade secret, or other intellectual property rights (does not apply to infringement in the insured's advertisement of copyright, trade dress, or slogan)

- Any offense committed by an insured whose business is an Internet search, access, content, or service provider
- An electronic chatroom or bulletin board the insured hosts or owns, or over which the insured exercises control
- Unauthorized use of another's name or product in the insured's email address, domain name, or metatag
- Arising out of war or warlike acts
- Arising out of violations of any law that prohibits or limits the distribution of material or information, including the federal Telephone Consumer Protection Act and CAN-SPAM Act

Coverage B also contains a blanket exclusion for any type of pollution loss. You may be wondering why an exclusion for pollution losses is needed for Coverage B. In the past, some insureds were able to recover pollution liability losses under Coverage B because the policy's definition of personal injury includes "wrongful entry into another's premises." The CGL now contains a pollution exclusion for Coverage B to prevent insureds from obtaining personal and advertising injury coverage for pollution liability.

15.8. COVERAGE A AND B SUPPLEMENTARY PAYMENTS

The following supplementary payments are also available for Coverage A and B. These payments do not reduce the limits of insurance.

Supplementary Payments
• All expenses incurred by the insurance company
• Up to $250 for the cost of bail bonds
• Cost of bonds to release attachments
• Reasonable expenses incurred by the insured to assist in the investigation and defense of a claim, including up to $250 per day for loss of earnings
• All court costs taxed against the insured in a suit (does not include attorney fees)
• Prejudgment and postjudgment interest
• Defense costs for an indemnitee

Earlier, you learned that a third party's defense costs assumed by the insured under an insured contract are covered damages if they are related to a loss that is insured by the policy. Since these costs are classified as covered damages, they will reduce the policy's limit of liability. The supplementary payments section provides that, if certain conditions are met, the insurer will:

- pay the defense costs for an **indemnitee**—a party who is not an insured who is under contract to provide goods or services to an insured—**in addition to** the policy's limit of liability; and
- provide a defense for the indemnitee.

Among the conditions that must be met for this coverage to apply are that the insured and the indemnitee must be named in the same lawsuit and the liability assumed by the insured must be covered by the policy.

15.9. COVERAGE C—MEDICAL PAYMENTS

15.9.1. Coverage

Coverage C of the CGL coverage forms is **medical payments.** It pays for medical expenses incurred for bodily injury caused by an accident on premises the insured owns or rents, on ways next to premises the insured owns or rents, or arising from the insured's operations. To be covered, the expenses must be incurred and reported to the insurer within one year of the date of the accident. Medical payments are made without regard to fault, unlike other coverages under the CGL forms.

15.9.2. Exclusions

Excluded under Coverage C of the CGL are injuries:

- to any insured or to a tenant or employee of the insured, including a person injured on a part of the insured's premises that he normally occupies (does not apply to the insured's volunteer workers);
- payable under workers' compensation or related laws;
- that occur to a person while he is taking part in athletics;
- included in the products-completed operations hazard (these would be paid under Coverage A);
- excluded under Coverage A; or
- related to war.

15.10. WHO IS AN INSURED

15.10.1. Named Insured

In the CGL, who is considered an insured under the policy depends on how the named insured is designated in the CGL declarations: as an individual, partnership or joint venture, limited liability company, trust or organization other than a partnership, joint venture or limited liability company.

Who is an Insured

Designation in Declarations	Who are Insureds	Restrictions
Individual	Named insured Named insured's spouse	Only in connection with sole proprietorships
Partnership or joint venture	Named insured Named insured's members and their spouses Named insured's partners and their spouses	Members, partners and their spouses are insureds only in connection with conducting the business
Limited liability company (a company structured like a corporation, but with additional tax and liability advantages for its members)	Named insured Members Managers	Members are insureds only in connection with conducting the business Managers are insureds only in connection with their duties as managers
Organization other than partnership, joint venture or limited liability company	Named insured Executive officers and directors Stockholders	Executive officers and directors are insureds only in connection with conducting the business Stockholders are insureds only in connection with liability as stockholders
Trust	Named insured Trustees	Trustees are insureds only in connection with their duties as trustees

15.10.2. Others

Each of the following is also an insured under the CGL:

- The named insured's employees for acts within the scope of their employment or while performing duties related to the conduct of the insured's business (does not include executive officers of a corporation or managers of a limited liability company)
- The insured's volunteer workers while performing duties related to the insured's business
- A nonemployee or organization while acting as real estate manager for the named insured
- If the named insured dies:
  - Any person or organization having temporary custody of the named insured's property, but only with respect to liability arising out of the maintenance or use of that property and only until a legal representative has been appointed for the insured
  - The insured's legal representative with respect to those duties

15.10.3. Newly Acquired Organizations

CGL forms automatically cover newly formed or acquired organizations as a named insured under certain circumstances.

- The named insured must maintain ownership or majority interest of the new organization.
- There must be no other similar insurance available to the organization.
- Automatic coverage will be provided for 90 days or until the end of the policy period, whichever is earlier.
- Coverages A and B do not cover losses that occurred before the organization was acquired or formed.

Coverage will continue after the automatic period expires if the insured reports the new organization to the insurer.

Coverage is not automatically provided for newly acquired or formed partnerships, joint ventures or limited liability companies.

15.11. LIMITS OF INSURANCE

The limits of insurance shown in the declarations are the most that will be paid, regardless of the number of insureds, claims made, suits brought, or persons bringing suit. There are several different coverage limits and sublimits that apply to payments made under the CGL.

The **general aggregate limit** is the most that will be paid for the sum of Coverages A, B, and C, except for damages arising out of the products-completed operations hazard. This limit can be modified by endorsement so that it applies separately to each of the insured's locations or projects.

There is a separate **products-completed operations aggregate limit** that represents the most that will be paid under Coverage A because of injury and damage arising out of the products-completed operations hazard.

The **personal and advertising injury limit** represents the most that will be paid under Coverage B for the sum of all damages due to personal injury or advertising injury sustained by any one person or organization. This limit is also subject to the overall general aggregate limit.

The **per occurrence limit** is the most that will be paid for the sum of damages under Coverages A and C because of all bodily injury, property damage, and medical payments arising out of any one occurrence. This limit is also subject to either the general aggregate limit or the products-completed operations aggregate limit, whichever is applicable.

The **damage to premises rented to the insured limit** represents the most that will be paid under Coverage A for liability for fire damage to premises rented to the insured or occupied by the named insured with the owner's permission arising out of any one fire. This sublimit is also subject to the per occurrence limit and the general aggregate limit.

Finally, the **medical expense limit** is the most that will be paid under Coverage C for all medical expenses because of bodily injury sustained by any one person. This sublimit is also subject to the per occurrence and general aggregate limits.

The limits apply separately to each consecutive annual period.

If the insured purchases the supplemental ERP endorsement for the claims-made form, separate aggregate limits apply to claims first received and recorded during the supplemental extended reporting period.

15.12. CONDITIONS

15.12.1. Duties in the Event of Occurrence, Offense, Claim, or Suit

The insured has certain duties in the event of an occurrence, offense, claim, or suit.

The insured must notify the insurer as soon as practicable of an occurrence or offense that may result in a claim, including how, when, and where it took place, the names and addresses of any injured persons and witnesses, and the nature and location of any injury or damage arising out of the occurrence. (Under the claims-made form, notice of an occurrence is *not* notice of a claim.)

If a claim is made or suit brought against any insured, the insured must immediately record the specifics of the claim or suit and the date it was received and notify the insurer as soon as practicable. The insured must also see to it that the insurer receives written notice of any claim or suit as soon as practicable.

The insured must also:

- immediately send the insurer copies of any demands, notices, or other legal papers received in connection with a claim or suit;
- authorize the insurer to obtain records;
- cooperate with the insurer in the investigation, settlement, or defense of a claim;
- at the company's request, assist the insurer in the enforcement of any right against someone who may be liable to the insured; and
- not voluntarily make a payment, assume any obligation, or incur any expense, other than expenses for first aid, without the insurer's consent, except at the insured's own cost.

15.12.2. Nonrenewal

The **when we do not renew** condition states that if the insurer decides to not renew the CGL policy, it must mail or deliver written notice of nonrenewal to the first named insured at least 30 days before the expiration date of the policy.

15.12.3. Other Insurance

The **other insurance** condition states that when the insured's CGL is primary and other primary insurance applies to the same loss, the loss will be divided between the policies by one of two methods:

- Contribution by equal shares
- Contribution by limits

Under **contribution by equal shares,** all insurers contribute equally up to the limit of the policy with the lowest limit. At that point, the insurer with the lowest limit stops paying since it has already paid its policy's limit, and the other insurers share the remainder of the loss. This continues either until the loss is paid in full or each company has paid its limit.

Here's an example. The insured has primary coverage with two companies. Company A's policy has limits of $25,000, and Company B's limits are $50,000. Both policies permit contribution by equal shares. If a $60,000 covered loss occurred, Company A would pay up to its limits ($25,000), and Company B would pay $35,000.

Contribution by equal shares applies when all policies involved specify this method of handling other insurance. If they don't, **contribution by limits** applies. Contribution by limits is a method you are already familiar with for apportioning losses. Each company pays a proportion of the loss equal to the proportion its policy limits bear to the total amount of insurance available.

The CGL is **excess** over some types of insurance, such as builders risk and commercial property coverage on the insured's own work.

15.12.4. Claim Information

The **your right to claim and occurrence information** condition is included in the claims-made form, but not the occurrence form. It provides that the insurer will give the first named insured certain information relating to the current CGL claims-made form and any previous claims-made forms the insurer has issued to the insured during the previous three years. The information includes:

- a list or record of each occurrence not previously reported to any other insurer of which this insurer has been notified according to policy provisions; and
- a summary, by policy year, of payments made and amounts reserved under any applicable general aggregate limit and products-completed operations aggregate limit.

If the insurer cancels or does not renew the policy, it will provide this information no later than 30 days before termination. In other circumstances, the insurer will provide the information only if it receives a written request from the first named insured within 60 days after the end of the policy period. The information will be provided within 45 days of the request.

15.13. OTHER COMMERCIAL GENERAL LIABILITY COVERAGE FORMS AND ENDORSEMENTS

There are several CGL forms and endorsements that are commonly used.

The **pollution liability coverage extension endorsement** overrides the Coverage A exclusion for BI or PD claims arising out of pollution losses. It does not, however, provide coverage for clean-up costs associated with pollution losses.

The standard CGL coverage forms cover the insured's liability for operations of independent contractors. The **owners and contractors protective liability (OCP) coverage form** is specifically designed to provide this coverage. It is purchased by someone other than the named insured to protect the insured against liability arising out of work performed for the insured by an independent contractor. It is most frequently used to protect an owner for liability arising out of operations being performed by a general contractor. Coverage applies only to the specific location and contractor named in the declarations and is written on an occurrence basis.

The **liquor liability coverage form** covers insureds who are in the liquor business. It covers liability for contributing to a person's intoxication or for providing liquor in violation of the law for businesses engaged in the liquor business. The standard forms exclude this liability, which is sometimes called **dram shop liability.** Coverage can be purchased on either a claims-made or occurrence basis.

The **pollution liability coverage form** and the **pollution liability—limited coverage form** cover certain pollution losses excluded under the standard form. Each covers pollution incidents, which are emissions of pollutants into or on land, the atmosphere or water that cause environmental damage. The only difference is that the pollution liability—limited form does not cover clean-up costs, but the pollution liability form does. Both pollution forms are only written on a claims-made basis.

UNIT TEST

1. List the three major business liability exposures that can be covered under the commercial general liability policy.
   A. ______________________________
   B. ______________________________
   C. ______________________________

2. Coverage under an occurrence CGL form is triggered
   A. when the claim is first made against the insured during the policy period
   B. by BI or PD that occurs during the policy period

3. Which of the following statements about the 60-day basic extended reporting period are true?
   A. It becomes effective automatically if needed when a claims-made policy expires.
   B. The insured must request it in writing within 60 days after the policy expires.
   C. It does not require additional premium.
   D. No separate endorsement is required to provide this extended reporting period.

4. What is the purpose of a retroactive date in the claims-made form?
   A. Extend the period of time in which a claim may be covered under the policy
   B. Stipulate a date as the first date on which an event may occur and be covered by the policy if a claim is filed
   C. Extend the policy period

5. Coverage under a claims-made CGL is triggered
   A. when the claim is first made against the insured during the policy period
   B. by BI or PD that occurs during the policy period

6. Which of the following is a personal and advertising injury?
   A. Broken leg
   B. Death
   C. Calling a client a cheat and a fraud
   D. Dog bite

7. For each of the following examples, list which CGL coverage would apply: Coverage A, B or C. If there is no coverage, write "None."
   A. A third party becomes ill after eating a meal catered by the insured. ______________
   B. One of the insured's competitors sues the insured for slander. ______________
   C. A third party is extremely embarrassed, but not physically injured, after slipping on a step in the insured's store.______________
   D. The insured incurs expenses administering first aid to a customer who faints and injures his head. ______________

8. For Coverage C to apply under the CGL, the insured (is/is not) __________ required to be at fault for the injury from which the medical expenses arise.

9. Which of the following are usually excluded under Coverage A of the commercial general liability policy?
   A. Property damage to property owned by the insured
   B. Property damage to property in the care, custody, or control of the insured
   C. Liability assumed under an insured contract

10. Which of the following represents an insured contract covered under the commercial general liability policy?
    A. CLM Construction has signed a lease for a building.
    B. CLM Construction has signed an easement agreement with the local telephone company.

11. All of the following reduce the CGL's general aggregate limit EXCEPT
    A. the medical payments sublimit
    B. the personal and advertising injury limit
    C. the fire damage limit
    D. the products-completed operations limit

12. In the CGL, who is considered an insured under the policy depends on
    A. how the named insured is designated in the CGL declarations
    B. who is listed in the who is an insured section of the policy

13. What two methods may be used to pay a loss when the insured's CGL is primary and other primary insurance applies to the same loss?
    A. ______________________________
    B. ______________________________

14. What is the difference between the pollution liability coverage form and the pollution liability—limited coverage form? ____________
    ____

15. A woman is injured when she breaks a tooth on a rock that mysteriously found its way into a box of cereal. This is an example of the
    A. premises and operations exposure
    B. products-completed operations exposure
    C. contingent liability exposure
    D. contractual liability exposure

16. Which of the following business liability exposures are either excluded altogether from the CGL or covered only in certain circumstances?
    A. Premises and operations
    B. Indirect/contingent liability
    C. Pollution
    D. Work-related injuries to employees
    E. Products-completed operations
    F. Contractual
    G. Ownership, maintenance, or use of autos, watercraft, and aircraft

17. Which one of the following is NOT required in a CGL coverage part?
    A. CGL declarations
    B. One or more CGL coverage forms
    C. Causes of loss form
    D. Common policy conditions

18. To avoid coverage gaps when replacing one claims-made CGL form with another claims-made CGL form, the retroactive date of the replacement policy should be (the same as/different from) __________the retroactive date of the policy being replaced.

19. If an event occurred and was reported during the policy period of a claims-made CGL, and a claim is first made 30 days after the policy expires, which basic extended reporting period applies?
    A. 60 days
    B. 5 years

20. Suppose the insured first reports an occurrence to the insurer 15 days after a claims-made CGL expires. No claim has been made yet. Which basic extended reporting period applies?
    A. 60 days
    B. 5 years

21. Which of the following would be considered mobile equipment under the commercial general liability coverage form?
    A. Truck used to transport personnel to construction sites
    B. Road construction grader
    C. Bulldozer

22. Power Oil Company, the insured, manufactures petroleum products. In addition to the products themselves, would the can in which motor oil was sold be considered the insured's product?
( ) Yes ( ) No
Explain your answer.______________________
____

23. Dooley Plumbing, the insured, has contracted with J&L Builders to do the plumbing work on a new office building. Because of completion deadlines for three other jobs Dooley is working on, Dooley subcontracts part of the J&L job to a local subcontractor. Does the subcontractor's work qualify as the insured's work?
( ) Yes ( ) No
Explain your answer.
____
____

24. While visiting the Rainbow Spray Paint Factory on a field trip with his kindergarten class, George Leland was invited to try out the new Rainbow spray paint product. The container leaked red paint on George's leather jacket. Would this loss fall under the products-completed operations hazard?
( ) Yes ( ) No
Explain your answer.______________________
____

25. Which of the following are excluded under Coverage A of the CGL?
    A. Damage the insured causes intentionally
    B. Pollution losses caused by the insured
    C. Liquor liability for those in the business of serving liquor
    D. All of the above

26. The CGL's pollution exclusion applies to
    A. Coverage A only
    B. Coverage B only
    C. Both Coverage A and Coverage B

27. The insured, Francesca Pirelli, is a furniture retailer who is advertising a sale to get rid of older inventory. Pirelli has a contract with HighStyle Furnishings that says she will not sell their line at lower than their suggested retail price. When she includes some HighStyle furniture in an ad at 40% off, HighStyle sues her for breach of contract. Would this claim be covered under Coverage B of the CGL?
( ) Yes ( ) No
Why?_________________________________

28. Which of the following would be excluded under Coverage C of the CGL?
    A. A shopper is injured in the insured's retail store when a box falls on him from an overhead shelf.
    B. The insured sponsors a foot race on the land surrounding his retail store. A participant is injured during the race.
    C. An individual hired by the insured to paint her business office falls off a ladder and is injured.
    D. One of the insured's employees is injured while on the job.

29. Which of the following types of newly acquired businesses qualify for automatic coverage under the CGL?
    A. Corporation
    B. Sole proprietorship
    C. Partnership
    D. Limited liability company

30. If an insurer decides to not renew the CGL policy, how many days notice of nonrenewal must be provided to the first named insured?
    A. 7 days
    B. 10 days
    C. 20 days
    D. 30 days

ANSWERS AND RATIONALES TO UNIT TEST

1. The three major business liability exposures that can be covered under a commercial general liability policy are premises and operations, products-completed operations, and indirect/contingent.

2. **B.** With an occurrence policy, the policy that was in effect at the time the loss occurred will apply to the loss, even if the injured party makes the claim years after the policy expired.

3. **A**, **C**, and **D** are correct. When a claims-made policy is terminated, a 60-day basic ERP automatically becomes available. The insured does not have to apply for it, and no premium is charged. It provides automatic coverage for any valid claim made during the 60 days after the policy expires, as long as the incident occurred between the expiring policy's retroactive date and its expiration date.

4. **B.** The retroactive date provides some protection against losses that occurred before the claims-made form was written.

5. **A.** Under the claims-made form, the policy that was in effect when the claim is first filed will apply to the loss, even if the loss occurred before the policy was in effect.

6. **C.** The other answer choices are examples of bodily injury.

7. **A.** Coverage A. This coverage pays sums the insured becomes legally obligated to pay as damages because of bodily injury or property damage to which the insurance applies.

   B. Coverage B. This coverage applies to offenses such as libel or slander.

   C. None. This would not be covered under Coverage A or Coverage C because the individual did not suffer actual damages or incur medical expenses. It would not be covered under Coverage B because embarrassment is not considered a personal or advertising injury.

   D. Coverage C. This coverage pays for medical expenses incurred for bodily injury caused by an accident on premises the insured owns or rents.

8. Is not. Medical payments are made without regard to fault, unlike other coverages under the CGL forms.

9. **A** and **B** are correct. Coverage A excludes property damage to property owned by the insured and property damage to property in the care, custody or control of the insured.

10. **A** and **B** are correct. Insured contracts include leases, sidetrack agreements, easement agreements, contracts with municipalities required by ordinance, elevator maintenance agreements, and contracts relating to the insured's business under which the insured assumes another's liability.

11. **D.** There is a separate products-completed operations aggregate limit that is not subject to the general aggregate limit.

12. **A.** In the CGL, who is considered an insured under the policy depends on how the named insured is designated in the CGL declarations: as an individual, partnership or joint venture, limited liability company, or organization other than a partnership, joint venture, or limited liability company.

13. Contribution by equal shares and contribution by limits. Under contribution by equal shares, all insurers contribute equally up to the policy with the lowest limit. At that point, the insurer with the lowest limit stops paying since it has already paid its policy's limit, and the other insurers share the remainder of the loss. This continues either until the loss is paid in full or each company has paid its limit. Contribution by equal shares applies when all policies involved specify this method of handling other insurance. If they don't, contribution by limits applies. Under this method, each company pays a proportion of the loss equal to the proportion its policy limits bear to the total amount of insurance available.

14. The difference between the two pollution liability coverage forms is that the pollution liability coverage form covers clean-up costs and the limited form does not.

15. **B.** The products-completed operations hazard includes all BI and PD occurring away from the premises owned or rented by the insured, and arising out of the insured's product or work, other than products that are still in the insured's physical possession and work that has not yet been completed or abandoned.

16. **C**, **D**, **F**, and **G** are correct. Businesses face a number of liability exposures, including work-related injuries to employees, pollution, contractual agreements in which the insured assumes liability, and ownership, maintenance, or use of autos, watercraft, and aircraft. However, because of the unique nature of these liability exposures, they are either excluded outright from the CGL policy or may be covered only in certain circumstances or for limited amounts. More complete protection for these liability exposures is available under contracts specifically designed to cover them.

17. **C.** Causes of loss forms are not used with the CGL coverage part.

18. The same as. Using different dates could create a coverage gap—a period of time during which the insured is without coverage.

19. The 60-day basic ERP automatically becomes available when a claims-made policy is terminated. It provides automatic coverage for any valid claim made during the 60 days after the policy expires, as long as the incident occurred between the expiring policy's retroactive date and its expiration date.

20. **B.** An insured has up to 60 days following policy expiration to report the occurrence or offense to the insurer, even if a claim has not yet been filed. Claims for damages arising from the reported occurrence can be brought any time during the five-year ERP.

21. **B** and **C** are correct. Both of these items are specifically listed in the policy's definition of mobile equipment. An auto is a land motor vehicle, trailer, or semitrailer designed for travel on public roads, including any attached machinery or equipment.

22. Yes. Containers are included in the definition of the insured's product.

23. Yes. Work performed on the insured's behalf is included in the definition of the insured's work.

24. No. The damage did not occur away from the premises.

25. **D.** All of these losses are specifically excluded under Coverage A.

26. **C.** Both Coverage A and Coverage B exclude pollution losses. There is no pollution exclusion for Coverage C.

27. No. Losses arising out of breach of contract are not covered.

28. **B, C,** and **D** are correct. Coverage C excludes injuries to the insured's employees and injuries that occur while participating in athletics.

29. **A** and **B** are correct. CGL forms automatically cover newly formed or acquired organizations as a named insured under certain circumstances. However, coverage is not automatically provided for newly acquired or formed partnerships, joint ventures or limited liability companies.

30. **D** is correct. The nonrenewal condition states that if the insurer decides to not renew the CGL policy, it must mail or deliver written notice of nonrenewal to the first named insured at least 30 days before the expiration date of the policy.

UNIT 15 EXERCISE ANSWERS

Exercise 15.A

1. A and B

Exercise 15.B

1. False—it extends the period for reporting claims for an unlimited time
2. True
3. False—it must occur during this time period to be covered
4. True

Exercise 15.C

In any order:

1. Liability the insured would have incurred even without assuming it under contract
2. Liability assumed under insured/incidental contracts

U N I T

16

Commercial Auto Insurance

16.1. LEARNING OBJECTIVES

After completing Unit 16—Commercial Auto Insurance, you will be able to do the following:

- Identify the required components of a commercial auto coverage part
- For the business auto, garage, truckers, and motor carrier coverage forms, describe the types of risks covered by the form; coverages that are automatically included in the form; and coverages that must be added by endorsement
- Describe how the following terms are defined in the business auto coverage form: *auto*, *bodily injury*, *property damage*, *covered pollution cost or expense*, *pollutants*, *mobile equipment*, and *diminution of value*
- Describe the numerical symbols used to identify covered autos in the business auto coverage form
- For liability coverage in the business auto coverage form, describe the conditions that must be met for a loss to be covered; who is an insured; situations and perils that are excluded; expenses that are covered as supplementary payments; the purpose of out-of-state coverage extensions; and the circumstances under which worldwide liability coverage is provided
- For physical damage coverage in the business auto coverage form, describe the three coverages available and the perils they cover; how deductibles apply under these coverages; the insured's options for covering glass breakage losses; the purpose of the towing and labor costs, transportation expenses, and loss of use coverages; losses that are excluded; and the three options available for settling claims
- Explain the provisions of the following business auto conditions: legal action against the insurer, other insurance, and two or more policies issued by the same insurer
- Describe the numerical symbols that are unique to the garage coverage form
- For liability coverage in the garage coverage form, describe the types of losses covered; who is considered an insured; and losses that are excluded
- Explain the purpose of garagekeepers insurance
- Describe the features of the physical damage coverage in the garage coverage form
- Describe the numerical symbols that are unique to the truckers coverage form
- Explain the purpose of trailer interchange coverage
- Describe the financial responsibility requirements for truckers and commercial carriers under the Motor Carrier Act of 1980

- Explain the purpose of the MCS-90 endorsement
- Describe the features of the following commercial auto endorsements: drive other car coverage, individual named insured, employees as additional insureds, additional insured—lessor, specified hired autos, and mobile equipment

16.2. COMMERCIAL AUTO COVERAGE PART

Like individuals, businesses need both liability and physical damage coverage for losses that arise out of autos owned by or used in the business. In this unit, we will focus on automobile coverages designed to cover the private passenger and commercial auto exposures of businesses that can be insured under the commercial auto policy.

The **commercial auto** policy can be written as a monoline policy or can be included in the CPP. A commercial auto coverage part must contain the following elements:

- Common policy declarations
- Common policy conditions
- One of five separate coverage forms: business auto, business auto physical damage, garage, truckers, or motor carrier
- Appropriate declarations for coverage form selected

The **business auto physical damage form** covers the insured's owned or hired business autos for physical damage only. We will discuss the remaining forms in more detail. This course will focus on the business auto coverage form; our discussion of the other commercial auto coverage forms will be limited to the ways in which they differ from the business auto form.

16.3. BUSINESS AUTO COVERAGE FORM

16.3.1. Introduction

The **business auto coverage form** is used to insure the private passenger and commercial auto exposures of all businesses other than garages, truckers, and motor carriers. Because of the specialized nature of these businesses and their unique coverage needs, separate forms were designed to cover these risks.

The business auto coverage form includes:

- liability coverage; and
- physical damage coverage (comprehensive or specified causes of loss and collision).

Uninsured motorists, medical payments, and underinsured motorists coverage can be added by endorsement.

16.3.2. Definitions

The **definitions** section of the business auto coverage form defines certain key terms used in the policy. These terms help clarify the intent of various coverages and conditions, as you will see as you progress through this unit.

An **auto** is a land motor vehicle, trailer, or semitrailer, including any attached machinery or equipment, that is:

- designed for travel on public roads; or
- subject to compulsory or financial responsibility laws or other motor vehicle laws.

It does not include mobile equipment. An exception is made under the policy's liability coverage when mobile equipment is being towed or carried by a covered auto. This provision fills an insurance gap, because the commercial general liability policy excludes coverage for mobile equipment while it is being transported by an auto that is owned or operated by an insured. Other exposures arising out of mobile equipment are covered under commercial general liability insurance.

Bodily injury means bodily injury, sickness, or disease, including death resulting from any of these. **Property damage** means damage to or loss of use of tangible property.

Covered pollution cost or expense means costs arising out of any statutory or regulatory requirement or any order by a government authority demanding that the insured test for, monitor, clean up, remove, contain, treat, detoxify or neutralize, or respond to or assess the effects of pollutants. It does not include the costs arising out of the escape of pollutants that are in property being transported or towed by, handled into, onto, or from the covered auto, or otherwise in the course of transit by the insured, or being stored, disposed of, treated, or processed in or on the covered auto. Also excluded are pollutants released before the property is moved to the place where they are accepted by the insured for movement into the covered auto, and after the pollutants are delivered by the insured. This exclusion does not apply to fuels, lubricants, fluids, exhaust gases, or other pollutants necessary for or resulting from the normal operation of a covered auto or its parts.

Diminution of value is an actual or perceived loss in resale or market value that results from a direct, accidental loss.

Pollutants means any solid, liquid, gaseous, or thermal irritant or contaminant, including smoke, vapor, soot, fumes, acids, alkalis, chemicals, and waste. Waste includes materials to be recycled, reconditioned or reclaimed.

In the previous unit, you learned the definition of **mobile equipment.** This definition is identical in the business auto and commercial general liability coverage forms. This allows the two coverages to fit together precisely and removes any doubt about which coverage applies to autos and which applies to mobile equipment.

16.3.3. Covered Autos

The insured selects what autos are to be considered covered autos for each coverage. These selections are contained in the business auto declarations and are based on a numerical symbol system described in the policy.

The insured may select from the following.

Symbol	Type of Auto Selected	Description
1	Any auto	■ Any auto the insured will use during the policy period, including autos that are owned, leased, hired, rented, or borrowed ■ Used to designate liability coverage only
2	Owned autos only	■ Any auto the insured owns ■ Designates other coverages besides liability coverage
3	Owned private passenger autos only	■ Any private passenger auto the insured owns ■ Designates any coverage provided by the business auto coverage form
4	Owned autos other than private passenger autos only	■ Other types of vehicles the insured owns, such as trucks, trailers, buses, and motorcycles ■ Designates any coverage provided by the business auto coverage form
5	Owned autos subject to no-fault law	■ Designates owned autos required to have no-fault benefits in a particular state
6	Owned autos subject to compulsory uninsured motorists law	■ Designates owned autos required to have uninsured motorists coverage in a particular state
7	Specifically described autos	■ Applies only to autos specifically listed in the business auto coverage form declarations
8	Hired autos only	■ Designates liability and/or physical damage coverage only ■ Only used for autos the insured has leased, hired, rented, or borrowed ■ Does not include autos rented or borrowed from employees or members of their households
9	Nonowned autos only	■ Only used for autos used in the insured's business that are not leased, hired, rented, or borrowed ■ Includes autos owned by employees but used in the insured's business or personal affairs ■ Designates liability coverage only
19	Mobile equipment subject to motor vehicle laws only	■ Autos that would be considered mobile equipment if they were not subject to compulsory or financial responsibility laws or other motor vehicle laws

Coverage may be tailored to the needs of the insured by selection of the appropriate symbols. Different symbols may be used for different coverages. The broadest coverage available is reflected by symbol 1, because "any auto" includes all owned, hired and nonowned autos. The most restrictive symbol is symbol 7, because it applies only to specifically described autos.

With the exception of specifically described autos, autos acquired during the policy period are automatically covered. For specifically described autos, an auto acquired during the policy period is only a covered auto for a particular coverage if the insured already insures all autos for this coverage or if it replaces a covered auto and the insured notifies the insurer within 30 days of acquisition.

If the insured has liability coverage under the policy, the following vehicles are also covered autos for liability coverage:

- Temporary substitute autos
- Trailers with a load capacity of 2,000 pounds or less
- Mobile equipment while it is being towed or carried by a covered auto

Exercise 16.A

1. Which business auto coverage form symbol is the "any auto" symbol and is used only to designate liability coverage ?

   ____

2. If an insured wants collision coverage for only a few autos out of an entire fleet, which symbol would be used on the declarations?

   ____

3. Which symbol is used to designate coverage for owned autos required to have no-fault coverage?

   ____

Exercise answers can be found at the end of the Unit 16 answers and rationales.

16.3.4. Liability Coverage

The liability coverage in the business auto coverage form is similar to that provided by the personal auto policy. The policy agrees to pay all sums an insured legally must pay as damages because of BI or PD to which the insurance applies caused by an accident and resulting from the ownership, maintenance, or use of a covered auto. Coverage for defense costs and supplementary payments is also included.

The insurer also agrees to pay all sums an insured legally must pay as a **covered pollution cost or expense** to which the policy applies. The pollution cost must be caused by an accident and result from the ownership, maintenance, or use of covered autos. The insurer will pay for covered pollution costs only if there is bodily injury or property damage caused by the same accident. Coverage for liability for pollution clean-up costs is also included under specific circumstances.

16.3.4.1. Who Is an Insured

In addition to the named insured, others have liability coverage while using a covered auto with permission. The policy also covers those who become liable for the conduct of an insured.

Those who are not insureds include:

- the owner of an auto hired or borrowed from an employee or family member;
- a person who is working in an auto-type business;
- people besides employees or lessees while moving property to or from a covered auto; and
- the owner of a hired or borrowed auto.

16.3.4.2. Exclusions

Business auto liability coverage contains many of the same exclusions as personal auto liability coverage and some unique exclusions as well, including liability:

- for expected or intended injuries;
- assumed under contract or agreement (does not apply to liability the insured would have had if there were no contract or agreement or to contracts that meet the policy's definition of an insured contract);
- for work-related injuries to employees, including those covered under workers' compensation and related laws and injuries caused to an employee by another employee;
- for damage to property owned by, transported by or in the care, custody, or control of the insured;
- for damage arising out of the movement of property by a mechanical device;
- for bodily injury or property damage arising out of the operation of self-propelled vehicles with attached cherry pickers that are used to raise or lower workers, or that have permanently attached equipment, such as air compressors, pumps, and generators;
- for completed operations;
- for pollution damage, except as specifically provided in the policy;
- for BI or PD arising out of war or warlike acts; and
- for covered autos while being used for, or while practicing or preparing for, organized or professional racing, demolition, or stunting activities.

16.3.4.3. Supplementary Payments

The liability section of the business auto coverage form will cover the following as **supplementary payments**:

- Expenses the insurer incurs
- Cost of bail bonds up to $2,000 for violations because of a covered accident

- Cost of bonds to release attachments, but only within the limit of insurance
- Expenses the insured incurs at the insurer's request, including the insured's lost earnings up to $250 a day because of time off from work
- Costs the insured is required to pay because of a suit
- Interest that accrues after a judgment and before it is paid

Note: Losses covered under the supplementary payments section do not reduce the policy's limit of liability.

16.3.4.4. Out of State Coverage Extensions

The business auto coverage form provides for situations where a business's autos are driven in more than one state. The **out of state coverage extensions** modify the policy's liability coverage to meet other states' financial responsibility requirements and other state laws concerning out-of-state drivers when the covered auto is being driven in that state.

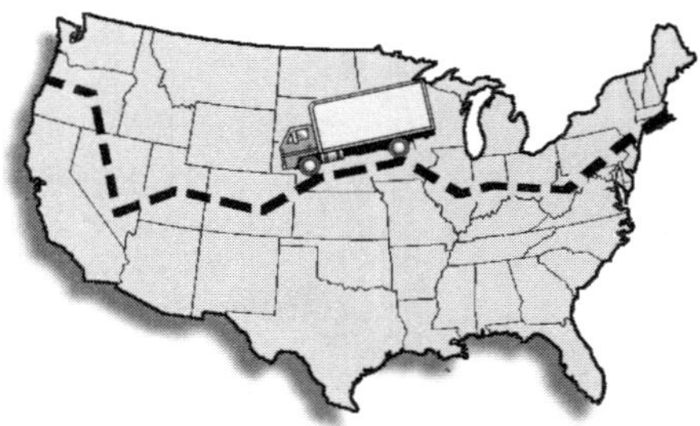

Exercise 16.B

1. Howard is driving his company-owned truck in another state and causes an accident. That state requires a minimum of $30,000 liability coverage, and his policy has a limit of $25,000. Howard is sued for $50,000 in damages arising out of the accident. How much will his policy pay?
   A. $25,000
   B. $30,000
   C. $50,000

Exercise answers can be found at the end of the Unit 16 answers and rationales.

16.3.4.5. Worldwide Liability Coverage

The coverage territory for the business auto coverage form includes the United States and its territories and possessions, Puerto Rico, and Canada.

In addition, the form provides worldwide liability coverage for private passenger autos the insured hires, leases, rents, or borrows without a driver for 30 days or less. The insured's liability must be determined in a settlement agreed to by the insurer or in a suit filed in the United States or its territories and possessions.

16.3.5. Physical Damage Coverage

The **physical damage** portion of the business auto coverage form contains three principal coverages.

- **Comprehensive** coverage covers any loss, other than collision or overturn, that is not excluded by the policy.
- **Specified causes of loss** is a more limited type of comprehensive coverage and covers only:
  - fire,
  - lightning,
  - explosion,
  - theft,
  - windstorm,
  - hail,
  - earthquake,
  - flood,
  - vandalism or mischief, and
  - sinking, burning, collision, or derailment of a conveyance transporting the covered auto (such as a ship).
- **Collision** covers overturn of the covered auto and collision with another object.

The insured may select different physical damage coverage options for different vehicles. For example, some vehicles may be insured for comprehensive and collision losses, whereas others are insured only for the specified causes of loss.

Collision and comprehensive coverages are written with a deductible. Under comprehensive coverage, the deductible does not apply to loss caused by fire or lightning. Under specified causes of loss coverage, a $25 deductible applies to loss by vandalism or mischief. No other losses have a deductible under this coverage.

If the insured carries comprehensive coverage, losses due to glass breakage, hitting a bird or animal, and falling objects or missiles are treated as comprehensive losses. This usually works to the insured's advantage, because comprehensive coverage is usually written with a lower deductible than collision coverage. However, the insured may also have glass breakage paid as a collision loss. This removes a possible double deductible if glass breakage and other damage result from a collision.

Also available is coverage for towing and labor costs incurred when a covered private passenger auto is disabled.

A **coverage extension** provides coverage for transportation expenses. It covers expenses incurred because of the theft of the insured's vehicle beginning 48 hours after the theft and ending when the auto is returned or the insurer pays the loss. Coverage is limited to a maximum of $20 per day or a total of $600.

Another coverage extension covers **loss of use** expenses to rented autos for which the insured is legally responsible under a contract or agreement. Coverage is limited to $20 per day, to a maximum of $600.

Exercise 16.C

1. A covered auto collided with a bird, which broke the windshield of the auto. The auto is insured for collision and comprehensive coverages under the business auto coverage form. Which coverage would pay for this loss?
   A. Collision
   B. Comprehensive
   C. Both collision and comprehensive

Exercise answers can be found at the end of the Unit 16 answers and rationales.

16.3.5.1. Exclusions

The physical damage coverage exclusions are similar to those found in the physical damage section of the personal auto policy, including loss:

- to sound reproducing and receiving equipment, tapes, and records;
- from wear and tear, freezing, mechanical or electrical breakdown, or road damage to tires;
- arising out of war;
- arising out of nuclear events;
- to covered autos while being used for, or while practicing or preparing for, organized or professional racing, demolition, or stunting activities; and
- due to diminution in value.

16.3.6. Conditions

The conditions in the business auto coverage form are similar to those you have studied in relation to other insurance contracts. We'll briefly cover those that are unique to the business auto coverage form.

16.3.6.1. Settling Physical Damage Claims

The insurer has three options for settling physical damage claims:

- Pay for, repair, or replace the damaged or stolen property
- Return stolen property to the insured at the company's expense and pay for any damages resulting from the theft
- Take the damaged or stolen property at an agreed or appraised value

In the event of a total loss, depreciation and physical condition will be considered when determining actual cash value. If a repair or replacement results in better than like kind or quality, the amount of the betterment is not covered.

16.3.6.2. Legal Action Against the Insurer

The insured cannot take legal action against the insurance company unless the insured has fully complied with all terms of the policy. If the lawsuit relates to the policy's liability coverage, the insurer must also agree in writing that the insured is obligated to pay or the amount of judgment must have been determined after a trial.

16.3.6.3. Other Insurance

The **other insurance** condition states that the business auto coverage form provides **primary coverage** for covered autos owned by the insured and, for liability losses, covered trailers that are connected to covered autos owned by the insured. The coverage is **excess** for losses involving nonowned covered autos and covered trailers while they are connected to nonowned motor vehicles.

When the business auto coverage form and the other insurance cover on the same basis, either primary or excess, the business auto coverage form pays only its proportionate share of the loss.

16.3.6.4. Two or More Policies Issued by the Same Insurer

If more than one policy or coverage form issued by the same insurer applies to a loss, the amount that the insured can be paid is limited to the highest single policy limit.

Exercise 16.D

1. Select all correct statements regarding the business auto coverage form conditions.
   A. An insured cannot take legal action against the insurance company unless she has fully complied with all terms of the policy.
   B. The business auto coverage form provides excess coverage for covered autos owned by the insured.
   C. When the business auto coverage form and other insurance cover on the same basis, the business auto coverage form pays only its proportionate share of the loss.
   D. Physical damage claims are always settled on a replacement cost basis.
   E. If more than one policy issued by the same insurer applies to a loss, the amount that the insured can be paid is limited to the highest single policy limit.

Exercise answers can be found at the end of the Unit 16 answers and rationales.

16.4. GARAGE COVERAGE FORM

16.4.1. Introduction

The **garage coverage form** is designed specifically for vehicle dealers, including dealers that have repair operations on the business premises. The form can be written to cover auto dealers, truck and truck-tractor dealers, motorcycle dealers, commercial trailer dealers, and recreational vehicle dealers.

The garage coverage form includes liability, garagekeepers, and physical damage coverage. Uninsured motorists, underinsured motorists, and medical payments coverage may be added by endorsement.

16.4.2. Covered Autos

Like the business auto coverage form, the garage coverage form uses a numerical system to determine which autos are covered autos. It is similar to the one used for the business auto coverage form, except the numbers are different. There are two symbols that are unique to the garage coverage form:

- **Symbol 30:** Customers' autos left with the insured for service, repair, storage, or safekeeping (this is garagekeepers coverage, which we'll cover later)
- **Symbol 31:** Physical damage coverage only for the dealers' autos, including owned autos, autos for sale, and autos on consignment

16.4.3. Liability Coverage

The garage coverage form covers both auto and business liability arising out of:

- the ownership, maintenance or use of covered autos (garage operations—covered autos); and
- garage operations (garage operations—other than covered autos).

Those protected as insureds under the garage coverage form for garage operations—covered autos are essentially the same as those insured for liability under the business auto coverage form, with one important exception. Garage customers are not covered if they have their own liability coverage. If customers do not have liability coverage of their own, the garage form protects them, but only up to the minimum limits of financial responsibility. The insured has the option of adding coverage for customers up to the full limits of the policy.

For garage operations—other than covered autos, those considered insureds include the named insured, the insured's employees, and the business's directors and shareholders while acting within the scope of their duties.

The garage coverage form contains many of the same liability exclusions as the business auto coverage form. It also contains some general liability exclusions, such as damage to property of others in the insured's care, custody, or control, property damage to the insured's own products or work, and product or work recalls.

16.4.4. Garagekeepers Coverage

The liability section of the garage coverage form excludes liability for damage to property of others in the care, custody, or control of the insured. For garages, this excludes a significant business exposure: the garage's liability for customers' autos in its care or custody. Coverage for this specific exposure is provided under the **garagekeepers insurance** section of the garage coverage form.

Garagekeepers insurance covers the insured's liability for damage to customers' property that the insured has for servicing, repair, parking, or storage. The insured also has the option of purchasing direct damage garagekeepers insurance, which pays for physical damage to customers' property in the insured's custody, whether or not the insured is liable. Direct damage garagekeepers insurance can be provided on either a primary or excess basis; the causes of loss that can be covered include comprehensive or specified causes of loss and collision.

16.4.5. Physical Damage Coverage

Garage physical damage coverage offers the same coverage as the business auto coverage form: comprehensive or specified causes of loss and collision. It specifically excludes false pretense coverage—coverage for losses when a dealer voluntarily parts with a covered auto because of a trick. (Such coverage is available by endorsement.)

Typically, auto dealers purchase physical damage coverage on a blanket basis. A few specialized exclusions apply to this blanket coverage, including:

- expected profits; and
- collision damage to autos being driven or transported from the point of purchase or distribution to the point of destination if this distance is 50 miles or more.

16.5. TRUCKERS COVERAGE FORM

16.5.1. Introduction

The business auto coverage form specifically excludes businesses that set themselves out for hire to haul the goods of others. So truckers must obtain coverage for their vehicles under the **truckers coverage form,** a modified version of the business auto coverage form that takes into consideration the special practices and regulations that apply to the trucking industry.

The truckers coverage form includes three coverages:

- Liability
- Trailer interchange
- Physical damage

The liability and physical damage coverages are similar to those provided under the business auto coverage form. We'll discuss trailer interchange coverage in a moment.

16.5.2. Covered Autos

Like the other commercial auto coverage forms you've studied so far, the truckers coverage form uses a numerical system to determine which autos are covered autos. It is similar to the one used for the business auto coverage form, except the numbers are different and the "owned auto" options do not include private passenger autos. It also contains two symbols to provide trailer interchange coverage:

- **Symbol 48:** Trailers borrowed or leased by the named insured for which liability for loss has been assumed under a written trailer interchange agreement; applies to comprehensive, specified causes of loss or collision coverages of trailer interchange coverage only
- **Symbol 49:** Trailers owned or hired by the named insured while the trailers are in someone else's possession under a written trailer interchange agreement

16.5.3. Trailer Interchange Coverage

Truckers frequently need to borrow or hire a trailer from another trucking business for use in their own business. Under the business auto coverage form, damage to such property is excluded from coverage. Under the truckers coverage form, **trailer interchange insurance** covers damage to a specific trailer under the policy of the trucker in whose possession the trailer is at the time of loss. For coverage to apply, the trucker must be liable under a written interchange agreement, and the damage must be caused by a covered peril.

16.6. MOTOR CARRIER COVERAGE FORM

The **motor carrier coverage form** is an alternative to the truckers coverage form. You learned earlier that a trucker is a person hired to haul the goods of others. A **motor carrier** is anyone who transports property by auto in a commercial enterprise, regardless of whether he was hired for that purpose.

Because this broad definition encompasses truckers, those who are eligible for coverage under the truckers coverage form could also be covered under the motor carrier coverage form. However, those who are eligible for coverage under the motor carrier form can be covered under the truckers form only if they transport goods for others by hire.

With the exception of those who can be covered under the form, the motor carrier coverage form is practically identical to the truckers coverage form. Like the truckers coverage form, it provides trailer interchange coverage. Unlike the truckers form, owned private passenger autos may be covered autos in the motor carrier coverage form.

16.6.1. Motor Carrier Act of 1980/MCS-90 Endorsement

Truckers and other commercial carriers are subject to a number of regulations, such as the **Motor Carrier Act Of 1980,** that require trucking companies to certify that they are able to meet financial obligations if they become liable for injury or damage arising from their trucking operations.

The most common method for satisfying these requirements is to obtain adequate truckers coverage to cover the automobile exposure, as well as commercial inland marine motor truck cargo insurance to cover the liability for cargo being hauled. If insurance is used to establish proof of financial responsibility, the **MCS-90 endorsement** must be attached to the policy. This endorsement provides public liability coverage for bodily injury, property damage, and environmental restoration.

The limits of liability required by the Motor Carrier Act affect vehicles that have a gross vehicle weight of 10,000 pounds or more. The required limits are divided into three categories, depending on the kind of hazardous cargo hauled:

- $750,000 for interstate transportation of nonhazardous property;
- $5,000,000 for interstate or intrastate transportation of large quantities of certain hazardous materials, such as compressed gas, radioactive materials, explosives, or oil; and
- $1,000,000 for interstate or intrastate transportation of oil or other hazardous wastes.

Vehicles that have a gross vehicle weight of less than 10,000 pounds must comply with the financial responsibility limit of $5,000,000 if the vehicle hauls explosives, any quantity of poison gas, or large quantities of radioactive materials.

16.7. ENDORSEMENTS

16.7.1. Drive Other Car Coverage Endorsement

There are a number of endorsements that can be added to the commercial auto coverage forms.

The **drive other car—broadened coverage for named individuals (DOC) endorsement** extends the definition of a covered auto to include autos the named insured does not own, hire, or borrow while being used by the person named in the endorsement. Coverage does not apply to autos owned by the person named in the endorsement or a family member.

DOC coverage might be especially important if the named insured under a business auto coverage form is furnishing an auto to an employee who has no personal auto insurance. Although the employee would have coverage under the business auto form while using the furnished auto or any other auto owned, hired, or borrowed by the named insured, the employee would have no coverage under the business auto form for an auto he borrowed or rented unless the DOC endorsement was attached to the business auto form.

Exercise 16.E

The insured has a business auto coverage form that covers all autos. She provides a company car to her top salesperson. Suppose this salesperson borrows a neighbor's car and, while on business for the company, has an accident.

1. Would this salesperson have liability coverage under an unendorsed business auto coverage form? ( ) Yes ( ) No
2. Would this salesperson have liability coverage under a business auto coverage form with the DOC endorsement attached? ( ) Yes ( ) No

Exercise answers can be found at the end of the Unit 16 answers and rationales.

16.7.2. Individual Named Insured

The **individual named insured endorsement** extends personal auto coverage to immediate family members of the named insured.

For example, consider a sole proprietor who operates a business and has business auto coverage, but no personal auto insurance. Under the business auto policy, the sole proprietor would have coverage for any auto. The sole proprietor's family members would have coverage while using autos owned, hired, or borrowed by the named insured and while using nonowned autos in the insured's business. However, they would have no coverage for their personal use of nonowned autos. Attaching the individual named insured endorsement to the business auto coverage form would extend coverage for the use of any auto to family members, subject to certain exclusions. It provides very similar coverage to that provided by the personal auto policy.

16.7.3. Employees as Additional Insureds

If a business has broad coverage for all autos, it would be covered in any suit arising out of an accident involving owned, hired, borrowed, or nonowned autos, including autos owned by employees while used for business purposes. Although the employees are insured under the business auto liability section while driving autos owned by the business, they are not insured while driving their own cars in the course of business. If a suit against a business also named an employee as the driver and owner of a vehicle, the business auto coverage form would only protect the business. If the employee had personal auto coverage, it would provide some protection, but claims resulting from a business-related accident might involve amounts well above the employee's coverage limits.

Employees can be protected under the business auto coverage form with the **employees as additional insureds** endorsement. It states that any employee is an insured while using an auto the business does not own, hire, or borrow when the autos are used in the business or personal affairs of the named insured.

This coverage insures employees for the business use of their own autos or autos owned by family members. It does not protect other family members who may own a vehicle being used by an employee.

Exercise 16.F

1. Misha is involved in an auto accident in which three people were killed. When the accident occurred, she was using her personal car to make a sales call for her employer. The victims' survivors file suit against Misha and her employer. Would Misha be an insured under the company's business auto coverage form, assuming that no endorsements apply?
( ) Yes ( ) No
2. Which endorsement would have provided coverage for Misha?

Exercise answers can be found at the end of the Unit 16 answers and rationales.

16.7.4. Other Endorsements

As we mentioned earlier, the insured may also add **medical payments, uninsured motorists,** and **underinsured motorists** coverage by endorsement. These endorsements provide coverage similar to that provided for personal auto coverage.

Leased vehicles can be considered owned vehicles for coverage purposes by attaching the **additional insured—lessor endorsement** to the policy.

An endorsement may be used to add coverage for specified hired autos as if they were covered autos owned by the named insured. When attached to a policy, the hired autos scheduled in the endorsement will be treated as if they were covered automobiles owned by the named insured.

Finally, when the **mobile equipment endorsement** is attached, mobile equipment is considered a covered auto.

UNIT TEST

1. Match each commercial auto coverage form with its correct description.

1) Business auto	____	A. Can be purchased by most businesses; provides very broad coverage for losses arising from owned and nonowned autos
2) Business auto physical damage	____	B. Covers businesses that set themselves out for hire to haul the goods of others
3) Garage	____	C. Provides broad coverage for liability arising out of autos and the business operations of vehicle dealers
4) Truckers	____	D. Provides physical damage coverage only for a business's owned or hired autos
5) Motor carrier	____	E. Covers businesses that transport property by auto in a commercial enterprise, regardless of whether the business was hired for that purpose

2. Which of the following coverages are provided by business auto physical damage coverage?
   A. Collision
   B. Transportation expenses
   C. Comprehensive
   D. Towing and labor costs
   E. Garagekeepers Insurance
   F. Specified causes of loss

3. Which portion of the garage coverage form covers liability for damage to property of others in the insured's care, custody or control?
   A. Liability
   B. Garagekeepers
   C. Physical damage
   D. Both A and B

4. Trailer interchange coverage is included in
   A. all commercial auto coverage forms
   B. the truckers coverage form
   C. the motor carrier coverage form
   D. the garage coverage form

5. Which of the following can be covered under a motor carrier coverage form?
   A. Truckers
   B. Motor carriers
   C. Both A and B

6. The garage coverage form covers liability arising out of
   A. ownership, maintenance or use of covered autos
   B. garage operations
   C. a trailer interchange agreement

7. Which of the following perils are included in the business auto coverage form's specified causes of loss coverage?
   A. Collision
   B. Earthquake
   C. Flood
   D. Theft
   E. Vandalism
   F. Mechanical breakdown

8. Which commercial auto endorsement extends personal auto coverage to immediate family members of the named insured?
   A. Individual named insured
   B. Drive other car—broadened coverage for named individuals

9. Medical payments, uninsured motorists, and underinsured motorists coverage
   A. is automatically included in all commercial auto coverage forms
   B. can be added by endorsement to any of the commercial auto coverage forms

10. Mobile equipment is usually excluded under the business auto coverage form. However, there is one exception under liability coverage. What is it?

    ____

    ____

11. Which of the following statements concerning business auto liability coverage are correct?
    A. It covers BI or PD caused by an accident.
    B. It does not cover pollution losses.
    C. It only covers sums for which the insured is legally liable.
    D. The BI or PD must result from the ownership, maintenance or use of a covered auto.

12. Who of the following would be considered an insured under business auto liability coverage?
    A. The named insured
    B. Others while using a covered auto with permission
    C. The owner of a borrowed auto
    D. Others who become liable for the conduct of an insured

13. Which of the following are excluded under business auto liability coverage?
    A. Liability assumed under a contract that is considered an insured contract
    B. Damage to the insured's own auto
    C. Injury to employees covered by workers' compensation laws
    D. Liability for property in the insured's custody

14. Which of the following losses would be paid under the business auto coverage form's comprehensive coverage?
    A. Gradual corrosion of the grillwork on a covered auto due to continuous exposure to salt air
    B. Overturn of a covered auto
    C. Collision damage to a covered auto
    D. Theft of a covered auto

15. Which of the following businesses might be covered under a garage coverage form?
    A. Used car dealer
    B. Catering company
    C. Auto body shop
    D. Service station

16. Which of the following coverages are included in an unendorsed garage coverage form?
    A. Garagekeepers
    B. Uninsured motorists
    C. Liability
    D. Physical damage

17. Which of the following can only be considered covered autos under the garage coverage form?
    A. Customers' autos left with the insured for service
    B. Autos the insured has leased to use in the business
    C. Autos held for sale by a dealer

18. What is the purpose of direct damage garagekeepers insurance?

    ____

    ____

19. What is the purpose of the truckers coverage form?

____

20. What type of coverage does the MCS-90 endorsement add to the commercial auto policy?

____

21. How does the mobile equipment endorsement affect the commercial auto coverage forms?

____

ANSWERS AND RATIONALES TO UNIT TEST

1. 1 A.; 4 B.; 3 C.; 2 D.; 5 E. The business auto coverage form covers a business's owned, nonowned and hired autos against liability and physical damage losses. The business auto physical damage coverage form covers a business's owned or hired business autos for physical damage only. The garage coverage form is designed for various types of vehicle dealers. It includes coverage for liability arising out of auto and garage operations, physical damage, and garagekeepers' losses arising out of owned, nonowned, and hired autos. The truckers coverage form is written specifically for the trucking industry. The motor carrier coverage form is an alternative to the truckers coverage form. It can be used to cover anyone who transports property by auto in a commercial enterprise.

2. **A**, **B**, **C**, **D,** and **F** are correct. The physical damage portion of the business auto coverage form contains three principal coverages: (1) comprehensive, (2) specified causes of loss (a more limited type of comprehensive coverage), and (3) collision. Coverage for towing and labor costs and transportation expenses is also available under physical damage coverage. Garagekeepers insurance is not included in the business auto coverage form.

3. **B.** The liability section of the garage coverage form excludes liability for damage to customers' autos in the insured's custody. Coverage for this exposure is provided under the garagekeepers section of the garage form.

4. **B** and **C** are correct. Trailer interchange coverage covers damage to a specific trailer under the policy of the trucker who has possession of the trailer at the time of loss, as long as certain conditions are met. It is included in the truckers and motor carrier coverage forms.

5. **C.** A motor carrier is anyone who transports property by auto in a commercial enterprise, regardless of whether the individual was hired for that purpose. Since this broad definition encompasses truckers, those who are eligible for coverage under the truckers coverage form could also be covered under the motor carrier coverage form. However, those who are eligible for coverage under the motor carrier form can only be covered under the truckers form if they transport goods for others by hire.

6. **A** and **B** are correct. Trailer interchange coverage is not included in the garage coverage form.

7. **B**, **C**, **D**, and **E** are correct. Specified causes of loss coverage is a limited type of comprehensive coverage. It covers fire, lightning, explosion, theft, windstorm, hail, earthquake, flood, vandalism or mischief, and sinking, burning, collision, or derailment of a conveyance transporting the covered auto.

8. **A.** The individual named insured endorsement provides coverage similar to that provided under the personal auto policy to family members of the named insured while using any auto.

9. **B.** These coverages are not included in any of the commercial auto coverage forms. They must be added to the policy by endorsement.

10. Mobile equipment is usually excluded under the business auto coverage form. However, an exception applies under liability coverage when the mobile equipment is being towed or carried by a covered auto.

11. **A**, **C**, and **D** are correct. This coverage pays all sums an insured legally must pay as a covered pollution cost or expense to which the policy applies as long as certain conditions are met.

12. **A**, **B**, and **D** are correct. The owner of a hired or borrowed auto is not an insured for liability coverage while using the covered auto.

13. **B**, **C**, and **D** are correct. The exclusion for liability assumed under contract or agreement does not apply to contracts that meet the policy's definition of an insured contract.

14. **D.** Losses from wear and tear are excluded. The other two losses are considered collision losses.

15. **A.** The garage coverage form is designed to cover vehicle dealers.

16. **A**, **C**, and **D** are correct. The garage coverage form includes liability, garagekeepers, and physical damage coverage. Medical payments, uninsured motorist, and underinsured motorists coverage is added by endorsement.

17. **A** and **C** are correct. There are two covered auto symbols that are unique to the garage coverage form. Symbol 30 is used for customers' autos left with the insured for service, repair, storage, or safekeeping. Symbol 31 is used for physical damage coverage only for the dealers' autos.

18. Direct damage garagekeepers insurance covers physical damage to customers' property that is in the insured's custody, regardless of whether the insured is liable for the damage.

19. The purpose of the truckers coverage form is to provide coverage for businesses that set themselves out for hire to haul the goods of others.

20. The MCS-90 endorsement adds coverage for public liability for bodily injury, property damage, and environmental restoration to the commercial auto policy.

21. The mobile equipment endorsement changes the business auto coverage form by allowing mobile equipment to be considered a covered auto under the policy.

UNIT 16 EXERCISE ANSWERS

Exercise 16.A

1. Symbol 1
2. Symbol 7
3. Symbol 5

Exercise 16.B

1. **B**

Exercise 16.C

1. **B**

Exercise 16.D

1. A, C, and E

Exercise 16.E

1. No
2. Yes

Exercise 16.F

1. No
2. Employees as additional insureds

UNIT

17

Commercial Crime Insurance

17.1. LEARNING OBJECTIVES

After completing Unit 17—Commercial Crime Insurance, you will be able to do the following:

- Identify the appropriate forms used to write a monoline crime policy, a package crime policy, crime insurance for commercial businesses, and crime insurance for government entities
- Compare and contrast the features of the loss sustained and discovery versions of crime policies
- Describe how the following terms are defined in crime policies: *burglary*, *safe burglary*, *robbery*, *theft*, *forgery*, *custodian*, *messenger*, *watchperson*, *employee benefit plan*, *money*, *other property*, and *securities*
- For each of the commercial crime insuring agreements, describe the type of crime loss covered, the type of property covered, requirements for where it is located for coverage to apply, and conditions that must be met for coverage to apply
- Describe losses that are excluded under employee theft coverage
- Compare and contrast employee theft coverage written on a per loss and per employee basis under a government crime form
- Explain the conditions required for defense costs to be paid under forgery or alteration coverage
- Identify losses that are excluded under all of the crime coverages
- Identify losses that are excluded only under certain crime coverages
- Compare and contrast how the crime policies value losses to money, securities, and property other than money and securities
- Explain the provisions of important conditions that apply to all crime coverages, including the insured's duties in the event of loss, legal action against the insurer, and other insurance
- Describe conditions that apply only to certain crime coverages
- Describe the purpose of the extortion—commercial entities and guests' property endorsements
- Discuss the losses covered by the kidnap/ransom and extortion coverage form
- Describe the purpose of fidelity bonds
- Define the roles of the three parties involved in a bond contract
- Explain the purpose of the following types of fidelity bonds: name schedule, position schedule, commercial blanket, and blanket position

17.2. TYPES OF CRIME FORMS

In this unit, you will learn about **commercial crime insurance**, which is insurance designed to protect businesses and government entities against property loss resulting from such crimes as burglary, robbery, theft, and employee dishonesty.

Crime coverage can be provided as a monoline policy or as part of a commercial package policy (CPP). However, unlike the other commercial lines coverages you've studied to this point, the same forms are *not* used for package policies and monoline policies. For crime insurance, coverage forms are used for package policies, and policy forms are the monoline versions. The primary difference is that a separate common policy conditions form is not required for a monoline policy because these conditions are incorporated into the policy. For a CPP, a separate form is required.

There are separate crime forms for commercial businesses and government entities. We will focus primarily on forms written for businesses.

Each crime form is available in two versions: the loss sustained form and the discovery form. The difference between the forms is what triggers coverage. We'll discuss these forms in more detail in a moment.

Here is a list of the most commonly used crime forms.

	Monoline Policies	Package Policies
Commercial	• Commercial crime policy—discovery version • Commercial crime policy—loss sustained version	• Commercial crime coverage form—discovery version • Commercial crime coverage form—loss sustained version
Government	• Government crime policy—discovery version • Government crime policy—loss sustained version	• Government crime coverage form—discovery version • Government crime coverage form—loss sustained version

Separate employee theft and forgery policies are also available. Other coverages may be added by endorsement.

17.2.1. Loss Sustained Form

Crime insurance written under a **loss sustained form** covers losses that are sustained during the policy period and discovered either during the policy period or up to one year after the policy expires. This one-year discovery period terminates immediately when the insured obtains other commercial crime insurance.

Note that the policy does not extend coverage beyond the policy expiration date. Losses that occur after policy expiration will not be covered, but losses that occur during the policy period and are discovered within one year after policy expiration are covered.

Suppose a pet supply store is insured under the loss sustained version of the crime policy. The policy period is January 1, 2003, to January 1, 2004. A loss occurs on April 6, 2003, but is not discovered until September 7, 2004. The crime policy will cover this loss because the loss occurred during the policy period and was discovered within one year after the policy expiration date.

The **loss sustained during prior insurance condition**, which appears only in the loss sustained forms, states that the policy will pay for a loss that occurred during the term of a previous policy but was discovered during the term of the present policy. For coverage to apply, three conditions must be met.

- The discovery period under the previous policy has expired.
- The current policy became effective on the date the prior policy expired.
- The loss is covered under both the current and previous policies.

The most that will be paid for the loss is the lesser of the current or previous policy limit.

Suppose the insured's commercial crime policy with Company A had an effective date of January 1, 2003, and expired January 1, 2004. The insured then purchased a policy from Company B that was effective from January 1, 2004, through January 1, 2005, and then renewed for another year. The insured had a crime loss that occurred in February 2003 but was not discovered until March 2005. The policies from both companies were written on a loss sustained basis. Assume that, without regard to the date, the loss would have been covered under either policy. This loss would be covered under Company B's policy.

17.2.2. Discovery Form

Certain crime losses, such as extortion and embezzlement, may not be discovered until weeks, months, or years after they occur. Crime insurance written on a **discovery** basis covers losses that are sustained at any time and discovered either during the policy period or up to 60 days after the policy expires (up to one year for losses related to employee benefit plans). A loss is discovered when the insured:

- first becomes aware that a loss has occurred or will occur, even if the actual amount of loss or details concerning the loss are not known; or
- receives notice of an actual or potential claim for a covered loss.

The extended periods to discover losses terminate immediately when the insured obtains other commercial crime insurance.

Exercise 17.A

1. The insured's crime policy is written on a discovery basis and is effective from March 1, 2004, to March 1, 2005. In December 2004, an audit of the insured's financial records reveals that the bookkeeper has embezzled over $50,000 from the business over the previous three years. This loss would
   A. be covered because the loss was discovered during the policy period
   B. not be covered because it occurred before the policy was in effect

Exercise answers can be found at the end of the Unit 17 answers and rationales.

17.3. DEFINITIONS

17.3.1. Types of Crimes

All of the crime forms include a **definitions** section that defines certain key terms used in the policy. These terms help clarify the intent of various coverages and conditions, as you will see as you progress through this unit.

Although burglary is not specifically defined in the crime forms, it still has a specific meaning in the insurance industry. **Burglary** is the taking of property from inside the premises by a person unlawfully entering or leaving the premises. There must be evidence of forcible entry or exit, such as marks made by tools, explosives, chemicals, or electricity.

Safe burglary is the taking of property from within a locked safe or vault by a person unlawfully entering the safe or vault, as evidenced by marks of forcible entry on the exterior of the safe or vault. It also includes the taking of the entire safe or vault from inside the premises.

Robbery is the unlawful taking of property from the care and custody of another person. The robber must have caused or threatened to cause bodily harm to the person being robbed or must have committed an obviously unlawful act that is witnessed by the person being robbed.

Theft means the unlawful taking of property. This broad term includes burglary, safe burglary, and robbery. However, unlike burglary, safe burglary, and robbery, which usually involve the use of force, theft also includes the taking of property by stealth (action designed to escape notice).

Forgery is signing the name of another person or organization with the intent to deceive.

Exercise 17.B

Match the loss described in the left-hand column with the type of crime it represents listed in the right-hand column. There is only one correct answer for each question.

1. ____	During a break-in at a business, the safe is removed from the premises.	A. Burglary
2. ____	Armed thieves tie up a struggling store clerk and customer and lock them in a back room. Then they load up several appliances from the showroom into their waiting truck.	B. Safe Burglary
3. ____	An unassuming, unarmed gentleman walks into a furriers at noon and walks out with three mink stoles. When an astonished clerk runs after him, she finds the gentleman has disappeared without a trace.	C. Robbery
4. ____	Professional crooks use dynamite to break into an isolated electronics warehouse after the building is closed for the day.	D. Theft
5. ____	While dining at a small eatery, a customer finds the owner's checkbook and slips it into his pocket. Later, he makes purchases using the checks and signing the restaurant owner's name.	E. Forgery

Exercise answers can be found at the back of the Unit 17 answers and rationales.

17.3.2. Other Definitions

A **custodian** is someone who has care or custody of property inside the premises. It includes the insured, the insured's partners or members, or any employee. It does not include a watchperson or janitor.

A **messenger** is someone who has care and custody of property while it is outside the premises. It can include the insured, a relative of the insured, the insured's partners or members, or any employee.

A **watchperson** is someone retained specifically by the insured whose sole duty is to have care and custody of property inside the premises.

An **employee benefit plan** is any welfare or pension plan subject to the Employee Retirement Income Security Act Of 1974 (ERISA), such as a 401(k), profit sharing, health, life, or disability insurance plan. Government plans, such as Social Security, are not employee benefit plans.

Money includes currency, coins, bank notes, travelers checks, register checks, and money orders.

Other property means any tangible property other than money or securities that has value. It does not include computer programs or electronic data.

Securities are instruments or contracts that represent money or property. Checks, drafts, bonds, certificates of deposit, stock certificates, stamps, and credit card receipts are all considered securities.

17.4. INSURING AGREEMENTS

The commercial crime forms include the following coverages as insuring agreements:

- Employee theft
- Forgery or alteration
- Inside the premises—theft of money and securities
- Inside the premises—robbery or safe burglary of other property
- Outside the premises
- Computer fraud
- Money orders and counterfeit paper money
- Funds transfer fraud

Although multiple coverages are listed in the form, the insured must select the coverages that will apply to the policy. For each insuring agreement selected, a limit of insurance and deductible must be listed on the declarations. The policy limit and deductible both apply per occurrence. Any insuring agreements the insured does not want must be designated as "Not Covered" on the declarations page. Each insuring agreement is subject to specific rules and has its own rating plan.

17.4.1. Employee Theft

Employee theft coverage pays for loss of or damage to money, securities, and other property resulting from theft or forgery committed by an employee, either acting alone or in collusion with others. The employee does not have to be identified for coverage to apply.

There is no coverage for:

- an employee who has previously had similar insurance canceled and not reinstated;
- loss resulting from trading, either in the insured's name or in a genuine or fictitious account; or
- loss resulting from fraudulent or dishonest use of warehouse receipts.

Proof of loss may not be based on an inventory shortage or profit and loss computation.

An employee benefit plan may be listed in the declarations as a named insured for employee theft coverage. No deductible applies to losses sustained by an employee benefit plan.

Under the government crime forms, employee theft losses may be written on a **per loss basis**, which means the limit of insurance applies regardless of how many employees were involved in the loss, or on a **per employee basis**, meaning all loss caused by one employee. Treasurers, tax collectors, and employees required by law to be individually bonded are not covered.

Exercise 17.C

1. Which of these statements about employee theft coverage are correct?
   A. It covers theft or forgery of money, securities, and other property by an employee.
   B. For a loss to be covered, the employee involved in the loss must be identified.
   C. An inventory shortage may be used as proof that a loss occurred.
   D. An employee benefit plan may be listed as an insured for this coverage.

Exercise answers can be found at the end of the Unit 17 answers and rationales.

17.4.2. Forgery or Alteration

Forgery or alteration coverage pays for loss resulting from forgery or alteration of checks, drafts, promissory notes, or similar instruments made or drawn by or on the named insured or the insured's agent. This includes documents that are forged or altered with a mechanically reproduced facsimile signature. Coverage is provided worldwide.

If the insured is sued for refusing to pay a forged or altered instrument and obtains the insurer's written permission to defend the suit, the insurer will pay reasonable defense costs incurred by the insured. These expenses are paid in addition to the limit of liability, with no deductible required.

17.4.3. Inside the Premises—Theft of Money and Securities

Inside the premises—theft of money and securities coverage pays for theft, disappearance, or destruction of money and securities while inside the insured premises or a banking premises. If the insured owns the premises or is liable for damage to it, it also covers damage to the interior or exterior of the premises that results from theft or attempted theft.

Damage to a locked safe, vault, cash register, cash box, or cash drawer that is inside the premises is also covered when the damage results from theft, attempted theft, or unlawful entry.

Exercise 17.D

1. After a convenience store closed for the night, a group of teenagers broke in by driving their car through the front door. While inside the store, they stole $100 worth of snack food and tried and failed to break into the safe. Which of the following would be covered under the store owner's Inside the premises—theft of money and securities coverage?
   A. Damage to the front door
   B. Damage to the safe
   C. Theft of the snack food
   D. All of the above

Exercise answers can be found at the end of the Unit 17 answers and rationales.

17.4.4. Inside the Premises—Robbery or Safe Burglary of Other Property

The fourth insuring agreement, **Inside the premises—robbery or safe burglary of other property,** has two primary coverages:

- Loss of other property (not money or securities) while inside the premises from actual or attempted robbery of a custodian
- Loss of other property from a safe or vault inside the premises from actual or attempted safe burglary

If the insured owns the premises or is liable for damage to it, it also covers damage to the interior or exterior of the premises that results from actual or attempted robbery or safe burglary. Damage to a locked safe or vault that is inside the premises is also covered when the damage results from actual or attempted robbery or safe burglary.

17.4.5. Outside the Premises

The **outside the premises** insuring agreement also provides two types of coverage:

- Theft, disappearance, or destruction of money and securities while outside the premises and in the care and custody of a messenger or an armored car company
- Loss of other property by actual or attempted robbery while outside the premises and in the care and custody of a messenger or an armored car company

17.4.6. Computer Fraud

Computer fraud coverage covers loss of or damage to money, securities, and other property due to the use of a computer to fraudulently transfer that property from inside the premises or banking premises to a place or person (other than a messenger) outside the premises. Coverage is provided worldwide. Proof of loss may not be based on an inventory shortage or profit and loss computation.

17.4.7. Money Orders and Counterfeit Paper Money

The next insuring agreement, **money orders and counterfeit paper money**, covers losses that result when the insured accepts invalid money orders or counterfeit money in good faith.

Suppose a customer at the insured's clothing store uses cash to purchase $1,000 worth of merchandise. When the insured attempts to deposit the money, she learns it is counterfeit. The money orders and counterfeit paper money coverage would pay for her loss.

17.4.8. Funds Transfer Fraud

The **funds transfer fraud** insuring agreement covers losses resulting from fraudulent instructions to a financial institution to pay money from an insured's transfer account. Loss resulting from the use of a computer to fraudulently transfer money, securities, or other property is not covered. Fraudulent instructions are defined as instructions by someone who is impersonating an insured or an employee to transfer money without the insured's knowledge or consent. A transfer account is an account maintained at a financial institution that allows money to be transferred electronically, either by phone or in writing.

17.5. EXCLUSIONS

17.5.1. For All Coverages

The following exclusions apply to all of the coverages in the crime forms:

- Theft or dishonest acts committed by the insured, partners, or members, whether acting alone or in collusion with others
- Loss caused by an employee if the employee had previously committed theft or another dishonest act prior to the policy period and the insured knew about that action
- Theft or dishonest acts committed by any of the insured's employees, managers, directors, trustees, or authorized representatives, except as covered under employee theft coverage; the exclusion applies whether

the person is acting alone or in collusion with others and while actually working for the insured or otherwise

- Unauthorized disclosure of insured's confidential information
- Unauthorized use or disclosure of another party's confidential information that is held by the insured
- Seizure or destruction of property by government authority
- Indirect or consequential losses
- Legal expenses, except as provided under forgery or alteration coverage
- Nuclear hazard
- Pollution
- War and similar actions

Exercise 17.E

1. Thieves dynamite the insured's safe, causing damage to the interior of the building. The insured has to close the business for two days while repairs are made. Would the commercial crime coverage form cover the two days of lost business revenue?
( ) Yes ( ) No
2. The insured's appliance store is burglarized. Among the merchandise taken is a video camera and monitor, which a wedding photographer left at the shop for repair. The photographer files suit against the insured for the loss of the equipment, claiming she was negligent in not providing enough security for the store. Would the insured's commercial crime coverage form pay defense costs arising from this suit?
( ) Yes ( ) No

Exercise answers can be found at the end of the Unit 17 answers and rationales.

17.5.2. For Selected Coverages

In addition to the exclusions that apply to all coverages in the crime forms, certain exclusions apply only to the **inside the premises—theft of money and securities, inside the premises—robbery or safe burglary of other property**, and **outside the premises** coverages. These coverages exclude loss:

- resulting from accounting or arithmetic errors or omissions;
- resulting from giving or surrendering property in an exchange or purchase;
- due to fire (does not apply to damage to safes, vaults, money, or securities);

- of property contained in any money-operated device, unless it is equipped with a recording instrument;
- to motor vehicles, trailers or semitrailers, including attached equipment and accessories; and
- of property when it is transferred or surrendered outside the premises or banking premises on the basis of unauthorized instructions or as a result of a threat.

This does not apply to loss of money, securities, or other property while outside the premises and in the custody of a messenger if the insured was not aware of a threat at the time the property left the premises:

- To the interior or exterior of the premises or to a safe, vault, cash register, cash box, cash drawer, or other property by vandalism or malicious mischief
- Resulting from the insured or anyone acting with the insured's authority being induced by any dishonest act to voluntarily part with title to or possession of property

The following exclusions apply only to the **computer fraud** insuring agreement:

- Loss resulting from the use of credit, debit, charge, stored value, and similar types of cards
- Loss resulting from funds transfer fraud
- Loss resulting from the insured, or someone acting on the insured's authority, being induced by a dishonest act to voluntarily part with title to or possession of property

17.6. CONDITIONS

Like the exclusions section, the crime conditions are divided into conditions that apply to all coverages and conditions that apply only to certain coverages. We'll begin with conditions that apply to all coverages.

17.6.1. Valuation

For loss or damage to property other than money or securities, the insurer will pay the lesser of the property's replacement cost, which is the amount needed to repair or replace the property, or the limit of insurance.

Losses to money are paid at face value, but loss of a foreign currency may be paid at its face value in that other currency or in the American dollar equivalent determined by the exchange rate on the day the loss was discovered. Losses to securities are paid at their market value at the close of business on the day the loss was discovered, but the insurer also has the option of replacing them in kind.

17.6.2. Other Insurance

If other insurance applies to a loss and the crime policy was written on a primary basis, the crime policy will pay its proportional share of the loss if the other policy is written on the same basis as the crime policy. If the other policy was not written on the same basis, the crime policy pays on an excess basis.

17.6.3. Other Conditions That Apply to All Coverages

If the insured establishes additional premises or hires more employees while the coverage is in effect (other than through a merger or acquisition), the additional premises and employees are automatically covered under the policy.

New employees and additional premises obtained through a consolidation, acquisition, or merger are automatically covered for 90 days. However, the insured is required to provide written notice to the insurer and pay any additional premium required. This condition does not appear in crime forms written for government entities.

If a loss is covered under more than one coverage in the crime form, the most the insurer will pay is the largest limit of insurance applicable to the loss.

The insured cannot take legal action against the insurer for 90 days after filing the proof of loss. Legal action must be instigated within two years of the date of loss.

The coverage territory includes the United States and its territories and possessions, Puerto Rico and Canada.

The insured's duties in the event of loss include the following:

- Notifying the insurer as soon as possible
- Notifying the police if a law may have been broken (does not apply to employee theft or forgery or alteration coverage)
- Submitting to examination under oath at the insurer's request
- Providing a sworn proof of loss within 120 days
- Cooperating with the insurer in the investigation and settlement of the claim

17.6.4. Conditions That Apply to Employee Theft Coverage

Two conditions apply only to the employee theft insuring agreement.

- Under the **cancellation as to any employee** condition, coverage for any employee is canceled immediately upon discovery by the named insured, partners, officers, directors, members, or managers of any theft or other dishonest act committed by the employee. This is true even when the dishonest act occurred before the employee was hired by the named insured. The insurance company also reserves the right to cancel coverage for any employee. The insured must be notified in writing at least 30 days before the effective date of cancellation.

- The **territory** condition provides coverage for losses that occur when the employee is temporarily outside the coverage territory for 90 consecutive days or less.

Exercise 17.F

1. Six months after a new employee is hired, the insured learns that the employee was fired from a previous job for stealing company property. How will this discovery affect the insured's employee theft coverage?
   A. Coverage for this employee will be canceled after 30 days.
   B. Coverage for this employee will be canceled at the end of the policy period.
   C. It will have no effect on coverage because the dishonest act occurred before the employee was hired.
   D. Coverage for this employee will be canceled immediately.

Exercise answers can be found at the end of the Unit 17 answers and rationales.

17.6.5. Conditions That Apply to Selected Coverages

- **Forgery or alteration coverage.** In addition to the proof of loss, the insured must submit the instrument involved in the loss or an affidavit describing the amount and cause of loss.
- **Inside the premises—robbery or safe burglary of other property and outside the premises coverages.** A $5,000 per occurrence limit applies for loss to precious metals, precious or semiprecious stones, furs, pearls, or other articles that contain these materials.
- **Outside the premises coverage.** The insurer will pay only the amount of loss that cannot be recovered under the insured's contract with the armored car company and from any insurance available from the armored car company.
- **Computer fraud coverage.** A $5,000 per occurrence limit applies for loss to manuscripts, drawings, or records, including the costs of reproducing or reconstructing information in them.

Exercise 17.G

1. Thieves break into a locked vault in a jewelry store and steal a necklace worth $15,000. The thieves also cause $1,000 in damage to the vault. The owner of the jewelry store has a $25,000 limit for inside the premises—robbery or safe burglary of other property coverage. How much would the insurer pay? Ignore any deductible that may apply.
   A. $5,000
   B. $6,000
   C. $15,000
   D. $16,000

Exercise answers can be found at the end of the Unit 17 answers and rationales.

17.7. OTHER CRIME FORMS AND ENDORSEMENTS

17.7.1. Extortion—Commercial Entities Endorsement

The **extortion—commercial entities** endorsement pays for loss of money, securities and other property resulting from extortion. The extortion—commercial entities endorsement covers payments made in response to threats of bodily harm to employees of the insured and relatives or invitees who are also captured in the covered territories. The territory is the United States (including its territories and possessions), Puerto Rico, Canada, and other locations shown on the endorsement Schedule. **Extortion** means the surrender of property away from the premises as the result of a threat communicated to the insured to do bodily harm to the insured or to an employee or a relative of the insured who is being held captive.

17.7.2. Guests' Property Endorsement

This endorsement covers money, securities, and other property owned by hotel guests while:

- on the insured's premises;
- in the insured's possession; or
- in a safe deposit box on the insured's premises.

17.7.3. Kidnap/Ransom and Extortion Coverage Form

This coverage form covers property surrendered as ransom for a kidnapping or alleged kidnapping of an insured person. It also pays for property surrendered as an extortion payment to prevent bodily harm, damage to property, a computer virus, contaminates or pollution to insured products, or the dissemination of proprietary or confidential information.

17.8. FIDELITY BONDS

A **bond** is a guarantee that a specific duty will be discharged, a certain performance maintained, or a specific obligation fulfilled. **Fidelity bonds** guarantee an employee's honest discharge of duty and are written to protect an insured against dishonest acts by employees. The employee dishonesty coverage we discussed earlier provides coverage comparable to that provided by fidelity bonds. There is another type of bond, called a surety bond, that we will discuss later in the course.

17.8.1. Parties to a Bond

There are many similarities between insurance policies and bonds (insurance companies often issue both), but there are some important distinctions as well. Insurance contracts include two parties—the insured and the insurance company. Bonds are contracts between three parties:

- **the principal**—the party who promises to do (or not do) a specific thing (this is the person or company bonded);
- **the surety**—the party (often the insurance company) who agrees to be responsible for loss that may result if the principal does not keep his promise; and
- **the obligee**—the party to whom the principal makes the promise, and for whose protection the bond is being written.

Suppose the XYZ Insurance Company issues a Fidelity bond to Baker and Company that covers Baker's treasurer. XYZ Insurance Company is the surety, Baker and Company is the obligee, and Baker's treasurer is the principal.

17.8.2. Types of Fidelity Bonds

There are several different types of fidelity bonds.

Name schedule bonds cover each employee named on the policy schedule for the amount listed in the schedule. The limit of liability may be different for different employees on the list.

Position schedule bonds list positions in the company that are covered, rather than the individuals who fill these positions. A new employee hired in a scheduled position is automatically covered.

Commercial blanket bonds cover losses arising from the dishonesty of one or more employees acting separately or together (in collusion). Neither the employees nor their positions are specifically named. The bond's limit of liability applies separately to each loss, regardless of the number of employees involved in a single loss.

Blanket position bonds are similar to commercial blanket bonds in that employees or positions are not specifically listed. However, the bond's limit applies separately to each employee involved in a loss.

Fidelity bonds are continuous and do not have an expiration date, although they may be terminated by the parties to the bond. Like commercial crime forms, fidelity bonds provide a discovery or cut-off period for losses that occurred during the term of the bond, but were not discovered until after its termination.

Exercise 17.H

1. What type of bond is used to schedule two or more employees by name?

   ____

2. What type of bond is used to schedule an amount of coverage applicable to each loss, regardless of the number of employees who are involved?

   ____

3. What type of bond is used to schedule coverage by position in the company?

   ____

4. What type of bond is used to schedule an amount of coverage that applies separately to each employee involved in a loss?

   ____

5. The period during which the insured may still be indemnified for losses that occurred during the term of the bond but were not discovered until after its termination is called the

   ______________________________.

Exercise answers can be found at the end of the Unit 17 answers and rationales.

UNIT TEST

1. George Hawthorn is employed by Moison Appliances as a shipping clerk. As he is stacking TVs in the storage room, he is surprised by two men, both carrying guns. They proceed to empty the warehouse of TVs. This is an example of
   A. burglary
   B. robbery
   C. mysterious disappearance
   D. a fidelity loss

2. Which of the following must be true in a burglary?
   A. Property must be taken from a custodian or watchperson.
   B. There must be no evidence of force or violence.
   C. The burglary must involve unlawful entry or exit from the premises.
   D. There must be visible evidence of forcible entry or exit.

3. Theft generally means
   A. any act of stealing
   B. any act of stealing, other than burglary or robbery
   C. burglary and robbery only
   D. employee dishonesty only

4. Employee theft coverage pays for loss or damage to what three types of property?
   A. ______________________________
   ____
   B. ______________________________
   ____
   C. ______________________________
   ____

5. Coverage for defense costs is included in
   A. computer fraud coverage
   B. forgery or alteration coverage
   C. all of the crime coverages
   D. none of the crime coverages

6. Who of the following would be considered custodians while having care and custody of company property inside the premises?
   A. A store clerk
   B. A company vice president
   C. A janitor
   D. A night watchperson

7. In a crime insurance policy, certificates of deposit are considered
   A. other property
   B. money
   C. securities
   D. either money or securities

8. True or false? When an insured purchases a commercial crime coverage form, all of the coverages listed in the form automatically apply to the policy. ( ) True ( ) False

9. A customer in a liquor store points a gun at the clerk and demands that she hand over several bottles of expensive whiskey. The clerk complies. Would this loss be covered under the store's inside the premises—robbery or safe burglary of other property coverage? ( ) Yes ( ) No

10. While on her way to make the daily deposit at the bank, the insured stops at a gas station. When she returns to her car after paying the cashier, she discovers that someone has taken the money from her unlocked car. Would this loss be covered under outside the premises coverage?
    ( ) Yes ( ) No

11. What type of property is protected under computer fraud coverage?
    A. Money
    B. Securities
    C. Other property
    D. All of the above

12. Burglars break into the insured's building and steal several thousand dollars. They also spray-paint graffiti on the building. Would the cost to clean up the graffiti be paid under the inside the premises—theft of money and securities insuring agreement? ( ) Yes ( ) No

13. An insured must file a proof of loss within how many days after a loss?
    A. 30
    B. 60
    C. 90
    D. 120

14. The insured sends an employee to Luxembourg for two months to oversee the opening of a new branch office. While on assignment, the employee embezzles over $5,000 from the company. Would this loss be covered under the insured's employee theft coverage?
    A. No, because Luxembourg is outside the coverage territory.
    B. Yes, because the employee was temporarily outside the coverage territory for less than 90 days.

15. What is the purpose of a fidelity bond?

____

____

ANSWERS AND RATIONALES TO UNIT TEST

1. **B.** In crime forms, robbery is defined as the unlawful taking of property from the care and custody of another person. The robber must have caused or threatened to cause bodily harm to the person being robbed or must have committed an obviously unlawful act that is witnessed by the person being robbed.

2. C and D are correct. Although burglary is not specifically defined in the crime forms, it still has a specific meaning in the insurance industry. Burglary is the taking of property from inside the premises by a person unlawfully entering or leaving the premises. There must be evidence of forcible entry or exit, such as marks made by tools, explosives, chemicals, or electricity. There is no requirement that the property be taken from a custodian or watchperson.

3. **A.** Theft means the unlawful taking of money, securities or other property. This broad term includes burglary, safe burglary and robbery.

4. Employee Theft coverage pays for loss or damage to money, securities and other property.

5. **B.** Under forgery or alteration coverage, if the insured is sued for refusing to pay a forged or altered instrument and obtains the insurer's written permission to defend the suit, the insurer will pay reasonable defense costs incurred by the insured.

6. A and B are correct. A custodian is someone who has care or custody of property inside the premises. It includes the insured, the insured's partners or members, or any employee. It does not include a watchperson or janitor.

7. **C.** Securities are instruments or contracts that represent money or property. Checks, drafts, bonds, certificates of deposit, stock certificates, stamps, and credit card receipts are all considered securities.

8. False. The insured must indicate which coverages will apply to the policy.

9. Yes. This insuring agreement covers loss of other property (not money or securities) while inside the premises from actual or attempted robbery of a custodian. The definition of custodian includes the insured's employees.

10. Yes. This insuring agreement covers theft, disappearance, or destruction of money and securities while outside the premises and in the care and custody of a messenger or an armored car company. The definition of messenger includes the insured.

11. **D.** Computer fraud coverage covers loss of or damage to money, securities, and other property due to the use of a computer to fraudulently transfer that property from inside the premises or banking premises to a place or person (other than a messenger) outside the premises.

12. No. Under this insuring agreement, damage to the exterior of the premises by vandalism or malicious mischief is excluded.

13. **D.** If a loss occurs, the insured must provide a sworn proof of loss within 120 days.

14. **B.** The coverage territory for the crime policy includes the United States and its territories and possessions, Puerto Rico, and Canada. Under employee theft coverage, losses that occur outside the coverage territory are covered when the employee is temporarily outside the territory for 90 days or less.

15. The purpose of a Fidelity bond is to guarantee an employee's honest discharge of duty and protect the insured against dishonest acts by employees.

UNIT 17 EXERCISE ANSWERS

Exercise 17.A

1. **A**

Exercise 17.B

1. **B**
2. **C**
3. **D**
4. **A**
5. **E**

Exercise 17.C

1. A and D

Exercise 17.D

1. A and B

Exercise 17.E

1. No—this is an indirect loss, which is excluded under the commercial crime form
2. No

Exercise 17.F

1. **D**

Exercise 17.G

1. **B** Loss to the necklace is limited to $5,000. Damage to the vault is paid in full.

Exercise 17.H

1. Name schedule bond
2. Commercial blanket bond
3. Position schedule bond
4. Blanket position bond
5. Discovery/cut-off period

18

Workers' Compensation

18.1. LEARNING OBJECTIVES

After completing Unit 18—Workers' Compensation, you will be able to:

- Describe how employees obtained reimbursement for work-related injuries prior to the passage of workers' compensation laws, and the common law defenses employers used to avoid paying for those injuries
- Explain the importance of the no-fault concept and the exclusive remedy doctrine in workers' compensation laws
- Identify the types of occupations usually covered under workers' compensation laws
- Describe the four general categories of benefits covered under workers' compensation laws
- Describe the requirements that must be met for an injury to be compensable under workers' compensation
- Compare and contrast permanent and temporary disabilities and partial and total disabilities
- Explain the difference between a compulsory workers' compensation law and an elective law
- Describe the various methods available for funding workers' compensation benefits
- Describe the purpose of each part of the workers' compensation and employers liability policy
- Identify losses that are excluded under the workers' compensation and employers liability policies
- Explain the purpose of the longshore and harbor workers' and voluntary compensation endorsements
- Describe the provisions of the Federal Employers Liability Act and the Jones Act
- Explain the procedures used to rate workers' compensation coverage

18.2. WORKERS' COMPENSATION LAWS

Workers' compensation laws give employees the right to collect from their employers for injury, disability, or death that occurs in the course of employment.

Prior to the enactment of such laws, a worker had to sue an employer and prove the employer negligent to be reimbursed for a work-related injury. Employers proved successful at avoiding liability through the use of three common law defenses.

Assumption of risk allowed the employer to deny liability on the basis that the employee knew what the situation was like before employment and assumed all of the risk of injury.

Contributory negligence was used to deny liability on the basis that, no matter how negligent the employer was, the employee also had been negligent, and therefore the employee should be responsible for the consequences.

The **fellow servant rule** was used to deny liability on the basis that the injury was caused by a fellow employee and, therefore, the employer could not be held liable.

When workers' compensation laws were adopted, they were designed to provide a fair means of handling work-related injuries, including occupational diseases. They are based on the idea that the cost of most work-related injuries and occupational diseases should be charged directly to the employer, regardless of who is at fault, and without complex court proceedings. The cost, in turn, would be passed on to the consumer as a cost of production. In return, the benefits stipulated in workers' compensation laws are the only means—the **exclusive remedy**—available to employees against employers for injuries covered by those laws. Employees cannot sue employers in court to obtain additional compensation.

18.2.1. Occupations Covered

The early workers' compensation laws applied only to very hazardous occupations. Over the years the scope of the laws has expanded to embrace more occupational groups. Every state has some exempt classifications, but the majority of the nation's employees are covered under workers' compensation laws. Although the exemptions are not the same in all states, the following classes of employees are typically exempt:

- Certain farm and agricultural groups workers
- Charitable organizations workers
- Domestic employees and casual laborers
- Newspaper vendors

In some states, the hours worked or wages earned determine whether an employee is exempt. Employers are not required to provide insurance or compensation benefits for exempt employees, but it is often recommended that they do. The fact that a worker is not covered under the law does not preclude legal claims against the employer. Benefits may be voluntarily provided by purchasing workers' compensation insurance to cover exempt employees.

18.2.2. Benefits Provided

Workers' compensation laws vary from state to state, but in general they pay benefits in four categories.

Disability/loss of income benefits compensate employees who are unable to work as the result of a work-related injury. These benefits are intended to replace a portion of lost income, but not all of it.

Medical benefits pay for the cost of various types of medical services required because of an employment-related injury. Nearly any type of related medical expense is covered with neither an upper dollar limit nor a limit on the period of time for which expenses will be paid.

Survivor/death benefits compensate a surviving spouse, children, or other relatives of an employee whose death results from a work-related injury. In general, survivor benefits include a weekly benefit and a stipulated amount for funeral and burial expenses.

Rehabilitation benefits include medical rehabilitation, such as physical therapy designed to improve physical functioning, and vocational rehabilitation, such as retraining for a different occupation. Workers' compensation rehabilitation benefits usually pay reasonably justifiable expenses for these purposes.

Exercise 18.A

1. Which of these statements regarding workers' compensation benefits are CORRECT?
   A. Payment of medical benefits is limited in terms of the types of services covered and the length of time benefits are paid.
   B. Survivor benefits pay a stipulated amount for funeral and burial expenses and a weekly benefit to surviving relatives.
   C. Disability benefits pay the full amount of the employee's lost income.
   D. Rehabilitation benefits cover both medical and vocational rehabilitation.

Exercise answers can be found at the end of the Unit 18 answers and rationales.

18.2.3. Compensable Injuries

Work-related injuries must arise out of employment and during the course of employment to be compensated under workers' compensation laws. Three factors are used to determine if the injury arose in the course of employment: time, place, and circumstances.

Time is important because a compensable injury must occur during the time work is being performed for the purposes of employment. Place and circumstances are important because the injury must either occur at the place of employment or occur away from the place of employment while employment duties are being performed.

18.2.4. Types of Disability

The level of disability suffered by an injured worker is categorized into one of four types:

- Permanent total
- Permanent partial
- Temporary total
- Temporary partial

A permanent **disability** is one that will affect the worker for the rest of his or her life. A temporary **disability** is one that will go away.

Determining the difference between a total and a partial **disability** depends on what standard the state uses to determine the degree of disability. In different areas, the determination is made by deciding first whether the worker is:

Industrially disabled, which refers to the individual's loss of earnings, or

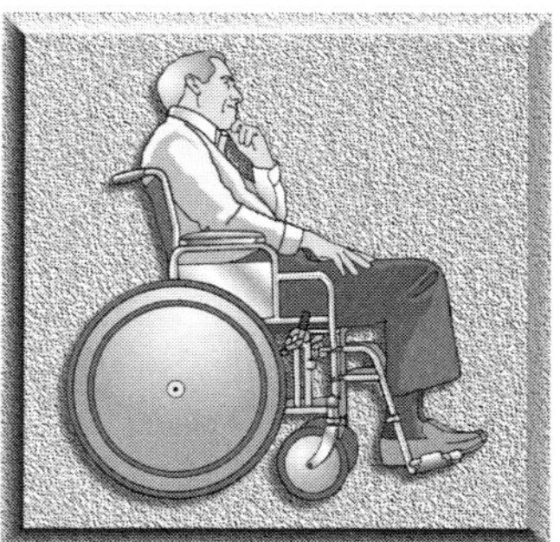

Medically disabled, which refers to the physical condition that affects functioning.

Where industrial disability is the standard, the difference between partial and total disability depends on whether the individual is able to earn at least some money by working or has completely lost the ability to work for a living. When medical disability is the standard, partial, or total disability depends on whether the individual has partial physical functioning after the injury or has sustained a complete loss of physical functioning.

Exercise 18.B

1. A disabled person capable of performing some type of gainful work is considered to be (totally/partially) ________ disabled in states that use the (industrial/medical) ____________ disability standard.
2. When the physical functioning of the injured worker is the prime consideration in determining total or partial disability, the state uses the (industrial/medical) ________________ disability standard, and a person who is completely disabled physically has a (total/partial) ____________ disability.
3. The type of disability that does not last for a lifetime is known as a (permanent/temporary) ________________ disability.
4. A disability that lasts for a lifetime is called a (permanent/temporary) _____________ disability.

Exercise answers can be found at the end of the Unit 18 answers and rationales.

18.2.5. Compulsory Versus Elective

State workers' compensation laws are either compulsory or elective. In most states, the law is compulsory, meaning the employer must accept and comply with all provisions of the law.

If the state law is elective, the employer may choose not to be subject to the law. However, an employer who does so is denied any rights provided under the law and loses the use of the pro-employer defenses against liability discussed earlier.

Even in elective states, there are certain occupations or groups for which workers' compensation is compulsory, such as government employees. And both elective and compulsory states often exclude certain classes of employees, such as farm workers or domestic servants.

18.3. FUNDING

Because workers' compensation benefits often are extended to employees over long periods of time, it is important that measures be taken to guarantee that the company will have the funds to pay benefits required under the law. There are five basic methods for funding these benefits. Each state requires that employers provide security through at least one of these methods.

One way employers meet their workers' compensation obligations is through insurance purchased from a **private insurer**. The employer transfers compensation obligations to the insurance company from which the policy was purchased. Then, the insurance company pays benefits required by law.

Some states have created **monopolistic state funds** that require employers to purchase workers' compensation insurance from them. Private insurance companies are not allowed to compete against these funds. To be insured against workers' compensation claims, the employer must buy coverage from the state fund.

Other states have created **competitive state funds** that give employers a choice between purchasing workers' compensation insurance from a state fund or a private insurance company. Thus, the state fund competes with private insurance.

Some employers assume their own workers' compensation liability through the **self-insurance method.** If this method is chosen, the employer will set up a fund to pay workers' compensation claims and file evidence of its existence with the state workers' compensation authority. The employer must handle benefit costs and claim expenses, as well as medical and legal services.

Many states allow individual employers to form **groups** to insure the group members' workers' compensation exposure in a particular state. Eligibility requirements vary from state to state. For example, in some states the group members must be involved in the same type of business; in others, the members must have a minimum amount of workers' compensation premium.

Exercise 18.C

1. A particular state gives employers the option of purchasing workers' compensation insurance from a state fund or a private company. This is an example of a (monopolistic/competitive) ________________ state fund.
2. A certain state requires employers to purchase workers' compensation insurance from a state fund. This is an example of a (monopolistic/competitive) ________________________ state fund.

Exercise answers can be found at the end of the Unit 18 answers and rationales.

18.4. WORKERS' COMPENSATION AND EMPLOYERS LIABILITY POLICY

18.4.1. Coverages

Nearly all states that allow private insurance companies to offer coverage use the standardized workers' compensation and employers liability policy filed by the National Council on Compensation Insurance (NCCI). A complete policy contains an information page (similar to the declarations used with other types of policies) and a policy form that contains the following sections:

- General Section
- Part One—Workers' Compensation

- Part Two—Employers Liability
- Part Three—Other States Insurance
- Part Four—Your Duties if Injury Occurs
- Part Five—Premium
- Part Six—Conditions

The General Section contains definitions and conditions that apply to the policy as a whole.

Part One—Workers' Compensation promises to pay all compensation and other benefits required of the insured by the workers' compensation law in the state or states where the insured's business operates (which are listed in the Information Page). No dollar limit applies, except for those that are a part of the law. Coverage applies to any work-related accident occurring during the policy period.

Part Two—Employers Liability provides coverage to the insured for sums the insured becomes legally obligated to pay under common law because of a work-related injury or occupational disease. Three separate limits apply and that the breakdown for the limits of a workers' compensation policy are as follows:

- Per accident—for all bodily injury arising from a single accident (regardless of the number of employees injured)
- Policy limit—for all bodily injury by disease during the policy term (regardless of the number of employees injured by disease)
- Per employee—for each employee injured by disease during the policy term

You may wonder why the insured needs employers liability coverage since workers' compensation laws were designed to make benefits payable on a no-fault basis. However, there are situations that are not covered by workers' compensation laws, such as exempt employments, illegal employments, and noncompensable injuries. An employee who is unable to collect workers' compensation under state law may still sue the employer for damages.

Part Three—Other States may be used to provide coverage for states that are not specifically listed in the information page for part one coverage. The state must be listed in the information page for other states coverage and the insured must provide notice to the insurer as soon as work begins in a new state.

Part Four—Your Duties if Injury Occurs addresses the insured's obligations when an injury occurs for which there may be coverage. The insured must provide medical services required for the injured party, report the injury to the insurer and cooperate with the insurer in the investigation and settlement of the claim.

Part Five—Premium explains how the cost of the policy is determined.

Part Six—Conditions sets forth the conditions that apply to the policy, such as cancellation procedures, subrogation and the insurer's right to inspect the insured's workplace.

18.4.2. Exclusions

There are few exclusions that apply to part one of the workers' compensation policy. The following exclusions apply to the employers liability:

- Liability assumed under contract
- Punitive damages awarded because a worker was employed in violation of the law
- Injury to a worker while employed in violation of the law with the insured's knowledge
- Obligations imposed by any workers' compensation, occupational disease, unemployment compensation, or disability benefits law
- Injury intentionally caused or aggravated by the insured
- Injury that occurs outside the United States, its territories or possessions, or Canada (does not apply to residents of these areas who are temporarily outside these areas)
- Damages arising out of violations of employment practices laws, such as discrimination or harassment
- Injury that is covered under a federal workers' compensation law
- Injury to the master or member of the crew of any vessel
- Fines and penalties imposed for violations of federal or state law
- Damages payable under the Migrant and Seasonal Agricultural Worker Protection Act and other federal laws awarding damages for violation of laws or regulations

Exercise 18.D

1. As punishment for illegally employing a 17-year-old, the state fines Jack Hammer $5,000 in addition to the amount for which he was held liable because of the boy's work-related injuries. Will part two of Jack's workers' compensation and employers liability policy reimburse him for the $5,000 fine?
( ) Yes ( ) No

Exercise answers can be found at the end of the Unit 18 answers and rationales.

18.4.3. Endorsements

Coverage for certain types of benefits or certain classes of employees may only be provided by endorsement.

Some workers are required to be covered under the federal Longshore and Harbor Workers Compensation Act, which takes precedence over any state law that may cover the same workers. Under this act, specified benefits must be paid to maritime employees injured while working on navigable waters or shore-site areas of the United States and its territories. Employers whose workers are subject to this act can provide coverage by attaching the **Longshore and Harbor Workers Compensation Act Coverage endorsement** to the policy.

Some types of workers are not covered under a state's workers' compensation laws, such as domestic employees and farm workers. An employer can provide coverage for excluded workers by adding the **Voluntary Compensation endorsement** to the policy.

18.5. FEDERAL WORKERS' COMPENSATION LAWS

Most workers are protected under their state's workers' compensation laws. However, there are some categories of employees that are covered under federal workers' compensation laws.

In most states, interstate railroad workers are covered under the **Federal Employers Liability Act (FELA)** instead of state workers'compensation laws. FELA allows the injured worker or a representative of a deceased worker to sue the employer for negligence and eliminates two of the common law defenses: contributory negligence and assumption of risk. Awards provided under FELA are often more substantial than those provided under state workers' compensation laws because FELA does not limit an injured employee's remedies to scheduled benefits.

The **Jones Act** is a federal law that allows members of ships' crews to sue the employer/shipowner at common law for injuries caused by the employer's/shipowner's negligence.

18.6. RATING WORKERS' COMPENSATION COVERAGE

Workers' compensation coverage is rated on the basis of the employer's payroll. Published manuals contain listings of rate classifications based on the type of work employees perform and their relative exposures to work-related injuries. For any given employer, one or more of these classifications will be selected.

For each classification, the manual provides a rate per $100 of payroll. The rate for each class is multiplied by each $100 of payroll applicable to the class. Rates for each class are totaled, and a premium discount that varies with the amount of total premium is applied. Since the employer does not know at policy inception what its payroll will be at any given time of the year, payroll is estimated for the purpose of determining a **deposit premium.** Later, the final premium is calculated.

Insureds that have premiums above a certain amount are eligible for **experience rating.** Premiums paid and losses incurred over the three years immediately preceding the policy period are evaluated. If the insured has a loss history that is better than average, an **experience modification factor** will be applied to reduce the premium. If the loss history is worse than average, a surcharge will be applied to increase the premium.

UNIT TEST

1. To obtain benefits under workers' compensation, the injured employee must prove that the employer was negligent for the injury.
( ) True ( ) False

2. Which one of the following injuries would qualify as a compensable injury under workers' compensation laws?
   A. A factory worker fractures her arm while working overtime on the assembly line
   B. A hotel maid falls down the stairs while cleaning her own home
   C. A secretary accidentally swallows his gum while in the company lunchroom and chokes when it gets lodged in his windpipe

3. Which of the following benefits are paid under workers' compensation laws?
   A. Medical
   B. Rehabilitation
   C. Disability income
   D. Pain and suffering

4. In a competitive state, an employer may obtain workers' compensation insurance from:
   A. a private insurance company
   B. a state fund
   C. Either A or B

5. Match the workers' compensation and employers liability policy coverage listed in the left-hand column with its correct description in the right-hand column.

1. Part One	____	A. Provides automatic coverage for states not specifically listed on the information page for part one coverage
2. Part Two	____	B. Explains how the cost of the policy is determined
3. Part Three	____	C. Pays all compensation and benefits required by state workers' compensation law
4. Part Four	____	D. Describes the insured's obligations when an injury occurs for which there may be coverage
5. Part Five	____	E. Covers the insured's legal obligations for work-related injuries under common law
6. Part Six	____	F. Contains the conditions that apply to the policy

6. In most states, workers' compensation laws apply
   A. only to workers in occupations that are considered extremely hazardous
   B. to most workers except those specifically excluded by law
   C. to full-time workers only

ANSWERS AND RATIONALES TO UNIT TEST

1. False. Workers' compensation laws eliminated the need to prove the employer's negligence.

2. **A.** Work-related injuries must arise out of employment and during the course of employment to be compensable. Time, place, and circumstances are all considered in making this determination.

3. **A**, **B**, and **C** are correct. Workers' compensation laws pay benefits in four categories: disability/loss of income benefits, medical benefits, survivor/death benefits, and rehabilitation benefits. They do not pay benefits for pain and suffering.

4. **C.** Competitive states give employers a choice between purchasing workers' compensation insurance from a state fund or a private insurance company. The state fund competes with private insurance.

5. 3 A.; 5 B.; 1 C.; 4 D.; 2 E.; 6 F.
The workers' compensation and employers liability policy is divided into six parts. Part One—Workers' Compensation pays all compensation and other benefits required of the insured by the workers' compensation law in the state or states where the insured's business operates. Part Two—Employers Liability covers the insured for sums the insured becomes legally obligated to pay under common law because of a work-related injury or occupational disease. Part Three—Other States may be used to provide coverage for states that are not listed in the information page for part one coverage. Part Four—Your Duties if Injury Occurs addresses the insured's obligations when an injury occurs for which there may be coverage. Part Five—Premium explains how the cost of the policy is determined. Part Six—Conditions sets forth the conditions that apply to the policy, such as cancellation procedures.

6. **B.** Every state has some exempt classifications, but the majority of the nation's employees are covered under workers' compensation laws.

UNIT 18 EXERCISE ANSWERS

Exercise 18.A

1. B and D

Exercise 18.B

1. Partially, industrial
2. Medical, total
3. Temporary
4. Permanent

Exercise 18.C

1. competitive
2. monopolistic

Exercise 18.D

1. No

U N I T

19

Miscellaneous Commercial Insurance

19.1. LEARNING OBJECTIVES

After completing Unit 19, Miscellaneous Commercial Insurance, you will be able to:

- Describe the coverages in the Farm coverage part and the exposures they cover
- Compare and contrast the provisions of the three Farm Property coverage forms
- Describe the different levels of coverage provided under the Farm Property—Causes of Loss form
- Identify property that may be insured under specialized Farm forms
- Describe the coverages available in the Farm Liability coverage form
- Identify losses that are excluded under the Farm Liability coverage form
- Describe the required components in a Boiler and Machinery coverage part
- Describe information contained in the Boiler and Machinery Declarations
- For the Equipment Breakdown Protection coverage form, describe conditions that must be met for a loss to be covered; what is and is not considered a breakdown; various coverages available under the form; losses that are excluded; the purpose of the suspension provision; how the policy limits apply; and options for settling losses
- Explain the purpose of the following Boiler and Machinery endorsements: Business Income—Report of Values, Refrigeration Interruption Coverage, Turbine Units Explosion, Pressure or Vacuum Equipment, and Production Equipment Exclusion
- Describe the types of losses covered by Aviation Physical Damage and Aviation Liability coverage
- Describe the purpose of Professional Liability insurance and the types of policies available
- Explain the purpose of the Consent to Settle Losses provision in a Professional Liability policy
- Describe the types of losses covered under Employment Practices Liability insurance
- Describe the features of Difference in Conditions insurance
- Identify losses covered under Commercial Umbrella policies
- Identify situations that require a surety bond instead of a fidelity bond
- Describe the following types of contract bonds: bid bonds, performance bonds, payment bonds, labor and materials bonds, supply bonds, and completion bonds

- Explain the purpose of fiduciary bonds and court bonds
- Identify situations where a public official or license and permit bond would be required
- Describe the purpose of surplus lines insurance and the general conditions that must be met to place coverage with a surplus lines insurer and
- Explain the federal government's role in providing coverage for terrorism losses

19.2. INTRODUCTION

Some commercial loss exposures are not covered by the policies we've studied so far. For example, the Commercial General Liability policy excludes losses arising out of professional liability and aviation, and the Commercial Property policy excludes losses resulting from boiler explosions. In this unit, we'll study some specialized commercial insurance policies that were developed to cover these exposures.

19.3. FARM INSURANCE

19.3.1. Introduction

Farmers' businesses and homes are often at the same location, so they need insurance that will cover both their personal and business exposures to loss. The Farm coverage part, which can be written as a monoline policy or included in the CPP, includes several Farm Property coverage forms that cover both the personal and business property of the farmer and a Farm Liability coverage form for the personal and business liability exposures of the farmer.

19.3.2. Farm Property Coverage Forms

19.3.2.1. Covered Property

The **Farm Property coverage forms** cover direct physical loss to a variety of properties. The insured can select any combination of three separate forms.

The **Farm Dwellings, Appurtenant Structures and Household Personal Property coverage form** is similar to Section I of the Homeowners policy. It contains the following coverages:

- Coverage A—Dwellings
- Coverage B—Other Private Structures Appurtenant to Dwellings
- Coverage C—Household Personal Property
- Coverage D—Loss of Use

Like the Homeowners form, Coverage D includes coverage for additional living expenses and fair rental value.

A special limit of $250 per occurrence applies to loss or damage to outdoor radio and TV antennas and satellite dishes.

In general, growing crops, trees, plants, shrubs, and lawns are excluded. However, a coverage extension for Coverages A, B, and C allows limited coverage for trees, plants, shrubs, or lawns within 250 feet of the covered residence, but only against loss by specified perils.

The **Farm Personal Property coverage form** covers scheduled and unscheduled farm personal property.

Coverage E—Scheduled Farm Personal Property covers property for the limit shown in the Declarations. Examples of property that can be covered under Coverage E include grain, farm products, poultry, livestock, machinery, and vehicles and equipment incidental to farm use.

Coverage F—Unscheduled Farm Personal Property covers farm personal property on a blanket basis both on and off the insured premises.

Coverage G—The **Barns, Outbuildings and Other Farm Structures coverage form** covers barns, silos, fences, radio equipment, and other farm buildings and structures that are not dwellings.

19.3.2.2. Causes of Loss and Other Provisions

The **Farm Property—Causes of Loss form** is a separate document that lists the perils property is insured against. This form offers three separate levels of coverage within the same form: Basic, Broad, and Special. These levels of coverage are very similar to those provided by the Commercial Property Causes of Loss forms you studied earlier. The Declarations indicates what level of coverage the insured has selected for each form. The insured may obtain coverage against earthquake by purchasing the separate Earthquake Causes of Loss form.

Perils covered under the Covered Causes of Loss—Basic section include:

- fire;
- lightning;
- windstorm or hail;
- explosion;
- riot or civil commotion;
- aircraft;
- earthquake or flood loss to livestock;
- vehicles;
- smoke;
- vandalism;
- theft;
- volcanic action; and
- sinkhole collapse.

Property insured under the Farm Property and Farm Structures forms is also covered for collision that results in damage to covered farm machinery or other farm personal property and death of covered livestock.

The **Covered Causes of Loss—Broad** section adds additional perils. Some that are unique to the farm risk include:

- electrocution of covered livestock;
- attacks on covered livestock by dogs or wild animals;
- drowning of covered livestock;
- accidents involving loading or unloading; and
- accidental shooting of covered livestock;

The **Covered Causes of Loss—Special** section provides open peril coverage. Among the **excluded** losses are:

- dishonest or criminal acts;
- pollutants or contaminants;
- transfer of property due to unauthorized instructions;
- voluntary parting with property; and
- failure to save and preserve property from loss.

Definitions, conditions, and additional coverages applicable to the three Property forms are contained in a separate form. They are essentially the same as those you studied in connection with other property insurance policies.

19.3.2.3. Additional Forms

Some items may be insured under their own specialized coverage forms instead of the Farm Property coverage part. The **Mobile Agricultural Machinery And Equipment coverage form** covers mobile agricultural equipment and machinery separately from other property. The **Livestock coverage form** is used to insure livestock separately.

19.3.3. Farm Liability Coverage Form

The Farm Liability coverage form provides these coverages for liability arising out of farming operations or personal activities:

- Coverage H—Bodily Injury and Property Damage Liability
- Coverage I—Personal and Advertising Injury Liability
- Coverage J—Medical Payments

The exclusions are similar to those found in other Liability policies. There is no coverage for losses arising out of:

- pollutants;
- injury to farm employees;
- motor vehicles, except as specifically described in the policy;
- the insured's performance of or failure to perform custom farming operations for others;
- the insured's own products; and
- aircraft spraying.

Other sections of the form, such as definitions, conditions, and additional coverages, are essentially the same as those you studied in connection with other Liability insurance policies.

Exercise 19.A

1. Which of the following coverages are automatically provided by the Farm Liability form?
   A. Personal liability
   B. Liability arising out of farming exposures
   C. Liability arising out of injuries to farm employees
   D. Medical payments

Exercise answers can be found at the end of the Unit 19 answers and rationales.

19.4. BOILER AND MACHINERY INSURANCE

19.4.1. Introduction

Most of the commercial lines policies we studied in previous units exclude loss resulting from boiler explosions.

Boilers are used to produce steam. Water in the enclosed vessel is heated to convert it to steam and then heated still further. Steam under pressure can generate the power to drive engines, turbines, and other heavy machinery, and the heat absorbed by the steam can be used in cooling and heating. This steam, however, can cause great destruction. Although boilers are built to withstand great pressure, and safety devices, such as safety valves, are designed to regulate pressure buildup, there was a time when accidents were all too frequent, resulting in substantial loss in lives and money.

To combat such problems, a group of engineers developed a boiler inspection service that they provided for their customers at a modest charge. As an added attraction, the engineers guaranteed their inspection service by offering insurance against loss that occurred in spite of their careful inspection.

This guaranteed insurance developed into Boiler and Machinery insurance, and the principles of boiler insurance were applied not only to boilers, but to loss exposures arising out of other machines, particularly those that generated power. The focal point of Boiler and Machinery insurance continues to be loss prevention, rather than loss protection, with a regular inspection service provided as an integral part of the package.

19.4.2. Boiler and Machinery Coverage Part

Whether boiler and machinery coverage is issued as a monoline policy or as part of a package, the policy will consist of:

- the Common Policy Declarations;

- the Common Policy Conditions; and
- a Boiler and Machinery Coverage Part (and one or more other coverage parts, if it is a package policy).

The boiler and machinery coverage part will consist of:

- the Equipment Breakdown Protection Coverage Declarations;
- the Equipment Breakdown Protection Coverage Form; and
- any applicable endorsements.

19.4.3. Boiler and Machinery Declarations

When boiler and machinery coverage is written, the Common Policy Declarations will show some basic information about the policy, but will only show that the coverage applies by listing an overall premium for the entire coverage part. The Equipment Breakdown Protection Coverage Declarations must be completed to provide additional information.

These Declarations will show a description of each covered premises, a schedule of the limits of insurance (or time limitations) that apply to each coverage that applies, a schedule of sublimits that may apply to certain exposures, deductibles that apply to various coverages, a list of the names and addresses of any additional insureds, a list of the forms and endorsements attached to the coverage, and a place for the date and signature of the producer who countersigned the policy.

19.4.4. Equipment Breakdown Protection Coverage Form

19.4.4.1. Covered Causes of Loss

While the term *boiler and machinery* is still used in the Common Policy Declarations and in the Commercial Lines Manual for classification purposes, the latest ISO coverage form is called the *Equipment Breakdown Protection Coverage Form.*

Under the Equipment Breakdown Protection Coverage Form, the only covered cause of loss is breakdown to covered equipment.

19.4.4.2. Definitions

Breakdown means the following types of direct physical loss that cause damage to covered equipment and necessitates its repair or replacement (unless the loss or damage is otherwise specifically excluded within the coverage form):

- Failure of pressure or vacuum equipment
- Mechanical failure, including rupture or bursting caused by centrifugal force
- Electrical failure, including arcing

- However, the term *breakdown* does not include any of the following:
  - Malfunction, including but not limited to adjustment, alignment, calibration, cleaning, or modification
  - Defects, erasures, errors, limitations, or viruses in computer equipment and programs, including the inability to recognize and process any date or time or provide instructions to covered equipment
  - Leakage at any valve, fitting, shaft seal, gland packing, joint, or connection
  - Damage to any vacuum tube, glass tube, or brush
  - Damage to any structure or foundation supporting the covered equipment or any of its parts
  - The functioning of any safety or protective device (such as one that turns off equipment to prevent further damage)
  - The cracking of any part of an internal combustion gas turbine exposed to the products of combustion

One breakdown means that if an initial breakdown causes other breakdowns, all will be considered a single breakdown. All breakdowns, at any one premises, that manifest themselves at the same time and are the direct result of the same cause will be considered *one breakdown*.

Covered property means property that the insured owns, or which is in the insured's care, custody, or control and for which the insured is legally liable.

Covered equipment includes:

- equipment built to operate under internal pressure or vacuum other than the weight of contents;
- electrical or mechanical equipment that is used in the generation, transmission, or utilization of energy;
- communication equipment and computer equipment; and
- any equipment that is owned by a public or private utility and used solely to supply utility services to the insured's premises.

Computer equipment means the insured's programmable electronic equipment that is used to store, retrieve, and process data, and associated peripheral equipment that provides communications including input and output functions (such as printing) or auxiliary functions (such as data transmission).

19.4.4.3. Coverages Provided

This form provides coverage only for that portion of loss or damage that is a direct result of a breakdown to covered equipment. Each of the following coverages is provided only if either a limit or the word *included* is shown for that coverage in the Declarations. If neither a limit nor the word *included* is shown, then that particular coverage is not provided. An insured may select from among the following coverages:

- property damage;
- expediting expenses;
- business income and/or extra expense;
- spoilage damage;
- utility interruption;
- newly acquired premises;
- ordinance or law;
- errors or omissions;
- brands and labels; and
- contingent business income and/or extra expense.

Property damage coverage applies to direct damage to covered property located at a premises described in the Declarations. The only difference between this coverage and commercial property coverage is the covered cause of loss—the damage must be caused by a breakdown of covered equipment (rather than fire, lightning, windstorm, and so forth).

Expediting expenses coverage will pay extra costs necessarily incurred by the insured to make temporary repairs and to expedite the permanent repairs or replacement of the damaged property.

Business income and extra expense coverage, or extra expense coverage only, is similar to these same coverages under the commercial property coverage part. The only significant difference is the covered cause of loss—the damage must be caused by a breakdown of covered equipment (rather than fire, lightning, windstorm, and so forth).

Spoilage damage to raw materials, property in process, or finished products may be covered if these items are in storage or in the course of being manufactured at the time of loss, the insured owns or is legally liable for these items under contract, and the spoilage is due to the lack or excess of power, light, heat, steam, or refrigeration. When this coverage applies, the insurer will also pay any necessary expenses incurred by the insured to reduce the amount of the loss, but only to the extent that the expenses do not exceed the amount of loss that otherwise would have been payable.

If the insured has business income and/or extra expense coverage, spoilage coverage, or both, coverage for **utility interruption** may be purchased. This coverage extends the business income, extra expense and/or spoilage coverage to apply to loss resulting from an interruption of utility services due to a breakdown of equipment that is not the insured's. It applies when there is a breakdown of equipment owned, operated, or controlled by a public or private utility that directly generates, transmits, distributes, or provides utility services received by the insured that are used to supply electric power, communication services, air conditioning, heating, gas, sewer, water, or steam to the insured's premises. When this coverage is written, a waiting period (stated in hours) must be shown in the Declarations. Once the waiting period is met, coverage will commence from the initial time of interruption and will be subject to any applicable deductibles.

If coverage for **newly acquired premises** is written, the insurer will automatically provide coverage at any newly acquired premises the insured purchases or leases. Coverage begins as soon as the premises is acquired and continues only for the number of days for this coverage shown in the Declarations. However, as a condition of the coverage the insured is required to notify the insurer, in writing, of the new premises and agree to pay an additional premium.

Ordinance or law coverage is virtually identical to the coverage available under other property coverages. If applicable, the ordinance and law exclusion will not apply and the insurer will pay increased costs resulting from the enforcement of laws or ordinances that regulate the demolition, construction, repair, or use of the building or structure. The only difference is that under this form, the loss must result from breakdown of covered equipment (rather than traditional perils such as fire, lightning, windstorm, and so forth).

Errors and omissions coverage will pay for loss or damage, which would not otherwise be payable under the coverage form, solely because of one or more of the following:

- any error or unintentional omission in the description or location of any property shown in the Declarations;
- any failure through error to include any premises owned or occupied by the insured at the inception date of the coverage part; and
- any error or unintentional omission by the insured that results in cancellation of any premises insured under the policy.

No coverage is provided as a result of any error or unintentional omission by the insured in the reporting of values for requested coverages. It is a condition of this coverage that errors or unintentional omissions must be reported and corrected when discovered.

Coverage for **brands and labels** is available for businesses that carry branded or labeled merchandise. If such property is covered property and is damaged in a breakdown, the insurer may take all or any part of the property at an agreed or appraised value. In such cases, the insured may stamp the word *Salvage* on the merchandise or its containers, or may remove the brands and labels, if doing so will not physically damage the property. The insurer will pay the reasonable costs for stamping or removing labels, but the total paid for these costs and the value of the damaged property will not exceed the applicable limit of insurance for such property.

Contingent business income and/or extra expense coverage is also available. When applicable, it will pay the insured's losses resulting from a breakdown of covered property at a premises shown in the Declarations that the insured does not own or operate. For example, a loss at another premises that prevents the insured from receiving services or materials, or from shipping them to others, or that results in a loss of sales at the insured's premises, might be covered. This is called coverage for dependent properties on commercial property coverage forms.

19.4.4.4. Exclusions

The Equipment Breakdown Protection coverage form lists a number of exclusions that apply to loss or damage regardless of whether any other cause or event contributes concurrently or in any sequence to the loss. A number of these are general exclusions found on many other commercial coverage forms, such as earth movement, water, nuclear hazards, and war or military action.

Additional exclusions also apply, and they address the unique nature of boiler and machinery coverage or the interface between this coverage and commercial property coverages. These exclusions merit some discussion.

Generally, explosions are excluded. This means internal or external combustion explosions resulting from the ignition of fuel or dust particles or something else, and not explosions caused by pressure or the centrifugal force of moving parts. The form makes an exception and states that it will cover loss or damage caused by an explosion of any covered steam boiler, electric steam generator, steam piping, steam turbine, steam engine, gas turbine, or moving or rotating machinery when the explosion is caused by centrifugal force or mechanical breakdown.

Any loss due to fire or combustion explosion is excluded—including those that result in a breakdown, occur at the same time as a breakdown, or ensue from a breakdown. The reason for this is that fire damage is covered by standard commercial property forms. If a fire causes a breakdown to occur, and the breakdown causes additional damage (perhaps because of a pressure explosion that blew out windows and destroyed furniture and fixtures), the fire is still the proximate cause of all resulting losses, which will be covered by property insurance even if some of the damage was not actually fire damage.

Also excluded are explosions within a chemical recovery type boiler or within the passage from the furnace to the atmosphere.

Damage to covered equipment undergoing a pressure or electrical test is excluded because during testing the technicians may push the threshold of tolerance of the equipment to the upper limits of specifications or beyond, and any resulting damage is not accidental and not what the insurance was designed to cover.

There is no coverage for damage caused by water or other means to extinguish a fire, even when the attempt is unsuccessful. Once again, the obligation for this loss should fall back on the property insurance coverage, under the doctrine of proximate cause.

Generally, there is no coverage for damage caused by depletion, deterioration, corrosion, erosion, or wear and tear. The insurer will not pay for upgrades to covered equipment. However, if a breakdown occurs, it will pay for any resulting loss or damage.

If coverage is provided by another policy, whether collectible or not, there will be no coverage for any loss caused by a limited number of the broad form perils found on commercial property causes of loss forms. Specifically, the Equipment Breakdown Protection form excludes losses caused by aircraft, vehicles, freezing, lightning, sinkhole collapse, smoke, riot, civil commotion, vandalism, or the weight of snow, sleet, or ice. But this exclusion applies only if there is other coverage—if it is not otherwise covered, the Equipment Breakdown Protection form will provide coverage within the scope if its provisions (damage resulting from a breakdown of equipment, even if due to one of these causes).

There is no coverage for any loss or damage resulting from a breakdown caused by windstorm or hail. Although this is similar to the previous exclusion, there is one major difference—it is absolute, and there is no exception when other insurance does not apply.

There is no coverage for any delay in or interruption of any business, manufacturing or processing activity, except as provided by the business income and/or extra expense and utility interruption coverages.

With respect to business income and/or extra expense coverage and utility interruption coverage, there is no coverage for the following:

- any business activity that would not or could not have been carried on if the breakdown had not occurred;
- the insured's failure to use due diligence and all reasonable means to operate the business as nearly normal as practicable; and
- the suspension, lapse, or cancellation of any contract following a breakdown extending beyond the time business could have been resumed if the contract has not lapsed, has not been suspended, or was not cancelled.

There is no coverage for lack or excess of power, light, heat, steam, or refrigeration, except as provided by the business income and/or extra expense, utility interruption, and spoilage damage coverages.

With respect to utility interruption coverage, there is no coverage for loss resulting from any of the following, whether or not the insured has coverage under another policy:

- acts of sabotage;
- collapse;
- deliberate acts of load shedding by a supplying utility;
- freezing caused by cold weather;
- impact of aircraft, missile, or vehicle;
- impact of objects falling from an aircraft or missile;
- lightning;
- riot, civil commotion, or vandalism;
- sinkhole collapse;
- smoke; and
- weight of snow, ice, or sleet.

There is no coverage for any indirect loss resulting from a breakdown of covered equipment except as may be provided by the business income and/or extra expense, utility interruption, and spoilage damage coverages.

There is no coverage for any loss resulting from neglect by the insured to use all reasonable means to save and preserve covered property from further damage at and after the time of loss.

19.4.4.5. Limits of Insurance

This form may show a variety of limits of insurance in the Declarations. The primary limit is an overall limit per breakdown—this is the most the insurer will pay for loss or damage resulting from any one breakdown under all applicable coverages.

For each applicable coverage, a limit of insurance or the word *included* must be shown in the Declarations. If a limit of insurance is shown, it is the most the insurer will pay for that particular coverage. If the word *included* is shown for any coverage, the limit for that coverage will be part of, and not in addition to, the limit per breakdown.

For some coverages, time limits must be shown in the Declarations. If coverage for an extended period of restoration is elected under the business income and/or extra expense coverages, or if coverage for newly acquired premises is elected, a number of days must be shown in the Declarations for these coverages. If utility interruption coverage is elected, a number of hours that will apply as a waiting period must be shown in the Declarations.

For the following coverages, the policy will automatically provide up to $25,000 per breakdown unless a higher limit (or the word *included*) is shown in the Declarations:

- ammonia contamination;
- consequential loss;
- data and media;
- hazardous substance; and
- water damage.

19.4.4.6. Deductibles

Deductibles apply separately for each applicable coverage, unless the deductibles are shown as combined for any two or more coverages. If a combined deductible applies, the insurer will subtract the combined deductible amount from the aggregate amount of loss to which the combined deductible applies.

Coverages may be subject to a dollar deductible, in which case the insurer will subtract the deductible amount from any loss it would otherwise pay.

Certain coverages may be subject to a time deductible, which is usually expressed as a number of days. If a time deductible applies, the insurer is not responsible for any loss that occurs during the deductible period immediately following a breakdown. For example, if business income coverage is elected with a time deductible of seven days, coverage would not begin until after the business has been shut down for more than seven days.

Deductibles may be expressed as a percentage of loss, in which case the insurer would not be liable for the indicated percentage of an aggregate loss.

For example, if a coverage was written with a percentage of loss deductible of 15%, the insurer would only be obligated to pay 85% of any covered loss.

Business income coverage may also be written with a multiple of daily value deductible, and with minimum or maximum deductible amounts that apply to the coverage.

19.4.4.7. Loss Conditions

The Equipment Breakdown Protection coverage form includes a number of standard loss conditions that are similar to those found on other commercial coverage forms, including abandonment, appraisal, other insurance, and subrogation.

Additionally, this form includes a provision for paying defense costs. If the insurer elects to defend the insured against suits arising from the owners of property, it will do so at its own expense.

The insurer also reserves the right to adjust losses with the owner of property. If there is loss or damage to property of others in the care, custody, or control of the insured, the insurer has the right to settle the loss or damage with the owner of that property.

Another condition addresses the issue of reducing the insured's loss. As soon as possible after a breakdown, the insured is required to resume business (partially or completely), make up for lost business within a reasonable period of time, and make use of every reasonable means to reduce or avert loss.

A valuation condition states that the insurer will determine the value of covered property when loss or damage occurs based on the cost to repair, rebuild, or replace the damaged property with property of the same kind, capacity, size, or quality. Some special provisions apply to particular types of property and circumstances.

For business income and/or extra expense coverage, a few additional conditions apply. These address the issues of providing annual reports of values, adjustments of premium, and coinsurance.

19.4.4.8. General Conditions

The Equipment Breakdown Protection coverage form includes a number of general conditions that are frequently found on other commercial coverage forms, such as concealment, misrepresentation or fraud, no benefit to bailee, and liberalization. It also includes some conditions that are unique to boiler and machinery insurance.

The coverage form includes a suspension provision. One of the unique things about boiler and machinery insurance is that the insurer or any representative of the insurer may immediately suspend the insurance against loss by breakdown for specific equipment whenever that equipment is found to be in, or exposed to, a dangerous condition. Advance notice is not required, but the insurer must mail or deliver written notice of the suspension to the insured's last known address or the address where the covered equipment is located. The suspension will only apply to the particular equipment. Once in effect, the suspension may be lifted and the insurance reinstated only by an endorsement for that equipment. If insurance is suspended, the insured will be entitled to a pro rata refund of premium for the period of suspension.

There is a joint or disputed loss agreement condition that is designed to facilitate payment when both a commercial property policy and equipment breakdown protection policy are in effect, damage occurs to property that is covered under both policies, and there is disagreement between the insurers as to whether there is coverage or as to the amount of the loss to be paid under its own policy. This condition applies only if both policies have a similar provision for resolving disputed losses. Generally, each insurer agrees to pay the full amount of any loss that it agrees is covered under its own policy and one-half of the loss that is in dispute. This condition does not apply when both coverages are written by the same insurer.

The last condition addresses final settlement between insurers. This condition applies only when two or more insurers are involved in settlement of a disputed loss or one that is resolved by arbitration. It requires the insurer found responsible for the greater percentage on the ultimate loss to return the excess contribution made by the other insurer(s), plus it must pay interest on the amount from the date the insured invokes this agreement until the date the other insurer(s) are actually reimbursed. Arbitration expenses will be apportioned between insurers on the same basis that the loss is apportioned.

19.4.5. Endorsements

A number of endorsements are available to modify the coverage provided by the Equipment Breakdown Protection coverage form.

Business income losses are settled based on estimates of income that might have been earned, because it can never be known with certainty how much income would have been earned had a loss not occurred. Past records of actual income provide one indication of potential income, but future estimates are also important (for example, a business may be expanding or contracting if an insured is increasing or decreasing its advertising budget and merchandise inventory by a significant amount, and comparable changes in income should be expected). The Business Income—Report of Values endorsement is used to report actual values of sales, earnings and net profit for a previous 12-month period and estimated values for the future 12-month period.

The Refrigeration Interruption Coverage endorsement is used to provide coverage for spoilage of the insured's owned refrigerated covered property while in storage due to an excess or lack of refrigeration because of a breakdown of covered equipment that is:

- owned by the insured;
- owned, operated, or controlled by a private or public cold storage warehouse that the insured has contracted with; and
- owned, operated, or controlled by a local private or public utility or distributor that provides utility services to the insured.

The endorsement includes a schedule where a description of the covered property and the locations of any owned premises or nonowned premises where coverage is to apply must be shown. A limit of insurance and deductible must also be shown.

Refrigeration interruption coverage is written on a reporting basis, and the Refrigeration Interruption—Report of Values endorsement must be used in conjunction with the coverage endorsement. It is used to schedule the total insurable values (based on current selling price) of covered property by month for a 12-month period at the described premises.

The Turbine Units Explosion coverage endorsement is used when coverage is desired for explosion of turbine units. When applicable, it deletes and replaces the definitions of *breakdown* and *covered equipment* in the main coverage form, but only for the turbine units listed as covered equipment in the schedule. Turbine units include any:

- turbine or auxiliary steam turbine;
- combustor, duct, piping, precooler, inter-cooler, regenerator, or heat exchanger forming part of a gas turbine; and
- compressor or pump on any shaft of the driving turbine.

To be covered, an explosion must be caused by the pressure of gas, liquid, or vapor within a turbine unit, or a breakdown must be caused by the breaking of the casing of a driving turbine or breaking of any spindle, rotor, or shaft of the equipment into two or more parts.

The Pressure or Vacuum Equipment endorsement is used when coverage is desired for pressure or vacuum equipment. When applicable, it deletes and replaces the definition of *covered equipment* in the main coverage form. Under this endorsement, *covered equipment* means any equipment built to operate under internal pressure or vacuum, which is subject to mandatory state or municipal jurisdictional inspection, and is located where the inspection requirements can be conducted by an authorized insurance company inspector. Note that the requirement for inspections is part of the definition.

Finally, the Production Equipment Exclusion endorsement is used to add an exclusion for certain types of production equipment. When attached, it amends the definition of covered equipment to state that it does not include production or process machines or apparatus that process, form, cut, shape, grind, or convey raw materials, materials in process, or finished products.

19.5. AVIATION INSURANCE

Insurance coverages for aircraft are similar to those available for automobile exposures. The most significant differences between aircraft and automobile insurance are the higher dollar exposure to loss and the high degree of care required by the operator of the aircraft. As in automobile policies, the two basic Aviation coverages are Physical Damage and Liability.

19.5.1. Physical Damage Coverage

Aviation Physical Damage coverage, called Hull insurance, is much like the Comprehensive and Collision coverages provided by auto insurance. It covers the complete aircraft, including its airframe, engines, controls, and electronic navigation and communications equipment. It does not cover personal effects. Either a fixed dollar or a percentage of the loss deductible usually applies. Coverage can be provided while the aircraft is:

- in the air or on the ground;
- on the ground only; and
- not in motion under its own power.

The Declarations indicate what coverage applies and any special restrictions or deductibles.

19.5.2. Liability Coverage

Aviation Liability insurance for owners of aircraft includes coverage for:

- bodily injury liability to persons other than passengers;
- bodily injury to passengers;
- property damage liability; and
- medical payments (payable for injuries to passengers, regardless of whether the insured is liable for their injuries).

19.6. PROFESSIONAL LIABILITY INSURANCE

Professional liability—liability arising out of rendering or failing to render services of a professional nature—is excluded under CGL policies. Special Professional Liability policies have been developed for many professionals, such as physicians, surgeons, dentists, lawyers, insurance agents, architects, accountants, and directors and officers of corporations. Each policy is tailored to fit a specific occupational need. Most policies are written on a claims-made basis.

Professionals have two kinds of legal duty to their clients. These are to perform the services for which they were hired and to perform them in accordance with the appropriate standards of conduct. Because of their special skills, professionals are held to a higher standard of conduct.

Professional Liability policies can go by several different names. *Malpractice insurance* is the term commonly applied to Medical Professional Liability policies written for medical professionals or institutions, including physicians, nurses, dentists, surgeons, opticians, optometrists, chiropractors, and veterinarians. *Errors And Omissions (E&O) insurance* is a broad term that refers to Professional Liability policies written for other professionals, such as insurance agents, accountants, architects, stockbrokers, engineers, consultants, and attorneys.

Another type of Professional Liability policy, the Fiduciary Liability policy, protects those who manage private pension and employee benefit plans against liability for violation of the federal ERISA law.

Early in our discussion of the insurance agent's role, we discussed the liability exposure that an insurance agent has and the need for her to be properly insured under an E&O policy. E&O insurance is also appropriate for directors and officers of corporations who may be sued as individuals by stockholders. Directors and officers have no coverage under a CGL for personal liability and no coverage under the Homeowners contract for liability arising out of business pursuits. This exposure is properly insured under a type of E&O insurance called *Directors and Officers Liability*.

Because Malpractice and Errors and Omissions insurance cover loss arising from professional acts or acts that fall within a professional's duties, it is extremely important to distinguish between professional and nonprofessional exposures. Unfortunately, courts have not always been consistent in their interpretations. If the insured wants full coverage against liability exposures arising from business, it may be advisable for the insured to maintain both a Commercial General Liability policy and the appropriate Professional Liability policy.

19.6.1. Consent to Settle Losses

Some professionals believe that settling claims out of court is an admission of an error that may harm their professional reputations. In the past, Professional Liability policies contained a provision that the insurer could not settle a claim without the insured's consent. Most policies now provide that such consent is not required.

19.7. EMPLOYMENT PRACTICES LIABILITY INSURANCE

Both the CGL and Workers' Compensation and Employers Liability policies exclude losses arising out of wrongful termination, discrimination, sexual harassment, and other employment-related practices. This coverage is provided by Employment Practices Liability (EPL) insurance.

EPL insurance may be issued as an endorsement to a Directors and Officers Liability policy or as a separate policy. Although standard ISO forms are available, many companies issue their own policies. Policy provisions differ greatly among insurers, particularly those regarding the types of wrongful employment acts covered. Most policies cover wrongful acts committed by the employer and its employees. Typical exclusions include:

- wrongful termination practices committed with dishonest, fraudulent, criminal, or malicious intent;
- mass layoffs of employees;
- deliberate fraud or purposeful violation of laws, rules, or regulations;
- BI or PD other than emotional distress, mental anguish, or humiliation;
- liabilities of others assumed under contract, except employment contracts; and
- circumstances reported under prior EPL policies.

19.8. DIFFERENCE IN CONDITIONS INSURANCE

In an earlier unit, you learned that while the Commercial Property coverage part provides extensive property coverage, it still contains several exclusions. Difference in Conditions insurance (DIC) provides broad coverage to fill those gaps. It is written to exclude the basic fire and extended coverage perils but include most other insurable perils. Consequently, it is written in conjunction with policies providing the basic coverage excluded by the Difference in Conditions policy.

DIC policies are usually written on large risks with a high deductible. Insurance companies issue their own DIC policies since there is no standardized form for this type of coverage.

Exercise 19.B

1. A Difference in Conditions policy (includes/excludes) ____________ basic fire and extended coverage perils.
2. A Difference in Conditions policy (is/is not) ___________ written in conjunction with policies providing basic fire and extended coverage perils.

Exercise answers can be found at the end of the Unit 19 answers and rationales.

19.9. COMMERCIAL UMBRELLA INSURANCE

Just as Personal Umbrella policies are available to cover the catastrophic liability exposures of personal risks, high-limit Commercial Umbrella policies are designed to provide catastrophic Liability coverage for business risks.

Because the Umbrella policy is not designed to handle usual or everyday exposures, the insured must have underlying Liability coverage, such as Commercial Auto or Commercial General Liability coverage, before an Umbrella policy will be issued.

A Commercial Umbrella policy provides coverage in three types of situations:

- The policy limits applying to a loss under an underlying policy have been exhausted
- A loss is excluded under an underlying contract but not excluded under the Umbrella (the insured must first meet the retention limit)
- Previous losses reimbursed under an underlying policy have reduced its aggregate limit so that a subsequent loss is not fully covered

Exercise 19.C

1. RV Industries has $500,000 in Commercial Auto coverage and a $1 million Commercial Umbrella policy. The retention limit under the Umbrella is $100,000. Which of the following losses would be partially or fully paid under RV's Umbrella policy?
   A. RV has a $400,000 loss that is fully covered under the Commercial Auto policy.
   B. RV has a $600,000 loss that is excluded by the Commercial Auto coverage. The Commercial Umbrella policy does not exclude losses of this nature.

Exercise answers can be found at the end of the Unit 19 answers and rationales.

19.10. SURETY BONDS

As part of our discussion of Crime insurance, we talked about Fidelity bonding, which is a way for employers to protect themselves against an employee's dishonesty. A Fidelity bond is essentially a guarantee that certain acts on the part of the employee will not be committed.

Surety bonds, on the other hand, emphasize that certain things will happen. In broad terms, Surety bonding guarantees that:

- **someone will faithfully perform** whatever he agrees to do; or
- **someone will make a payment** as agreed upon by that person and another party.

One of the key differences between Fidelity and Surety bonding lies in the fact that, in Fidelity bonding, it is the obligee (the employer) who seeks and pays for the bond. The principal (the employee) often does not even know the bond exists. With Surety bonds, on the other hand, the principal is always the party that both arranges and pays for the bond for the benefit of the obligee.

Before a Surety bond is issued, the principal must submit an application that contains not only the information needed for underwriting, but also an indemnity agreement through which the principal agrees to indemnify the surety for any loss sustained. This is necessary because suretyship does not anticipate losses, although they do occur. Instead, it is expected that the principal will perform as agreed and, if not, that the principal will otherwise make it up to the obligee.

If the principal does default, however, the surety company will indemnify the obligee and then attempt to collect from the principal. The premium paid is actually a charge for using the credit of the surety company, without allowance for losses. In addition, in some cases the surety may require that the principal deposit money, called collateral security, to protect the surety against possible loss.

Exercise 19.D

Suppose the principal is a contractor who must purchase a Surety bond to guarantee that she will complete a job according to contract specifications.

1. What is the first step she must take to obtain a surety bond?
____
____

2. What does the principal agree to do if her actions cause a loss for the surety? ____
____

3. If the principal does not complete the job as the bond guarantees, the surety will indemnify the obligee and

   A. write off the loss
   B. attempt to collect the loss from the principal

4. In some cases, when the bond is provided the surety may protect itself against loss by requiring that the principal

   A. assign her rights of subrogation to the surety
   B. provide collateral security

Exercise answers can be found at the end of the Unit 19 answers and rationales.

19.10.1. Contract Bonds

There are many different types of bonds available for a variety of needs. One of these is **Contract bonds**, which guarantee the fulfillment of contractual obligations. Common among Contract bonds are:

- **Bid bonds**—Guarantee that if a contractor's bid is accepted, the contractor will enter into a contract and provide the required Performance bond
- **Performance bonds**—Guarantee that jobs will be completed by the contractor according to contract specifications
- **Payment bonds**—Guarantee that bills for labor and materials will be paid by the contractor as they are due. These are sometimes called *Labor and Materials bonds* and are frequently included as part of a Performance bond
- **Supply bonds**—Guarantee that a supplier will furnish supplies, products, or equipment at an agreed-upon price and time
- **Completion bonds**—Guarantee that when contractors borrow money to fund construction projects, the project will be carried out and the work will be delivered free and clear of liens or encumbrances

Exercise 19.E

1. Which type of bond is used to guarantee that supplies will be furnished at an agreed-upon price and time?

   ____

   ____

2. What are the two different names for bonds that guarantee that a contractor will pay bills for labor and materials?

   ____

   ____

3. Which bond is used to guarantee that a contractor will complete a job as specified?

   ____

   ____

4. A bond that guarantees that a contractor, upon acceptance of a bid, will enter into a contract is called a

   ____

Exercise answers can be found at the end of the Unit 19 answers and rationales.

19.10.2. Judicial Bonds

Judicial bonds guarantee that the principal will fulfill certain obligations set forth by law. There are two classes of judicial bonds:

- **Fiduciary bonds** are commonly used to bond guardians, administrators, trustees, and executors, all of whom are fiduciaries, or persons appointed by a court of law to manage the property of others.
- **Court bonds** are used to settle legal arguments that do not involve monetary damages. Their primary purpose is to protect obligees against loss in case principals are not able to prove that they are legally entitled to the legal remedy they sought against the obligees.

19.10.3. Other Types of Bonds

Public Official bonds, which are required by law, guarantee that public officials will handle public money correctly and otherwise perform their duties faithfully and honestly.

License and Permit bonds are sometimes required in connection with the issuance of licenses by government agencies. They guarantee that the person who posts the bond will comply with all applicable laws pertaining to their activities.

19.11. SURPLUS LINES

19.11.1. The Unauthorized Market and Surplus Lines

Generally, an insurer is not allowed to transact business in a state without having a current Certificate of Authority or license issued by the insurance department specifically authorizing the insurer to transact particular lines of business. These insurers are known as authorized or admitted insurers, and they transact traditional lines of insurance. In most states, the law prohibits anyone from acting as an agent for an unauthorized company, and prohibits an insurer from transacting any line of business for which it is not authorized.

In almost every state, the insurance law makes exemptions that apply to certain transactions that may be legally conducted by unauthorized or non-admitted insurers without requiring a Certificate of Authority. These transactions usually include certain types of transportation and Ocean Marine risks, reinsurance, and surplus lines coverages. **Surplus lines coverages** are those that are not available or cannot be procured from authorized insurers within a state. Although surplus lines are considered an unregulated area of insurance, the business must be procured and conducted in accordance with the surplus lines insurance law of the state.

19.11.2. Conditions for Obtaining Coverage

Although there are variations from one state to another, generally three conditions must be met before surplus lines insurance may be obtained from an unauthorized insurer.

- The business must be obtained through a licensed surplus lines broker.
- It is determined after a diligent search that the full amount of insurance cannot be obtained from authorized insurers who market the insurance in the state.
- Coverage may not be obtained as a surplus lines coverage solely for the purpose of obtaining a better contract or a lower premium than an authorized insurer could provide.

Although surplus lines insurers are unauthorized, many states issue an approved list of surplus lines carriers and require brokers to place surplus lines business with those insurers.

19.12. FEDERAL TERRORISM RISK INSURANCE ACT OF 2002

We'll conclude our discussion of miscellaneous commercial insurance policies by covering a federal program that affects most commercial lines of insurance—the Federal Terrorism Risk Insurance Act of 2002.

19.12.1. Background

Insurance protection is vital for economic development and stability. Without insurance protection, builders might not build, potential buyers might not buy property, and potential businessowners might not be willing to operate a business. When faced with catastrophic losses, the insurance industry has often backed away from providing needed coverages and the federal government has stepped in to provide subsidies, loss sharing, or excess reinsurance in order to make insurance available. The FAIR Plan program was created to make property insurance available in urban areas after the riots during the 1960s. The Federal Crop Insurance Program was implemented when insurers were unwilling to assume the full risk of crop hail damage. The National Flood Insurance Program was a response to the unavailability of flood insurance in high risk areas.

After the terrorist attacks on the United States on September 11, 2001, insurers started to attach terrorism exclusion endorsements to commercial property and casualty policies. They did not want to assume the potential catastrophic losses that might result from future attacks. But without insurance for such losses, businessowners who were no more capable of assuming such losses would have to bear the risk. This situation created a lot of uncertainty in the US economy, which could have many negative consequences.

As a result, in 2002, Congress enacted, and the President signed into law, the Terrorism Risk Insurance Act (TRIA) of 2002. This federal law provides a federal backstop for defined acts of terrorism and imposes certain obligations on insurers. It is designed to limit the exposure of individual insurers and the insurance industry as a whole, and to make insurance available and affordable, under a system where the federal government participates and shares the risk of loss. The act voids terrorism exclusions, and state approval of such exclusions, in property and casualty insurance contracts to the extent that they exclude losses that would otherwise be insured losses.

19.12.2. Temporary Program

The program is intended to be a temporary federal program that provides for a system of shared public and private compensation for insured losses resulting from acts of terrorism, in order to protect consumers by addressing market disruptions and ensure the continued widespread availability and affordability of property and casualty insurance for terrorism risk. The program will terminate December 31, 2014, unless it is extended by Congress.

19.12.3. Definitions

Not all acts of terrorism are covered by TRIA. To be deemed an act of terrorism, the act must:

- be a violent act or an act that is dangerous to human life, property, or infrastructure;
- have resulted in damage within the United States, or outside of the United States in the case of an air carrier, vessel, or the premises of a United States mission;

- have been committed in an effort to coerce the civilian population of the United States or to influence the policy or affect the conduct of the United States Government by coercion;
- not be committed during the course of a declared war (except for workers' compensation coverage);
- result in property and casualty losses exceeding $5 million; and
- be certified as an act of terrorism under TRIA by the Secretary of the Treasury, in concurrence with the Secretary of State and the US Attorney General.

For purposes of the act, **insurer** means any entity and affiliate that is licensed or admitted to engage in the business of providing property and casualty insurance on a primary or excess basis in any state, including eligible surplus line carriers and residual market insurance entities. All insurers, as defined in the act, are required to participate in the Terrorism Insurance Program and make available coverage for insured losses in all of their covered commercial lines policies.

Insured loss means any loss resulting from an act of terrorism, including an act of war (in the case of workers compensation losses) that is covered by primary or excess property and casualty insurance issued by an insurer if the loss occurs:

- within the United States;
- in an air carrier or to a United States flag vessel regardless of where the loss occurs; or
- at the premises of a United States mission.

19.12.4. General Overview of Program

The program allows for risk sharing when the proper conditions are met. Generally, insurers are subject to deductibles (amounts they must pay before federal contributions begin), and when multiple insurers are involved in a loss the Secretary will determine the pro rata share of insured losses to be paid by each insurer. The federal government will pay 85% of insured losses that exceed insurer deductibles. However, there is an annual cap on the maximum obligation of insurers and the federal government under the law.

19.12.5. Deductibles and Marketplace Aggregate Retention

Coverage for an insurer's losses are subject to a deductible equal to 20% of the insurer's direct earned premiums during the prior calendar year.

The insurance marketplace aggregate retention is $27.5 billion.

19.12.6. Cap on Annual Liability

If the aggregate insured losses exceed $100 billion during any program year under the shared program, the federal government will not be liable for any portion of insured losses in excess of $100 billion, and no insurer that has met the deductible requirement will be liable for the payment of any portion of insured losses that exceeds $100 billion. The Secretary will notify Congress no later than 15 days after an act of terrorism stating if terrorism losses are expected to exceed this amount.

19.12.7. Conditions for Federal Payments

No payment may be made under the program with respect to an insured loss that is covered by an insurer, unless:

- the person that suffers the insured loss, or a person acting on behalf of that person, files a claim with the insurer;
- the insurer provides clear and conspicuous disclosure to the policyholder of the premium charged for insured losses covered by the Program;
- the insurer processes the claim for the insured loss in accordance with appropriate business practices, and any reasonable procedures that the Secretary may prescribe; and
- the insurer submits to the Secretary a claim for payment of the Federal share of compensation for insured losses under the Program, written certification of the underlying claim, and of all payments made for insured losses, and certification of the insurer's compliance with all applicable provisions of the law. **(15 U.S.C. s 6701)**

UNIT TEST

1. The Farm coverage part insures a farmer's
   A. personal loss exposures
   B. commercial loss exposures
   C. Both A and B

2. The Farm coverage part provides
   A. property coverage only
   B. liability coverage only
   C. both Property and Liability coverage

3. Which of the following are covered under a Farm coverage part?
   A. Farm buildings, equipment, and livestock
   B. Liability arising from farm operations
   C. Growing crops
   D. Farm dwelling and its personal property
   E. All of the above

4. A breakdown of equipment covered under the Equipment Breakdown Protection coverage form results in the simultaneous breakdown of 2 other pieces of covered equipment. According to the form, how many breakdowns occurred in this loss?
   A. 1
   B. 2
   C. 3

5. The insured knows it may take several months for his damaged turbine to be fully repaired, so he authorizes $500 for temporary repairs so production can resume. This expenditure would be covered under which coverage in the Equipment Breakdown Protection coverage form?
   A. Spoilage
   B. Errors or omissions
   C. Expediting Expense

6. Under the Equipment Breakdown Protection coverage form, which of the following causes of damage to covered equipment would NOT be a covered breakdown?
   A. Electrical failure, including arcing
   B. Leakage at any valve, fitting, shaft seal, gland packing, joint, or connection
   C. Failure of pressure or vacuum equipment
   D. Mechanical failure, including rupture or bursting caused by centrifugal force

7. Briefly define the purpose of each of the following types of Aviation policies.
   A. Hull

   ____

   ____

   B. Aviation Liability

   ____

   ____

8. Professional Liability policies
   A. cover the insured's liability arising from the rendering or failure to render services of a professional nature
   B. duplicate the coverage provided by the Commercial General Liability policy
   C. are tailored to fit specific occupational needs

9. A business that wants coverage for its liability for employment-related acts can obtain it by purchasing
   A. Commercial General Liability insurance
   B. Workers' Compensation and Employers Liability insurance
   C. Employment Practices Liability insurance
   D. Any of the above

10. What is the purpose of Difference in Conditions insurance? ______________________________

    ____

    ____

11. Commercial insureds who need more Liability coverage than that provided by a certain policy or who want coverage for losses that are excluded by a certain policy should purchase a
    A. Difference in Conditions policy
    B. Commercial Umbrella policy
    C. Surety bond

12. Which of these statements regarding Difference in Conditions insurance are CORRECT?
    A. It excludes coverage for basic perils such as fire, lightning, and windstorm.
    B. It is written in conjunction with policies that cover basic perils.
    C. It does not have a deductible requirement.

13. What is the difference between a Fidelity bond and a Surety bond?
    A. A Fidelity bond guarantees that certain acts will not be committed; a Surety bond emphasizes that certain things will happen.
    B. A Fidelity bond emphasizes that certain things will happen; a Surety bond guarantees that certain acts will not be committed.
    C. None of the above are correct; Fidelity and Surety bonds serve the same purpose.

14. Which one of the following answer choices lists all of the parties to a Surety bond?
    A. Principal and obligee
    B. Principal, obligee, and surety
    C. Surety and obligee

15. Identify each of the following as contract bonds (C), judicial bonds (J), or other types of bonds (O).

A.	____	Public Official bond
B.	____	Court bond
C.	____	Bid bond
D.	____	Supply bond
E.	____	License and Permit bond
F.	____	Completion bond
G.	____	Fiduciary bond
H.	____	Performance bond
I.	____	Payment bond

16. What items can be insured under the Farm Property coverage forms or separately under their own specialized coverage forms? ____________
____
____

17. All of the following types of losses may be covered by the Equipment Breakdown Protection coverage form EXCEPT
    A. business income losses and/or extra expenses
    B. expediting expenses
    C. losses due to spoilage damage
    D. damage caused by fire or combustion explosion

18. What 2 coverages are typically provided in Aviation policies?
    1. ____________________
    2. ____________________

19. How do deductibles apply in the Equipment Breakdown Protection coverage form?
    A. Deductibles apply separately for each applicable coverage unless the deductibles are shown as combined for any 2 or more coverages.
    B. A single deductible applies to all applicable coverages.
    C. Deductibles are always stated as a specific dollar amount.

20. Under the terms of the Suspension provision in the Equipment Breakdown Protection coverage form, coverage on dangerous equipment can be suspended
    A. on 30-days' advance notice to the insured
    B. at the end of the policy period
    C. immediately upon delivery of written notice to the insured

21. Which of the following would be covered by Aviation Physical Damage insurance?
    A. Airframe
    B. Engine
    C. Personal effects
    D. Navigation and communications equipment
    E. Controls

22. An insured professional who wants full coverage against liability exposures arising from business should purchase
    A. a Commercial General Liability policy only
    B. the appropriate Professional Liability policy only
    C. both a CGL and the appropriate Professional Liability policy

23. What is the purpose of Directors and Officers Liability insurance? ______________________________
____
____

24. What general surety bond category guarantees that the principal will fulfill certain obligations set forth by law? ______________________________
____

25. Individuals who are entrusted with the care, control, or management of others' property might require what type of bond? ______________________________
____

26. The newly elected treasurer of a certain state must post a bond to guarantee that she will handle money correctly and perform her duties honestly. What type of bond would she obtain?
____
____

ANSWERS AND RATIONALES TO UNIT TEST

1. **C.** Farmers' businesses and homes are often at the same location, so they need insurance that will cover both their personal and business exposures to loss. The Farm coverage part includes several Farm Property coverage forms that cover both the personal and business property of the farmer and a Farm Liability coverage form for the personal and business liability exposures of the farmer.

2. **C.** The Farm coverage part includes both Property and Liability coverage.

3. **A, B,** and **D** are correct. Growing crops are not covered under a Farm coverage part.

4. **A.** One breakdown means that if an initial breakdown causes other breakdowns, all will be considered a single breakdown. All breakdowns at any one premises that manifest themselves at the same time and are the direct result of the same cause will be considered one breakdown.

5. **C.** This coverage extension covers the reasonable cost of temporary repairs and expedition (speeding up) of permanent repairs.

6. **B.** Under the Equipment Breakdown Protection coverage form, breakdown means the following types of direct physical loss that cause damage to covered equipment and necessitates its repair or replacement: failure of pressure or vacuum equipment, mechanical failure, including rupture or bursting caused by centrifugal force, and electrical failure, including arcing. Choice B is specifically excluded under this definition.

7. **A.** Hull coverage provides Physical Damage coverage for the aircraft.

8. **B.** Aviation Liability insurance covers various liability exposures of owners of aircraft.

9. **A** and **C** are correct. Liability arising out of rendering or failing to render services of a professional nature is excluded under CGL policies. Special Professional Liability policies have been developed for many professionals, such as physicians, lawyers, and insurance agents. Each policy is tailored to fit a specific occupational need.

10. **C.** This coverage is provided by Employment Practices Liability insurance. The other policies listed specifically exclude losses arising from employment-related practices.

    The purpose of Difference in Conditions insurance is to cover most of the exclusions in the Commercial Property coverage part.

11. **B.** Commercial Umbrella policies provide catastrophic Liability coverage for business risks. Because the Umbrella is not designed to handle usual or everyday exposures, the insured must have underlying Liability coverage before an Umbrella will be issued. The Umbrella may cover certain losses that are excluded by the underlying insurance.

12. **A** and **B** are correct. Difference in Conditions insurance is written to exclude the basic fire and extended coverage perils but include most other insurable perils that are not covered under Commercial Property coverage. Consequently, it is written in conjunction with policies providing the basic coverage excluded by the DIC policy. DIC policies are usually written on large risks with a high deductible.

13. **A.** A Fidelity bond is essentially a guarantee that certain acts on the part of the employee will not be committed. Surety bonds guarantee that certain things will happen. In broad terms, Surety bonds guarantee that someone will faithfully perform whatever he agrees to do, or someone will make a payment as agreed upon by that person and another party.

14. **B.** There are 3 parties to a Surety bond: the principal, the obligee, and the surety.

15. O A.; J B.; C C.; C D.; O E.; C F.; J G.; C H.; C I.
Contract bonds guarantee the fulfillment of contractual obligations. Types of contract bonds include bid bonds, performance bonds, payment bonds, materials bonds, supply bonds, and completion bonds. Judicial bonds guarantee that the principal will fulfill certain obligations set forth by law. Fiduciary bonds and court bonds are 2 types of judicial bonds. Other types of bonds are public official bonds and license and permit bonds. Public official bonds guarantee that public officials will handle public money correctly and otherwise perform their duties faithfully and honestly. License and permit bonds are sometimes required in connection with the issuance of licenses by government agencies. They guarantee that the person who posts the bond will comply with all applicable laws pertaining to their activities.

16. There are 2 types of property that can be insured under the Farm Property coverage forms or separately under their own specialized coverage forms: mobile agricultural machinery and equipment and livestock.

17. **D.** Business income and/or extra expense losses, expediting expenses, and spoilage damage are all coverage options in the Equipment Breakdown Protection coverage form. Damage caused by fire or combustion explosion is excluded because it is covered under Commercial Property insurance.

18. Aviation policies typically include Liability and Physical Damage coverage.

19. **A.** Deductibles apply separately for each applicable coverage unless the deductibles are shown as combined for any two or more coverages. Depending on the coverage, the deductible may be expressed as a dollar amount, a time limit, a percentage of loss, or a multiple of daily value.

20. **C.** The insurer may immediately suspend coverage whenever covered equipment is found to be in or exposed to a dangerous condition. Suspension applies only to that particular equipment and takes effect as soon as written notice is delivered to the insured.

21. **A**, **B**, **D**, and **E** are correct. Aviation Physical Damage insurance is similar to the Comp and Collision coverages provided by auto insurance. It covers the complete aircraft, including its airframe, engines, controls, and electronic navigation and communications equipment. It does not cover personal effects.

22. **C.** Because Malpractice and Errors and Omissions insurance cover loss arising from professional acts or acts that fall within a professional's duties, it is extremely important to distinguish between professional and nonprofessional exposures. Unfortunately, courts have not always been consistent in their interpretations. If the insured wants full coverage against liability exposures arising from business, it may be advisable for the insured to maintain both a Commercial General Liability policy and the appropriate Professional Liability policy.

23. Directors and Officers Liability insurance provides Liability coverage for directors and officers of corporations who may be sued as individuals by stockholders.

24. Judicial bonds. This category of surety bonds guarantees that the principal will fulfill certain obligations set forth by law.

25. A Fiduciary bond. Fiduciary bonds are commonly used to bond persons appointed by a court of law to manage the property of others.

26. A Public Official bond. Public Official bonds guarantee that public officials will handle public money correctly and otherwise perform their duties faithfully and honestly.

UNIT 19 EXERCISE ANSWERS

Exercise 19.A

1. A, B, and D

Exercise 19.B

1. Excludes
2. Is

Exercise 19.C

1. **B**

Exercise 19.D

1. Apply for bond
2. Indemnify the surety
3. **B**
4. **B**

Exercise 19.E

1. Supply bond
2. Payment bond and labor and materials bond
3. Performance bond
4. Bid bond

Glossary

A

Abandonment condition A condition often contained in property insurance policies that states that the insured cannot abandon damaged property to the insurer and demand to be reimbursed for its full value

Absolute liability Type of liability imposed by law on those participating in certain activities that are considered especially hazardous; a person involved in such operations may be held liable for the damages of another even though the individual was not negligent

Accident A loss that occurs at a specific time and place

Accounts receivable insurance Filed commercial inland marine form that insures against loss the insured suffers because of an inability to collect from customers when accounts receivable records are damaged or destroyed

Actual cash value (ACV) The cost to replace an item of property at the time of loss, less an allowance for depreciation; often used to determine the amount of reimbursement for a loss

Additional coverages Supplemental insurance coverages that apply only in certain circumstances, have reduced or separate limits of liability, or require the insured to meet certain requirements before they are applicable; also called *coverage extensions, other coverages, and extended coverages*

Additional insured An individual or company, in addition to the insured, who is listed in the declarations; an example is a mortgage company that has an insurable interest in the property insured

Additional insured—Lessor endorsement commercial auto endorsement used to make leased vehicles considered owned vehicles for coverage purposes

Adhesion contract A contract where one party has more power than the other party in drafting the contract; an insurance policy is an adhesion contract—the insurer is the one with more power

Admitted insurer See *Authorized insurer*

Adverse selection The tendency of insureds with a greater-than-average chance of loss to purchase insurance

Agency Principles governing the authority of any agent that represents a principal

Agent An individual or organization that legally represents another; a state-licensed professional who represents the insurance company in the sale and servicing of insurance; the direct link between the insurance company and the policyholder

Aggregate limit Type of policy limit found in liability policies that limits coverage to a specified total amount for all losses occurring within the policy period

Agreed amount policy See *Valued policy*

Agreed value condition Condition found in some property insurance policies that stipulates a certain value that will meet the coinsurance requirement; if the policy limit equals or exceeds this amount, the insured will not be assessed a coinsurance penalty; also called *stated amount condition*

Agreement See *Offer and acceptance*

Aleatory contract A contract that is contingent on an uncertain event (a loss); an insurance policy is an aleatory contract

Alien company An insurance company incorporated in a country other than the United States that is doing business in the United States

All risk policy See *Open peril policy*

A.M. Best Company Organization that rates the financial stability of insurance companies doing business in the United States

Annual transit policy Nonfiled commercial inland marine transportation form that insures a property owner's incoming or outgoing shipments of goods during a year

Apparent authority Legal doctrine that states that an agent has whatever authority a reasonable person would assume she has

Application Questionnaire filled out by an agent and the prospect who is seeking insurance; the form contains information used to underwrite and rate the policy

Appraisal condition Policy condition that outlines a procedure for when the insured and insurer disagree on the amount of a loss—the insured and the insurer each select an appraiser; the two appraisers select an umpire; if the appraisers cannot agree on the amount of loss, the umpire is consulted; the amount agreed to by any two of the three parties is the amount paid for the loss

Appurtenant structures Buildings of lesser value that are on the same premises as the main building insured under a property policy; they are usually covered by the policy

Arbitration condition Policy condition that is similar to the appraisal condition; may be used to resolve other areas of disagreement besides those regarding the value of a loss

Assessment mutual company Mutual insurance company that charges members a pro-rata share of losses at the end of each policy period. See *Mutual company*

Assigned risk plan See *Automobile insurance plan*

Assignment condition Condition in insurance policies that specifies that the policy cannot be transferred to another unless the company consents to the transfer in writing

Assumption of risk Defense against liability based on the common law principle that a person who knowingly exposes himself to danger or injury assumes the risk of loss and cannot hold another person responsible for the loss

Audit See *Premium audit*

Authorized insurer Company that meets a state insurance department's standards and is authorized to do business in that state; also called an *admitted insurer*

Automatic increase In Insurance Endorsement Dwelling policy endorsement that provides an annual increase in the Coverage A amount of 4%, 6%, or 8%

Automobile insurance plan A state-sponsored plan that provides automobile insurance to those who are uninsurable under standard auto insurance policies

Aviation hull insurance Insurance that provides coverage for physical damage to aircraft

Aviation liability insurance Insurance provided for owners of aircraft that covers liability for bodily injury, injury to passengers, and property damage; also provides medical payments coverage

B

Bailee A person or organization that has temporary possession of someone else's personal property

Bailee's customer policy Nonfiled commercial inland marine form obtained by a bailee to cover loss or damage to customers' property in the bailee's custody without regard to liability

Bailment Delivery of property by the owner to someone else to be held for some special purpose and then returned to the owner

Barratry Illegal acts committed willfully by a ship's master or crew for the purpose of damaging the ship or cargo—includes hijacking, abandonment and embezzlement; this peril is covered in ocean marine insurance

Best's Organization that rates the financial stability of insurance companies doing business in the United States

Bid bond Type of surety bond that guarantees that if a contractor's bid is accepted, the contractor will enter into a contract and provide the required performance bond

Bill of lading Standardized contract of carriage issued by common carriers to the business for which it is shipping goods

Binder Oral or written statement that provides immediate insurance protection for a specified period; designed to provide temporary coverage until a policy is issued or denied

Blanket insurance Type of insurance policy that covers more than one item of property at a single location or one or more items of property at multiple locations

Blanket position bond Fidelity bond that covers losses arising from the dishonesty of one or more employees acting separately or in collusion; provides a single limit of liability applicable to each employee involved in a loss

Boat owners policy See *Watercraft package policy*

Bodily injury (BI) Defined in most policies to include injury, sickness, disease, and death resulting from any of these at any time

Boiler and machinery insurance Insurance that covers the insured for losses arising out of the use of steam boilers or other machinery or equipment; may be included in the commercial package policy

Broad theft coverage endorsement Dwelling policy endorsement that covers theft, attempted theft and vandalism, and malicious mischief resulting from theft; property is covered while it is on or off the premises

Broker Individual who represents the prospect, instead of the insurance company, in the insurance transaction

Builders risk coverage form One of the commercial property coverage forms; covers commercial, residential, or farm buildings that are under construction

Builders risk reporting form Optional form used with the commercial property builders risk coverage form; allows insured to purchase a smaller amount of insurance that gradually increases as the value of the building under construction increases

Building and personal property coverage form Commercial property coverage form that covers buildings, the insured's business personal property, and the personal property of others located at the business premises

Burglary As defined in crime insurance forms, the taking of property by a person unlawfully entering or leaving the premises as evidenced by visible signs of forced entry or exit

Business auto coverage form One of the commercial auto coverage forms; covers a business's owned, nonowned, and hired autos against liability and physical damage losses

Business auto physical damage coverage form One of the commercial auto coverage forms; covers a business's owned or hired business autos for physical damage only

Business income coverage forms Commercial property coverage forms that pay for loss of income that the insured sustains due to a direct physical loss from a covered peril that forces the insured to suspend operations until the property can be repaired, rebuilt, or replaced with reasonable speed; available with or without extra expense coverage

Business income from dependent properties Broad form commercial property coverage form designed for insureds whose business income is dependent on the ongoing operations of other businesses they do not own

Business liability Liability that arises out of the conduct of a business

Business pursuits endorsement Homeowners policy endorsement that provides liability coverage for a business conducted away from the residence premises

Businessowners policy (BOP) Package policy designed to provide broad property and liability coverage for small businesses; eligibility requirements are more strict than the CPP's

C

Camera and musical instruments dealers coverage form Filed commercial inland marine form written to cover camera and musical instruments dealers; covers the insured's stock in trade as well as customer property in the insured's care, custody, or control

Cancellation Termination of an insurance policy by the insured or the insurance company during the policy period

Capital The accumulated, permanent resources a company gets from owners and customers; the value of the portion of assets that a company owns and that are not restricted by obligations to creditors

Captive agent See *Exclusive agent*

Cargo insurance Type of ocean marine insurance that covers goods while they are in transit over water

Casualty insurance Line of insurance that includes a wide variety of unrelated coverages, including liability, auto, workers' compensation, aviation, crime, and surety bonds

Causes of loss form Separate form used with the commercial property coverage part of the commercial package policy that lists covered perils and exclusions; several different versions provide increasingly broader coverage from basic to broad to special; a causes of loss form takes the place of the policy's perils insured against provisions

Certificate of insurance Written form that verifies a policy has been written; provides a summary of the coverage provided under the policy

Claim adjuster Person employed by or acting on behalf of an insurance company to evaluate and settle insurance claims; the adjuster must determine the cause of loss, whether the loss is covered by the policy, the value of the loss, and the amount of loss payable by the policy

Claims-made form Commercial general liability coverage form that pays for BI or PD losses for which a claim was first made against the insured during the policy period

Class rating See *Manual rating*

Coinsurance Policy condition that requires an insured to pay part of a loss if the amount of insurance carried on property is less than a specified percentage of the value of the property at the time of loss

Coinsurance penalty The amount not paid by the insurance company because the insured failed to comply with the coinsurance condition

Collision coverage In auto insurance, a type of physical damage coverage that covers loss that occurs when the insured auto strikes another object or vehicle; may also include upset or overturn of the insured auto

Combined ratio The sum of the loss ratio and the expense ratio; a ratio of 100% is the breakeven point; a ratio below 100% indicates an underwriting profit; a ratio above 100% indicates a loss; see *Loss ratio* and *expense ratio*

Combined single limit See *Single limit*

Commercial articles coverage form Filed commercial inland marine form that covers photographic equipment or musical instruments used commercially

Commercial auto coverage Part A part of the commercial package policy that provides liability and physical damage coverage for a business's autos, including garage, trucking, and motor carrier businesses

Commercial blanket bond Type of fidelity bond that covers loss arising from the dishonesty of one or more employees acting separately or in collusion; the limit of liability applies separately to each loss, regardless of the number of employees involved

Commercial crime coverage Part A part of the commercial package policy that covers various crime exposures of businesses

Commercial general liability (CGL) coverage Part A part of the commercial package policy that provides liability coverage for businesses

Commercial inland marine insurance See *Inland marine insurance*

Commercial lines Insurance designed for businesses, institutions, or organizations

Commercial package policy (CPP) The insurance services office (ISO) commercial lines policy that contains two or more lines of insurance or two or more coverage parts; it will include some forms and/or endorsements that are common to all lines of insurance or coverage parts, as well as the individual forms and endorsements required for the individual coverages selected; the CPP can include almost any commercial coverage the insured might need, with the exception of ocean marine, aviation, and workers' compensation insurance; most commercial risks are eligible for the CPP

Commercial property coverage Part A part of the commercial package policy that provides insurance for a business's real and business personal property

Commercial property floater risks Category of the nationwide definition that includes a number of commercial inland marine forms, such as Bailee's customer forms, equipment forms, business floaters, and dealers policies

Commercial umbrella policy See *Umbrella policy*

Common policy conditions Form that must be included in the commercial package policy; it contains conditions that apply to all coverages issued under the CPP

Common policy declarations Form that must be included in the commercial package policy; contains information about the insured that applies to all coverages issued under the CPP

Comparative negligence Law that allows an injured party to collect from another party for a loss, even when the injured party contributed to her own loss. Damages are reduced to the extent of the injured party's negligence

Compensatory damages Damages that reimburse an injured party for losses that were actually sustained; see *General damages* and *Special damages*

Competent parties One of the requirements of a legal contract; states that for a contract to be valid, it must be made between parties who are considered competent under the law

Competitive state fund Method of providing workers' compensation coverage in some states; employers may either purchase insurance from a private insurance company or from a state fund

Completion bond Type of surety bond that guarantees that when contractors borrow money to fund construction projects, the project will be carried out and the work will be delivered free and clear of liens or encumbrances

Comprehensive coverage In auto insurance, a broad physical damage coverage that covers all property losses except collision and those perils or property that are specifically excluded; also called *other than collision coverage (OTC)*

Concealment The withholding of a material fact involved in the contract on which the insurer relies

Concurrent causation A situation where two or more perils act concurrently (at the same time or in sequence) to cause a loss; some courts ruled that losses from concurrent causation are covered even when one of the perils that contributed to the loss is excluded under the policy; these rulings led property insurers to revise policy language to clarify the intent of the policy

Conditional contract A contract that contains a number of conditions that both parties must comply with; an insurance policy is a conditional contract

Conditions Portion of an insurance policy that describes the rights and duties of the insured and the insurance company under the policy

Condominium association coverage form Commercial property coverage form that covers the buildings in a condominium complex; does not cover the condominium owner's personal property

Condominium commercial unit-owners coverage form Commercial property coverage form that may only be purchased by owners of commercial condominiums; covers the condominium's contents, including business personal property and the personal property of others

Consequential Loss See *Indirect loss*

Consideration A characteristic of a legal contract; the thing of value exchanged for the performance promised in the contract; with insurance contracts, the consideration that the insured gives is the premium payment; the consideration that the insurer gives is the promise to pay for certain losses suffered by the insured

Consultant Insurance professional who, for a fee, offers advice on the benefits, advantages, and disadvantages of various insurance policies; sells advice, not insurance

Contract A legal agreement between two competent parties that promises a certain performance in exchange for a certain consideration

Contract bonds Category of surety bonds that guarantee the fulfillment of contractual obligations; includes bid bonds, labor and materials bonds, performance bonds, payment bonds, supply bonds, and completion bonds

Contractors equipment floater Nonfiled commercial inland marine form that covers the heavy machinery, equipment, and tools a contractor uses in business

Contribution by equal shares Type of other insurance condition found in liability policies; it calls for all insurers to contribute equally up to the limit of the policy having the smallest limit, whereupon that company stops paying; the other companies share in the remainder of the loss until the loss is paid in full or all policy limits are exhausted

Contribution by limits See *Pro rata other insurance*

Contributory negligence Common law defense against negligence that states that if an individual contributes to her own loss in any way, then someone else cannot be held liable for the loss

Countersignature Signature of a licensed agent that, in most states, must appear on the policy to validate the contract

Court bond Type of surety bond used to settle legal arguments that do not involve monetary damages

Coverage extensions See *Additional coverages*

Coverage form Document that contains insuring agreements, coverages, exclusions, and conditions; must be attached to a policy jacket to make a complete policy; also called a *policy form*

Coverage part Combination of forms and endorsements used to provide a particular commercial coverage; the forms and endorsements available under each coverage part can be used to issue a policy covering a single line of insurance or combined to provide a commercial package policy

Coverage trigger Event that activates (triggers) coverage under a commercial general liability coverage form Under the occurrence form, the coverage trigger is bodily injury or property damage that occurs during the policy period; under the claims-made form, the trigger is BI or PD that occurs on or after the retroactive date, if any, for which a claim is first made against an insured during the policy period

Custodian As defined in crime insurance forms, an insured, partner, or employee who has care and custody of insured property within the premises; does not apply to watchpersons or janitors

D

Damages Monetary compensation awarded by a court to an injured party

Declarations Section of an insurance contract that shows who is insured, what property or risk is covered, when and where the coverage is effective, and how much coverage applies

Deductible Dollar amount the insured must pay on each loss to which the deductible applies; the insurance company pays the remainder of each covered loss, up to the policy limits

Defense costs Legal expenses incurred by the insurer to defend suits brought against insureds; defense costs are paid in addition to payments for BI or PD claims

Definitions Section of an insurance policy that clarifies the meaning of certain terms used in the policy.

Degree of care Extent of legal duty owed by one person to another; also called *standard of care*

Deposit premium Premium paid at the beginning of the policy period that is based on an estimate of what the final premium will be; this premium is adjusted based on reports submitted by the insured to the insurer; also called an *estimated premium*

Difference in conditions insurance (DIC) Type of commercial property policy that covers most insurable perils but excludes basic fire and extended coverage perils

Diminution of value An actual or perceived loss of an auto's resale or market value that results from a direct, accidental loss

Direct loss Financial loss resulting directly from a loss to property

Direct response system Insurance company that sells insurance through the mail or over the phone; no agents are involved

Direct writer Insurance marketing system where the company's agents are also employees of the company

Directors and officers liability insurance (D&O) Type of errors and omissions policy written for directors and officers of corporations who may be sued as individuals by stockholders

Disability insurance Line of insurance that protects the insured against loss of income resulting from injury or sickness

Discovery form Commercial crime form that covers losses that are sustained at any time and discovered either during the policy period or up to 60 days after the policy expires; the discovery period for losses related to employee benefit plans extends for up to one year after policy expiration

Doctrine of reasonable expectations Legal principle that provides that an insurance policy includes coverages that an average person would reasonably expect it to include, regardless of what the policy actually provides

Domestic company Insurance company doing business in the state in which it is incorporated

Domestic shipments Category of the nationwide definition that includes coverage for cargo in transit over land.

Drive other car (DOC)—Broadened Coverage For Named Individuals Endorsement Commercial auto endorsement that extends the definition of a covered auto to include autos the named insured does not own, hire, or borrow while being used by the person named in the endorsement

Duties following loss Condition found in property-casualty policies that explains the insured's responsibilities after a loss occurs

Dwelling policy Policy that provides property coverage to individuals and families; covers dwellings, other structures, personal property, and fair rental value; some versions also cover additional living expense; the unendorsed policy does not provide liability coverage

Dwelling under construction endorsement Dwelling policy endorsement used to provide provisional limits of liability for dwellings under construction; the limits of liability increase as construction of the building progresses

E

Earned premium Premium an insurance company has actually earned by providing insurance protection for the designated period of time

Earthquake insurance Insurance that covers damage to a structure, its contents, or both as the result of an earthquake; available as a separate policy and as an endorsement to the dwelling, homeowners, and commercial property policies

Electronic data processing equipment floater Nonfiled commercial inland marine policy that provides open peril coverage for computer hardware, computer software, and data that is owned by the insured or in the insured's care, custody, or control. Breakdown coverage, extra expense, and business interruption coverage may also be included

Employees as additional insureds endorsement Endorsement used with the business auto coverage form that covers employees while they are using an auto not owned, hired, or borrowed by the business in the business or personal affairs of the named insured

Employers liability coverage Coverage included in the Workers' Compensation and Employers Liability policy that covers the employer's liability at common law arising out of employees' work-related injuries and occupational diseases

Employment practices liability insurance Type of policy that covers a business's losses arising out of wrongful termination, discrimination, sexual harassment, and other employment-related practices

Endorsement Document attached to an insurance policy that changes the policy in some way

Equipment breakdown protection coverage form Title of ISO coverage form used to write what is traditionally called boiler and machinery insurance. See *Boiler and machinery insurance*

Equipment dealers coverage form Filed commercial inland marine coverage form that covers mobile equipment and construction equipment dealers; covers the insured's stock in trade as well as customer property in the insured's care, custody, or control

Errors and omissions insurance (E&O) Professional liability coverage that protects the insured against liability for committing an error or omission in the performance of professional duties

Estimated premium See *Deposit premium*

Estoppel Principle that states that if one intentionally or unintentionally creates the impression that a certain fact exists, and an innocent party relies on that impression and is injured as a result, the guilty party may be legally prohibited from asserting that the fact does not exist

Excess electronic equipment endorsement Personal auto policy endorsement that allows an insured to add coverage for tapes, records, and disks used with electronic media and to increase the limit of insurance for electronic equipment that is permanently installed in an area of the auto not normally used for installing this equipment

Excess insurance When two or more policies or coverages apply to the same loss, the one that applies only after the limits of the primary coverage have been exhausted

Excess lines agent Agent licensed by the state to handle the placement of business with nonadmitted insurers; also called *surplus lines agent*

Exclusions Section of an insurance policy that lists property, perils, persons, or situations that are not covered under the policy

Exclusive agent An agent who markets insurance for a single company; also called *captive agent*

Exclusive remedy doctrine One of the precepts upon which the workers' compensation system was founded; stipulates that the only means available to employees to receive compensation from employers for injuries covered by workers' compensation laws is through the benefits mandated by those laws

Exemplary damages See *Punitive damages*

Expense ratio Ratio that indicates the cost of doing business; it is calculated by dividing the amount of underwriting expenses by the amount of written premium

Experience modification factor In experience rating, the factor applied to reduce the premium when loss experience is better than expected

Experience rating Type of merit rating that determines premium based on previous loss experience

Exports Category of the nationwide definition that includes risks eligible for ocean marine insurance

Exposure A condition or situation that presents a possibility of loss

Express authority Legal doctrine that states that an agent has the authority specifically given to the agent, either orally or in writing, by the principal

Extended coverages See *Additional coverages*

Extended nonowned coverage—Vehicles furnished or available for regular use endorsement Personal auto policy endorsement that eliminates most exclusions applicable to autos that are furnished or available for the regular use of the named insured or family members

Extended reporting period (ERP) Period of time provided by the claims-made commercial general liability coverage form during which coverage will be provided for claims made after the expiration date of the policy if certain conditions are met; the basic ERP runs 60 days and can be extended to five years; the supplemental ERP runs for an unlimited duration, but is available only by endorsement for an additional premium

Extortion—Commercial entities endorsement Endorsement used with the commercial crime policy that covers loss of money, securities, and other property when surrendered away from the premises as a result of a threat to do bodily harm to the insured, an employee or a relative of either who is being held captive

Extra expense coverage form Commercial property coverage form that covers additional expenses incurred by the insured business to continue operations following a direct loss by a peril insured against

F

Fair Credit Reporting Act Federal law that allows consumers who are denied insurance because of information contained in a credit report to be notified and allowed to obtain the information used in the report from the reporting agency

Fair access to insurance requirements (FAIR) plan Program established by law that makes property insurance available to insureds who might otherwise be uninsurable in the standard market

Farm coverage Part of the commercial package policy that provides property and liability insurance to farmers for both their personal and business exposures

Federal Employers Liability Act (FELA) Federal law that provides benefits to injured railroad workers who are exempt under state workers' compensation laws

Fellow servant rule Common law defense against liability that allowed employers to escape liability for injury to an employee if another employee's carelessness had contributed to the loss

Fidelity bond Class of bonds that guarantees an employee's honest discharge of duty; written to protect an insured from dishonest acts by employees

Fiduciary Person who stands in a special relationship of trust to another person

Fiduciary bond Type of surety bond that guarantees that a fiduciary will fulfill its obligations set forth by law

Fiduciary liability policy Insurance that protects people who manage private pension and employee benefit plans against liability for violation of the federal ERISA law

Field underwriting Selection of clients by the agent in accordance with company standards

File and use Method of rate and form ratification used by some state insurance departments that allows a company to begin using forms or rates as soon as they are filed by the department; the department eventually reviews the filing and officially accepts or rejects it

Filed form Standardized inland marine form that can be written under the commercial inland marine coverage part of the commercial package policy

Film coverage form Filed commercial inland marine form that covers exposed motion picture film until production is complete and positive prints are made

Financial responsibility laws State laws that require owners or operators of autos to provide evidence that they have the funds to pay for automobile losses for which they might become liable. Insurance is the usual method for providing this evidence to the state

First-named insured First person listed in the declarations as an insured; the first-named insured may have a higher level of duties or rights under the policy

First party loss Property insurance loss

Flat cancellation Cancellation of a policy by the insured or the insurance company on its effective date

Floater Insurance policy that covers property wherever it is located

Flood insurance See *National Flood Insurance Program*

Floor plan coverage form Filed commercial inland marine form that covers stock that is subject to a *floor plan arrangement*, where a dealer borrows money from a lender with which to pay for merchandise

Foreign company An insurance company doing business in a state other than the one in which it is incorporated

Fraternal Benefit Society An incorporated society or order, without capital stock, that is operated on the lodge system and is conducted solely for the benefit of its members and their beneficiaries and not for profit; Fraternal benefit societies offer insurance that is available only to members

Fraud A deliberate misrepresentation that causes harm; an all-out effort by one party to deceive and cheat the other

Freight insurance Type of ocean marine insurance that protects the insured against the loss of shipping costs

Functional replacement cost Method to determine reimbursement for some losses, particularly those to antique, ornate, or custom construction; the damaged property is repaired or replaced with less expensive, but functionally equivalent, materials

G

Garage coverage form Commercial auto coverage form that provides liability, garagekeepers, and physical damage coverages for vehicle dealers, including dealers that have repair operations on the business premises

Garagekeepers insurance Coverage that is part of the garage coverage form; covers a garage risk's legal liability for customers' autos in the care, custody, or control of the garage; at the insured's option and for an additional premium, can also apply without regard to fault

General average loss Ocean marine term used to indicate a partial loss resulting from a sacrifice of cargo to save remaining property (jettison); each party shares in the loss in proportion to his total interest in the property being transported

General conditions form Separate form that lists the conditions that apply to a policy

General damages Type of compensatory damages that reimburse the injured party for such things as pain and suffering and disfigurement.

H

Hazard Something that increases the chance of loss

Health insurance Line of insurance that protects the insured against financial loss due to medical bills

Hired and nonowned auto liability endorsement Businessowners policy endorsement used to cover hired or nonowned autos used by the business

Hold harmless agreement Contractual arrangement where one party assumes the liability of a situation and relieves the other party of responsibility

Home day care coverage endorsement Homeowners policy endorsement used to provide coverage for home day care businesses

Homeowners policy Personal multiline policy for homeowners that includes both property and liability coverages; there are different forms that provide varying degrees of property coverage; liability coverage is the same in all forms

Hull insurance Ocean marine insurance that provides coverage for physical damage to the ship

I

Implied authority Authority given by the principal to the agent that is not formally expressed or communicated

Implied warranties In ocean marine insurance, warranties that are not written into the policy, but have become a part of the policy by custom

Imports Category of the nationwide definition that includes risks eligible for ocean marine insurance

Imputed liability See *Vicarious liability*

Incidental contract See *Insured contract*

Incidental occupancy A business conducted in a dwelling used primarily as a residence with no other businesses operating on the same premises; individual insurers have specific guidelines about the types of incidental businesses permitted, but examples include business or professional offices and private schools or instructional studios

Incurred losses One of the components used to calculate the loss ratio; it includes paid losses and certain expenses associated with claim handling

Indemnity Principle of insurance that provides that when a loss occurs, the insured should be restored to the approximate financial condition he occupied before the loss occurred, no better or no worse

Independent adjuster Claim handler who works independently instead of for a particular insurer

Independent agent Agent who represents many insurance companies, rather than a single company; also called a *nonexclusive agent*

Indirect loss Loss that is the result or consequence of a direct loss; also called a *consequential loss*

Individual named insured endorsement Commercial auto endorsement that provides coverage similar to that provided under the personal auto policy to family members of the named insured while using any auto

Inland marine insurance Form of insurance originally designed as an extension of ocean marine coverage to insure transportation of goods over land; today it covers a variety of portable property, in addition to goods in transit; available as personal or commercial insurance; commercial inland marine insurance can be included in the commercial package policy

Installation policy Nonfiled commercial inland marine policy that covers loss to machinery, equipment, building materials, and supplies in transit to or being used with or during the course of installation, testing, building, renovating, or repair

Instrumentalities of transportation and communication Category of the nationwide definition that includes a variety of forms closely related to transportation or communication, such as bridges, pipelines, and television towers

Insurable interest Any actual, lawful, and substantial economic interest in the safety or preservation of the subject of the insurance from loss or destruction or financial damage or impairment

Insurance Contract or device for transferring the risk of loss from a person, business, or organization to an insurance company that agrees, in exchange for a premium, to pay for losses through an accumulation of premiums

Insurance Commissioner Head official of a state insurance department; may also be called an *Insurance Director* or *Insurance Superintendent*

Insurance department State department charged with controlling insurance matters within the state

Insurance guaranty association State funds created by law that pay claims of insurers domiciled in that state that become insolvent; funds are generated by making assessments against other insurers operating in the state

Insurance Services Office (ISO) Organization established for the benefit of its member insurance companies and other subscriber companies; ISO gathers statistics, provides loss costs, drafts policy forms and coverage provisions, and conducts inspections for rate-making purposes

Insured contract Term used in the CGL and businessowners liability forms to describe contracts for which contractual liability coverage is available under the policy, such as leases, sidetrack agreements, and elevator maintenance agreements; also called *incidental contract*

Insuring agreement Section of an insurance policy that describes what is covered and the perils the policy insures against

Interline endorsement An endorsement that modifies two or more lines of insurance

Intervening cause An independent action that breaks the chain of causation and sets in motion a new chain of events; when this occurs, the intervening cause becomes the *proximate cause*; can serve as a common law defense against liability

Invitee A person invited onto a premises for some purpose involving potential benefit to the property owner

J

Jettison A voluntary action to rid a ship of cargo to prevent further damage or peril. Jettison is a covered peril in ocean marine policies

Jewelers block coverage form Filed commercial inland marine form for jewelers that covers the insured's stock in trade and the property of others while it is on or off the premises

Joint ownership coverage endorsement Personal auto policy endorsement that allows the policy to be issued to two or more persons who live in the same household or two or more individuals who are related in another way besides husband and wife

Jones Act Federal law that allows members of ships' crews to sue their employer/ship owner at common law for injuries caused by the employer's/ship owner's negligence

Judgment rating Method of rating that establishes premiums based on a careful evaluation of each individual risk without the use of manuals or tables

Judicial bond Category of surety bond that guarantees that the principal will fulfill certain obligations set forth by law—includes fiduciary bonds and court bonds

L

Labor and materials bond See *Payment bond*

Law of large numbers Principle that states that the more examples used to develop any statistic, the more reliable the statistic will be

Legal liability coverage form Commercial property coverage form that covers the insured for liability arising out of negligent damage to the property of others while it is in the insured's care, custody, or control

Legal purpose One of the characteristics of a legal contract; means that contracts are only enforceable if they are not obviously illegal, immoral, or against the public good

Liability insurance Type of insurance that protects an insured from financial loss arising out of liability claims by transferring the burden of financial loss from the insured to the insurance company

Liberalization condition Condition found in property insurance contracts that provides that if the insurer broadens coverage under a policy form or endorsement without requiring an additional premium, then all existing similar policies or endorsements will be construed to contain the broadened coverage

License and permit bond Type of surety bond that is sometimes required in connection with the issuance of licenses by government agencies. They guarantee that the person who posts the bond will comply with all applicable laws pertaining to their activities

Licensee Person on the premises with the property owner's consent but for the sole benefit of the visitor

Life insurance Insurance that pays a stipulated sum to a designated beneficiary upon the death of the insured; protects the insured's beneficiary against the financial consequences of the insured's premature death

Limitations Policy language that eliminates or reduces coverage under certain circumstances or when specified conditions apply

Limit of coverage, limit of insurance, limit of liability See *Policy limit*

Liquor liability coverage form CGL coverage form that provides coverage for liquor liability excluded by standard CGL policies for those who are in the business of manufacturing, distributing, selling, serving, or furnishing alcoholic beverages

Livestock coverage form Farm coverage form used to provide separate coverage for livestock

Lloyd's Association A voluntary association of individuals or groups of individuals who agree to share in insurance contracts; each individual or syndicate is individually responsible for the amounts of insurance they write

Longshore and Harbor Workers' Compensation Act coverage endorsement Endorsement used with the Workers' Compensation and Employers Liability policy that covers the additional benefits required by federal law for maritime workers injured while working on navigable waters or shore-site areas

Loss cost Factor used in figuring insurance rates that represents how much an insurance company needs to collect to cover expected losses

Loss payable condition See *Mortgage condition*

Loss provisions General term used to describe policy conditions that specify what the insured and insurer must do after a loss

Loss ratio Method used to determine an insurance company's success in covering current losses out of current premium income; determined by dividing incurred losses by earned premium

Loss sustained during prior insurance condition Condition found in loss sustained version of the commercial crime forms that allows losses that occurred during a prior policy period to be covered under the current policy if certain conditions are met

Loss sustained form Commercial crime form that covers losses that are sustained during the policy period and discovered either during the policy period or up to one year after the policy expires

M

Mail coverage form Filed commercial inland marine form that covers property in transport by registered mail, first class mail, certified mail, or express mail

Malpractice insurance Term used to describe professional liability insurance issued to medical professionals or institutions

Manual rating Method of premium determination that uses rates based on collected statistics. The rates, which apply per unit of insurance, are published in manuals; also called *class rating*

Market value The amount property could be sold for at the time of loss. May be used to determine the amount of reimbursement for a loss

Material fact A fact that would cause an insurer to decline a risk, charge a different premium, or change the provisions of the policy that was issued

MCS-90 endorsement Endorsement attached to the truckers coverage form to provide public liability coverage

Merit rating Method of determining premiums where a manual rate is modified to reflect the risk's unique characteristics; see *Experience rating, Retrospective rating and Schedule rating*

Messenger As defined in crime insurance forms, an insured, partner, or employee who has care and custody of insured property outside the premises

Miscellaneous type vehicle endorsement Personal auto policy endorsement that provides coverage for vehicles that are usually excluded by the policy, such as motorcycles, motor homes, golf carts, mopeds, and other recreational vehicles

Misrepresentation Written or verbal misstatement of a material fact involved in the contract on which the insurer relies

Mobile agricultural machinery and equipment coverage form Farm coverage form that provides separate coverage for a farmer's mobile agricultural machinery and equipment

Mobile equipment endorsement Commercial auto endorsement that makes mobile equipment considered a covered auto for coverage purposes

Mobile home insurance Coverage that protects both a mobile home structure and its contents; some companies have mobile home package policies that provide property and liability insurance for owners of mobile homes. In addition, there is a mobile homeowners endorsement that can be attached to an HO-2 or HO-3 to modify coverage for mobile homeowners

Monoline company Insurance company that writes a single line of insurance

Monoline policy Insurance policy that provides one type of insurance coverage

Monopolistic state fund Method of providing workers' compensation coverage used in some states; employers must purchase workers' compensation insurance from a state fund; private insurance companies are not allowed to compete

Moral hazard Hazard created by an individual who would be willing to create a loss situation on purpose just to collect from the insurance company

Morale hazard Hazard created by an individual's tendency to contribute to a loss through his own irresponsible actions or carelessness

Mortgage condition Condition found in property insurance policies that specifies the rights and duties of the mortgagee under the policy; also called the *loss payable condition*

Mortgagee rights Rights granted to a mortgagee under a property contract issued to a mortgagor by virtue of the mortgagee's financial interest in the property

Motor Carrier Act of 1980 Federal regulation that requires truckers and other commercial carriers to certify they are able to meet financial obligations if they become liable for injury or damage arising from their trucking operations

Motor carrier coverage form Commercial auto coverage form that is an alternate to the truckers coverage form; it can be used to cover anyone who transports property by auto in a commercial enterprise

Motor truck cargo policy Nonfiled commercial inland marine policy that protects a carrier against its liability for damage to domestic shipments in its custody

Multiline company Insurance company that writes more than one line of insurance

Multiline policy See *Package policy*

Mutual company Insurance company owned by its policyholders; the policyholders share in profits made by the company through dividends or reductions in future premiums

Mysterious disappearance Vanishing of property with no explanation

N

Name schedule bond Type of fidelity bond that covers loss only from named employees

Named insured Person, business, or other entity named in the declarations to whom the policy is issued.

Named nonowner coverage endorsement Personal auto policy endorsement that provides coverage for the use of nonowned autos to individuals who do not own a car

Named peril policy Insurance policy that insures only against perils specifically listed in the policy; also called *specified peril policy*

National Association of Insurance Commissioners (NAIC) Organization made up of individual state insurance commissioners whose purpose is to promote uniformity in regulation by drafting model laws and regulations

National flood insurance program Program run by the federal government that makes flood insurance available to eligible communities at subsidized rates; includes coverage for both buildings and personal property

Nationwide Definition Document that categorizes and classifies risks that are eligible for ocean or inland marine insurance

Negligence The lack of reasonable care that is required to protect others from the unreasonable chance of harm

No benefit to bailee condition Condition found in some property insurance contracts that states that a bailee is not covered under an insured's policy while the bailee has possession of the insured's property

No-fault insurance Form of automobile insurance where each insurance company pays the damages of its own insureds, regardless of who was at fault for the accident; no-fault insurance has been enacted in several states

Nonadmitted insurer Company that is not authorized to do business in a particular state; also called an *unauthorized insurer*

Nonconcurrency Situation that exists when the same property is covered by more than one policy, but the policies are not identical as to the extent of coverage provided

Nonexclusive agent See *Independent agent*

Nonfiled form Type of commercial inland marine form that is not standardized and cannot be included in the commercial inland marine coverage part of the commercial package policy

Nonrenewal Decision made by an insured or insurance company to not continue coverage for another policy period after the current policy period expires

Nonreporting policy Type of insurance policy for which a flat premium is charged every time the policy is renewed

O

Obligee In bonds, the party to whom the principal makes the promise and for whose protection the bond is written

Occurrence A loss that occurs at a specific time and place or over a period of time

Occurrence form Commercial general liability coverage form that covers bodily injury or property damage that occurs during the policy period, regardless of when the claim is made

Ocean marine insurance Insurance designed to provide broad coverage for cargo and ships in transit over sea; includes cargo insurance, hull insurance, freight insurance, and protection and indemnity insurance

Offer and acceptance One of the elements of a legal contract; means that a contract must involve two parties: one who makes an offer and another who accepts the offer; also called *agreement*

Open competition Method of rate and form regulation used by some state insurance departments that allows insurance companies to compete openly with the forms and rates they select, subject only to requirements of adequacy and nondiscrimination

Open peril policy Insurance policy that protects the insured from losses caused by any peril that is not specifically excluded by the policy; also called *all risk* and *special coverage*

Optional limits transportation expenses coverage endorsement Personal auto policy endorsement that allows the insured to select the daily and maximum limits of coverage provided for transportation and loss of use expenses

Ordinance or law coverage endorsement Endorsement used with the commercial property coverage part to provide coverage for demolition costs and increased construction costs required or regulated by law or ordinance

Other coverages See *Additional coverages*

Other insurance condition Policy condition that sets out how any other insurance that applies to the same loss will affect reimbursement under the policy; see *Contribution by equal shares*, *Excess insurance*, *Primary insurance*, and *Pro rata other insurance*

Other than collision coverage (OTC) See *Comprehensive coverage*

Outboard motor and boat insurance Insurance against physical damage to boats; usually provided by inland marine forms

Owners and contractors protective liability coverage form Commercial general liability coverage form that covers claims caused by the negligence of a contractor or subcontractor hired by the insured

P

Package policy Policy that includes more than one type of insurance coverage; also called a *multiline policy*

Pair or set condition Loss settlement condition found in property insurance contracts that states that when part of a set is damaged or destroyed, the insured will not be reimbursed for the value of the entire set; various methods are used to determine the amount of reimbursement

Parcel post policy Nonfiled commercial inland marine policy that covers mail sent by parcel post

Particular average loss In ocean marine insurance, any partial loss that does not arise from a general sacrifice of property (jettison)

Payment bond Type of surety bond that guarantees bills for labor and materials will be paid to the contractor as they are due; also called *labor and materials bond*

Peak season endorsement Endorsement attached to the commercial property coverage part to provide increased coverage during particular seasons of the year when the insured's inventory is at higher levels than usual.

Performance bond Type of surety bond that guarantees that jobs will be completed by the contractor according to the contract specifications

Peril The cause of loss

Perils of the sea Perils to which property in transit by water is exposed; includes unusual action of wind or waves, stranding, lightning, collision, and sinking

Permitted incidental occupancies endorsement Homeowners policy endorsement that covers the insured's business activities conducted on the residence premises

Personal articles form Personal inland marine form that provides scheduled coverage for nine optional classes of personal property: jewelry, furs, cameras, musical instruments, silverware, golf equipment, fine arts, stamp collections, and coin collections

Personal auto policy Auto policy that provides property and liability coverage for both owned and nonowned autos used, maintained, or operated by the insured and her family members

Personal contract One of the characteristics of an insurance contract; means that an insurance contract insures a person, not property

Personal effects form Personal inland marine form that covers an insured's personal belongings, such as baggage, while traveling

Personal injury Injury other than bodily injury arising out of such things as libel, slander, false arrest, wrongful entry, violation of privacy, and malicious prosecution

Personal injury endorsement Homeowners policy endorsement that modifies the definition of bodily injury to include personal injury

Personal inland marine insurance See *Inland marine insurance*

Personal liability and medical payments to others endorsement Endorsement to the dwelling policy that provides liability coverage similar to that provided by Section II of the homeowners policy; may also be purchased as a separate policy

Personal lines Insurance coverages that protect individuals and their families

Personal property form Personal inland marine form that provides open peril coverage for personal property

Personal property floater risks Category of the nationwide definition that includes risks eligible for personal inland marine insurance

Personal property replacement cost endorsement Homeowners policy endorsement that adds replacement cost coverage for personal property

Personal umbrella policy See *umbrella policy*

Personal yacht insurance Type of personal watercraft policy written for large pleasure boats

Physical hazard Hazard that arises from the condition, occupancy, or use of the property itself.

Physicians and surgeons equipment form Filed commercial inland marine form that covers medical instruments on and off the premises and furniture and fixtures at the doctor's office against direct physical loss.

Policy An insurance contract

Policy form See *Coverage form*

Policy jacket Document used to assemble an insurance policy; contains general conditions or the declarations page, but provides no coverage in and of itself; a policy form must be attached to make it a complete policy; also called a *skeleton policy*

Policy limit Maximum amount the insurance company will pay for a particular loss or for losses sustained during a period of time; also called *limit of coverage*, *limit of insurance* and *limit of liability*

Policy period The date and time specified in the declarations for when coverage begins and ends

Policy territory Place where coverage under a policy applies

Pollution liability coverage extension endorsement Commercial general liability endorsement that provides coverage for BI and PD claims arising out of pollution losses; excludes coverage for pollution clean-up costs

Pollution liability coverage form CGL coverage form that provides certain pollution coverages that are excluded under the standard CGL; includes coverage for pollution clean-up costs

Pollution liability—limited coverage form CGL coverage form that provides certain pollution coverages that are excluded under the standard CGL; does not include coverage for pollution clean-up costs

Position schedule bond Fidelity bond that covers specifically named positions in the company, rather than the individuals who hold these positions

Post-judgment interest Interest accruing on a judgment after an award has been made, but before payment is made by the insurance company; usually covered as a supplementary payment in liability policies

Prejudgment interest Interest awarded to compensate a third party for interest he might have earned if compensation had been received at the time of injury or damage, rather than at the time of judgment.

Premises and operations Business liability exposure arising out of the business location or the activities of the business; covered under the CGL

Premium audit Survey of the insured's financial records to gather information used to calculate the premium, such as exposures and limits

Primary insurance When two or more coverages or policies apply to the same loss, the one that pays first, up to its limit of liability or the amount of the loss, whichever is less

Principal In bonds, the party who promises to do or not do a specific thing; in agency law, the person or company being represented

Prior approval Method of rate and form ratification used by some state insurance departments that requires a company to obtain official approval before using new forms or rates

Producer General term used to describe someone who sells insurance, such as an agent, broker, or solicitor

Products and completed operations Business liability exposure arising out of defects in the company's products or completed operations; covered by the CGL

Professional liability Liability arising out of rendering or failing to render services of a professional nature

Professional liability policy Insurance coverage issued to a professional that covers the rendering or failing to render services of a professional nature; policies are tailored to fit specific occupational needs

Proof of loss Form completed by an insured after a loss that provides an official inventory of damages

Property damage (PD) Damage to or destruction of property, including loss of use of the property

Property insurance Line of insurance that includes many types of coverages designed to handle the risk that a person will suffer financial loss because something she owns is damaged or destroyed

Pro rata other insurance Method of handling insurance when more than one coverage applies to a loss; each coverage pays a portion of the loss in proportion to the relationship its limit of liability bears to the total limit of liability under all applicable insurance; also called *contribution by limits*

Protection and indemnity Form of ocean marine liability insurance that covers a variety of types of liability, such as damage to cargo through negligence and damage to other property or another boat resulting from collision

Protective safeguards endorsement Businessowners policy endorsement that requires the insured to maintain fire or security service on specified property as a condition of the policy

Proximate cause An action that, in a natural and continuous sequence, produces a loss

Public official bonds Type of surety bond furnished by principals who are elected or appointed to fill positions of trust that guarantee their faithful and honest performance in office

Punitive damages Type of damages intended to punish the defendant and make an example out of her to discourage others from behaving the same way; also called *exemplary damages*

Pure risk A risk in which there is no chance of gain, only loss

Q

Quotation A summary of coverages and premiums proposed by an agent to a prospective client

R

Rate The basic charge an insurance company sets for various types of insurance

Reasonable person rule Principle of law that states that each person must behave like a prudent person following those ordinary considerations that guide human affairs

Rebating Giving or offering some benefit other than those specified in the policy to induce a customer to buy insurance; rebating is illegal in most states

Reciprocal company An unincorporated group of members that share insurance responsibilities with other members; it is managed by an attorney-in-fact

Reinsurance Acceptance by an insurer, called a reinsurer, of all or part of the risk of loss of another insurer

Repair cost The cost to repair a damaged or destroyed item of property. May be the basis of reimbursement for a loss

Replacement cost The cost to replace a damaged or destroyed item of property without deduction for depreciation; may be the basis of reimbursement for some losses

Reporting policy Type of policy that does not charge a flat premium; the insured pays a deposit premium, then submits periodic reports to the insurer showing the status of the factors on which the premium is based; from these status reports, premiums are calculated and charged against the deposit

Representation Statements on an insurance application that the applicant believes are true; a representation is not considered a matter to which the parties contract, so a policy cannot be voided on the basis of a representation

Residual market insurance Insurance that is not ordinarily available from private insurers and may be provided by the government; examples include flood insurance, which is provided by the federal government, and workers' compensation benefits, which may be provided by state funds

Retention limit In an umbrella policy, the amount the insured must pay for a loss that is not covered by an underlying policy before the umbrella will begin to cover the loss; also called the *self-insured retention*

Retroactive date Under the claims-made CGL form, a date stipulated in the declarations as the first date on which an event may occur and be covered by the policy if a claim is filed

Retrospective rating Type of merit rating that bases the insured's premium on losses incurred during the policy period

Risk The chance or uncertainty of loss

Risk retention group Insurance company formed by several organizations to cover those organizations' liability loss exposures; risk retention groups are exempt from most state laws that govern insurance companies

Robbery In crime insurance, the taking or attempted taking of property by one who has caused or threatened to cause bodily harm, or committed a witnessed, obviously unlawful act

Running down clause Provision found in ocean marine hull policies that provides protection if the ship owner is held liable for the negligent operation of the vessel in damaging another ship

S

Salvage Damaged property that can be retrieved, reconditioned, and sold to reduce an insured loss

Schedule rating Type of merit rating that applies a system of debits or credits to reflect characteristics of a particular insured

Scheduled coverage Property that is specifically listed in the declarations and covered for a specific amount; also called *specific insurance*

Scheduled personal property endorsement Homeowners policy endorsement that provides open peril, scheduled coverage for nine optional classes of property

Self-insurance Alternative to purchasing insurance where a company or individual assumes the risk of paying for its losses and sets aside the necessary funds to pay for such losses

Self-insured retention See *Retention limit*

Service bureau Organization that gathers, pools, and analyzes statistics from its member insurance companies to establish loss costs used to determine insurance rates

Signs coverage form Filed commercial inland marine form that insures businesses against loss to neon, fluorescent, automatic, or mechanical electric signs and lights

Single limit One policy limit that applies to both BI and PD losses; may also be called a *combined single limit*

Skeleton policy See *Policy jacket*

Solicitor Insurance professional who sells insurance and collects premiums but cannot issue or countersign policies

Special coverage See *Open peril policy*

Special damages Type of compensatory damages that reimburse the injured party for direct and specific expenses involved in the loss, such as medical expenses and lost wages

Specific insurance See *Scheduled coverage*

Specified Causes of Loss One of the physical damage coverage options in the commercial auto coverage forms; provides more limited coverage than comprehensive coverage, insuring only against specified perils such as fire, flood, or explosion

Specified peril policy See *Named peril policy*

Speculative risk A risk that may result in a loss or gain

Split limits Policy limit that provides separate limits for BI and PD

Spoilage endorsement Endorsement used with the building and personal property and condominium commercial unit-owners commercial property coverage forms; it adds coverage for the insured's perishable stock—personal property that must be maintained under controlled conditions to protect it from loss or damage

Spread of risk Principle of insurance that states that insurers should spread their insured risks over a large geographical area, rather than insuring a large number of people in a small area

Standard & Poor Organization that rates the financial stability of insurance companies doing business in the United States

Standard of care See *Degree of care*

Stated amount condition See *Agreed value condition*

Statute of limitations Law that provides that certain types of suits must be brought within a specified time of the occurrence to be valid under the law

Stock company An insurance company owned by its stockholders; profits are shared by the stockholders; policyholders are not entitled to share in company profits

Subrogation The transfer to the insurance company of the insured's right to collect damages from another party

Supplemental extended reporting period See *Extended reporting period*

Supplementary Payments Provide extra coverage over and above the insured's limit of liability; commonly included are defense costs, first aid expenses, bond premiums, and post-judgment interest

Supply bond Type of surety bond that guarantees that a supplier will furnish supplies, products, or equipment at an agreed-upon time and price

Surety In bonds, the party (often the insurance company) that agrees to be responsible for loss that may result if the principal does not keep his promise

Surety bond Bond that guarantees that someone will perform faithfully whatever she agrees to do or that someone will make an agreed-upon payment to another party

Surplus The difference between what a company owns (assets) and what it owes (liabilities)

Surplus lines agent See *Excess lines agent*

T

Terrorism Risk Insurance Act of 2002 Federal law designed to ensure that insurance coverage for terrorism losses under commercial lines policies will be available and affordable; it requires insurers to pay a specified amount for terrorism losses in a given calendar year; once that limit is reached, the federal government will reimburse insurers 85% of insured losses that exceed the limit

Theatrical property coverage form Filed commercial inland marine form that covers scenery, props, and costumes used by a theater group in a specific production

Theft In crime insurance, a broad term encompassing any unlawful taking of property, including burglary and robbery

Third party loss A liability loss

Time element coverage Coverage for the loss of business income over a period of time that results from direct physical loss

Tort A civil wrong for which monetary damages may be provided; does not include losses arising out of contracts

Towing and labor costs endorsement Personal auto policy endorsement that covers towing and the costs of labor performed at the site the car was disabled

Trailer interchange insurance A coverage provided under the truckers and motor carrier coverage forms; covers damage to a specific trailer under the policy of the trucker who has possession of the trailer at the time of loss, provided that: the trucker is liable for the damage under a written interchange agreement, and the damage is caused by a covered peril

Trespasser A person who is on the premises without the property owner's express or implied permission

Trip transit policy Nonfiled commercial inland marine policy that covers a single shipment of goods

Truckers coverage form Commercial auto coverage form written specifically for the trucking industry

Twisting Illegal activity in which an agent convinces a prospect to cancel existing insurance and buy another policy from the agent to the detriment of the prospect

U

Umbrella policy Type of policy that provides broad coverage for an insured's liability over and above liability covered by an underlying contract; may also cover losses that are excluded by the underlying policy; available as personal or commercial insurance

Unauthorized insurer See *Nonadmitted insurer*

Underinsured motorists coverage Auto coverage that pays the difference between the insured's actual damages for bodily injury and the amount of liability insurance carried by the at-fault driver; may be added to the personal or commercial auto policy by endorsement

Underwriting Insurance company function that involves researching and evaluating insurance applicants to decide which ones are acceptable to the company as insureds

Underwriting expenses One of the components used to calculate the expense ratio; includes all costs required to acquire and maintain a book of business, such as expenses for commissions, salaries, and other administrative and regulatory costs

Unfair discrimination Applying different standards to insureds that have the same risks of loss

Unilateral contract A type of contract that is one sided; an insurance policy is one sided because only the insurance company is legally bound to perform its part of the agreement

Uninsured motorists coverage Automobile coverage designed to provide protection for the insured if she is involved in an accident in which an uninsured motorist is at fault; uninsured motorists include those who do not carry insurance, motorists whose insurance does not meet the state's minimum financial responsibility laws, drivers whose insurance companies are insolvent, and hit-and-run drivers who cannot be identified

Unoccupancy The absence of people from a premises; property coverage is often restricted if there are long periods of unoccupancy

Use and file Method of rate and form ratification used by some state insurance departments that requires insurance companies to file rates and forms within a certain period of time after they are first used

Utility services—Direct damage coverage endorsement Businessowners policy endorsement that covers loss or damage to property caused by an interruption in water, communication, or power service; for coverage to apply, the property must be listed on the endorsement and the utility equipment must be damaged by a covered cause of loss

Utility services—Time element coverage endorsement Businessowners policy endorsement that covers loss of business income and extra expense that occurs because of an interruption in water, communication, or power service; for coverage to apply, the property must be listed on the endorsement and the utility equipment must be damaged by a covered cause of loss

Utmost good faith A characteristic of insurance contracts meaning that the insurance company must be able to rely on the honesty and cooperation of the insured, and the insured must rely on the company to fulfill its obligations

V

Vacancy The absence of both people and property from a premises; property coverage is often restricted when there are long periods of vacancy

Valuable papers and records insurance Filed commercial inland marine form that provides coverage for valuable papers such as manuscripts, blueprints, records, and other printed documents

Valuation Method used by the insurance company to determine the appropriate payment for a loss

Valued policy Policy written for a specified amount that lists the value of the insured property as agreed to by both the insured and the insurer; this amount is used to value losses; also called an *agreed amount policy*.

Value reporting endorsement Endorsement used with the commercial property coverage part to provide coverage based on the actual values of property at certain locations at specific times

Vandalism and malicious mischief (V&MM) Coverage provided in many property insurance policies that protects property against damage caused by vandals

Vicarious liability Liability that a person or business incurs because of the actions of others, such as family members or employees; also called *imputed liability*

Voluntary compensation endorsement Endorsement used with the workers' compensation and employers liability policy that adds coverage for employees who are excluded from the state's workers' compensation law

W

Waiver The intentional relinquishment of a known right

Warehouse to warehouse clause Provision found in ocean marine cargo policies that extends coverage for the cargo from its point of origination to its point of destination

Warranty A specific agreement between the insured and the insurer that becomes a part of the insurance policy; a breach of warranty can void the policy

Watchperson As defined in crime insurance forms, someone retained specifically by the insured whose sole duty is to have care and custody of property inside the premises

Watercraft endorsement Homeowners policy endorsement that provides coverage for BI or PD arising out of the use of watercraft

Watercraft package policy Package policy that provides property, liability, and medical payments coverage for losses arising out of the ownership, maintenance, or use of watercraft

Workers' Compensation and Employers Liability Policy Insurance that covers an employer's obligations under workers' compensation laws, which make the employer responsible for stated damages in the event of a work-related injury or illness; also covers the insured's liability for work-related injuries under common law

Written premium One of the components used to calculate the expense ratio; it is the gross amount of premium income on the company's books, which includes both earned and unearned premium

Index

Symbols

A

B

C

W

Y

Notes

Notes

Notes

Notes

Notes

Notes

Notes